THE HOUSE OF BECKHAM

THE HOUSE OF BECKHAM

Money, Sex and Power

TOM BOWER

HarperCollins*Publishers*

HarperCollins*Publishers*
1 London Bridge Street
London SE1 9GF

www.harpercollins.co.uk

HarperCollins*Publishers*
Macken House, 39/40 Mayor Street Upper
Dublin 1, D01 C9W8, Ireland

First published by HarperCollins*Publishers* 2024

1 3 5 7 9 10 8 6 4 2

A catalogue record of this book is
available from the British Library

ISBN 978-0-00-863887-0
TPB ISBN 978-0-00-863888-7

Printed and bound in the UK using 100%
renewable electricity at CPI Group (UK) Ltd

To Sophie

Blind Eye to Murder: Britain, America and the Purging of Nazi Germany – A Pledge Betrayed

Klaus Barbie: Butcher of Lyon

The Paperclip Conspiracy: The Battle for the Spoils and Secrets of Nazi Germany

Red Web: MI6 and the KGB Master Group

Maxwell: The Outsider

Tiny Rowland: A Rebel Tycoon

The Perfect English Spy: Sir Dick White and the Secret War 1935–90

Heroes of World War II

Maxwell: The Final Verdict

Nazi Gold: The Full Story of the Fifty-Year Swiss-Nazi Conspiracy to Steal Billions from Europe's Jews and Holocaust Survivors

Blood Money: The Swiss, the Nazis and the Looted Billions

Fayed: The Unauthorized Biography

Branson

The Paymaster: Geoffrey Robinson, Maxwell and New Labour

Broken Dreams: Vanity, Greed and the Souring of British Football

Gordon Brown: Prime Minister

Conrad and Lady Black: Dancing on the edge

The Squeeze: Oil, Money and Greed in the 21st Century

No Angel: The Secret Life of Bernie Ecclestone

Sweet Revenge: The Intimate Life of Simon Cowell

Branson: Behind the Mask

Broken Vows: Tony Blair – The Tragedy of Power

Rebel Prince: The Power, Passion and Defiance of Prince Charles

Dangerous Hero: Corbyn's Ruthless Plot for Power

Boris Johnson: The Gambler

Revenge: Meghan, Harry and the War Between the Windsors

CONTENTS

CHAPTER 1

GLASTONBURY, JUNE 2017

The sun was shining. The music was blaring. The atmosphere was fevered. Expectations were soaring.

Like a rock star, he stood by the bar deep in the Rabbit Hole, the VIPs private club. Famous among music fans as a June weekend of drink, dance, dalliance and a great deal more, David Beckham was enjoying three days of hectic partying at the Glastonbury Festival.

As Radiohead blasted 200,000 fans from the Pyramid Stage, the national treasure was in deep conversation with Mary Charteris, a 30-year-old married party girl, the ultimate cool Sloane Raver. A member of London's fast-living Primrose Hill set, Lady Mary had been introduced to Beckham by Dave Gardner, the closest friend of the retired footballer. Paid annually about £250,000, Gardner provided business advice to Beckham and scurried around to make sure his friend was happy. So it fell to Gardner and his wife, actress Liv Tyler, to tell Charteris to wait for Beckham in the VIPs club.

The atmosphere was less stressful than in previous years. Unusually, the Somerset fields were not waterlogged but bathed in sunshine. Those gazing at Lady Mary probably recalled the recent photograph of her posing naked in a bath filled with goldfish.

Just a few weeks earlier, Charteris had been seen with Beckham having dinner at London's fashionable Chiltern Firehouse. Inevitably, an admirer stopped by their table. 'She's with me,' Beckham told the man.[1] Famous for her wild life and being present at parties where others enjoyed cocaine, the socialite model and DJ daughter of an eccentric Scottish aristocrat, the 13th Earl of Wemyss and 9th Earl of March, had featured in all the newspaper society pages after her 2012 wedding to the electronic rock musician Robbie Furze. Everyone latched on to her father's excited reaction to the unusually revealing dress she wore and on to her stepmother known as 'Lady Mindbender'.

Although in Glastonbury Beckham appeared to be smitten by Charteris, he also attracted the attention of a glamorous Australian bikini model. As his companions smirked: 'What happens in the Rabbit Hole, stays in the Rabbit Hole.'

Also at the festival was Beckham's 18-year-old-son, Brooklyn, protected by the judo champion and fitness instructor Bobby Rich. Brooklyn was fascinated by the singer Rita Ora and superstar model Cara Delevingne.[2] Journalists had already reported Brooklyn's recent embrace with Rita Ora at the Electric Diner restaurant in London. Few were surprised that their friendship continued in Glastonbury. Spurred on by the festival's intoxicating atmosphere, Ora confessed to a friend, above the roar of music, about her romance with Delevingne.[3]

During that weekend Brooklyn was not only chasing women but also promoting his own career as a photographer. His pictures in a new book called *What I See* were being exhibited at Christie's in London's St James's. Brooklyn seemed unaware about the swirl of comments about his talent. 'I like this picture' was one caption under a photograph called 'Dinner' snapped in a restaurant. 'It's out of focus but you can tell there's a lot's going on,' wrote Brooklyn.

By Friday afternoon Glastonbury's frenzy had strained Beckham's nerves. Standing with friends in the backstage Park Bar he spotted a fan taking a photo. 'Don't you dare!' he shouted. Barging across the room he forced the man to delete his picture. That evening, Beckham's publicist Simon Oliveira would correctly tell the *Sun* newspaper, 'David did not turn down any of the hundreds of requests for pictures.' But that particular fan's unauthorised photo happened to include a woman close to Beckham – and he preferred the association not to be recorded. In his media-saturated life, Beckham welcomed exposure – so long as everything was carefully orchestrated. Turning off the non-stop publicity blitz that weekend was similarly planned. As Gardner repeated, 'It's David's first chance to let his hair down.' He was off the football treadmill, and in control of his life.

Thirty minutes later, Beckham rushed from the Park Bar to the privacy of the Winnebago area.[4] That night his entourage did not sleep in the comfortable caravans or even in the luxury tents rented for about £14,000. Instead, they all headed for the nearby Babington House. Their partying at the new establishment's headquarters continued until 4 a.m. Several guests were seen taking Ecstasy, but these did not include Beckham or Brooklyn.

Late the following morning, in an unusual 30-degree heatwave, Beckham's gang returned to Worthy Farm, the festival's headquarters. The Three Musketeers – Beckham, Gardner and Oliveira – were not interested in the Labour Opposition leader Jeremy Corbyn receiving a rapturous reception as he regaled a huge crowd from the Pyramid Stage. Instead, they partied in the Hole and elsewhere until 5 a.m. on Sunday. They resumed at lunchtime until interrupted by a telephone call. Victoria 'Posh' Beckham had arrived. 'There was no hassle and a great mood until she landed,' complained one of the group.[5]

The former Spice Girl had flown in from New York. In the latest instalment to rescue her fashion business, Victoria had told *Vogue* in their Manhattan office, 'I love the development process and the packaging. David thinks I'm so boring talking about boxes and stuff.' He wasn't keen, either, to hear her complaints about his party lifestyle.

Insiders knew about Victoria's opinion of Dave Gardner and his racy lifestyle. 'Dreggy,' she called his party crowd. In 2003, she had been particularly unhappy about Beckham being best man at Gardner's £2 million first wedding to the soap actress and socialite Davinia Taylor. His presence, she complained, increased the financial value of Gardner's contract with *OK!* magazine. She also didn't like the presence of Atomic Kitten Jenny Frost as chief bridesmaid. David and Jenny, she suspected, had kissed after a party.[6]

Two years after the wedding, Victoria was irritated by the publicity surrounding Gardner's 'crisis talks to save his marriage'. His wife had become notorious for lesbian affairs with her Primrose Hill neighbours and treatment for alcoholism and drug addiction at The Priory.[7] Their separation and eventual divorce increased the time Gardner and Beckham spent together, especially after Beckham stopped playing professional football. Without the demands of a strict training routine, Gardner had helped fill the vacuum by introducing him to glittering parties. He also encouraged his new friendships with model and TV presenter Alexa Chung and the actress and socialite Poppy Delevingne, both fellow bit-part actors in Guy Ritchie's latest film *King Arthur: Legend of the Sword*.

On that hot Sunday afternoon in 2017, Victoria's helicopter landed in a Somerset field close to the festival. With her entourage she headed in a golf buggy through the scruffy campers to the VIP zone. She was furious that her husband had failed to reply to her telephone calls and had dispatched a search party. Eventually, David appeared. Within seconds, they were embroiled in a ferocious argument.

Onlookers saw Brooklyn act as the peacemaker: 'Don't worry, Dad, I'll get you a drink.' Returning with a bottle of water and a double gin-and-tonic, their eldest son became Victoria's shoulder to cry on. 'They looked quite miserable,' said one eyewitness, 'but they managed to pose for the cameras.'[8] As accomplished media stars, the image of a blissful couple underpinned their whole business. Victoria always worked hard to establish an impression of harmony. The question was whether there was a deeper truth behind their appearance together. Known on occasion to be sulky, uncommunicative and domineering, Victoria's outbursts were resented by Beckham. Many believed that trust between the Beckhams had been seriously damaged over the last few years.

In her own autobiography *Learning to Fly*, Victoria admitted in 2001 that 'Fooling people becomes part of the buzz.'[9] Performing had become natural to Victoria. She protected herself, her business, her relationships and most other things too by giving interviews, interpreting the facts with a self-serving tilt. She made no attempt to spin a myth about herself using the power of silence.

Like most celebrities, David and Victoria were obsessed by media reports about themselves. Everything was focused upon their style. Studiously, they avoided saying what they represented. Or whether they represented anything. His smile and her pout filled the vacuum. In a crisis, they relied on memories of his magical goals to distract attention.

To remain a global brand, worth at the time about £250 million, required constant public interest. Any prospect of their fame fading was intolerable. 'The moment we have a problem is when the fans don't want to take a selfie,' was a familiar celebrity truism. 'When the music stops, will the public still want me?' was another showbiz cliché whispered by the narcissistic and insecure. If the public became indifferent to the Beckhams, their fortunes would disappear. Fear of losing their wealth had made the couple exceptionally money-conscious. In self-protection they had occasionally sacrificed a happy marriage, regarding it as being of less importance than everlasting fame. Every public appearance was pure theatre.

Victoria had come to Glastonbury to watch Ed Sheeran perform the festival's final set. Both Beckhams were invited to sit at the edge of the stage in full view of the audience. After partying for three days, David could not conceal his exhaustion. In spite of the ear-splitting noise, he kept falling asleep. In the accustomed management of the media, their spokeswoman simply said, 'They had a great night.' Nothing in the couple's life was left to misinterpretation or beyond their control.[10] Lapses were regretted, not least at the end of the festival. The Beckhams were unaware of a photographer snapping Victoria with her familiar pout and her arm draped possessively around David. Lady Mary Charteris was standing nearby. Just the picture David hoped to avoid.[11]

One year later, Beckham admitted to Australian television that his marriage was 'hard' and 'complicated'. In an unusually candid interview his confession devastated Victoria. For years she had cultivated the image of a Domestic Goddess. The Beckham team was always presented as a happy family based on true love between herself and her husband. Image-making was critical to their fortunes. Any cracks revealing the truth were vigorously sealed. Everything was about Brand Beckham. Rekindling memories of the Darkness in 2003 was forbidden.

CHAPTER 2
MADRID, JULY 2003

'Not my type,' thought Rebecca Loos as David Beckham stepped out of a private jet at Madrid's Torrejón airport. Dressed in a white suit, and with striking blond highlights, the footballer's diamond studs dazzled Loos under the bright sun. 'I'm just a regular bloke,' he had said recently, although he was wearing jewellery worth £40,000.[1]

Next to him on the aircraft steps, dressed in an identical white suit, was Victoria Beckham. Her diamonds also glinted in the sunlight. Employed solely to manage the Beckhams' first days in Spain, Loos, their new 26-year-old Dutch personal assistant, was intrigued by the challenge.

Beckham was not a stranger to Loos. Over several months, while working for his London agent SFX, Loos had watched the famous footballer amble through the Grosvenor Street office. He always looked as though he was evaluating each woman. Some longed for his attention. Others would later say he was rather creepy. Loos, a multi-lingual graduate, was not interested. After leaving SFX to work for another agency, Loos forgot about the star. A telephone call in June 2003 from Tony Stephens, the footballer's trusted agent, changed her life.

David Beckham's decision to leave Manchester United and sign for Real Madrid, the world's most successful football club, was global news. Aware that Loos spoke fluent Spanish, Stephens offered her a short contract to help the Beckhams settle in Madrid.

David Beckham's first hours in Spain were frenetic. Escorted by police cars, his convoy sped from the airport to the La Zarzuela hospital. Doctors were to certify that Real Madrid's £25 million purchase was in perfect health. The publicity was intense. An estimated two billion people were watching as Real Madrid's live TV cameras followed the 28-year-old star and nurses around the Sanitas clinic. With the gift of modest charm, Beckham effortlessly generated admiration and love.

The clinic's certificate of Beckham's fitness was only marred by their discovery that his left leg was shorter than his right leg. Subsequently, Beckham quipped that the doctors were wrong. After checking, he discovered that one leg was indeed longer than the other.

Outside the building the following day, over 200 broadcast cameras and about 400 journalists were waiting for Beckham to sign his contract. His pen, his publicists told the favoured reporters, was a gift from Victoria. 'Thank you very much,' Beckham told the club's chairman Florentino Pérez, a 56-year-old billionaire industrialist, after signing. 'You've made me a very happy man.'

'You have come to us from the Theatre of Dreams,' replied Pérez, 'to join the team of your dreams.' Presented by the president with the white number 23 shirt – a number made iconic by the legendary NBA player Michael Jordan of the Chicago Bulls. Beckham beamed towards the cameras. Like a professional model, he turned slowly to allow each cameraman to snap the perfect shot. Pérez was thrilled. Eight thousand replica shirts costing £58 each had already been sold in Madrid. Sell-outs were reported by shops across Spain. Pérez calculated that the world's most lucrative footballer would earn his new club an unprecedented fortune.

One thousand girls – many with Beckham's name written on their faces and arms – were chanting in the club's training ground: 'Beckham, cojonudo corno: Beckham, no hay ninguno.' After hearing the translation, the star smiled: 'No one has bigger balls than Beckham.' The fans' only irritation, some suggested, was directed at Posh. Worshipping him meant resenting her. Victoria smiled and waved.[2] 'My family are moving over,' Beckham told Real Madrid TV. 'My wife's going to be happy here.'

That night the Beckhams slept in a suite at the boutique hotel Santo Mauro. At the end of the second day Victoria asked Loos, 'You make things happen. Do you have a boyfriend?'

'Yes,' lied Loos, anxious to get a well-paid permanent job.[3]

'Would you like to work for us?'

Loos agreed to move to Madrid within one month. With that settled, Victoria returned to London.

Days later, Loos drove Beckham to his first training session. From habit he arrived early. Unnoticed, they waited in the car park. He could barely control his nerves and nearly retched. He did not want to stand alone in the changing room. Playing with Ronaldo of Brazil, the great French star Zinedine Zidane and other Galacticos was a challenge. News of his arrival had prompted the footballing heroes to grouse that Pérez had bought a shirt salesman from Manchester United rather than a world-beating player. Beckham was a very fine footballer, but in their eyes he did not rank as exceptional. In private, Florentino Pérez and his fellow directors did not disagree with the players' opinion, but Beckham's celebrity was hugely valuable to the club. His first match appearances would take place during Real Madrid's promotional trip to the Far East.

Four weeks earlier in June, Pérez had been amazed by Beckham's commercial success in Japan. Four thousand screaming fans had mobbed David and Victoria at Tokyo airport. Beatlemania had been reinvented with a dash of Cool Britannia, the brilliant merger of football and music. Tokyo was awash with Beckham memorabilia. His face was plastered over greeting cards, Meiji Almond Chocolate dolls, key-rings, wallpaper, bed linen and second-hand cars. 'This is unbelievable,' Beckham had said, smiling. Obeying a 32-page instruction book compiled by his publicists, his clothes, hairstyle and his every word had been carefully prepared. Posh stoked Beckham-mania by revealing that her husband liked his nails manicured and enjoyed facials.[4]

On the eve of his return to Japan with Real Madrid, the club had pocketed £7 million including an unprecedented £5.5 million from the sale of shirts. Over 300,000 of them were Beckham's number 23. Real Madrid charged 1.5 million euros to stage friendly games in Japan and China, three times more than Manchester United. Because of Beckham, the following year they would charge 5 million euros for the tour.[5] After the team bus arrived in Tokyo's city centre from the airport, thousands of hysterical girls prevented Beckham leaving his hotel. 'It's an extraordinary feeling,' Beckham admitted.[6] In the stadium, thousands of girls squealed whenever Beckham touched the ball. Forty-five thousand fans paid merely to watch him train. Ronaldo and other Galacticos watched in silence.

In Tokyo, Beckham's SFX's publicists had allowed trusted British journalists to interview Beckham. Pérez was annoyed. To control the new superstar SFX was told that only the club could organise interviews. Failure to obey would mean Beckham's instant dismissal. SFX scoffed. Managing Beckham's media appearances was essential to his brand – and that was SFX's sole interest.[7] Amazed by his extraordinary popularity, the football boot manufacturer Adidas concluded: 'He's the most popular athlete ever.' Seeing the unrivalled power of Beckham's image, the corporation increased its sponsorship offer. Instead of £4 million a year for seven years, he agreed to a life-time deal, subject to renewal every five years.[8]

With other sponsorship deals including Vodaphone, M&S, Police sunglasses and Pepsi, Beckham's annual income in 2003 was esti-mated at £18 million, including £92,000 per week he received from Real Madrid.[9] The Pepsi contract gave Beckham global recognition. Beckham's authenticity made the brand unbeatable.

Yet in August 2003 the world's highest-paid footballer's debut in the Bernabéu, Real Madrid's stadium, fell under close scrutiny. In two previ-ous away matches in Spain his performance had been poor. Football journalists described him as 'awkward', 'clumsy' and 'frustrated'. His credibility was on the line. But after 72 minutes on Real Madrid's home turf against Real Mallorca in the Spanish Super Cup he scored with a classic header from a cross by Ronaldo, to seal a 3–0 victory. It helped dispel the gossip that he was bought by Real Madrid just to sell shirts. With the roar of the stadium ('Beckham, Beckham') still echoing, the superstar admitted: 'It's the happiest I've been for two years.'[10]

At that moment his reputation was unchallengeable. Throughout his career Beckham had shown he could summon exceptional reserves of strength that would astonish his critics. Proving them wrong made his day. 'You know, I am in love with David Beckham,' Florentino Pérez told the British writer John Carlin.[11]

The impressive debut by England's captain in Madrid was hailed by his cheerleader the *Sun* newspaper in August: 'He is the perfect role model for every generation. A clean-living, honest, decent, caring, gentle bloke ... with old-fashioned values.'[12] To feed their 10 million readers' insatiable appetite for Beckham stories, the newspaper had sent two journalists to Madrid – one to cover Beckham's football career and the other to monitor the family's private lives – plus a photographer. The newspaper's executives knew that Beckham stories added sales.

Eric Beauchamp was given the *Sun*'s golden prize of living in Madrid to follow Beckham's football career. Standing in a cramped

pen by the players' exit, dubbed 'The Mix Zone', Beauchamp's intro-
ductory shout at Beckham elicited a friendly but short reply: 'Nice to
meet you,' and a handshake. Thereafter, three times a week,
Beauchamp was granted five minutes of the star's time. Everything was
controlled by Simon Oliveira, Beckham's tough spokesman. Oliveira
knew that the *Sun* needed to keep the tap flowing but his terms were
draconian. If the newspaper failed to tow the line, Beauchamp would
not be allowed even one minute with Beckham. In that claustrophobic
world, most journalists in The Mix Zone knew their place. Few dared
to risk losing their access, even with the limitations.

By contrast, the *Mirror*'s Oliver Holt was seen as independently
critical of Beckham. To get him into line, Beckham's housekeeper,
business manager and fixer Terry Byrne and Oliveira gave Holt a
scoop over the *Sun* – an interview with Beckham. 'Are you addicted
to fame?' asked Holt on the *Mirror*'s front page. The *Sun* was furious
to be scooped by their arch-rival. But the ploy worked. Thereafter,
Holt was more sympathetic towards Beckham.

Unlike other footballers, Beckham refused to socialise with journalists, not even over a beer. 'He'll never cross the line,' those sent to
Madrid understood. Even when journalists saw Beckham drinking at
the Irish Rover pub in central Madrid, he was never approached. 'We
treated him like royalty,' recalled one journalist.

The first hint of trouble was soon obvious. Contrary to her promises, Victoria did not move to Madrid with their two sons. Beckham
remained living alone in his hotel suite. When Beckham was substituted as Real Madrid lost 2–1 to Real Mallorca in a second match
between the clubs, Posh was in Chalk Farm in north London having
hair extensions put in. She was about to fly to New York.

Watching his humiliation in the Bernabéu stands was his old friend
Dave Gardner, as well as Beckham's mother Sandra and his assistant
Rebecca Loos. His unexpected substitution after 73 minutes, Beckham
revealed, made him 'sore'.[13] His loneliness in Madrid was aggravated
by the absence of one particular person, his father. Ted Beckham, a
gas fitter still living in their small Leytonstone family home, was the
architect and mentor of his son's success.

As a passionate Manchester United fan, Ted had started teaching
his young son the skill to control a football. In 1982, at the age of
seven, David was playing for a local club and regularly training under

Ted's supervision. Constantly, from every position, his son was learning to kick the ball into a goal. As a hard taskmaster Ted drilled discipline into the football-mad boy. Self-control, remaining calm in the face of challenges, he said, was critical for strength. Ted nurtured his son's competitive ego to believe he could achieve anything. He should never give up. Quitting was unimaginable. Stubborn ambition, in Ted's mantra, was essential. Perfecting skills was another.

In particular, Ted created his son's mastery of the deadball kick – kicking a stationary ball into the goal. After months of endless practice every day, the kick became instinctive. For young David Beckham, playing football became natural. When he was 15, in 1991, he was rewarded. Alex Ferguson, Manchester United's fearsome manager, personally recruited him to join the club's youth academy. Until then Ted had been David's sole mentor. Ferguson, who began to adopt and shape the young player, became his new mentor.

Born on New Year's Eve in 1941, Ferguson was brought up in Govan, Glasgow's notorious area for hard men, ship-workers, crime and deprivation. After playing professional football in Scotland and an astonishingly successful stint as manager of Aberdeen, which he had led to victory in the UEFA Cup Winners' Cup against Real Madrid in 1983, he moved to Manchester United in 1986. Known as 'The Boss', his outstanding 27-year reign was built on an iron determination to control every player, instil a hard work ethic, demand excellence and live by the mantra 'I have to win,' not only on the pitch but also in the dressing room. 'I made up my mind that I would never give in,' he said about his management style. Finding exceptional young players to mould them into stars as part of close team friendships was the background to Ferguson signing Beckham.

Thereafter, every week Ted and Sandra drove 200 miles to Manchester to watch their son train, and eventually play for, the club. Thanks to Ferguson, both parents were embraced as members of United's family, enjoying the directors' hospitality suite in Old Trafford and flying with the team to away matches.

Ted's privileges disappeared on the day his son was sold to Real Madrid. 'I've lost him,' Ted complained to a journalist. David, said Ted, had been 'forced out' of Manchester United. 'It's disgusting. This has been our life for the last 14 years and now it's over. I don't know what we'll do.'

Even worse was the personal schism between father and son. 'I'm upset the way things have gone. We've lost that comradeship we had between us. Unfortunately, David has got bigger than anything we could have dreamed of. His football was my life and once you have it you don't want to lose it.' Ted had created a man he no longer recognised. Communication was often through lawyers.[14]

Pouring out his distress, Ted admitted that his son's fame had been 'devastating for me and the whole family'. Even before his move to Madrid, their family relationships had disintegrated. 'My biggest fear is that it's all over for us.' Not only had Ted stopped regularly speaking to David, but after 32 years of marriage he and Sandra, a hairdresser, had divorced in 2002. In the bitter battle over cash and their house, Ted felt that David had not been overly generous. Despite earning millions of pounds, he had only paid off their small mortgage three years earlier and installed new windows in their modest house.

On a personal level, Ted blamed Victoria. She didn't conceal her dislike of her father-in-law, and once her own children were born David became more distant.[15] Ted also blamed Victoria's parents, Tony and Jackie Adams. The wealthy middle-class couple, he thought, were snobs. Both enjoyed the Beckhams' hospitality and placed themselves at the centre of their world. They had become intensely involved in the couple's personal lives and played a key role during the couple's arguments about their future.

Ted also blamed Alex Ferguson. 'I feel he has stabbed us in the back. David didn't want to go.' Not surprisingly, Ted did not sympathise with Ferguson's opinion of his son, which was that David's showbiz lifestyle and Victoria's influence were interfering with the player's professional dedication. Only 100 per cent commitment to Manchester United, to the exclusion of everything else, was acceptable. 'He's not a womaniser,' protested Ted. 'He's not a gambler, he doesn't get drunk. That's why I'm disappointed Ferguson has treated him like this.'

Surprised by Ted's outspokenness, Beckham called his father to protest.[16] Beckham was critical of his father. Not only did he complain that Ted had never praised him – not once – but was also, he believed, 'quite hard-faced and can be sarcastic. He also gets fired up easily'.[17]

Beckham's move to Madrid in 2003 broke Beckham's relationship with two mentors, the guiding spirits who had been critical to his success. Although he was stubborn he relied on his mentors to guide him through his career and marriage. As his later close advisers would discover, Beckham was 'malleable' but he could also move on. Without Ferguson and Ted, his only support was Tony Stephens, his loyal agent, and Victoria. Stephens had taken a sabbatical and Victoria had dramatically refused to move to Madrid. He was alone. None of those tensions were evident to the public when Beckham signed for the Spanish club.

Also hidden were the financial advantages of Beckham playing abroad. Not only had his income soared from £3.5 million in 2002 to £18.7 million in 2003,[18] but if he had stayed in Britain most of his personal income would be taxed at 40 per cent. By moving to Spain he not only escaped British taxes on all his profits earned outside Britain but he also benefited from 'Beckham's law', a special Spanish exemption reducing income tax for foreigners from 47 per cent to 24 per cent.

Money obsessed the Beckhams. Thrilled to be rich, they were terrified by the prospect of sliding back into a constrained standard of living. Opportunities to legally avoid taxes abounded. Beckham's 2003 company accounts showed that when he moved to Real Madrid he was not paying National Insurance contributions, and had effectively become a non-dom.[19]

Taking advantage of the move offshore, his accumulated income in 2003 was received by Beckham's company Footwork in 2004. The British company's cash deposit increased from £134,000 to £12,780,000. Simultaneously, he established a Spanish company also called Footwork described as 'acting as a representative office'. That company's profits in 2004 were just £29,000. Footwork's profits, it appeared from their filed accounts, were not being taxed in Britain and there were no taxable profits earned in Spain. A spokesman for Beckham said that he was at the time taxed fully on all his income earned in Spain and his income earned elsewhere in the relevant jurisdictions.

Allowing him to remain a non-dom, Beckham would reject the possibility of returning to the UK to play for Chelsea, would move to America rather than return to Britain, and would play for a season in France before the financial year ended.

Over the rest of his career, Beckham gave the impression that playing the tax card had become nearly as important in his life as kicking the ball.

CHAPTER 3
LONDON, JULY 2023

Twenty years after his move to Spain, Beckham told an audience in London's St John's Wood that he had been utterly surprised in 2003 by Manchester United's decision to sell him. 'My friend Dave Gardner called,' explained Beckham. 'He said, "Turn on the TV. Manchester United have accepted an offer from Barcelona." That was the first I heard about it.' He continued his story by recounting that in his next telephone call he had protested to Manchester United's managing director Peter Kenyon, 'I don't want to go to Barcelona.' He was not allowed to speak to Ferguson, he told his audience. 'One and a half days later I was sold to Real Madrid.'

Few in the audience of 700 would have any reason to doubt Beckham. With glowing charm, his East London twang gave his recollection utter authenticity. But as Beckham ought to have recalled, his version gave his audience a somewhat misleading impression.[1] Whether Beckham had over the years forgotten the complete truth was uncertain. His agents and the club, as he knew, had spent one year negotiating his transfer to Real Madrid. The Barcelona announcement was just Manchester United's negotiating tactic to extract a better price from Madrid, and a gimmick by an aspiring president of the Barcelona club. His mistaken recollection about his life-changing move to Spain was not exceptional. Over years of hype to boost Brand Beckham, both David and Victoria Beckham had altered the reality of many milestones in their lives.

Beckham had good reason to reinterpret the circumstances surrounding his 2003 transfer. Convinced at the outset of his career that he would forever play at Manchester United, his transfer had destabilised his marriage and, more important, threatened the cultivated image of a happy family man with a loving wife.

By any measure, as a member of the Spice Girls, Victoria had been part of a global phenomenon. The group had sold 85 million albums and earned millions of pounds from shows and merchandise. But ever since the group disintegrated in 2000 after four best-selling years and two years after Geri Halliwell had abruptly walked out, Victoria feared losing her celebrity status. When she married David in 1999 she was the star, but since 2000 she had reluctantly hitched herself to Beckham's ever-growing international superstardom. Posing as the happiest couple in showbusiness, Victoria had said before his transfer to Madrid: 'He's the incarnation of everything I want. I'm very faithful because he's faithful.'[2]

In a bid to renew her public glory, Victoria had invited the *Sun*'s columnist Lorraine Kelly to accompany her shopping in 2001. 'Posh' was not really posh, Kelly knew, but she was to the newspaper's readers.

Her parents, Tony and Jackie Adams, had brought up their three children in The Old School House in Goff's Oak in Hertfordshire. Tony Adams' electrical wholesale business had paid for a second-hand Rolls-Royce and a comfortable lifestyle for Jackie, who had worked as an insurance clerk and hairdresser. Both parents were credited with instilling their daughter with ferocious ambition and a passion for performing. The family's remarkably close bonds sustained Victoria through repeated pitfalls before she became famous. By 2003, she had perfected a performance for the public as self-confident, pouting Posh and, in private, as a master of media manipulation.

Accordingly, after their shopping trip, Lorraine Kelly revealed that her preconception of a 'right little madam' had been mistaken. Victoria, she wrote, was 'an utterly charming, bright-eyed young woman with a gorgeous smile'. The Beckhams, Kelly continued, should be 'hailed as the most positive of role models'. Kelly concluded that the couple, blessed with extraordinary talent and rewarded for their sheer hard work, were the victims of 'sour people's unhealthy streak of jealousy'.[3] Kelly's judgement had delighted her readers.

Ever since David Yelland became the *Sun*'s editor in 1998, he had decided that the Beckhams would sell newspapers. They glowed with glamour, just like the late Princess Diana. Yelland's newspaper treated the couple as royalty. In the newspaper's portrayal, they represented the Best of Britain. The combination of football and sex was magic. Putting them on the front page automatically increased the newspaper's 3.8 million circulation by 4 per cent. Most of the 10 million readers loved the Beckhams.

Backing Beckham proved to be a money-spinner after the 21-year-old Beckham, playing for Manchester United, scored a spectacular goal in August 1996 from the halfway line against Wimbledon. 'That one swing of a new boot ... kicked open the door to the rest of my life,' Beckham admitted. 'Watching it still leaves me with goose-pimples.'[4] Although his goal was scored in injury time and Manchester United were already in the lead, his star thereafter had shone. 'I have always been convinced of my own ability,' he said the following year, after scoring another sensational goal for England against Italy from 25 yards. 'It is a pressure I enjoy living with.'

The *Sun*'s readers had arrived at the Italy match with masks of Beckham's face. 'The *Sun* proudly backs Beckham' pronounced the newspaper knowing that football fans wanted a hero. 'Beckham', the newspaper predicted, 'is going to be a huge star and a great player for years. He makes things happen and the crowd are excited every time he touches the ball.'[5]

Stunningly handsome, modest and clean-living, Beckham was a British dream boy. Living first as a lodger opposite Old Trafford and then in his own townhouse, with steady girlfriends – Deana and then Helen – he forged lifelong friendships among the club's young players, including brothers Gary and Philip Neville. Under Ferguson, Manchester United was a family demanding loyalty and unquestioning obedience to the coaches. The routine was demanding. Every day Beckham trained hard and then played even harder, until in 1995 he won his place in the first team. Seeking a mentor on the pitch, he picked out the legendary French attacker, Eric Cantona. Hero-worshipping one of the club's greatest ever players, Beckham spotted Cantona's unspoken 'edge' separating him from the ordinary. Specialness was precisely what Beckham aspired to replicate.

Brylcreem was to be the end of Beckham's innocence. In 1997, Sara Lee, the company's new American owner, was looking for a star to relaunch the hair cream using the tag 'Brylcreem Boy'.

The advertising agency's approach to Tony Stephens, Beckham's agent, produced an unexpectedly quick reply. Jumping at the opportunity as 'interested and honoured', Stephens accepted £200,000 for a two-year deal.

'We were genuinely shocked,' the advertising executive who signed the deal said later. 'We signed him up so easily, and so cheaply.' They did not appreciate the tax advantages for Beckham. The costs of his image rights could be offset against his income from the club. Brylcreem's only condition was that Beckham's hair would never be shorter than a 'Number 2' cut: one-quarter of an inch.

Invented in Birmingham in 1928, Brylcreem was a mixture of water, mineral oil and beeswax. Its popularity had declined since the cricket and football star Denis Compton had been its 'face' during the 1950s. Forty years later, WCRS, a British advertising agency, urged Lee that Beckham's fame after the Wimbledon goal made him a natural for Brylcreem's working-class market. Aged 22, he was the quiet, good-looking, unpolished young bloke with perfect hair who lived down the road. Among Beckham's other strengths was his innocence. He was not a rasping celebrity, but a passionate footballer. Eventually, Lee agreed.

Beckham's spokesman told the media that Brylcreem had paid £4 million for a four-year contract.[6] There was good reason to lie. Beckham's new girlfriend, the business-savvy Victoria Adams, alias 'Posh Spice', complained that her boyfriend was worth much more than £200,000 a year.[7] Stephens, she added, had made the same mistake by signing a four-year deal for Beckham with Adidas for £800,000.

Victoria's influence did not stop at the fees. While a Brylcreem TV advertisement was shot at Brentford's football ground, Griffin Park, she continued to interfere. 'Hello, Vicks,' Beckham said in his frequent calls. The footballer was filmed kicking the ball from the penalty spot into the goal, and then turning to the camera and saying, 'I've always used Brylcreem since I was a kid.' There were problems, he confided to Victoria.

'We were shocked by his voice,' recalls a creative at WCRS. 'It was flat and robotic. It was really awkward getting him to say his lines again and again. We couldn't get a performance out of him.'

A director had intervened. 'Say it again, David, with a bit more gravitas.' Silence. Everyone realised that shy Beckham with his high-pitched voice didn't understand the meaning of 'gravitas'. Flummoxed, an executive for the PR agency Shilland reported: 'He is very acutely aware of his voice. He is obviously self-conscious about it.' In the end, his words to the camera were junked and replaced by the song 'There She Goes'.

Even more worrying during the shoot were Beckham's misses. Instead of kicking the ball into the open goal, the ball went repeatedly over the bar. 'Christ,' moaned a member of the crew. 'It's just weeks before the World Cup.' But at least his image as a genuine bloke was authentic. At lunchtime, he was asked to choose a meal from a sophisticated menu. After hesitating he asked, 'Could I have a Hawaiian Pizza from Pizza Express?'

Victoria was 'negative' about the finished TV advert. So was the agency. It was ditched. Only the women at the advertising agency's office watched it. During their lunch break, they repeatedly replayed the tape. 'They thought he was a dream,' sighed the frustrated creative director.

There was not the slightest hint of those problems during the public unveiling of Beckham as the 'Brylcreem Boy'. He smiled at the photographers, played with his hair and said nothing. 'He appeared shell-shocked by the interest,' recalled an advertising man. 'He was quiet. There was nothing polished about him at all.'[8] Although known to be modest, the PR executive also realised that Beckham was a showman. He loved to perform in front of a packed Old Trafford. And he loved the camera. David Beckham had become a face for sale.

Beckham's relationship with the tabloid press had become critical. Football journalists were fond of Beckham, not least because on trips to away games he brought coffee to them at the back of the bus. Chatting with the football writers about his favourite subject made even experienced journalists give the sincere player the benefit of any doubt.

Primed by Tony Stephens, Beckham understood that he shared with the tabloids a mutual interest: to keep the story going. 'Speak to them but don't tell them anything,' Stephens ordered his client. 'Less is more.' The lesson was clear: promise the headline, 'Beckham Opens His Heart' but never deliver. Every interview was transactional. Journalists would be given access, but were never regarded as friends. Those who thought they were close were mistaken. Journalists were to be used. In the early days of his relationship with Posh Spice, there were exceptions.

'Trust Andy Coulson', ordered Alan Edwards, the Spice Girls' publicist. Coulson, the *Sun*'s ambitious 29-year-old showbiz editor, was a trusted friend of Edwards, who ranked as one of the music world's most influential publicists. Among his clients were David Bowie, Prince, Blondie and the Rolling Stones. Edwards' work for the Spice Girls focused on their personal lives while the record companies promoted their discs. Among the prominent employees of his company, The Outside Organisation, was Caroline McAteer, the daughter of an Ulster policeman. She was known by journalists as the 'attack dog'. McAteer was tasked by Edwards to devote herself to Victoria.

Coulson, said Edwards, would deliver the Beckhams' ambition. With soft aggression coated with modest charm, Coulson had first ingratiated himself in November 1997. 'She's sitting tantalisingly close to me,' he wrote, claiming that Victoria had broken eight months of silence to finally speak about her relationship with Beckham. 'For the first time in my life I'm happy,' she told Coulson, flashing a gold Rolex watch, a present from Beckham. 'Sincerely happy. I've never felt like I do now.'[9]

David and Victoria had met exactly one year earlier. In November 1996 she had been a guest with the Spice Girls' manager Simon Fuller at a record company's box at Stamford Bridge. Arriving during the match between Manchester United and Chelsea, the famous Spice Girl pointed at Beckham on the pitch. 'I fancy that bloke,' she told an executive. At her request Fuller introduced the two of them to one another in the players' lounge. Both would say it was love at first sight, but there was also an unusual attraction between the two stars. Both were trophy hunters.

In January 1998, with Edwards' approval, the 'lovestruck' Posh, aged 23, and Becks, 22, again confided in Coulson and the *Sun*'s readers. Showing off their engagement rings – a £40,000 solitaire ring for her and a £50,000 diamond band for him – they revealed the 'secrets of their love story'. How soccer ace David fell for Victoria Adams as he watched a Spice Girls video, and how she was captivated watching him play for Manchester United.[10]

Their marriage, predicted Coulson, would be 'the showbiz wedding of the decade'. The wedding took place on 4 July 1999 in Luttrellstown Castle outside Dublin. It was the beginning of a unique relationship between the Beckhams and the media. Victoria would call it after the association soured 'an unhealthy obsession with Posh and Becks'.[11]

Richard Desmond, notorious for his abrasive manner, owner of pornographic publications and *OK!* magazine, paid an unprecedented £1 million for the exclusive picture rights to the wedding. Victoria had set the terms. On their wedding night she spent hours selecting the right photographs for the magazine's special edition. To Desmond's fury, the *Sun* arranged for photos of the ceremony to be secretly shot and published before *OK!*'s special edition was even printed.

After the extraordinary ceremony, Victoria set the terms for obtaining the two velvet thrones on which the couple sat during the celebrations. Bought by the *Sunday Mirror* for £1,500, the thrones were offered by the newspaper to the reader who won a competition. Once chosen, the newspaper suggested to Caroline McAteer, Victoria's trusted spokeswoman, that the singer could present them to the reader.

'No,' replied McAteer. 'Vic wants them. For nothing.'

Surprised, the newspaper's executive agreed, but only if Victoria agreed to be photographed accepting the newspaper's gift. McAteer concurred, but there was a hitch. Without a fanfare the thrones were taken off the lorry outside her house. The doorbell was rung.

McAteer voiced outrage. 'Victoria wants to be surprised,' she said in a fury.

The delivery had to be contrived as a revelation. 'You mean staged?' asked the journalist.

From that moment, the *Sunday Mirror* and every other tabloid journalist understood that Victoria and Beckham wanted to 'play' coy. They would appear to resist media intrusion while agreeing to stage 'impromptu' photographs. Their collusion with the media was to be disguised.

In the year after their media-blitz wedding in Ireland, David Yelland spoke about his newspaper's creation of the 'icons of our age'. Everyone was interested in the Beckhams. Tabloid readers adored the celebrities' lives.

The *Sun*'s new showbiz editor Dominic Mohan summarised the country's 'addiction to our premier couple'. As 'ambassadors of their generation, we love them because both are completely normal', he wrote. 'They have become cultural icons and role models to millions.

They are just like you or me. They have captured our imaginations with their style and sometimes questionable tastes.' Good-looking, polite and genuinely in love, the showbiz couple had become the new royalty. Having 'conquered the world' they evoked 'special emotions in us'. Their appeal to tabloid readers was that neither were 'contrived or cultivated. As unsure of themselves as we all are.' Posh could be the girl working behind the counter at the local Tesco.[12]

Yelland also grasped that he had underestimated Victoria. She had seen the bigger picture before others. She had listened and learned, not least from her father, a self-made businessman. 'Don't mess around,' was his gospel. 'You're there to make money.' After watching the mechanics of manufacturing publicity for the Spice Girls, Victoria knew that her best tactic was to remain an enigma. The Beckhams' success depended upon creating fascination about every detail of their lives. If the public remained intrigued, their fame would continue. Victoria and David, Yelland realised, had broken the mould of the usual football or pop stars. They were moving far beyond what their advisers and mentors expected.

By 2001, Alex Ferguson had good reason to be suspicious of the Beckhams' 'faithful' image conjured through the media. Football players live as a family, especially during foreign tours. Infidelity was not a big issue among footballers. But rumours had seeped back to Old Trafford that in early August Beckham had met a party girl in Singapore's Shangri-La hotel, the team's stopover during an Asian tour. Her vivid account of their meeting would be published three years later.

Sarah Marbeck described how four hours after they met they were in bed. 'I looked down,' recalled Marbeck, 'and there was David Beckham kissing my breasts. David Beckham!'[13] Marbeck kept Beckham's text message sent on 8 August 2001. The previous night, he wrote, was 'amazing and ... I want some more nites like that.'[14] In Marbeck's version, Beckham fantasised that she was a call-girl like Julia Roberts in the film *Pretty Woman* while he was the rich married businessman portrayed by Richard Gere. In his texts Marbeck was called 'Tinkerbell' and Victoria was 'Wendy'.

On 10 August 2001, Beckham had sent a series of explicit texts to Tinkerbell about his sexual fantasies. Asked for a description of underwear he had bought for her, he replied: 'It is a surprise. It's very sexy but very filthy.' Then he fantasied about drizzling champagne and licking the drops from her naked flesh: 'When I've had a drink, I get very dirty. Imagine candles, champagne, chocolate, cream, strawberries and a massive bed. U can trust me that when I c u I'll be so in your ***** you'll never get me out. I'm just imaging u in the shower and how I wish I was soaping you down and down and down.'[15] Marbeck kept all those text messages.

During their two-year affair Marbeck flew to Leeds in March 2002 to watch England v Italy. In a text he urged her to behave 'discreetly' because 'you have to remember Wendy' (Victoria's codename). Later, they had sex in the team hotel. Afterwards Beckham texted her: 'I would love to see you on the bed naked. Do you know you have the best set of lips I have ever kissed?' Marbeck did not reveal whether she had told Beckham that she was working as a prostitute in Sydney, Australia.

Shortly afterwards, on 17 August 2002, Celina Laurie was in bed with Beckham in Denmark. They had met at a hotel bar in the team's hotel. At 4 a.m. in his bedroom, she recalled that 'I had to pinch myself to make sure I wasn't dreaming. I was utterly seduced by him. He had a charm that is irresistible.' Picking up girls after matches, Laurie later realised, 'was quite normal for Beckham'.[16] What Laurie and Marbeck's experiences also indicate is Beckham's excitement about taking a risk.

During those months, Victoria told *Glamour* magazine she would 'die of a broken heart' if David were unfaithful.[17] Secretly suspecting him of an affair, she had become hysterical. 'I actually physically beat him up. I punched him in the face,' she said.[18] Her jealousy extended to forbidding Beckham to appear in a Pepsi advert with Britney Spears. The American singer's sin was to call him 'cute'.[19]

Aware of the facts and the rumours, one of the Beckham's employees leaked the possibility of a divorce. 'They have nothing in common and have grown tired of each other,' reported the *Sun*.[20] The report was quickly buried.

CHAPTER 4

FLASHPOINT

Years later, Beckham would tell an admiring audience in London that his private life 'never affected my game'. He added, 'I never let fame get in the way. Nothing changed in my football because of fame and publicity.' Alex Ferguson disagreed. Too often, he believed, Beckham's celebrity had started to undermine the footballer's performance.

The breathtaking publicity machine that created the Beckham Brand was not just a consequence of his enviable good looks, flawless charm and some magical goals, but also – as Beckham himself admitted – he 'loves the adulation'.[1] Rhetorically he asked: 'What can I do? I would be lying if I said that I did not enjoy most of the publicity. I believe I have come to terms with being in the public eye. I have accepted that it will not go away, nor change, and I am handling it. In fact, you get used to it.' Seven days later, he said the opposite: 'I still find it odd when I am on the front pages because I dyed my hair blond.'[2]

Deliberately he generated attention. Not only did Beckham drive around Manchester's Deansgate area in his open-top Ferrari, waving at fans, but when heading for a local sandwich shop he ignored a parking space outside the shop and left his car several hundred yards away. He enjoyed being recognised on his walk to buy a sandwich.[3]

'It would be brilliant if I could become as big as Gazza,' Beckham had said. 'I would love to be that big.' To identify Paul Gascoigne, who became an unstable alcoholic, as his role model did not reassure Alex Ferguson. Equally surprised was Glenn Hoddle, the England team manager charged with winning the World Cup in France in summer 1998. Both managers had become wary of Beckham's stubborn impatience and insubordination.

Those characteristics had already been obvious to a schoolteacher. 'As a youngster, I did have a dodgy temperament,' admitted Beckham.

'If things did not go my way, I would shout and yell.' In a 1987 school report his teacher wrote that 'David is continuously silly' and suffers a 'lack of self-discipline'.[4] Years later, after being sent off in a match against France for an explosive tirade against a referee, he admitted: 'My reaction was over the top. I do get hyped up before games. It starts on the morning of the match … I cannot sleep after matches, never. I have to control that frustration.'[5]

The fans ignored that flaw. They were desperate for a football hero. Ferguson was less sure. Once the team had to wait at an airport for Beckham, who had forgotten his passport. During a match against Chelsea in March 1998 he got his fifth yellow card, and there had also been several lucky escapes when the referee was looking the other way. He justified his aggression: 'I'm doing what I think is right to win.'[6]

Glenn Hoddle shared Ferguson's doubts. In the summer of 1998 Hoddle carried a heavy responsibility. England was electrified by the imminent World Cup tournament in France. Nostalgic about England's sole triumph in 1966, the fans, encouraged by the media, were convinced of another victorious return to London. Naturally, Hoddle could leave nothing to chance. Was Beckham's modesty a mask, he wondered? Was his charm sincere or skin-deep? And was his multi-millionaire lifestyle with Victoria destabilising him? In the run-up to the World Cup, Hoddle noticed Beckham's 'suspect temperament'. 'He's a notorious moaner,' said Hoddle. 'I have seen things go on this season that will lead to a red card. We can't afford that to happen in the World Cup.'

Beckham saw himself in a different light: 'I have never been sent off in my professional career and I do not think I have got a problem with my temperament.'[7] Great players, he reasoned, must have 'an edge to their character'. Hoddle disagreed. In a 'friendly' match against Portugal in April 1998, Beckham failed to produce a single cross. In the second half Hoddle pulled him off the pitch. England won 3–0.

To Beckham's fury he was dropped from England's opening game in the World Cup against Tunisia. 'He was not focused on the tournament,' explained Hoddle later. 'He was vague.'[8] Hoddle blamed this on Victoria's use of Beckham to promote her own career. After he wore a sarong in a restaurant she told the *Sun*'s Victoria Newton that

Beckham also wore her knickers. She also boasted about 'a sex romp in the back of her Mercedes sports car'.[9] On the eve of the first World Cup match, Hoddle judged that Beckham was 'shattered'. Instead of being wholly focused on football, Beckham was distracted by the tabloid's headlines – about his fame and romance with Victoria. 'I was devastated,' admitted Beckham, hours after being dropped by Hoddle, 'and I still can't come to grips with it even now.'[10]

Beckham's inner strength confounded his critics. Seven days later he was sent on as a substitute against Romania. An almighty roar from 25,000 fans swept across the Toulouse stadium, followed by the crowd singing 'You'll Never Walk Alone'. 'It sent a shiver down my spine,' said Beckham. Within minutes he had the ball at his feet, wrong-footed two defenders and charged down the wing. But there was no goal. England lost the match 2–1 after Romania scored in the 90th minute.

Hoddle rightly chose Beckham four days later for the third match against Colombia. Sensationally, he drove a curving free kick from 30 yards to score a goal. 'It's just unbelievable,' swooned one football writer after England's 2–0 victory. 'A wonder goal.' England would now face Argentina.[11]

The night before the game, Victoria called from New York to announce her pregnancy. Beckham has never explained whether that news influenced what Hoddle called his 'mental state' during the crucial match.

The events that unfolded in the 47th minute indelibly defined not only Beckham but also English football forever. Falling to the ground after a foul by Argentina's Diego Simeone, Beckham, who was face-down on the pitch, impetuously kicked out in retaliation at Simeone standing above him. Simeone fell to the ground. The Danish referee showed Beckham the red card. Crushed and crying he staggered back to the dressing room, devastated. He feared becoming an outcast after the remaining ten Englishmen battled to a draw, but lost in yet another penalty shoot-out. Beckham's misery was not relieved by Hoddle. In a television interview the disappointed manager blamed Beckham for England being eliminated from the tournament. Ever since, Beckham resented Hoddle's refusal to console him and for openly heaping the blame on him. Hoddle became the villain in Beckham's crafted auto-biography.

Ferguson, his loyal mentor, offered the shattered player some reassurance. Priding himself that 'sometimes you have to be a doctor, or a teacher, or a father,' Ferguson said in a telephone call, 'Son, get back to Manchester, you'll be fine.'[12, 13]

Later, Simeone would admit that Beckham's kick never touched him.

Beckham returned to England as a pariah. In the stadiums and the streets he was a target of vicious abuse. The yobs were at their worst. They would scream: 'We're going to kill your baby'; 'We hope your kid dies of cancer'; and 'Your wife's a whore.'

'This is not for us,' declared Brylcreem's Sara Lee. She ended the sponsorship without an announcement. But others ignored the furore and spotted opportunities. British PR expert Jackie Cooper was among the few who predicted a lucrative future for the footballer: 'We would recommend any firm with a big budget to try and get David Beckham to launch an advertising campaign. He's the boy of the moment, doing heroic things that every boy aspires to – scoring for England and playing for Manchester United. He's drop-dead gorgeous to boot. He even looks good in a skirt.'[14]

Deep down, the crisis turned Beckham into a harder man. While he recognised his errors, he could never totally control his rage. Months after the World Cup, his temper produced a warning and a yellow card for reckless tackles in club matches in Poland and Germany. He was unapologetic, as always: 'I'm not only better but a stronger person because of all the stick I've taken.'[15]

During 1999, sheer will power fuelled Beckham's return to superhero status. In March two crosses for Manchester United against Inter Milan produced two goals. 'He was brilliant,' said Ferguson with rare praise. 'He is now top of his game.'[16] Two months later a 30-yard curling free kick gave Manchester United a win against Aston Villa. Beckham was hailed as a 'midfield magician', 'unstoppable' and 'world class'.[17] Shortly after, against Barcelona, he led the charge, and was once more acclaimed by Ferguson. 'All he wants to do is play football.' Then in 'one of the most nail-biting climaxes for years', he scored against Spurs to give Manchester United the Premiership title.

One week later he played in a 2–1 victory against Newcastle United in the FA Cup. Days later, Beckham's corners produced two goals for a 2–1 victory against Bayern Munich and the UEFA Champions

League trophy. Unassailable Manchester United had won three trophies – the Premier League, the FA and the European Cups: the Treble. Ferguson was an international hero – and Beckham shone. 'It has been pure character,' concluded Kevin Keegan about Beckham's recovery. 'He has shown us what he has got. He has been a great example for so many others.'

Every appearance – and he loved performing in front of tens of thousands – confirmed his stardust. No less than 23 of United's goals that season came from his crosses. After his astonishing passes produced two winning goals against Southampton, their manager Dave Jones said: 'I just drool when I watch him play. There's quite simply nobody in the world better at crossing the ball than him.' Beckham adored the showers of praise.

Commuting between his in-laws' home in Hertfordshire and his luxury flat in Manchester, he revelled at parties and on the street as the style-setter and pin-up. Every outfit, every smile, every comment was minutely detailed by newspapers and magazines. One evening he wore a handkerchief bandana on his head. Another day a woman's knitted Tibetan peasant hat, complete with bobble and earflaps. 'I like to dress in a fashionable way,' he told the *Sun*.[18] To men and women he was an object of aspiration or desire. 'From Ongar to Oldham,' wrote an observer, 'dedicated fans of fashion are mad for the Beckham look. And you don't even have to be able to afford designer prices if you want your man to look like the trend-setting soccer ace, because now the High Street have rushed out versions of his most fashionable outfits.'

Even the *Sun*'s football writer Neil Custis recorded from his Old Trafford eyrie, 'Publicity-wise, himself and Posh Spice have taken the place of the Royal Family. The couple's looks, fortune and fame have made them an insatiable subject for the masses.'[19] *GAY* magazine described the 24-year-old as having 'the face of an angel and the bum of a Greek god'.[20] Gay men's attention, Victoria told the G-A-Y TV show, excited him: 'He walks around the kitchen going, "I'm a gay icon. I'm a gay icon."' After Posh insisted that she too was an icon, Beckham teasingly said: 'But they love me. You've got nothing on me, baby.'

Victoria helped to shape his lifestyle and fashion image. But in private she was at the end of her tether. In the midst of blistering rows she urged him not sign another contract with Manchester United. She hated living in Manchester, away from her family. She wanted him to join a London club. 'I did all I could to get David away from Manchester,' she told her London-based family and friends.[21] She neither liked commuting to Manchester, nor did she like their flat in Cheshire's Alderley Edge. Fellow residents in the converted mansion had started a petition urging the family to move out. Regardless of the couple's fame, some could no longer live with Victoria's screaming outbursts and the demand that they move to London. Others resented being forced by the Beckhams' bodyguards to leave the communal garden. Desperate to live near her parents, she pronounced: 'At some point he will move from Manchester United. I think playing abroad is something he would like to do.'[22]

Shortly after her unhappiness was exposed, Victoria summoned Rav Singh, a trusted *Sun* showbiz editor, to say the exact opposite. 'These reports are unfair and hurtful to both David and me,' she told Singh. 'The fans have made me feel very welcome in Manchester. I have no reason to want David to quit. I know how much it means for David to play for United, so I'd never put him in a position like that.'[23] To protect them both, David repeated the script. 'Victoria loves Manchester,' Beckham told the newspaper. 'There's been a lot of rubbish about her not liking the city. It's a load of nonsense.'

CHAPTER 5

SEPTEMBER 1999

After the summer of Treble glory, the problems could not be hidden from football writers. 'There was something very worrying about the performance of David Beckham in Graz,' wrote Neil Custis in September 1999 after a European Champions League game in Austria. 'From the first whistle, he looked like a man on a mission to self-destruct. From word go, he was charging around like a lunatic, flying into tackles and snarling at the opposition.'

Ferguson was appalled by Beckham's *kung-fu*-style kick that could have broken the leg of Sturm Graz's Tomislav Kocijan. Whenever Beckham performed badly, Ferguson usually blamed Victoria for the player's poor behaviour. The night before the team flew from Manchester to Austria, Beckham had been with Victoria at a showbiz party in London's Covent Garden. The next morning, photographed wearing a £75 headscarf, he had sped up the motorway and he was one of the last players to arrive at the airport at 8.30 a.m.[1] Hyped up, he committed a second offence in the Graz match and was suspended from playing in the second leg. Branded 'arrogant and provocative' after his night of fury in Austria, Ferguson fined his player £40,000.

Instead of retreating contrite into the shadows, Beckham got on a plane and flew to see Victoria in Los Angeles. The 48-hour round trip was meant to be secret, but Victoria could not resist giving 'exclusive access' to the *Sun*'s Victoria Newton. The journalist 'spotted' the couple enjoying a Halloween dinner at the Mondrian Hotel with Rolling Stone Mick Jagger and supermodel Kate Moss at nearby tables. With Beckham beside her, Victoria got Newton's co-operation to write a puff-piece: 'Victoria had to be in Los Angeles for business reasons. She is very much in demand in America. They love her and think she would make a great TV personality. She hasn't ruled out a solo pop career but she is looking at all the options. She is in demand for all sorts of film and TV roles but she has not yet signed anything final.' The pay-off was certain to infuriate Ferguson: 'Becks joined her on the trip but he didn't want a big fuss made because of all the attention he attracts wherever he goes.'

Ferguson's disillusionment with Beckham was growing. Whenever he saw a newspaper photograph of the player – and that was on most days – his face turned thunderous. On one day Posh and David were snapped at a star-studded party hosted by designer Donatella Versace at her West End store. Both wore matching black leather outfits. 'I want another baby' was the headline of Victoria's interview with her 'special friend', Dominic Mohan.[2] Another day, both appeared in his-'n'-hers Gucci biker outfits, and then in leather and PVC trousers. High Streets were full of PVC and leather trousers 'thanks to the trend-setting couple,' wrote Mohan. Victoria's Gucci designer pair 'cost a whopping £1,400, but even prices in your local stores can put a strain on the purse – the M&S version costs £175'.

As the Beckhams' fortunes soared, Ferguson complained, 'I saw his transition to a different person.'[3] Victoria's influence, said the manager, 'changed everything'. Before their marriage Beckham practised every day after training was over. That had changed. At the end of the session, Beckham sped off. And then, Ferguson noticed that while the Beckhams complained about publicity they were constantly promoting themselves on the catwalk and at film premieres. They clearly adored being Britain's most famous celebrity couple. 'I had to think about control of the club,' recalled Ferguson. 'David Beckham thought he was bigger than Alex Ferguson. That was the death knell for him.'[4]

Brooklyn Beckham's birth on 4 March 1999 was a momentous life-changer for both parents. Ferguson understood Beck's emotions and told him to stay with the baby in London and return to Manchester just before the next match.[5] The amenability was short-lived. Over the next four months, Ferguson's patience snapped.

Arriving at the training ground, Michael Jackson was blasting from Beckham's Rolls-Royce's 12-speaker stereo. It got worse when 'the car crazy soccer star' roared into Old Trafford alternately driving his £150,000 Ferrari, Porsche, Jaguar XK8, BMW, Range Rover or his £250,000 gleaming Bentley. Teammate Roy Keane ironically observed, 'He upped everyone's game in the car park, I'll give him that.' Victoria was more enthusiastic. 'David just loves the Bentley,' she said. 'It's a real status symbol.' Her spokeswoman added, 'It oozes class and sophistication.' Ferguson had a different opinion: 'As a Londoner, Beckham is a bit flash at times. I think it's something in the water down there.'[6]

The trigger for the first showdown was Beckham's decision in July 1999 not to drive from his London home to training in Manchester. Soon after leaving his house, he was told that four-month-old Brooklyn was ill. He was needed to care for the child. On the same day Victoria was photographed shopping in London. Ferguson was outraged. Players' families, Ferguson believed, should come second to the club. His control was being challenged by the celebrity circus. Beckham's talent, Ferguson raged, was being diminished by 'that woman's' hectic lifestyle and Beckham's extravagance'. Victoria could not forgive Ferguson when he ruined their honeymoon. Not only had he refused them two extra days away, but he also ordered Beckham to train with the reserves while the rest of the team had four days off.

After baby Brooklyn recovered, Beckham drove to Manchester. He arrived after the day's training was finished and saw Ferguson in his office. During 'the biggest dressing down I've ever had in my career', Ferguson told him the club came before family. 'I didn't back down,' admitted Beckham, insisting that his family came first.[7]

To re-establish his control, Ferguson dropped Beckham from a critical match against Leeds and fined him £50,000 for missing the training session. He also allowed the rumour to spread that Beckham might be sold for £22 million. Beckham was given an ultimatum. Move permanently to Manchester to stop the 400-mile commute to and from London and end the showbiz lifestyle, or leave the club.[8]

Ferguson's approach was beyond Beckham's comprehension. The manager was always focused on a player's life cycle – his current value and his future potential.[9] He believed in winners and questioned whether Beckham might start deteriorating in two years. If he was a problem, then best for him to be sold sooner rather than later. Ferguson would remove anyone seeking to become stronger than himself. 'If you give in once you'll give in twice,' was his motto. 'You can never lose control.'

Ferguson's punishment for Beckham's first absence from training in nine years created a national furore. In retaliation, Beckham 'opened his heart' to the *Sun*. 'I am devastated by the events of the past few days,' he confessed. 'I have never wanted to play for any other team since I was a boy and really want to carry on doing that.'[10]

Even the *Mirror*'s shrewd columnist Carole Malone was seduced. Beckham, she wrote, was 'over-hyped, overrated and over the top' but the national vilification for missing a training session 'borders on the insane'. Malone pointed out that unlike all the sleazy footballers who got drunk, took drugs, smashed up hotel rooms and beat up women, Beckham 'loves his wife, he doesn't cheat on her and he's one of the only footballers who holds any decent values'.[11] His only serious critic was his father Ted. Ferguson, he told his son, was right. His place was on the pitch.[12]

Certain of his invulnerability, it seemed that Beckham was encouraged by Victoria to provoke Ferguson again. In early February 2000, dressed in near-identical clothes with the same dyed hairstyle and fringe, they posed at a charity screening of the movie *Withnail And I*. With similar mannerisms and accents, the celebrity couple seemed to be morphing into one.[13]

Weeks later, with some massive publicity organised by their publicist Caroline McAteer, the Beckhams celebrated Brooklyn's first birthday at a Cheshire hotel. The party cost £12,000. One-hundred and twenty-five guests, including many Manchester United players and their families, were fed a 'sumptuous' banquet and entertained by clowns, magicians and an indoor bouncy castle. 'They're going to roll out the red carpet on this one,' said McAteer for the story headlined 'Money happy returns.' She continued, 'But this isn't going to be some glitzy showbiz bash – it's very much a family occasion.[14] Despite their demand for privacy, the 'superstar couple' featured in all the following day's sell-out newspapers. The Beckhams' collaboration with the media hit a new peak. No one reported that Brooklyn had slept throughout the party.

The year 2000 was the turning-point.

As Manchester United's triple crown was challenged in England and Europe, Beckham appeared more interested in his showbiz life than defending his club's supremacy.

In the same week as Victoria revealed on Channel 4's *Breakfast* programme that Beckham wore her G-string, McAteer tipped off photographers that he would be walking down a London street wearing a handkerchief on his head and later wearing a Tahitian skirt.

Beckham even encouraged journalists to ask what colour thong he was wearing. The tabloids loved it, but the stunt backfired. 'It is time for David Beckham to grow up,' wrote Neil Custis in desperation.[15] Three months later, Manchester United's reign as European champions was over after a 3–2 defeat by Real Madrid. Beckham scored one goal but otherwise was ineffective. Ferguson was desolate.

All eyes now switched to the Euro 2000 championship in July hosted by Holland and Belgium. 'David Beckham is key to England's hopes,' wrote Gary Lineker. 'He is a genuine world star.' To temper Beckham's complaints to the *Sun* about its recent criticism of him, he was signed up to 'write' a weekly column for £75,000 a year. 'England can win Euro 2000,' Beckham told readers.[16] With mixed feelings, the *Sun*'s lead football writer Steven Howard urged all supporters to 'get behind David Beckham' for the 'biggest game' England had faced since the 'heartbreak' defeat by Argentina in 1998.

England's first match in Eindhoven was against Portugal. Beckham crossed for the second goal and England were coasting to a 2–0 victory. Then disaster struck. Portugal scored three goals in 37 minutes. 'This horror show left them propping up the table,' reported the *Sun* about England's deflated team. In the next match against Germany, good luck gave England, after a 'nail-biting night', a 1–0 victory. The third match in the group was against Romania and was heading for a draw until the last two minutes. Enough to qualify. Then Phil Neville committed a foolish foul. Romania converted the penalty and won 3–2, 'a shattering blow to England'.[17]

The tabloids were merciless. England's team was composed of 'rotting, decaying, second-rate backwoodsmen', all 'high-profile millionaires, unable to pass the ball who have won nothing since 1966'. And no one, some fulminated, was more pampered than Beckham. Mollycoddled by sycophants, he was blamed for playing his own game. Even his *Sun* column was axed.

Weeks later, the 25-year-old's first autobiography was published. The book's success was calculated to aggravate Ferguson. Once again the footballer had put himself first. His family and his money-making operations were more important to him than the club. The Beckhams' lives had become a jigsaw of vanity, contradictions and hypocrisy. Directed by the Beckhams, Caroline McAteer spoke about their 'desperation' for privacy.

'I have never done a photoshoot with my kids. I never have and I never will,' Beckham wrote in his book. Just six weeks earlier at Old Trafford he had held one-year-old Brooklyn aloft for thousands to see his baby wearing a Number 7 shirt with 'Daddy' emblazoned on top. 'We want Brooklyn to keep his anonymity as much as possible,' said Victoria. After a blizzard of publicity to promote his autobiography, Beckham demanded 'a little privacy and respect'.[18] That did not interfere with his release of pictures to millions of followers of the 'private family moments' during Brooklyn's second birthday party at a Wacky Warehouse play-centre.[19]

The public remained unaware of the machinations behind the photos.

'I hear that Becks had a golf buggy converted into a Hummer at Harrods for Brooklyn,' a journalist told Caroline McAteer. 'Not true,' snapped McAteer. 'That's strange, because I've got a copy of the invoice.' McAteer's denials, journalists discovered, were misleading. 'A power-crazed woman' and 'the devil publicist' was the journalists' response to her increasing intimidation.[20] McAteer had fashioned her craft to deny the obvious truth sometimes. Only journalists and newspapers who followed her orders would be given access to the Beckhams.

'Send a photographer to the Trafford Centre,' McAteer told a *Sunday Mirror* executive. 'Victoria's buying baby clothes for Brooklyn.' The photographer, Andy Stenning, found Victoria. 'Hi! Shall we do the pics here?' he asked. 'That's not what Victoria expected,' McAteer screamed at the executive while Stenning waited near the shop. 'It's meant to be impromptu. Victoria wants to be shocked by a pap surprise.'

McAteer received better coverage after she revealed that the Beckhams had made a 'secret visit' to a children's cancer hospital. 'They want no publicity,' she had told the hospital's administrators. One week later, newspapers were given quotations praising Posh and Becks for their generosity during their 'secret visit'.[21] For the Beckhams, these visits and similar appearances at charity events in Britain and elsewhere showed their huge commitment to help the disadvantaged. A critic might suggest that, considering the Beckhams' wealth, they were insufficiently generous.

Months later, in advance of arriving at Elton John's annual ball near Windsor to raise money for his AIDS foundation, Victoria's staff demanded that photographers sign contracts that she would not be photographed. Escorted by three bouncers to enforce the rule, one revealed overhearing Victoria talk about the Russian Cossack dancers, 'Oh look, Spanish dancers. I love them.'[22]

'The media getting into my life is terrible,' Victoria told the *Sun*'s Dominic Mohan. With a straight face she sat at home with her mother and sister Louise criticising journalists as they flicked through their own newspaper cuttings books with innumerable photographs of Victoria. Jackie and Louise joined the chorus of complaints. 'There are so many people who use us for publicity,' griped Victoria. Mohan was puzzled. One of their best sources for stories about Victoria – 'a regular caller peddling tittle-tattle for a quick buck' – was her own sister Louise.[23] And Victoria's complaint about an ex-boyfriend selling his story to a newspaper was odd from a woman who sold her own wedding to *OK!* magazine for £1 million.[24]

Little about the Beckhams was normal anymore. Many students at the University of Staffordshire had joined a 12-week 'Beckham studies' course led by Professor Ellis Cashmore and devoted to the cultural importance of the 'icon of icons'. Cashmore called the Beckham phenomenon 'inescapable', but dismissed Beckham as 'a vacuous personality' who ten years earlier would have been known as just another good footballer. His marriage to Posh Spice had created the celebrity. People's interest in Beckham, said Cashmore, was 'compensation for their own powerlessness'.

Other academics adopted a different opinion. John Harris and Ben Clayton described Beckham, the 'new man', as a 'conceptualisation of Englishness in the 21st century'. Left-wing academics judged Beckham's 'contemporary celebrity' as a product of 'neo-liberal democracy and consumer capitalism'.

Outsiders were magnetically drawn to Beckham, but Ferguson knew he was witnessing Beckham's self-destruction as a footballer. 'I could see him being swallowed up by the media or publicity agenda,' he wrote in his autobiography.

In March 2000, Beckham's nonchalance reached a new peak. During two days of training he wore a beanie hat. To get maximum exposure Beckham planned to take off his hat just before Saturday's kick-off against Leicester. It would reveal a completely shaven head. Haircuts, Beckham knew, fuelled the power of his image. Ferguson was suspicious and ordered Beckham to take off the hat or be dropped from the team. 'I tended to act quickly,' Ferguson recalled, 'when I saw a player become a negative influence.' The footballer, wrote Ferguson, went 'berserk'.[25]

'I never did it for attention,' Beckham would later say. 'Publicity never changed my football.'[26]

'SKINHEAD BECKHAM' was the *Sun*'s headline. The newspaper also published 'the first exclusive pictures' of the Beckham family 'showing off their trendy new hairstyles'. Walking in London's West End, 'Baldy' David took off Brooklyn's hat for Dominic Mohan, 'showing he was just like Dad'. Equally eager for publicity, Victoria pronounced, 'I absolutely love David's haircut. It makes him look sexier than ever.'[27]

Everyone assumed that Beckham had sabotaged his £4 million contract with Brylcreem. Victoria called a radio station, 'I just wanted to clear up some things. When you said he has no brain for shaving off his hair because he lost £4 million you were wrong. He has not lost a penny.' She added: 'I would go crazy if he lost £4 million by having his hair cut.' Caught in the crossfire, a Manchester United spokesman said, 'There is nothing in his contract to say how long his hair should be.' All the misinformation was profitable. 'We got twenty to thirty times more coverage than we paid for,' Brylcreem's executives chortled. And their £200,000 contract with Beckham had ended more than a year previously.

Just as the 1999–2000 football season finished, the Beckhams headed for a private family holiday to Disneyland in Los Angeles with Brooklyn. The *Sun*'s Victoria Newton was delighted to meet them at the outset of their holiday. As they posed for photos of hugs and kisses with Brooklyn, the Beckhams spoke about their terror of kidnappers, murder plots and media intrusion. Under the newspaper's 'exclusive' headline, 'Shall we buy the lot, Daddy?' Brooklyn was revealed as having caught 'the shopping bug off his famous mum and dad'. The one year old had chosen to wear Ralph Lauren clothes. Inevitably, there was a suspicion that the Beckhams enjoyed a lucrative tie-in with the brand.[28]

Curiously, a few years later the Beckhams 'went ballistic' after a Ralph Lauren press release boasted that Brooklyn and his brother Romeo had worn Ralph Lauren blazers at Geri Halliwell's daughter's christening. 'Victoria and David are fiercely protective of their three sons,' wrote Caroline Hadley, the *Mirror*'s mouthpiece for the Beckhams, 'and went apoplectic when they discovered what Ralph Lauren had done.'[29]

Among Beckham's new critics was the *Mirror*'s Carole Malone. 'I don't like the fake life about himself,' she wrote. 'He's always focused on the endgame. And Posh's lies have become the truth in her head.'[30] Malone particularly disliked Beckham posing with a bottle of Moët wearing a T-shirt bearing the face of Adolf Eichmann, one of Nazi Germany's architects of the Holocaust. 'Got shirt in post from American fan,' noted Beckham. 'Beckham probably thought that Eichmann was a footballer,' wrote Malone, 'or that Auschwitz is a German car.'

CHAPTER 6

REVIVAL

During early 2001, Beckham's performance for Manchester United slumped. He scored a goal for the club in late April against Middlesbrough during the penultimate match of the season, but had otherwise scored only once since the Manchester derby the previous November. His crosses had been generally poor. Repeatedly, Ferguson left the stale midfielder on the bench.[1] The manager was not impressed when Beckham arrived at Old Trafford in his seventh car, a 200 mph Lamborghini Diablo worth £185,000.[2]

Nor did Ferguson like Beckham's new Mohican haircut. 'I've not done it to create attention,' said Beckham. 'It's just me.' Shortly afterwards, Brooklyn was seen at a London restaurant with the same haircut. 'He likes showing off weird new looks,' said McAteer.[3] The truth emerged soon after. Beckham had been paid by the style magazine *The Face* to have the haircut and to speak about his love for scented candles. GQ magazine then paid £30,000 to photograph Beckham posing in 'snug' Dolce & Gabbana trunks, his body glistening with baby oil, flashing black nail varnish, a face make-up and a white silk scarf.[4] Shortly after the magazine's publication, Beckham was spotted by a football journalist at an airport news shop searching the shelves for features about himself. On the plane, Ferguson fumed about the supposedly modest, privacy-seeking footballer parading before the adoring public as an effeminate exhibitionist.[5]

Worse for Ferguson was the reality of Beckham's career as a 'star' footballer. Compared to his teammates Roy Keane, Eric Cantona, Paul Scholes, Ryan Giggs and Ruud van Nistelrooy, he was not an exceptional player. Instead, with solid but stiff grace he could still occasionally deliver a winning pass or execute a stunning deadball kick. As for players at other clubs, Paul Gascoigne, Ferguson believed, had been better.

Beckham's good fortune was playing for England. Unexpectedly, a temporary manager, Peter Taylor, appointed him in 2000 as the team's captain. The stubborn will power which had threatened his downfall fuelled his revival. Resilient in adversity whenever his fortunes ebbed, he could summon inspiration to deliver a spectacular winner.

On 6 October 2001, England were on the brink of failing to qualify for the 2002 World Cup in Japan and South Korea. Despite a stunning 5–1 victory in Germany on 1 September that included a Michael Owen hat-trick, England's performance against Greece at Old Trafford in October was incoherent. Not least because Owen was injured. Towards the end of the game, England were 1–2 down. Only a draw would guarantee qualification.

In the second minute of injury time, England were given a free-kick. Although he had already missed the target with as many as seven free kick goal efforts during the game, Beckham insisted as captain on taking the final one. 'I knew that was the last throw of the dice,' he later said.[6] The Greek goalkeeper expected Beckham to target the right corner. But with an astonishing swerve, the ball sped over the wall of Greek players, fooled the goalkeeper and went into the top-left corner of the goal.

The effortless elegance of his movement provoked an intoxicating roar. Sixty-six thousand screaming fans hailed their hero for saving England from disaster. In the dressing room, Beckham called Victoria. He was crying. 'Thinking back to the red card,' he said, 'for me personally, that [goal] was redemption. It's been an incredible year for me.'[7] Even his critics hailed him as a saviour. That single goal consolidated his brand. To his good fortune, most fans remembered his successful efforts and forgot his many misses. In 115 games for England, he would score only 17 goals, many from set-pieces, compared to Manchester United legends Bobby Charlton and Wayne Rooney, who scored 49 and 53 goals for England, respectively.

Unlike Ferguson, England's new manager Sven-Göran Eriksson was seduced by Beckham's charm. The 52-year-old Swede had been an undistinguished player before turning to management. As the manager of Lazio, his seventh managerial position, he had achieved impressive results. Lazio was top of Italy's Serie A league and had won the last ever European Cup Winners' Cup in 1999. His personality belied his success. Without charisma and somewhat dry, he possessed few endearing characteristics for British football writers to latch on to.

The Swede was completely won over by Beckham's style. Beckham was blessed by the qualities Eriksson lacked. As the coin was tossed at the start of a match Beckham looked beautiful and his strut across the turf to deliver a free kick was memorable. Besotted by his captain, Eriksson built his team around Beckham. That caused many problems, not least because Beckham demanded that he play on the right. Consequently, players better suited for the position struggled to be selected.

A second problem in the aftermath of the goal against Greece was Beckham's captaincy. Few realised that Beckham's character was unsuited to leadership. Unlike previous England captains such as Bobby Moore, Bryan Robson and Tony Adams, Beckham did not understand the psychology of authority. He was neither strategic nor aggressive, commanding his players to deliver victory. Passive at best, he believed his determined energy alone would inspire the team to follow his example. He never performed as the king on the pitch.

'Fergie went nuts when I asked him about the Greek goal at a luggage carousel,' recalled Neil Custis. 'I'll drop him,' Ferguson seethed. Ferguson believed in the team, not the individual, and faced a huge dilemma. At Manchester, Beckham was a distraction. No man could be bigger than the club. Yet the player was beloved by the club's merchandising team. Faced with the threat of Beckham leaving, Manchester United agreed a four-year deal in May 2002 worth £16.5 million. Beckham would be paid a record £90,000 per week and receive £2.5 million back pay.[8]

Three months later, Manchester United lost to Zalaegerszegi in Hungary. Beckham was booed by the fans. In the months before Christmas 2002 he regularly sat on the bench at the start of each match. Finally, after Christmas, and for the first time in eight weeks, he was allowed to start. In his unique way he overcame the pressure and scored a goal from 25 yards. 'We should have scored a lot more,' Ferguson said dismissively.[9] Any chance of controlling the stubborn celebrity was slipping away.

Boosted by three competing publicity machines – the club's and those of Alan Edwards and Tony Stephens' SFX – Beckham's self-confidence soared. In the past, after entering Ferguson's office, he said 'your lip starts to quiver and your mouth goes dry'. But times had changed. 'I think,' said Beckham, 'maybe he saw he didn't have that effect on me anymore, because I'd grown into a man.'[10] Like Ferguson, Beckham was obsessive about controlling everything. Contrary to what he would say later about playing forever at Manchester United, he started to think about his exit.

His increasing self-belief contrasted with Victoria's self-doubts. As the Spice Girls' legacy evaporated, she was increasingly relying on Beckham's celebrity. The ambitious woman wanted to find new fame on her own terms.

Each of the other Spice Girls had developed a solo career since the group broke up in 2000. Only Victoria had failed to score a solo success. Mel C had made two No. 1 records. Mel B and Emma Bunton had each registered a hit. But the most successful was Geri. In May 2001, 'Raining Men' became her fourth No. 1.

Victoria faced several problems. She was not a talented singer. As she later admitted, the Spice Girls' producers occasionally switched off her microphone during stage performances to prevent the show being ruined.[11] Loving the publicity, she was nevertheless waiting in August 2000 for the release of her first single 'Out of Your Mind'. To make sure it would be a number-one hit, McAteer was feeding the media with a stream of stories and new angles. Everything was geared to keep alive Victoria's rank as one of the nation's top celebrities.

Victoria's pitch was to be confessions about her wretched sense of inadequacy. 'Deep down,' she admitted, 'I feel like a spotty teenager.'[12] She traced her insecurity back to her school days and then training as a teenage dancer at Betty Laine Theatre Arts school in Epsom in Surrey. Harshly disciplined to focus on hard work, the image was conjured that each girl was weighed on Monday morning, to scrutinise whether they had eaten too much. 'Can we have the crane to lift Miss Adams on to the stage?' Laine once roared. That created the spiteful atmosphere which tended to turn the girls against one another. Victoria graduated with a set-piece performance – somewhat aloof, with her mouth fixed in an unsmiling pout – and a searing ambition to be famous. Unlike others suffering low self-esteem, Victoria believed that self-pity would sell discs.

To answer speculation about her breasts, she adamantly denied resorting to surgical enhancement when she appeared on Michael

Parkinson's TV show in September 2001. 'There's nothing wrong with boob jobs,' she said, 'but I don't feel the need to do it.' She added, 'A push-up bra and tape can do wonders.'

The issue had arisen after her catwalk show for Maria Grachvogel during London Fashion Week at the Natural History Museum. 'I'm the only one here with boobs,' she told Rav Singh. 'When I was walking down the catwalk, I was really worried about them coming out.' Constantly she exposed her breasts for photographers. In particular, at footballer's wife Sarah Bosnich's 31st birthday in London's Ivy restaurant. 'Those boobs just stood out,' said a friend.[13] 'Her new boobs', wrote Carole Malone, 'resemble two beach balls in a sack.'[14] Yet Victoria's explicit denials of any surgery continued for two years. 'Honestly, I've just got a really big set of breasts,' she told the *Sun*. 'I'm completely natural,' she told the BBC, 'except for my fingernails, and I have a bit of help with my hair.'

'Why do you think people think you've had a boob job?' asked an ITV interviewer. 'Because I have got a big old pair of boobs,' she replied. It was just one of what Fleet Street's finest called 'Posh's Little Porkies' or 'Victoria telling a fib or three.'[15] Thirteen years later, Alison Boshoff traced Victoria's emotional biography by dating the varying sizes of her breasts, alternating from torpedoes to flat-chested. Their size changed depending on her misery (enhanced) or happiness (reduced).

In their competition for publicity, Victoria confronted the celebrity Jordan, alias Katie Price, in a Chinese restaurant's bathroom. The self-publicist Jordan – carrying 34FF about-to-burst beach balls – soon after recalled in a broadcast interview how Posh had taken out her breasts and asked, 'Do you think I need a boob job?' adding, 'David likes big ones.'[16]

In retaliation for that supposed breach of privacy, Victoria called Jordan 'vile', 'a second-rate celebrity'. A catfight had started. Seeing Jordan enter the Old Trafford players' lounge, Victoria carped loudly, 'Who let the dogs out?' To seal her antagonism, Victoria said during an ITV documentary, 'Jordan does full frontals with her crotch and tits out and says that I'm a bad influence for wearing a fake lip-ring.' Jordan's counter-attack was limp: 'Posh is a conniving little cow.'[17] Carole Malone listed the women's similarities: fake boobs, fake hair and shovels of make-up.

All that grief was generated by Victoria's miscalculation. She blamed her sister Louise's ex-boyfriend for leaking the details about her plastic surgery. 'Poor Louise,' said Victoria. 'It was so hurtful.' But Louise and her ex-boyfriend did not betray her sister's breast secrets. Victoria had told the truth in her own autobiography: 'I don't have any [boobs] and never did.' Victoria's misfortune was she had never read her ghosted autobiography. She was unaware of her 'truth'.[18] She was also unaware that the *Sun* had bought from an employee of London's Wellington hospital a photograph taken on 4 September 1999, showing the explicit aftermath of Victoria's first breast-implant operation. For £10,000 her original A cups had been enlarged by 2001 to DD.[19]

Victoria was less coy about her love life. Asked whether she wanted more children she replied, 'We are both so busy. That's not to say our sex life isn't great, though. It's fantastic and always has been, thank you very much.' Posing in a see-through dress for photographers outside London's Ivy restaurant, she swung a bag labelled 'Sex'. 'I'm blissfully satisfied with my man,' she said about their first sexual experience. It happened, she chortled, hours after meeting Prince Charles. Thereafter, she said, Beckham was 'a total animal' in bed. Even scoring goals, she insisted, was 'not as good as having sex with me'.[20]

Little had been more calculated than telling Michael Parkinson in a television interview – while constantly pulling at her sharply revealing dress to cover her breasts – that David was 'Golden Balls'. With a crafty smile, she posed as the clever minx, the check-out girl at the supermarket who everyone claims to fancy.

Beckham sat speechless next to her during that Parkinson interview. Tightly holding Posh's hand, a slight smile of satisfaction registered. He liked being Golden Balls. 'One of those things I shouldn't have said,' said Victoria, laughing about her prepared quip. Some viewers might have been shocked, casting Posh as vulgar, but Posh knew how to please her market. Living the life her fans would like to enjoy, she rarely said anything offensive. Few were jealous of her looks, only of her proximity to Beckham himself.

Parkinson nodded sympathetically as Beckham complained during the interview about press intrusion of Brooklyn. 'He's never going to get a bit of privacy in his life,' said the father, forgetting that Victoria had allowed a team from a Virgin website to film Brooklyn in his bedroom.[21] He also overlooked their frequent collaborations with Jason Fraser, the paparazzi famous for his stunning photos of Princess Diana during her 1997 Mediterranean romance with Dodi Fayed. At the height of his success, Fraser was paid £50,000 for a single sequence of Diana posing in her turquoise bathing suit. 'Enough to buy a bungalow,' said the *Sun* executive who agreed the astronomical fee. Exclusive photos taken by Fraser of the Beckhams, such as Victoria playing with Brooklyn at Paradise Wildlife Park in Broxbourne, were rarely worth more than £3,000.[22]

Beckham denied that he had ever been paid by the media for photographs, but he had allowed Fraser to call the *Sun*'s picture editor Geoff Webster from their private jet. 'I'm over the Atlantic with David and Posh,' boasted Fraser. Beckham's voice could be heard in the background. Fraser was in the plane because he shared his fee for exclusive pictures with the Beckhams. Neither Beckham believed the photographer should pocket all the financial benefit of pictures of themselves. Michael Parkinson was among many who ignored that reality.[23]

'Thin and thick' was how the jokers described Posh and Becks. 'We're definitely going to get Brooklyn christened,' said Beckham, 'but we don't know into which religion.'[24] The enigma remained. Which of the two was dominant? Who controlled their home life? In public, he exercised remarkable self-control. She was brash but unthreatening.

Some would say that Victoria's brashness reflected the average perception of an Essex girl. She was born in 1974 in the post-war new town of Harlow but lived in neighbouring Hertfordshire. But she revealed ignorance about the county when asked in a TV show whether David had bought an island off Essex. 'There isn't a coast in Essex, is there?' she replied. Seeing incredulous faces, she snapped: 'I said the most stupid thing just now, didn't I?'

Her unawareness was matched by fantasy. While promoting her bestselling 528-page autobiography *Learning to Fly* she told TV host Graham Norton with a smile that 'I wrote the book'. She added, 'So I'm good on a typewriter now.' That surprised her ghost-writer, Pepsy Dening. Not least because Victoria also admitted, 'I've never read a book but I do love fashion magazines.' She also denied reading any articles about herself: 'We just look at the pictures, to be honest.'

For good measure, Beckham revealed that he also couldn't read Posh's autobiography. 'I'm halfway through it,' he said unconvincingly. Later he admitted, 'I haven't read a book in my life.'[25] At Chingford High School he had studied Home Economics, some cooking and some drawing. And he played football.

One truth Victoria could not deny. Weighing seven stone and 5 foot 5 inches tall, she appeared to be on the borderline of illness. Posing in hot-pants and a tight T-shirt at London Fashion Week for Maria Grachvogel, the audience was shocked by her figure. 'Skeletal Spice' was the headline over a startling photograph of Victoria in a red leather dress. To conceal her frailty she insisted on changing clothes alone. Other women were forbidden to be in the same room.[26]

After feeling dizzy and tired during a family holiday in Mustique she was told by Jackie and Sandra to seek help. Asked by the *Sunday Mirror*'s Ian Hyland about Victoria's visit to Mustique, McAteer replied: 'That's bollocks. Victoria is in London.' Hyland had tired of McAteer's style. 'Well, you say Victoria's not in Mustique,' he countered, 'but I'm looking at photos of her taken yesterday there.' There was a pause. 'I'll call you back,' said McAteer.

Denying that she was anorexic or bulimic, Victoria claimed at first to suffer an eating disorder caused by allergies to most food and milk. Eating only vegetables, especially steamed spinach and carrots, she mentioned a hormone imbalance and a blood disorder diagnosed by a Chinese herbalist as a zinc deficiency and a yeast infection. In another version, she blamed Geri for urging her to diet to get thinner and to shrink her bum. Jackie Adams also denied the problem. 'My Posh eats like a pig,' she pronounced while waving a glass of wine at an art gallery party.[27]

Exposing their fantasies rarely embarrassed the Beckhams. Regardless of their missteps, the public and the media loved them. As a couple embracing football, pop music, style and the family, no other couple so completely reflected modern British life. As the August deadline to release her single 'Out of My Mind' drew closer, maintaining the wholesome image depended on constant publicity.

As part of the publicity drive, she sang solo in front of 100,000 in Hyde Park. 'If it doesn't work,' she said afterwards, 'I'll just go back to singing to myself and leaping around the living-room.' Unfortunately, in the same week as her single was released by Virgin, the same record company released Spiller's 'If This Ain't Love'. Compared to Victoria, the vocalist Sophie Ellis-Bextor, former singer in the rock band The Audience, was less well known. Yet Spiller's disc hit No. 1, beating Victoria to No. 2, albeit with 180,584 sales in the first week. Virgin had not imagined that Spiller would trump Victoria. Weeks later Victoria began a new media bandwagon for the release in 2001 of her second single, 'Not Such an Innocent Girl'.

To repair any damage McAteer called journalists with a list of Victoria's successes. She had been auditioned for film roles in Hollywood, lined up for a six-part television series about shopping in America, was offered a part by Andrew Lloyd Webber in *Starlight Express*, and would be a *Pop Idol* panellist – even though she had said, 'I've never watched *Pop Idol*.' Months earlier she had also said, 'I'm absolutely addicted to the show.' Other than one stiff and unfunny appearance on *Pop Idol* alongside Simon Cowell, all those 'offers' disappeared.[28]

Desperate for more publicity, she persuaded Beckham to appear with her in an Ali G television interview for Comic Relief on Red Nose Day. 'So will Brooklyn be a good footballer like his dad or a good singer like Mariah Carey?' asked Ali G. 'Sing like Mariah Carey,' replied Victoria with perfect self-control. Shaven-haired Beckham uttered single-word replies or awkwardly laughed during ten minutes packed with double entendres. In one exchange Ali G asked Victoria: 'Is your little boy starting to put whole sentences together?' and when Victoria replied that he was, Ali G then inquired: 'And what about Brooklyn?' Victoria's relaxed reaction won her a lot of fans.

The public's sympathy towards Beckham was overwhelming. 'Everyone thinks I'm stupid,' he had said in a recent documentary. 'I've learnt not to say too much in interviews.'[29]

'David can't afford any slip-ups,' his spokesman admitted before a previous appearance on the show. Coaching from Parkinson's producers and elocution lessons to strengthen his mousey voice had been part of a charm offensive to get him out of Victoria's shadow.[30] Everyone loved Beckham. Victoria was different. Increasingly, she was outspoken and provoked retaliation.

'I can't stand Geri,' she said about her former best friend. 'She is one of the most disloyal people I've ever known.' Twisting the knife, she even scoffed at Geri for going out with DJ Chris Evans. 'She'll do anything to get publicity. Geri doesn't care what she does as long as she gets in the paper.' Victoria was getting even for Geri telling *Vogue* earlier that year: 'Posh Spice, she's a cheap, common, uneducated, talentless, greedy little moron. Sorry don't like her at all.'[31]

'Not Such an Innocent Girl' was released in September 2001. Entering the charts at No. 10, it sold 9,274 copies on day one. On the same day Kylie Minogue's 'Can't Get You Out of My Head' sold 77,174 copies. Three weeks later, Victoria's disc had fallen to No. 70. Only 20,000 copies were sold. Even Beckham, after urging his friends to buy Victoria's record, admitted: 'It's not my kind of music.'[32]

To humiliate Victoria, Kylie's Minogue's sister Dannii revealed that both of them 'fancied' David.

At the time, he was deep into a relationship with Sarah Marbeck.

CHAPTER 7

DISMAY

On 10 April 2002 a metatarsal bone in Beckham's left foot dominated Britain's headlines. As he came off the pitch at Old Trafford he recalled, 'I could tell it was broken and I thought: "That's it."' An Argentinian playing for Deportivo La Coruña against Manchester United in a Champions League match had plunged the country into a crisis. Would Beckham be fit for June's World Cup tournament in Japan and South Korea? 'England woke up yesterday,' wrote one effusive journalist, 'to learn that its modern-day Nelson, its Wellington and Raleigh rolled into one, had been injured in battle.'[1] Experts predicted that only divine intervention could repair the bone in time for the opening match against Sweden. Eriksson had good reason to pray for the bone to heal, because other key players would definitely not be fit.

At their home in Manchester the fate of Beckham's foot took second place to Victoria's latest crisis. Knowing that Victoria was uninterested in football, McAteer was ordered to revive her stalling career. The publicist was consoling a contrary employer. In public, immaculately dressed and made-up, Victoria appeared solidly serene. In private, her moods swung between chatty gossip, 'hard arsed' and wild emotion. Victoria was still complaining about an £8 taxi that an employee had charged without her approval. She felt under pressure.

Whereas Kylie had closed Sydney's 2000 Olympics, Victoria was opening an obscure ski contest in Austria. Her fee was £45,000. To her embarrassment the organisers admitted that she was chosen because Tom Jones and Cher were too expensive. At a solo concert in Leicester she was spotted miming out of sync. Fans threw onions and apples at the stage.[2] Unable to sing live anymore, she cried out for salvation.

Before Beckham's accident, Victoria's new manager John Glover had obeyed her demand for more engagements. He landed an offer to feature in a 40-second advertisement promoting Walkers Sensations crisps. The scenario for filming at Blenheim Palace was straightforward. She would step down from her carriage, walk through the palace and shout, 'I'm starving'. Given a packet of Sensations, she would eat the crisps sitting on a throne. 'Posh crisps from Walkers' read the caption. Poking fun at herself by promoting a popular brand, cooed the advertising executive, would help to rebuild her status. Anxious for publicity, she accepted a £200,000 fee, much less than the agency expected to pay.

The two-day shoot, the production crew would recall, was marred by 'stressful and tense' arguments. The body double used at her insistence for the shot of her leg getting out of a carriage told Victoria, 'I'm such a fan of yours.'

'You look nothing like me,' snapped Victoria, furious when the exchange was published on *popbitch.com*. Glover failed to get the post removed.

Hovering on the set, Glover watched Victoria refusing to swallow the crisps. Instead she spat them out. Introduced to the heir of the estate Jamie, the Marquis of Blandford, Victoria quipped, 'I thought that was a tent.' (She had confused the word 'marquis' with 'marquee'.) At the end, she refused to sign the visitors' book, previously signed by Bill Clinton and Nelson Mandela. 'Her trademark sense of humour is not evident,' said a Walkers executive after a fraught dinner at the nearby gourmet restaurant Le Manoir aux Quat'Saisons. Everyone ate the specialities except Victoria. As usual she asked for steamed fish, steamed vegetables and green grapes. During dinner Beckham telephoned to report on a successful match. 'I'll call you back,' interrupted Victoria.

At the end of filming, she wanted to keep the shoes provided for the shoot. 'No,' she was told. The expenses Glover submitted included M&S fat-free crisps. 'What a cheek!' Glover was told. 'No way.'

Inevitably, after viewing the rough cut she demanded retakes. 'It's OK,' her mother Jackie soothed. Everyone breathed a sigh of relief.

One unseen sequence was Victoria eating crisps in a bath. 'She's super, super sensitive about being photographed in the bath,' the team had been told before filming. Entry to the bathroom was strictly controlled. Looking through the rushes, the producers decided that even beneath the soap bubbles her body was too thin and her breasts would need retouching. The scene was dropped.

Nevertheless, Victoria decided that hyping herself as a sex symbol would sell her next single 'Mind of Its Own', taken from her first album. Wearing a skimpy bikini she posed in raunchy positions for *Arena* magazine's cover.[3] She also arranged for Italian *Vogue* to photograph her with Beckham. He wore a push-up skirt while she, crouched in a doggy position, was dressed in bondage. 'I'm not a sex symbol,' Victoria pronounced during the same week. 'Pop stars posing near-nude to promote their discs,' she declared, 'are cheap. I am an artist.'[4] Two days later on 11 February, 'Mind of Its Own' was released.

Victoria hoped that a primetime ITV documentary, *Being Victoria Beckham,* her personal story, would boost disc sales. 'My life has been an emotional rollercoaster,' she said, remembering her lonely childhood, shunned by other children. Added to other familiar stories, she was filmed saying to Beckham, 'I just love giving birth.'

'What do you mean?' he replied. 'You had a caesarean – you didn't even feel it.'

'I wonder why they call you thick, David,' Victoria fired back.[5]

In *Victoria's Secrets*, a Channel 4 documentary shown simultaneously, she regaled viewers with the usual list of glories and sadnesses – as well as the pleasure of shopping in Sainsbury's. The impression of an ordinary mum was ruined by the fleeting presence of Mark Niblett, a bodyguard hired to deter potential kidnappers and murderers. After the cameras were turned off, Niblett pushed Victoria's trolley.

'Mind of Its Own' started at No. 6 in the charts but then slid down. Even after she insisted that Beckham appear with her at Woolworths in Oldham to promote the song, her solo career was not taking off. The single and the album flopped. Virgin decided that Posh, alias the Queen of Mime, would be dropped. Accompanied by John Glover, Victoria rushed into the office of Virgin's vice chairman Nancy Phillips. Falling to her knees, she tearfully begged, 'Give me another chance. Let's try another single.' Even the revelation that she was two months pregnant failed to move Phillips. Her only concession was to make no announcement that Victoria had been fired.

Phillips' kindness was not rewarded. Victoria's publicist persuaded some tabloids that Victoria had sacked Phillips. In the published scenario, Victoria strode into Phillips' office and pronounced: 'Why did it go wrong? You chose the wrong single. The whole promotion was

wrong. I just can't believe it. This has got to change. This is horrible.'
Phillips was guilty of allowing Posh to be 'over-exposed'.[6] To hide the
true story, Glover even announced that Virgin had agreed to release
another single. Although untrue, Virgin executives said nothing.

Secluded with her parents, her sister Louise and McAteer, Victoria
raged about the unfairness of life. Her surroundings suggested the
opposite. After extensive work to convert a former children's home,
Rowneybury House in Sawbridgeworth, she had moved into the
seven-bedroom mansion, renamed Beckingham Palace, which was set
in 24 acres. It had been bought in 1999 for £3.14 million.

As a testament to the happy family's talent and hard work, the
Beckhams revelled in excess. As one of the People's Royals her fans
praised the Essex girl for getting a lifestyle they would love. 'It's a
tart's boudoir,' she boasted about one bedroom with a mirrored ceiling. 'If you've got it, flaunt it,' Victoria told a journalist during a tour
around her new home. To their fans' delight, the Beckhams proved
there was no birthright to being rich and privileged.

But there was another effect on Victoria as she settled into her new
house and lifestyle. Unnecessarily, she started an argument with Tarts,
a local fashion boutique. She accused the shop of using her visits to
promote sales – and demanded payment.

'I'm scared of Posh,' said the manager, Dimitri Stylianides. 'We've
managed without her for 25 years.'

The owner, Brenda Green was more forthright: 'She's just so
greedy. She was really, really rude and she was swearing.'[7]

Forever seeking control of the couple's image, Victoria also
launched a legal action for copyright against Peterborough United for
using the nickname Posh, a name the club had used since 1923.[8] The
case was dropped. Soon after this she accused a trader at Bluewater
shopping centre of selling phony David Beckham autographs. She had
even stood in the shop loudly telling the public shoppers not to buy
the 'fakes'. The autographs, however, were genuine. She paid the
shop's owner £155,000 for damage to his business.[9]

Those around Victoria thought she seemed oblivious to any hurt
caused. Some spotted an imperiousness when she welcomed the rich
and famous to Beckingham Palace in May 2002.

On the eve of the Queen's Jubilee the Beckhams hosted a fundraiser
for UNICEF, the United Nations Children's Fund, although some

believed it was for the NSPCC.[10] The white-tie, diamond Gucci and sushi party with a Japanese theme was presented by Victoria's publicist as a £350,000 extravaganza. The event, she said, was decorated with 60,000 orchids. The champagne alone was said to cost £75,000. Among the 400 guests were a galaxy of stars including Ray Winstone, Mick Hucknall, Joan Collins, Mohamed Fayed, Richard Branson and Natalie Imbruglia.

As usual at a charity fundraiser, some guests were asked to pay for their ticket for their dinner, and unusually they were also asked to sign confidentiality agreements forbidding them from taking photographs or discussing the party. Mobile phones were banned. Most guests did not realise that the party was not funded by the Beckhams but by *OK!* and *Hello!* magazines in return for exclusive picture rights.[11]

By endorsing UNICEF the Beckhams wanted to prove their commitment to make the world a better place. Filling a marquee with like-minded celebrities, the guest-list projected the Beckhams as powerbrokers sharing their spotlight. No one minded about their employment of a team of publicists to parade their deeds and lifestyle, but they were failing to persuade Establishment insiders to rank them among the great and the good. Unchallenged by moral or political conflicts, the Beckhams' inability to express any thoughts beyond repeating their lifetime experiences showed that they represented nothing other than themselves. Despite their celebrity, they still remained firmly outside the conventional Establishment's tent.

The party anticipated England's victorious World Cup. Seven weeks after his injury, the nation rejoiced as Beckham was declared 'fit enough' to play. Manchester United fans were also delighted that he had finally signed a new three-year contract. Only the footballers understood how the party exposed Beckham's misunderstanding of the captain's responsibilities.

Beckham's teammates were seated at the back of the marquee next to the Portaloo toilets. In the front were the party's stars. Celebrity took priority over football. To his irritation, the closest England's right-back Danny Mills got to Beckham was in the Portaloo. 'Please don't spray it over him,' Mills thought as his three-year-old son stood in a nearby stall to Beckham. The party was 'a surreal experience', Mills decided, not least because he realised its real purpose was to promote the Beckhams' brand in Asia.[12]

Hysterical Japanese fans chanting 'England' and 'Beckham' greeted the captain's arrival in Tokyo. He had reached a turning-point. Beckham was a global star.

I've got a feeling my time has come,' he said on the eve of the first match against Sweden. 'I am a patriot and this is going to be a special moment for me. We want the World Cup.'[13]

After England slumped in the second half, the match ended in a 1–1 draw. No one mentioned the captain's failure to galvanise his team.

Next, England faced Argentina. That evening, Britain's streets were deserted. In the 44th minute, England were awarded a penalty, when the Argentine defender Mauricio Pochettino, destined to become the manager of both Spurs and Chelsea, was adjudged to have tripped Michael Owen. 'I had to take some very deep breaths,' recalled Beckham, 'as I walked towards the ball. It was an emotional time. The game meant so much to me. There were certain flashbacks from four years ago especially when the ball went into the net. I just felt the burden of it all lifted.'[14] A 1–0 win for England.

Beckham cried after the whistle. 'It doesn't get any sweeter than this,' he said. Victoria added, 'I was so nervous when David was taking the penalty. I thought I was giving birth.' After the wild, cele-bratory party, England's mediocre performance against Nigeria produced a draw.

Next, they faced Brazil's finest. In the 23rd minute Owen scored and then England went downhill. Shortly after half-time Ronaldinho scored a second for Brazil, but soon after he was given a red card. Against ten Brazilians, England had a new advantage. But exhausted and fading away, Beckham failed to drive the advantage. Soundly defeated 1–2, England were soon on a plane back home. Beckham sat silently, reported the accompanying journalists, frequently apologis-ing to his team for his failure.

In Japan, Brazil's Ronaldo delivered a resounding judgement: 'Normally when you swap shirts, especially after a game in the heat like that, they absolutely stink and are soaked in sweat. So it was a surprise, to say the least, that Beckham's shirt smelled only of perfume.' Fearing public criticism, Beckham refused Elton John's invi-tation to a White Tie & Tiara Ball at his Windsor home.[15]

English football had reached a moment of reality. At Old Trafford, Ferguson reversed his decision to retire from football. Manchester

United, he lamented, had failed to win any trophy in 2002. Everything had to change. Even selling Beckham was on the agenda if he did not improve.[16]

By contrast, Geoff Thompson, the FA's self-important chairman, failed to grasp that the idea of building the team around Beckham was fatally flawed. Instead of curtailing the Eriksson–Beckham alliance, the team's plight was barely discussed.

CHAPTER 8

DOUBLE-DEALING

In July 2002, John Glover had good news for Victoria. Pete Hadfield, the A&R man of Telstar, a successful record company over the previous 20 years, was offering a £1.5 million contract for five albums.

Victoria was not a stranger to the record label's executives.

Seven years earlier, before the Spice Girls' success she had worked with Telstar. 'Now she could dictate to us,' recalled an executive. 'Events ran on her command.' Over the next six months, the best writers and producers hired by Hadfield produced 'Open Your Eyes', her single to be released in 2003. By the end, everyone was exhausted. 'Victoria's very expensive to run and hard work,' complained Hadfield. 'She's terribly difficult.' But there was also a nasty surprise.

The Telstar executives had introduced Victoria to Damon Dash, a 32-year-old mercurial New York businessman. Famously forward, he had demanded that a *Daily Mail* journalist interview him in the Jacuzzi at his Chelsea house. She refused.

Controlling an array of businesses, Dash co-owned Roc-A-Fella Records with the rapper star Jay-Z, his childhood friend in Brooklyn. Together, they had also created Rocawear, a clothing retailer. By 2003 the relationship between Dash and Jay-Z was fraught, not least because of Dash's excessive spending. Surrounded by an entourage of at least 20 people, including his personal chef and valets, Dash was filmed 24 hours every day by a cameraman, even during his transtlantic flights on a large private jet.

Dash appointed Victoria as the 'face' of Rocawear. Dumping her pouting image posing for magazines wearing Dolce & Gabbana clothes and carrying large Louis Vuitton bags, she would become his fashion icon. She would be plastered over billboards from Times Square to Los Angeles. She would also star as Rocawear's face at Dash's European launch in Selfridges. He said: 'Victoria embodies everything Rocawear is on an international level, from fashion to music. She's beautiful. Incredible.' Asked whether she was now a professional model, Victoria replied 'Do I look that unintelligent?'[1]

For Steve Grayson, the British Rocawear licensee across Europe, Victoria's Selfridges' launch was 'great'. Dash as a personality was less attractive. 'He was the biggest self-publicist I've ever met,' said Grayson. 'It was all about showing off. The gossip in Britain was she had a special relationship with Dash. But nothing was known. At parties they stood apart.'

Clearly bewitched by Dash, Victoria frequently flew to New York hoping that Roc-A-Fella Records, a hugely successful label, could revive her own singing career. 'I can make Victoria a star here,' Dash declared. At her expense, American songwriters were commissioned to produce blockbuster hits. In London, Hadfield did not dare to interfere.

Just as Telstar was about to release 'Open Your Eyes' in June 2003, Victoria demanded that Hadfield first release her hip-hop album. Unaware that she had even recorded an album for Dash, Hadfield complained. 'She's adamant and the album's rubbish. And she has refused to promote our single.' No one dared to tell Victoria the truth about her American album. Especially not Glover, a floundering manager.

Unlike Glover, Alex Ferguson was determined to impose his will on Beckham.

Ferguson's antagonism towards Beckham was reaching a climax. Manchester United, he believed, came third in Beckham's priorities. First, there was himself, then the England team, and only then the club. Just as Gary Neville, Beckham's best friend, explained: 'He wanted to be a global superstar. Football was never enough for him. He always wanted to be bigger.'[2] Beckham's ability, Ferguson concluded, had been sacrificed because he and Victoria were 'desperate for fame'. The longing for adulation, he believed, had robbed the player of the hunger to play outstandingly. His protégé, he decided, would never deliver his full potential. Certainly, he would not reach football genius levels.

In Ferguson's judgement Victoria was the troublemaker. Her hunger for headlines fuelled the media circus. He was puzzled. How, he wondered, could a compulsive actress whose career as a singer was effectively over forget that Beckham's success as a brand – for sunglasses and hair gel – depended on Beckham being a great footballer. Only one person could decide that – the manager.

'Too many suck up to your son,' Ferguson told Sandra. He criticised Beckham for accepting the Queen's invitation to visit Buckingham Palace with the England team before going to Japan. His dismal performance on 14 February 2003 during a FA Cup 5th round match against Arsenal in Manchester had proved Ferguson's point. The home side was defeated 2–0.

After the match, Ferguson entered the dressing room. He was furious with Beckham for allowing Arsenal to score a second goal. He advanced to launch an explosive outburst known throughout football as his 'hairdryer'.

'I felt I was being bullied and being backed into a corner for no reason other than spite,' recalled Beckham. 'I was trapped. I swore at him.'[3]

In Ferguson's version, 'David swore, I moved towards him and as I approached kicked a boot. It hit him right above the eye.'

Blood poured from the wound. 'Fucking hell!' shouted Beckham, 'My head's covered in blood.' Ferguson called it a 'freak act of nature'.

As the blood flowed, Beckham rose to attack the manager in what he called 'some mad scene out of a gangster movie'.

'Sit down!' spat out Ferguson as the player was restrained by his teammates. 'You've let your team down. Just fucking patch him up,' he ordered.

Beckham 'stormed' out of the ground. Normally, the incident would have been concealed by the dressing room *omerta*. But that night an Arsenal player told the *Sun* about the altercation. The newspaper's explosive headline, 'FERGIE DECKS BECKS', sealed the player's fate.

The following day, Beckham drove from his Manchester home with an Alice band pulling his hair back. Waiting photographers could clearly see two sticking plasters on his face. At the training ground, there was no apology. 'If any player wants to take me on,' Ferguson would later say, 'to challenge my authority and control, I deal with them.' Beckham did not respond as expected.

Two weeks later relations deteriorated even further. To Ferguson's fury, on the day before a crucial match against Leeds, Beckham hosted a party for the team.[4] The party was held just after Manchester United had been beaten by Liverpool. Ferguson ordered all the players not to drink and be home by 9 p.m. Anyone disobeying his order would be fined one week's wages.

To further infuriate Ferguson, Beckham posed for photos as he took delivery of a new Range Rover. It would be garaged next to two Bentleys, a Ferrari, a Porsche and countless other cars. 'David thought he was bigger than Alex Ferguson,' wrote the manager. 'The minute they threaten your control, you have to get rid of them.' He correctly anticipated that Manchester United's supporters would not complain if Beckham were sold. 'They support the shirt, not the occupant of the shirt,' was a favoured expression.

Back in January, Ferguson had told the board that he would drop Beckham to see how the team played without him. Ferguson had already agreed that the outstanding 17-year-old Cristiano Ronaldo would move from Lisbon to Manchester in 2004. Beckham, he said, should be sold.[5] But to get a good price – £30 million was the target – he told Jorge Valdano, Real Madrid's transfer negotiator, a sale was 'totally out of the question. No way would we sell him.'[6] On the eve of a critical match, he would not be distracted.

On 23 April 2003, Ferguson faced a dilemma. Two weeks earlier, Manchester United had been humiliatingly defeated 3–1 by Real Madrid's outstanding play in the Champions League. Beckham had missed a critical goal. To win on aggregate in the second leg at Old Trafford, Real Madrid would need to be defeated by at least two goals. In choosing his team, Ferguson decided to leave Beckham on the bench. Statistics were showing that Manchester United got better results when Beckham was not playing.[7]

Humiliated, the forlorn player watched the Brazilian Ronaldo score three incredible goals. In the 63rd minute Ferguson panicked. Beckham was sent on. At those critical moments, Beckham's stubborn survival gene galvanised the footballer. Bursting with angry pride, he ran on to the pitch 'like a man on a mission from God'.[8] He would score two remarkable goals. Standing on the touchline as the whistle blew, Ferguson was devastated. Manchester United's 4–3 victory was not enough. Real Madrid had won 6–5 on aggregate. Beckham's admirers would say that Ferguson's antipathy towards him had blown it.

Forty minutes after the match, Beckham met his agent Tony Stephens at Manchester's Malmaison hotel. With Victoria beside him he told Stephens to finalise a deal with Real Madrid. With the world's best players, Europe's most profitable club was the obvious choice for the ambitious star.[9] Despite his protestations about staying with Manchester United forever, he and Victoria had decided it was time to leave.

In football's murky world, Beckham's transfer would produce an estimated £2 million commission for the agents. Among the beneficiaries would be Ferguson's son Jason, a partner of Stephens at Elite Sports Group and SFX. Aware of his client's commercial value, Stephens became obstructive when on 14 May the club's managing director Peter Kenyon told Stephens that the club was offering Beckham a new four-year contract. Stephens replied that he would seek alternative offers in Barcelona and Madrid.[10]

On 24 May, Stephens began negotiations with Real Madrid's chief executive José Ángel Sánchez in Nice. Assuring Sánchez that Beckham's desire to move to Madrid was a 'heartfelt decision', Stephens agreed that he could not earn more than other players, namely 5.5 million euros a year. Simultaneously, through another agent, Beckham began discussions with Barcelona.

Peter Kenyon could not conceal that Beckham would inevitably be sold, but Beckham's insistence that he would only be transferred to Real Madrid restricted Kenyon's instinct to play hard and extract a high price. Beckham no longer needed to pretend that he was dedicated to Manchester United.

Simultaneously, encouraged by Damon Dash, Victoria had engaged publicists to raise her own and Beckham's profile across America. She had landed in New York in mid-May for a *Vogue* party. Wearing a shimmering transparent Dolce & Gabbana dress, she arrived hand in hand with Naomi Campbell. The next day, the British media were told by their publicists that the two women would be visiting the Twin Towers site.[11] However, they were not on the best of terms.

Three years earlier on a television show, Posh had called Naomi a 'bitch' and a 'complete cow'. 'Who's Posh Spice?' Campbell retaliated a few days later. Naomi's mother now weighed in. Posh, she said, was a 'talentless cow' and a 'crap' singer who 'doesn't know when to shut her gob'. Not only was she 'stupid and thick' but she was also 'a major league attention-seeker.'

Now in New York, publicists revealed, Naomi Campbell had asked, 'Why exactly do they call you Posh?'

'And why exactly do they call you beautiful?' Victoria hit back.[12]

In her autobiography, Victoria had stated that she wanted to be 'bigger than Persil washing powder'. To achieve global fame she understood it was in her interest to bury any bitterness. Hanging around New York for the next 11 days she plotted reinventing her career. David's fame was central to her sell.

Beckham mania had erupted after the release of the feature film *Bend It Like Beckham*.[13] Although the film was made without his co-operation he exploited its success. The previous month, Beckham had played for Manchester United against Barcelona in Philadelphia. Within one hour 66,000 tickets had been sold. On the same day, 80,000 tickets were sold in New York for the Manchester United match against Juventus. Naturally, Victoria tapped into that new fame. She imagined both becoming a brand representing family values and a pop star. The breakthrough, she hoped, would be featuring on the cover of *Vogue* magazine. For years Victoria had longed for that prestige.

Joined in New York by Beckham on 27 May 2003, they both headed out for dinner with Anna Wintour, the long-standing editor of *Vogue*. Wintour enjoyed adding celebrities to her family of 'friends'. Beckham, she knew, was not just sporty but beautiful. His presence enhanced her magazine's appeal. Victoria, she knew, was a harmless diva who would never be a heavyweight, but she exuded an attractive certainty. The publicity surrounding Wintour's dinner – which included David Bowie, Donna Karan and Calvin Klein – was spewed out by several agencies, including an American PR company retained by Victoria. Posing for photographers before entering Manhattan's Soho House, both Beckhams wore hip-hop clothes. Classed as 'street', they wore baggy jeans, baseball hats and bling jewellery.

After the dinner Victoria could not resist ordering her publicist Caroline McAteer to whisper 'exclusively' to the *Sun* that four-year-old Brooklyn had been taken for lunch in New York wearing a £32,000 Jacob & Co diamond-encrusted watch. The result was not entirely successful. 'Victoria,' scoffed her former admirer Dominic Mohan, 'is a nouveau riche kid who used to be a sickly-sweet Spice Girl. She's not "street".'[14]

One carping comment could easily be forgotten after Wintour rewarded Victoria for playing the game. The famous photographer Mario Testino – Princess Diana's favourite – was commissioned to immortalise the couple for the magazine's important September cover. In Victoria's mind, that was total victory.

The couple's next stop was Los Angeles to present the MTV awards.[15] Once again Mohan had a dig. Victoria's ambition to be the new J-Lo, he wrote, was 'ridiculous'. The disillusioned journalist, irritated by the Beckhams' media manipulation, scoffed that no one took her seriously as an artist. Instead of talent, Mohan sniped, there was 'just a void'. The only noteworthy fact was that her 'boobs' appeared to have become smaller.[16] Even the *Sun* could not protect her.

Arriving at the awards ceremony wearing a dazzling white suit and jewellery, David Beckham expected applause. Instead there was silence. While McAteer persuaded journalists in London that the couple were 'besieged' in Los Angeles, the *New York Post*'s headline DON'T COME BACK classed their three-week trip as 'a failure'. The couple, reported the newspaper, were 'going home as anonymously as when they arrived'. *Sports Illustrated*, a mighty magazine, ridiculed their potential for cracking the US. Their segment presenting one of the MTV prizes was not broadcast in America.[17] Being ignored hurt Victoria. McAteer, she complained, had failed to organise sufficient media attention.

Back in England, Beckham assumed he would be playing his last matches at Old Trafford.[18] His tearful exits from the ground were followed by defiant gestures against Ferguson. To enrage the manager he would arrive at Old Trafford wearing an Alice band. After one match he went back on to the Old Trafford pitch with Brooklyn. While they kicked the ball around, Ferguson saw Brooklyn's bike in the players' dressing room. 'What the fucking hell is that?' he bellowed. 'This is a dressing room, not a fucking playground. Get it out of here.'

In the mind and media games conjured by the Beckhams and their publicists, Beckham told the *Sun* he was 'surprised' that Ferguson was 'forcing him out' and how Manchester United was 'stabbing him in the back'.[19] Most newspapers adopted Beckham's version.

Beckham even pretended that he did not want to leave the club. On his return from filming a Pepsi advertisement in Spain, he complained about suffering 'the worst experience of my life. A nightmare.' Spain's aggressive media, he groaned, had 'put me off ever considering a move abroad'. They were 'worse than the English'. Then he insisted: 'I have always found the attention difficult. I get fed up of seeing myself in the papers. Everyone thinks I live this high life, but I'm just a normal lad really.'[20]

Beckham had forgotten that 'normal lads' are not photographed stripped to the waist for a *GQ* fashion shoot. 'My style?' he had asked rhetorically about the image of his sweating body as if he was pumping iron. 'It's from another planet. There is literally no photo-shoot I regret. They were all great opportunities to actually do something different. And I wasn't scared to do it.'[21]

He adored the hero-worship of *GQ*'s editor Dylan Jones. Like Wintour, Jones created an extravagant aura around celebrities. Jones even provided a dresser to make sure that Beckham always wore the best clothes. Beckham had ceased to be a normal footballer.

Amid the wave of publicity, Peter Kenyon, Manchester United's managing director, was undermined. He could not conceal that Beckham was being sold. Kenyon lost the media's sympathy.

To sell Beckham without consulting him, complained the players' trade union leader Gordon Taylor, was treating the player 'like a piece of meat'. The *Sun* agreed. Hawking him around to the highest bidder was wrong. Treating Beckham like 'a yellow duster', wrote Mohan, was a 'shabby episode' by a manager too old to handle young players. 'Allowing him to leave would be a catastrophic own-goal.'[22] Some disagreed. Beckham was not a brilliant footballer, judged the *Mirror*, and Manchester United was not Europe's greatest club.

That was a disservice to Beckham. Since playing for Manchester United he had played a key part in 80 goals, more than most Premier League players. But his tally had peaked in 2001.

In early June 2003, after ruling out Barcelona and Milan, Kenyon met Real Madrid's Pedro Lopez and José Ángel Sánchez in Sardinia. Kenyon knew that Adidas was pushing for Beckham's transfer to Real Madrid. The club's players wore Adidas shirts and Adidas's chief, Herbert Hainer, reflected that 'People in Asia are crazy for Beckham.' With Beckham in Madrid, sales of Adidas would be boosted across the region.[23]

José Ángel Sánchez could not believe Kenyon's lacklustre negotiating skills. Repeatedly, Sánchez swallowed hard to conceal from the Englishman his own folly. Instead of selling the most profitable football player for over £30 million, Kenyon agreed to £25.6 million. Even the headline sum was a fig leaf. Manchester United would receive just £18 million over four years and the last £7.6 million was conditional on Real Madrid's success in the Champions League. Sánchez had secured a steal, as he said, for 'peanuts. We've bought him for a song.' Luis Figo had cost 60 million euros and Zidane 70.5 million (about £70 million). Kenyon had forfeited about £25 million. At best, Sánchez expected to earn 500 million euros over four years from Beckham's shirts and appearances. Asia would be his best market.[24]

Simultaneously, Tony Stephens negotiated with Real Madrid a four-year contract at £100,000 per week, about £20,000 less than Beckham's Manchester United salary.[25] Stephens discovered there was a hitch. Like all players Beckham would be compelled to hand over to Real Madrid half the income from his image rights. But the 50 per cent rule applied only to new sponsorship deals introduced by Real Madrid. Beckham could keep the income from the existing deals and any renewals. He could also avoid the 50 per cent payment if the sponsorship was tied to the Beckham Academy, or if Victoria's appearance was included in any deal.

The transfer was signed at 8.55 p.m. on 17 June 2003. 'We were glad to see the back of him,' recalled one Manchester United's director echoing Ferguson's relief. 'Becks was too big for his boots and Jon Holmes [SFX's managing director] was far too pushy.'

The sale was national news. Beckham's departure appeared in the front and the back of the newspapers. In the front, the showbiz and gossip writers enjoyed nothing more than glorifying or trashing the Beckhams. At the back, football writers genuinely favoured the transfer.

On his last day, there was no farewell party. Manchester United's fans trusted Ferguson's judgement. Few lamented the end of an era. Most assumed Beckham was leaving because he was no longer focused on football. His successor, Cristiano Ronaldo, would mesmerise fans as 'a butterfly with a machine gun'. Manchester United's serious weakness was the lack of good defenders, not midfielders like Beckham. Fans of Beckham would thereafter swear that he was never genuinely happy as a footballer again. Partly because he missed his real family, his close friends in the dressing room.

The truth was the first casualty. The Brand required a confected version of Beckham's departure. Tony Stephens arranged for David Harrison, a *News of the World* writer, to interview Beckham. As Harrison had long experienced, 'Posh always told Becks what to say.'

Harrison described a Sunday barbecue lunch in Beckingham Palace on 15 June. After weeks of negotiations with Real Madrid, Stephens briefed Beckham about the final offer. 'After 28 calls with Stephens, we thought about it,' said Beckham. 'At 1 a.m. we chose Real Madrid.'[26] Victoria told Harrison that she had persuaded her husband to move to Madrid and promised him that she would join him there. Harrison wrote down Beckham's words: 'She will follow me anywhere in the world. As long as it benefits my career.'[27]

Harrison's version did not resemble Beckham's account 20 years later to his London audience, expressing his absolute surprise to be told he was being sold to Barcelona while he was in America. Nor was what followed in Madrid accurately reflected in the Beckhams' Netflix series. The couple's memories became hazy in what they described as a 'difficult' time.

Victoria never intended to move immediately to live in Madrid with her husband.

After returning to Madrid to work permanently for the Beckhams, Rebecca Loos witnessed a series of ferocious rows between the couple. His wife, Beckham complained to Loos, was spending the whole day on her mobile to promote her music career. He grumbled that she ignored him and their children. She had refused to move permanently to Spain. After declining all the houses she visited as unsuitable to rent, she decided she didn't like Spain. 'The streets of Madrid', she said later, 'smell of garlic, and it was very difficult to be a woman in Spain because of the inequality of the sexes.' She admitted later, 'I was lonely and fed up in Madrid. I really was bored.'[28]

Loos was surprised by Beckham's candour. To Loos – an intelligent, sophisticated woman – Victoria appeared vulnerable. To make her feel welcome in Spain, Loos invited the whole Beckham family for lunch with her mother and father, a Dutch diplomat. The introduction was not a success. 'My parents didn't like Posh,' she recalled. 'They thought she was a conniving, manipulative woman.'[29]

Instead of staying in Madrid, Victoria began commuting between London and New York. Wearing a T-shirt with the logo 'Pillow Talk is Extra', she stood in front of photographers at Heathrow in five-inch heels advertising her search for a new career as a solo singer.[30] Her bad news was buried.

Appalled by the images of Victoria produced by Testino, and by the Beckhams' publicity flop in America, Anna Wintour cancelled *Vogue*'s September cover featuring the couple. Victoria, some said, looked unhealthy. What survived of Testino's work later appeared in a men's fashion supplement.[31] Victoria's cure for the stalemate was brutal. She dumped her manager, John Glover. She had already considered his replacement.

Ever since the £1 million deal with Richard Desmond's *OK!* magazine for their wedding, the Beckhams enjoyed close relations with the proprietor. Despite Desmond's crude behaviour, the Beckhams often visited his office, especially after he bought Express Newspapers in 2000. 'I can make you the biggest brand in the world,' Desmond boasted as he strutted across his pornography-financed publishing domain. Eventually, despite endless fawning features about them in his newspapers and magazine, Victoria understood Desmond's toxicity. To Desmond's fury she shunned his offer, and to revive her career she signed with the self-promoting Simon Fuller. 'There's no one better than Simon Fuller to help me achieve my dreams,' she said about her new manager.[32]

Aged 43, Fuller gave the impression that the Spice Girls were entirely his creation. In reality, the world's most successful all-girl group had been established in 1994 by Chris and Bob Herbert. After the Herberts were dumped by the five girls as inadequate to secure their success, the women arrived in Fuller's Battersea office. Before their audition, their name had been agreed, their first album was in production and their slogan – Girl Power – had been devised by the five girls.[33] Later, some had the impression that Fuller was exclusively responsible for all three milestones. In reality, Fuller masterminded their meteoric rise to fame and fortune. Among his skills was manipulating the media to make money from the new brand.

At the height of their success in 1997 there was little gratitude for his work. He was unceremoniously fired while recuperating from a back operation. Ostensibly, the reason was his excessive demands on them to work without a week off. In reality, they thought Fuller was vain and greedy. Not only did he like standing with the Girls in the photo-calls as the group's 'sixth member', but he directed his publicist Julian Henry to glorify him as their 'Svengali' and 'Simon the Genius'. Memorably described by journalist Paul Morley as a 'death dwarf', Fuller expected the world to unquestioningly accept his self-evaluation as a genius. He was even accused of exaggerating his wealth for the *Sunday Times Rich List*. 'Critics probably don't like me because I'm so nice,' Fuller fulminated. 'I'm incredibly articulate, thoughtful and moral, and I think about what I do.' Rivals castigated him as 'Simon Fullershit'.[34]

'Get out!' Mel B shouted at Fuller, once she realised that under the contracts Fuller had written he was earning more than each of the Spice Girls.[35] That arrangement was similar to his management of the band S Club 7. While Fuller's management company was reported to have earned about £50 million from the group, each member of the band pocketed about £590,000.[36]

'We had been numbed by Simon,' Victoria wrote in her autobiography. 'To survive, you have to be ruthless. It's kill or be killed.'[37] Shortly after Fuller's departure, Victoria would damn those who had in turn betrayed her – especially those who sold sordid accounts about their personal lives with the Beckhams to the tabloids. But from Victoria's perspective, that was different. Her inheritance from Fuller was an understanding of the media world's marketing, strategy and rules.[38]

Since the Spice Girls' break-up, Fuller's fame had soared. In 2002 he created the smash-hit musical TV show *American Idol,* which was based on his earlier British version *Pop Idol*. By 2003 the format had been sold to over 50 countries. His 19 Entertainment Group's annual income would rise in 2004 from £2 million to £53 million. As an international media mogul, Fuller claimed to own five homes, including ones in Sussex, the south of France and Los Angeles. He drove a designer Mercedes Maybach and owned a private jet.

Among his fiercest critics was Simon Cowell, the music producer and star of *American Idol*. 'It's all about Fuller,' Cowell told a friend. 'He's not interested in anyone else. He doesn't deliver on his promises.' Cowell also accused Fuller's spokesman Julian Henry of planting false stories about his rivals. Exhausted by other doubts about Fuller's character, Cowell had left *American Idol* and launched a rival show, *The X Factor*.

All that was irrelevant, Victoria decided. She needed someone to save her career. Fuller was her man. Mindful of what she felt in 1997 – 'To survive you have to be ruthless' – she also dumped Alan Edwards, the loyal publicist she had in 2001 called 'supportive from the start'.[39] He had run his course. Good for the music business, he was considered too vague to promote the Brand. Aware of Victoria's intentions, Caroline McAteer also abandoned Edwards and joined Fuller's 19 Management. Edwards' business suffered. An investor cancelled a lucrative deal. Edwards was furious but powerless. His feelings were irrelevant to Victoria and to Fuller.

Fuller knew that Victoria's career was in trouble. Obsessed with Damon Dash and fighting against Telstar's executives, she was constantly seeking advice, consulting publicists, fashion designers and music executives about her future. Fuller knew that her future depended entirely on Beckham.

In his first statement, Fuller's intentions were clear – he hoped to oust Tony Stephens and become David Beckham's manager too: 'With the Beckham name so renowned the world over for music, fashion and football, there are no boundaries for what we can achieve together.' Fuller knew about Beckham's financial potential, but nothing about football and little about his personal life in Madrid. In Beckham's first autobiography *My Side*, which was published in September 2003, he could have read about Beckham's unconditional love for Victoria. 'It's still a powerful relationship,' said Beckham.[40]

Before the book's publication, the *Sun*'s editor bumped into Beckham in a Manchester nightclub's lavatory. 'You don't know me,' David Yelland said to the footballer, 'but we've just bought the serialisation rights to your autobiography.'

'What autobiography?' asked Beckham, genuinely surprised.

'Just paid you £100,000 for it,' replied Yelland.

Watching Beckham sitting in a corner drinking a Coke, Yelland concluded that the sober star was a decent bloke. Fortunately, over the previous four years he had not published any negative stories about him. Even tips about his love affairs had been ignored. If true, those stories would have lost more readers than would be won. The *Sun* was Beckham's true friend.

CHAPTER 9
MARRIAGE CRISIS

'I've got a hot one,' a woman caller told Ben Todd, the *Sunday Mirror*'s showbiz editor. 'About the Beckhams.'

With charm, long hours and a big budget, Todd had successfully schmoozed many stars to share their own secrets or divulge the secrets of others. He had built a network of informers about the stars' private lives – drivers, housekeepers, hairdressers, beauticians, masseurs, spray-tan specialists, barmen, bodyguards and, most critically, the celebrities' trusted friends and acquaintances. All those relationships were valuable for getting the truth about celebrities, not least the Beckhams. In return for brown envelopes with thousands of pounds, Todd got tips to write gossip stories, or even a front-page splash. Occasionally, Todd was given a story by the news desk, unaware of its source.

In early September 2003 a source of Todd's who described herself as a friend of a teacher at Brooklyn Beckham's Hertfordshire school called. She told Todd that Victoria had said to Brooklyn's teacher: 'I'm not fucking going to Madrid. I've told him, "There's no fucking way"'.

Inevitably, Todd was excited. Any truth that punctured the official story of the happily married Beckhams was dynamite. Still unknown to Todd, the Beckhams were ferociously arguing about Victoria's refusal to move into a Madrid villa he had rented for £32,000 a month. Not only was she focused on her own career in New York, she said, but she also appeared to be unconcerned about the pressure on Beckham to prove himself.

While Beckham played his debut match in the Bernabéu in August, Victoria was in a New York recording studio with Damon Dash. Despite the distance, she was hyper-sensitive. After seeing a newspaper photo of Rebecca Loos alongside her husband's friend Dave Gardner in the stadium, Victoria had telephoned Loos. 'It's not your job to go to David's matches,' she snapped. Loos apologised and agreed to work only from the SFX office. Not surprisingly, Victoria did not complain when Loos arranged through private contacts for Brooklyn to enter immediately Madrid's elite English-speaking Runnymede school. Yet, bizarrely, Victoria would later claim that she could not relocate to Spain during the first year because there were no schools for her children, four-year-old Brooklyn and one-year-old Romeo.[1]

Telephoning his contacts, Todd heard how Victoria had discussed with Dash using Brooklyn and Romeo in a Rocawear advertisement. That eyewitness told Todd that Sandra Beckham, caring for the boys, had witnessed the discussion in a New York hotel room. Dash, Sandra had told her son, was 'sprawled over the bed. It was not appropriate.'

Other calls by Todd to Beckham's friends revealed how Victoria did not want to leave her parents and sister; and how she also wanted Brooklyn to continue in his English school. Finally, she demanded a private jet for any flight to Madrid.[2]

To confirm the sensational story, Todd called Caroline McAteer, the Beckhams' spokeswoman. Around that time, McAteer had been asked: 'What happens if a client is embroiled in a scandal and you're asked to lie for them?'[3]

'I've never been in that position,' replied McAteer. 'And I wouldn't like to be.'

When Todd asked McAteer whether the Beckhams had marital problems, she instantly roared: 'Not true!'

In the *Sunday Mirror*'s office, Todd was overheard calling Alan Edwards. He had bonded with Todd over football and David Bowie concerts. The spurned publicist no longer felt loyal towards the Beckhams. And despite his dismissal Edwards had retained good relations with many close to the family. Edwards confirmed to Todd the Beckhams were in trouble. He had heard their marriage was in crisis.

'Trouble in Paradise', Todd chortled. Under the headline 'REAL MAD' the *Sunday Mirror* revealed for the first time in September 2003 the Beckhams' arguments. The Beckhams were rattled. Until then their control over the media had suppressed even the slightest hint of unhappiness.

Without delay, on the Beckhams' orders, their lawyers accused the newspaper of defamation. There was absolutely no truth, wrote

Gerrard Tyrrell of Harbottle & Lewis, about any problems. The lawyer called the editor Tina Weaver at home, although she was on maternity leave. Issuing threats, the lawyer demanded substantial damages and a published retraction admitting that the story was untrue. The newspaper rejected the Beckhams' demands.

Todd's revelation spooked the *Sunday Mirror*'s competitor, the *News of the World*. Little was more important for Andy Coulson, its editor, than halting the slow decline of the newspaper's 4 million circulation. Every Sunday, at least 10 million readers enjoyed the newspaper's exposes about famous celebrities. Angry that he was being scooped by a newspaper with a mere 1.7 million circulation, Coulson tasked Rav Singh, renowned as a feisty showbiz editor, to get more than Todd had published. Coulson then flew to Portugal on holiday.

In another part of the newspaper's Wapping offices, one of the news editors was paying telephone hackers to glean selected celebrities' secrets from their mobile telephones. One target for the illegal operations were the Beckhams.

Singh would always insist that his story about the Beckhams on 21 September 2003, the week after Todd's, was gathered by traditional and legal methods – from informers close to the Beckhams.

Talking to his contacts, Singh heard that the footballer had been seen that week with women and other team players in a Madrid nightclub. In particular, Beckham had been spotted with a tall brunette. No name was forthcoming. Another paid informant also revealed that Victoria had said to a friend in a restaurant, 'It's over.' Something sensational, he was persuaded, was definitely going on. Automatically, he telephoned McAteer. Without hesitation, the publicist denied the story.

Convinced the Beckhams' marriage was indeed shaky, Andy Coulson flew back from his holiday to oversee the story's publication. His first call was to Alan Edwards, an old friend. He confirmed that the marriage was troubled. Coulson, Edwards knew, had enjoyed a close relationship with one of the Spice Girls, and was therefore well connected.

Coulson now needed to consider whether the advantageous co-operation between the Beckhams, the *Sun* and the *News of the World* should be endangered. After calculating that there was no gain in allowing his competitors an advantage – the truth would eventually emerge – he executed a 'reverse ferret', a journalist's term for a U-turn. This, he reasoned, would be revenge against the Beckhams' threatening lawyers and their publicists promoting fake news. 'POSH AND BECKHAM IN MARRIAGE CRISIS' was his blazing headline. Adding the tag 'Exclusive' was redundant on a report shattering the image of England's most celebrated loving family.

'The marriage of David and Victoria Beckham has hit trouble,' wrote Singh. 'The famous pair are suffering serious strains over Victoria's bid for fame and their new life in Spain. A friend says, "There are real tensions in the marriage for the first time. The family hope they can be resolved before it gets out of control."' 4

To add gravitas Coulson added a personal comment: 'We take no pleasure revealing tensions in the Beckham household. No marriage is easy and being famous certainly doesn't help make it easier despite the riches. We sincerely hope Britain's favourite family ride out this storm.'

To celebrate their splash, Coulson took his journalists to Mayfair's Met Bar. He would have been aware of the twist of fate. He took the credit for helping to create the Beckhams in 1996. Now he could claim to have exposed their drift towards the abyss. Good journalists owe favours to no person, only to the truth. First editions of the newspaper had long been on sale outside King's Cross station when the celebrating journalists staggered into the dawn.

That Sunday, Beckham effortlessly pretended that the report had no effect on him. After scoring a stunning goal against Malaga he spoke to Eric Beauchamp, the *Sun* sports writer sent to Spain to follow Beckham's football career. Stories about a 'rift in our marriage', Beckham told Beauchamp as he left the dressing room, are 'a load of rubbish'. Living apart from Victoria was normal. 'I'm really enjoying Spain,' he said with a smile as he headed for the airport to return to Madrid. He planned that evening to go to a bar with a special friend, and the following day he would celebrate Ronaldo's birthday. The Brazilian had planned a huge party. 5

Beckham knew that his comment to Beauchamp was inaccurate. 'Things are ropey,' he told a friend later that Sunday. 'I don't know what to do.'[6] Geoffrey Wansell in the *Daily Mail* reported that eyewitnesses had overheard Beckham 'screaming his heart out', pleading with his wife not to spend time with Dash and to come to Madrid.[7] But, obsessed by her own fame, Victoria's friend described her being 'utterly entranced' by Dash. 'He makes her feel special and she loves the glamour he brings her.'

Whatever the truth, Beckham was unable to fully understand his wife. Preoccupied by his own performance and appearance, he gave little thought to Victoria's fears. Seven years earlier, when they met, she was the global star, much more famous than himself. Now, living under his shadow, she was unsettled and unhappy. Her pulling power was declining. With doubts about her looks she lacked the sensitive foresight to anticipate the consequence of sidelining her husband while she sought to rebuild her own career. She wanted to shine in her own right.

That same Sunday evening, surrounded by four bodyguards, she hosted a London Fashion Week party in Mayfair. Tirelessly, she sought to boost her profile.[8] Voted earlier that month in a *Prima* magazine poll as the world's best-dressed woman for the second year running, she had, on Simon Fuller's advice, hired a film crew to follow her to shoot a TV documentary. So far, they had footage of her shopping, getting beauty treatments in Madrid and travelling with Beckham in Asia. During the London party she was filmed speaking about her new style of rap music: 'Damon brings the hip-hop and I bring the pop culture. Together we make hip-pop.'

Before midnight she left the club with Dash, heading for the Ministry of Sound. Dancing until 2.30 a.m., Victoria gave a good impression of being unconcerned about the *News of the World* story.[9] 'I don't read the stuff that's written about us,' she said. 'I'm not interested in gossip.'[10] In reality, after hearing about the gossip among SFX's staff she had called Beckham that Sunday morning. What really bothered her, she had admitted in her autobiography, was the accuracy of the media reports.[11]

Who, she screamed, was leaking the stories? In what a *News of the World* journalist called 'a cat-and-mouse chase to discover our sources,' the Beckhams suspected agents, employees, Fuller's staff and friends. They also suspected phone-tapping. But in their publicity-seeking world the couple expected McAteer's denials of the story to be believed. The truth, they insisted, must in all circumstances be suppressed.

The scene in Beckham's Madrid hotel room after Victoria's phone call that Sunday morning was clearly recalled by one eyewitness: Rebecca Loos.

'The shit has hit the fan,' Beckham told Loos. 'Victoria knows what's been going on. We'll have to be more careful.'

From the vantage of his hotel bedroom, Loos did not witness Beckham showing any contrition. Rather, he was dispassionately calculating his next steps. Convinced that no journalist in London would discover the truth, Beckham expected that the recent newspaper reports would be forgotten. Similarly, he was not a person to ask himself how he ended up in his bed with Rebecca Loos. He was not a man filled with regrets who wanted to wind back to the beginning. 'He's become brooding, self-conscious, meaner, more self-obsessed,' a friend had noticed. Stardom and bachelor life in Madrid had transformed him. 'He can do what he wants.'

Some people close to the Beckhams believed that SFX had hired Rebecca Loos to undermine Victoria. But that raised contested assumptions.

No one could have assumed that Loos would find Beckham attractive when she arrived in Madrid. In the summer of 2003 she was involved with Emma Basden, a television presenter living in London. Nor could anyone have anticipated Victoria's refusal to move to the Spanish capital.

In Victoria's absence Loos was responsible for furnishing the rented villa in Madrid. Frequently, Victoria sent Loos instructions, which in turn David overruled. 'What shall I do?' Loos asked Beckham after a disagreement arose over the swimming pool. 'Do it my way,' he replied. 'It will be our secret. We don't have to tell anyone.'

Some would say that Beckham was bored. After training in the morning and then lunching with the team, he was alone for the rest of the day – and night. Not only was his family in England but during their conversations Victoria seemed uninterested in his career. Rolling her eyes whenever he spoke about football, she seemed to turn up at matches only to be photographed.[12] To fill his empty hours in Madrid, Beckham headed for the gated community where Ronaldo lived. The Brazilian was famous for his loud parties, described by one commentator as wild girls falling out of the windows at 8 a.m. At Real, the hobby was not alcohol or drugs, it was women.

Beckham would later say, 'I wasn't about parties,' but the evidence was contradictory.[13] In the hills outside Madrid was an isolated house used by Real Madrid players to entertain endless girls. No one ever discovered whether Beckham joined those parties, but he was seen at others.

Rebecca Loos says now that she was attracted by Beckham's vulnerability. And inevitably his looks. A one-hour video shot by Sam Taylor-Johnson of Beckham asleep in his Madrid hotel room revealed a stunning Adonis. Bare-chested with flopping blond hair, Taylor-Johnson captured the Sleeping Beauty, the icon who decided to chase Loos. Apparently forgotten was his love for Victoria expressed just 18 days earlier on the publication of his updated autobiography: 'I loved the whole package: her looks, her personality, her energy.'[14]

Thursday 18 September was a warm evening in Madrid. After meeting at the Santo Mauro hotel, Loos and Beckham were driven by his Cuban bodyguard Delfin Fernandez to the Thai Garden restaurant. A back-up car with two more bodyguards followed. Four SFX employees were waiting for him in the restaurant.

Beckham was depressed. After ordering champagne, he started a Truth or Dare game. Beckham was asked if he had ever had sex in a plane. He perked up. Yes, he replied, but offered no more information. After 40 minutes of laughter and jokes, Beckham declared 'This is the first time I have had any real fun since I came here two months ago.' At midnight, to avoid the paparazzi, he and Loos left the restaurant by the back door. As he drove to the Ananda nightclub, Fernandez saw the couple kissing in the back. While dancing, Beckham asked Loos to come back to his hotel. They returned to the Santo Mauro after 4 a.m.

In his suite, Loos discovered that 'David was a sensational lover – the sex was highly charged and explosive. David's stamina was extraordinary.' Repeatedly he said, 'I know we shouldn't be doing this but I can't help it. It makes me so happy.' Loos would add, 'He'd been going weeks without sex, trying to stay faithful to Posh.'[15]

One exchange in bed that night impressed Loos. 'You're so lucky,' she said. 'You could have anyone.'

'No,' replied Beckham, 'I've never done this before.'

The following night, Friday, they met again, at a tapas bar in the Old Town. Loos was waiting with several friends. After dinner, Beckham and Loos left by a back door. Before driving away, Beckham signed autographs and played football with a boy on the street. They returned to his hotel suite. On Saturday morning he flew to Malaga to play a match, unaware that the *News of the World* was planning to publish its revelations the following morning.

After returning to Madrid on Sunday evening, 21 September, he went to a nightclub with some team friends. Waiting for them was Esther Canadas, a blonde 28-year-old lingerie model and actress also known as Miss Big Lips. Their encounter was reported by Spain's television talk-show *Con T de Tarde*. By then a mobile phone video had surfaced of Beckham with Loos at the Ananda nightclub. The exclusive rights were bought by the *News of the World*. But that was all. 'Fishy,' muttered one old-timer. Coulson still appeared not to know the woman's name.

That same Sunday night, after returning to his hotel from the nightclub, Beckham sent Loos a series of texts. Despite that day's *News of the World* report he listed in breathlessly graphic language his appetite for a succession of sex acts. 'I want to hear you scream,' he wrote. She kept the text messages on her phone.

'Very heavy stuff,' she thought. 'I was his lover, his pimp and his wife,' she later said.[16] Beckham's texts had been sent on a mobile phone he used for messaging his girlfriends. When not used, he entrusted it to his new right-hand man Andy Bernal,[17] an Australian and former professional footballer. Among the messages was his agreement with Loos to meet the following day, Monday 22 September, at Ronaldo's birthday party. To conceal their relationship they would arrive separately. His caution was pointless. At least 12 people knew about Loos's affair with Beckham: SFX employees, hotel staff, his bodyguards and especially Loos's friends. She had shown them Beckham's sexually explicit text messages.

Ronaldo's house parties were as legendary as his love of women. 'I need love,' he told Real Madrid's manager when asked about his endless girlfriends. When asked about Beckham's arrival at Real Madrid, Ronaldo replied, 'Terrific. He is a great player and a good guy. Plus he attracts so many women that there are bound to be plenty left over for me.'[18] Ronaldo's parties with stunning girls 'in the house up the hill' were famous in the football world.

Arriving at 10 p.m. at Ronaldo's beautiful villa, Beckham was not disappointed. There was an intoxicating atmosphere and the garden was filled with glamorous girls drinking champagne. The chef was a celebrated Argentinian. Loos arrived to discover Beckham chatting 'intensely' on a garden bench to Esther Canadas. From a distance she watched the couple disappear into the house. Followed by a bodyguard they went into a bedroom and locked the door. Once inside, Beckham turned off his phone. Beckham's bodyguard stood outside.

In England, Victoria had become frenzied. Aware from SFX employees that Beckham and Loos had been seen earlier that week at a nightclub, she called her husband. Unable to reach him she called Loos at around 1 a.m. Before answering, Loos moved into an empty room.

'I can't get hold of David,' said Victoria. 'Where the hell is he?'

'I don't know,' Loos lied.

'What the fuck are you doing with my husband? It's not your job to be out with him at nightclubs. Just back off.'

Two years earlier, Victoria had described her reaction to a newspaper kiss-and-tell story by a girl who had met Beckham.

'I'm screaming and shouting and swearing and going hysterical,' Victoria admitted in her autobiography. 'It was the most awful thing that happened to me.' Since then, she wrote, she had stopped panicking: 'I had to remember that I could not wish for anybody as faithful and kind and caring as David. I was just being a spoilt brat because I thought someone was trying to take what was mine. He would never do anything that would jeopardise our relationship.'[19]

Now she was seriously jealous – and worried.

At 3 a.m. Victoria called Loos again. Screaming, 'I know you both went to the same party!' Victoria demanded: 'Fucking find him.' Loos went upstairs and asked the bodyguard to get Beckham from the bedroom.

'David, I have your wife on the phone.' Minutes later, Beckham opened the door. Fully clothed, he took the phone.

Loos saw Canadas in the bed. 'I looked at him, very hurt,' she would tell a friend. 'I thought I was the only one.'

Beckham went back inside the room. After speaking to Victoria, he reopened the door. Without showing any emotion he returned the phone to Loos. He left the party at 3.30 a.m. After returning to his hotel room, Loos arrived and stayed for the rest of the night. 'I was too tipsy to remember what happened,' she later recalled.[20]

Two amazing women in one night had a profound influence on Beckham's relationship with Victoria. All the pluses built up over the previous seven years of their mutual dependency, trust and inter-changeable characters changed dramatically.

At daybreak on Tuesday, Victoria boarded a plane and headed for Madrid. She would not be alone in the city. Alerted by the *News of the World* and the *Sunday Mirror*, all the tabloids had sent reinforce-ments to Madrid to find evidence of Beckham's activities. Against them stood Victoria.

Over the previous years, Victoria had learned better than most how to manage the media. In her calculation, the Beckhams' mystique was enhanced by sticking to the formula that less is more. To prove the happy marriage, Victoria ordered McAteer to stage a photo opportu-nity. At an agreed spot in Madrid, Victoria was recorded pecking her husband on his cheek. 'Our marriage', said their statement, 'is not in crisis. We are extremely happy together.'[21] Asked about Beckham and Canadas at Ronaldo's party, McAteer told Rav Singh, 'It's all nonsense. Esther's presence was a complete coincidence.'

That evening, Victoria went alone to the Spanish *Elle* Style awards. Her face, said some, looked like 'thunder'. After the awards she ate dinner with Beckham at the Salamanca restaurant. 'They looked really happy together,' pronounced McAteer about the display of unity. The following morning, after a blazing row, Beckham headed off for training. In the evening they posed together again over dinner. McAteer pronounced that they were close.

The following morning, instead of watching Beckham play Valencia, Victoria flew back to London to present the Lycra awards. 'David', she told the audience in Old Billingsgate market, 'is not getting the award for being best dressed but he's the best at undressing me. David, I love you and I love Spain.' Some in the audience later asked, 'Why is she back?'[22] In Madrid, Beckham was fuming. As he told a friend, 'I've been in Madrid for 89 days. She's been here for 35 days.'[23]

Leading the pack to expose the Beckhams' version of events was the *News of the World*. Ulrika Johnson spoke for many in her regular column by criticising Victoria: 'You claimed you loved to be at home, but you're never at home, or with your husband. You arrive at school dressed in a Dolce & Gabbana cocktail dress, high heels and sunglasses. It's the arrogance of a woman who believes she is indispensable.'[24]

While Victoria visited Madrid, Coulson was chivvying his reporters to obtain legally watertight evidence of an extramarital relationship. Aware that the Beckhams were preparing to sue the *Sunday Mirror*, Coulson held back from suggesting an outright affair based on the video of Beckham and Loos in the Ananda club. Nevertheless, under the *News of the World*'s screaming headline 'BECKHAM AND THE BRUNETTE' the newspaper's five-page report was graphic: 'Touching shoulders, flirting, what will Posh say? It's 2.30 a.m. and the lonely English ace cosies up with a girl in a Madrid club.' Under the video image of the couple in the club was the bold caption. 'Pictures that Victoria just hasta see.' Readers were left in no doubt about the implication. 'Message to Posh' headed a body expert's warning: 'You'd better watch out.'

Loos was furious about the publicity. According to a neighbour she was 'in tears' because of the 'false accusations'. Unspoken, she was also upset that Beckham was pursuing Canadas and possibly even other women. After all, he had told her on their first encounter that he had never been unfaithful before. For the moment her intimate relationship with Beckham slipped beyond her control. Similarly distraught, Victoria's suspicions were wreaking havoc on her own life.

Victoria knew that that she increasingly relied on her husband's fame to maintain her own profile. Without him she knew that her celebrity and career would fade. But she knew that together they had a unique bond, not just with a large section of the British public but across China and Japan. To keep their unrivalled status as Britain's most revered celebrity couple, the public's adulation was best preserved by sticking to their joint message of hard work, family values and a happy marriage. Her challenge was to prove those realities to her husband. The financial implications for both were huge.

Beckham appeared unconcerned by the *News of the World*'s latest revelations. That Sunday, his denials to Victoria of any wrongdoing were designed to bear a ring of truth. Convinced he was protected by Britain's libel laws, he invited Canadas to his hotel suite on the following day. On Tuesday morning he left the hotel for the training ground. Canadas remained asleep in his bed. Outside his room sat two bodyguards, Delfin Fernandez and Arsenio Ruiz. An unexpected call announced that Victoria was heading to Madrid on a private jet. 'You've got minutes to get your things together,' a bodyguard told Canadas, 'and go.'[25]

That same night the Beckhams staged what McAteer called 'a romantic dinner' at Madrid's Ritz hotel. The *Sun*'s photographer was told where to see them walking hand-in-hand. With consummate professionalism, they kissed and hugged for the camera.[26]

Shortly after Victoria returned to London, Beckham texted Canadas: 'Have a safe flight, baby and I really wish we was in your bed now.'[27] Asked by Todd about her relationship with Beckham, Canadas denied any personal involvement. 'It is nothing,' she said.[28]

Sighing in relief as he prepared for that weekend's match against Espanyol, Beckham was unaware of his escape from another explosion. In Australia, the *News of the World*'s investigative journalist Neville Thurlbeck had spent six weeks with Sarah Marbeck. After deciding to sell her story, the prostitute gave Thurlbeck all the details of her two-year affair with Beckham. All that was needed was proof that she was telling the truth. Repeatedly, with Thurlbeck at her side, she texted Beckham on his usual number. She received no reply. Simultaneously involved with Loos and Canadas he was uninterested in Marbeck. At the end of October 2003, Thurlbeck returned to London with a large expenses claim and an unpublishable story.[29]

CHAPTER 10

WRECKAGE

Sitting with her family in her Hertfordshire mansion, Victoria cried, 'heartbroken' about Beckham letting her down.[1] Frustrated that she could not express her anger, she felt paralysed by the uproar. At the end of September 2003, Girl Power was not uppermost in her mind. She was more concerned about her career crumbling.

'Posh's comeback is going pear-shaped,' observed a Telstar executive. Her efforts to relaunch herself as a singer were a disaster. Not only did Telstar refuse to release her hip-hop album but they also rejected Dash's financial demands. 'Telstar are fucking retarded,' retorted Dash. 'We are fighting about money.' He threatened to sue Telstar.[2]

'We've lost £500,000 on our own dud album,' a Telstar executive complained. In her misery, Victoria pulled out of singing at a Prince's Trust concert at the Royal Albert Hall. The Trust complained about losing money.[3] Telstar also complained about Victoria's failure to arrive at a meeting to discuss promoting her single. What's more, she broke her promise to Telstar to ditch Dash.[4]

Regularly, she was seen around London with Dash – one night at Nobu, then two days later at Soho House, and next at a party in Covent Garden. 'I've seen Victoria a lot this week,' Dash cooed. 'She's a cool girl.'[5] It would be only six months later that Dash denied for the first time having an affair with Victoria.[6] Most believed he was telling the truth. Victoria was not known to be promiscuous. Before her marriage she had enjoyed single, committed relationships. Yet four years later Dash said, 'I wouldn't blame David if he was jealous.'[7]

Dash's interference in the Beckhams' married life disturbed David. His telephone calls with Victoria suggested she was seriously unsettled. At the end of a Real Madrid press conference in early November, Beckham burst out: 'All this speculation about my wife not being happy, it can't carry on – it's all rubbish. She's very happy here in Madrid. There are no problems in our marriage.'[8] No journalist dared reply, 'But she's not in Madrid.' To safeguard their access to Beckham, they said nothing. No one mentioned that one-year-old Romeo had just been taken to a Madrid hospital for a head injury after a fall, his third visit to a hospital in two months.[9] Victoria was in New York. She had no plans, said her spokeswoman, to interrupt her recording session with Damon Dash and fly to Madrid. In the previous six weeks she had spent barely 15 days in Spain.

'I'm incandescent with rage about Telstar,' Victoria complained to the *Sun* after a trip from Sawbridgeworth to London to arrange the release of her single and album.[9] The promotion had started in November but then backfired. *Beckham's Body Parts*, an ITV documentary focusing on Victoria's lifestyle, was derided as 'vacuous'.[10] Beckham's staged reaction after a doctor apparently wrote to tell him that he suffered from Obsessive Compulsive Disorder (OCD) merely raised a smile. One shot of Beckham's bathroom showed a vast range of toiletries laid out in straight lines – moisturisers, hair gels, face make-up, aftershave lotions and endless gadgets. Alongside were brushes and towels – separate towels for his feet, his face and his body.

To create a point of interest in himself Beckham often admitted suffering from OCD. 'I have to have everything in a straight line,' he frequently explained, including the Coke cans in his fridge. Among his other foibles was wiping the inside of the candle-holders each night to eradicate hated smoke-marks. On this occasion, asked by Victoria if he suffered from OCD, he replied jokingly: 'Yes, I have. And I've got lots of DVDs as well.' In another bid for publicity she later disclosed that her OCD husband hoovered in straight lines 'wearing a pinny'.[11] Other men who have suffered from OCD include Steve Jobs, the co-founder of Apple, and Elon Musk, the co-founder of Tesla, the Falcon rocket and the owner of Twitter/X.

Caroline McAteer asked Victoria Newton the following day, who wrote about the result of Victoria's filming over the previous eight months. 'Television companies are battling over the rights to the footage,' a 'friend' told Newton. 'The recordings are dynamite. There is so much great stuff, it's impossible to cut it down to one show.'[12] Insiders were not fooled. Victoria's bid to win a global audience as a solo star had hit a new crisis.

To clear the path – and manage both Beckhams – Fuller persuaded Victoria that she should break from Telstar. He bought a ticket for a Telstar executive to fly to Nice to hear his offer: he would buy out Victoria's contract and pay compensation for the unreleased single. Back in London the executive confessed, 'We're sick of her. She's been a complete waste of time. Fuller's taken the sting out of it. Let's take the cash.'

Victoria was present for the final rites in Telstar's London office. Fuller offered to pay, at Victoria's expense, for the single's release by Telstar at the end of December. The A-side was 'Let Your Head Go' and the B-side was a hip-hop single called 'This Groove'. Dash's hip-hop album was ditched. Or as Fuller said, 'buried'.[13] That did not stop sightings of Victoria around London with Dash.

As Beckham had left Old Trafford after England's 2–3 defeat by Denmark on 16 November, Beckham told a trusted journalist, 'I'm fed up. I love my wife. She loves me. There have never been any problems. People should stop making up silly stories.' Three weeks later he met Loos in a bedroom in Madrid's Fenix hotel.[14]

On 23 November the Beckhams' charade was exposed by the *Sunday Mirror*. In a telephone call Victoria had told her husband she was not coming to Madrid. Instead she would continue to socialise with Damon Dash and he should return immediately to England. 'It's my way or the fucking highway,' Todd reported as Victoria's ultimatum.[15] The source, apparently a friend of Victoria's, was paid £3,000 in cash.

Interpreting Victoria's ultimatum was difficult at the time. Few realised that Beckham was intimidated by Victoria's parents' control over his life, as well as his estrangement from his own father. 'Sandra also got very, very upset', Rebecca Loos had noticed, 'at the way the Adams family acted in general and towards her.' In what Loos called a 'power struggle', Beckham was 'angry by the way his mum was treated by the in-laws'.[16] Most assumed that Victoria dominated their marriage. No one had yet pieced together the truth about Beckham's affairs. The vast majority of his fans still believed in the magical marriage.

The *Sunday Mirror* headline on an inside page, 'IT'S MY WAY OR THE FUCKING HIGHWAY', terrified the Beckhams. Unaware of the source of the report they ordered Gerrard Tyrrell to extract an apology. McAteer was also ordered to complain to the Press Complaints Commission. Both insisted that the *Sunday Mirror*'s journalists were lying. The newspaper's circulation soared.

That morning, Victoria called one of the Spice Girls, Emma Bunton. During an emotional conversation about the state of her marriage she disclosed, 'We could be splitting up. We have a long-distance relationship.'[17] She disclosed that she had given Beckham an ultimatum that their marriage was over 'unless he returned to England'. She had also refused, she told Bunton, to watch Beckham play for England against Denmark.[18]

On reflection, Victoria realised the importance of burying the rumours. She turned to her trusted advocate, Michael Parkinson. An interview with both Beckhams on BBC TV, she calculated, would be invaluable. It was recorded on the same day as Beckham received an OBE from Queen Elizabeth. Victoria was introduced as 'one of the most talked about women in the world'. Parkinson asked the previously agreed question: 'Are you getting divorced?'

'Apparently so,' she laughed, as Beckham sat silently impassive next to her.

'Where do those rumours come from?' asked Parkinson.

'A lot of people don't like that we're the golden couple and that we're very happy.' She added, 'Even though the Beckhams are a commodity to a certain extent, we're married and we're normal people and we're very much in love.' She continued, 'Those who say there's a rift are jealous. Moving to Spain, we just got a house and we're getting settled. It's been great for us.'[19]

Victoria's version was not challenged by 'Parky'. By then her refusal to move into the rented house in Madrid had cost Beckham £432,875 at the Santa Maura hotel. His bill included two suites, separate rooms for his visiting family and friends, garaging, an English chef, plus food and drinks from the bar and restaurant.[20]

Asked by Parkinson about her solo career as a rapper, Victoria replied 'The thought of me rapping is ridiculous.'

A publicity blitz had been organised to promote her hip-hop record. She was booked to appear on *The Jonathan Ross Show*, *Top of the Pops* and dozens of radio stations, as well as having a part in a TV soap and making four pre-recorded appearances on Christmas Day. She would also feature on Christmas Eve in *The Real Beckhams*, a 110-minute fly-on-the-wall television documentary featuring Beckham's move to Madrid and then living alone. 'David, that's not fair,' she is filmed saying during a telephone argument. 'I am around. It's really difficult talking sometimes.' She also admitted to being jealous when Beckham spoke to other women: 'They're always trying it. I don't like it.'

To capture a headline she revealed her use of Brazilian waxes – 'Brazilians ought to be made compulsory,' she said – and recounted that she and Beckham enjoyed telephone sex; and that after shopping at Dolce & Gabbana she would be eating dinner with Beckham at Mayfair's Nobu. She did not disclose that Beckham had flown in specially for the dinner and returned that night on the private jet to Madrid. In anticipation she had spent five hours having hair extensions at a specialist salon in Chalk Farm. The work also concealed a patch of grey hair.[21]

All that effort proved unsuccessful. A *Daily Mirror* poll on the eve of her single's release reported that Victoria topped the list of Britain's most unpopular celebrities.[22] Two weeks after entering the charts at No. 3, the disc went into freefall, selling fewer than 10,000 copies.[23]

To prove herself undaunted, she staged an unusual photo opportunity at 1 a.m. for the paparazzi waiting outside Nobu. After allegedly celebrating the release of her disc, she and Beckham got into their waiting Bentley. Instead of the chauffeur driving away, the photographers witnessed an aggressive sex scene, starting with her unbuckling Beckham's belt and taking off his jeans. Calculated to show that their marriage was perfect, the chauffeur just stared ahead.[24]

Two reasons persuaded the Beckhams to stage the stunts: fear and money. In plain language Victoria had warned Beckham that if their marriage broke up he would lose his children. Sole custody would be granted to her. He would find access difficult. The footballer's deep love for his children – he telephoned them every day – made that prospect unthinkable. Simultaneously, he was told that Jackie and Tony Adams would cut him off. The threat was serious. The Adams were more his family now than Ted and Sandra. Fearing that loss glued him to Victoria.

For her part, Victoria's fear for her career without Beckham's fame kept her onside. Money united the couple. Fuller, she was convinced, should replace SFX's Tony Stephens as Beckham's agent.

Fuller's pitch to Beckham was enticing. Now 28 years old, Beckham's football career was peaking. He needed to consider his post-retirement income. While SFX had secured Beckham about £15 million per annum, Fuller explained that 19 Entertainment's management team could generate much more money in the long term. His pitch was made easier by Stephens taking a sabbatical after Beckham went to Madrid. Beckham's relationship with Jon Holmes, SFX's prickly chief executive, was unsatisfactory. Equally unsatisfactory was Alex Ferguson's decision to allow his son Jason to be inserted into many lucrative Manchester United transfer deals.[25] Jason and Tony Stephens were partners. All those relationships offended Beckham's mantra: 'I'm always in control of what's going on.'[26]

To prove his value to the Beckhams, Fuller had been discussing a sponsorship deal for David as the face of Gillette.[27]

In 2003, Gillette was searching for a personality to promote the new 'Power Shave'. While Gillette controlled 80 per cent of the European market, the corporation sought inroads into Asia. Its initial target was to convert just 1 per cent of Chinese to wet shaving using 'G Razors', alias the 'M3 Power micro-powered shaving system'. As a Galactico, the advertising agency was certain that Beckham would be a 'global face' of masculinity, especially in Asia. After the World Cup tournament in Japan, his annual earnings in the region were about £10 million and still rising. Gillette's tagline since the late 1980s was 'The Best a Man Can Get'.

Throughout Gillette's negotiations for 'Project Bond', the managers were often told by Beckham's lawyers, 'We've spoken to Victoria ...' Hearing about Gillette's insistence that Beckham's 'appearance' must not change, Victoria was adamant. She insisted his looks constantly changed depending on his mood. As a style icon he needed 'style autonomy'.

Gillette's American headquarters resisted contracting the footballer until the film *Bend It Like Beckham* was a confirmed box-office hit. All that remained was to finalise the finances. The money, Fuller assured Beckham, would be huge – about £4 million a year. And, promised Fuller, there was much more to come if he abandoned SFX.

In Beckham's version, the change was anodyne: 'I now felt that SFX and I were moving in different directions. I talked to Victoria and she agreed it was time to bring things back to basics.'[28]

Beckham's announcement that he was leaving SFX in mid-October 2003 shocked Holmes. 'We are very surprised to learn of the statement,' he spluttered about the loss of his prize asset. Tony Stephens, however, was not surprised by the move. Meekly, he emerged from his sabbatical to say, 'He still has a two-year contract with SFX.' 'It's not binding,' replied Fuller.[29]

To disguise his plan, Fuller added: 'Considering the pressure of the European Championship and Real Madrid, he will be focusing entirely on football and not taking on any new commercial activity in the short term.'[30] On that same day, Beckham was filming in Spain for Adidas. For five hours, surrounded by a hairdresser and a make-up artist, he kicked a ball, time and time again.

Four weeks later, Holmes lost the battle. In the final deal Beckham paid SFX £2 million to end his contract, but initially retained Stephens to represent his football interests. That would soon end. The new era required different skills. Without any emotion, Beckham abandoned another friend and mentor.

Under the new regime Beckham's earnings would be channelled through Footwork Productions. Fuller would take a 10 per cent commission on his new contracts. The simplicity of Beckham's operations did not last long. Fuller, a former accountant, believed in a complex corporate structure. For his own business he was the controlling director of 76 companies in Britain and more in the United States. His revenues did not justify all the complications that followed, but they reflected his focus on legally managing the best tax advantages.

Despite Beckham's departure from SFX and the strain on their relationships, Stephens told Rebecca Loos to continue working for Beckham in SFX's Madrid office. She was left dangling with conflicting orders. Fuller was among those suspicious about SFX's reasons for hiring and then retaining Loos.

In his first move before the Loos saga became public, Fuller searched for an experienced publicist, a man who, having trodden in enough cow pats, would know how to avoid stepping into another one. Out of the blue he called Simon Oliveira, a 30-year-old sports publicist and Arsenal fan. Unaware of the purpose of Fuller's vague conversation, Oliveira was eventually appointed as Beckham's spokesman, starting in June during the Euro 2004 championship in Portugal.[31]

While Victoria retained McAteer as her aide she took Fuller's advice and dismissed Loos. Neither Fuller nor Victoria considered the consequences. Just four months after leaving London, Loos unexpectedly found herself unemployed in Madrid. She also feared being abandoned by Beckham.

The footballer had asked his assistant Andy Bernal to get Loos's mobile and delete all his text messages on her mobile.[32] Bernal failed and was fired shortly after, just three months after he was employed. Then Sam Rush, SFX's operating officer and a solicitor, arrived in Madrid. He demanded that Loos sign a confidentiality agreement. She refused. She also retained all of Beckham's text messages. Foolishly, Rush did not offer Loos any money for her silence. He offered nothing at all. In the hiatus, neither of the Beckhams considered the danger they faced. Past experience should have alerted them to the risks.

Three years earlier, Mark Niblett, hired as a bodyguard, resigned partly because his father was dying of cancer. Five weeks later, on Victoria's evidence, he was arrested on charges of threatening to kill Brooklyn. Eventually, the charges were dropped. Outraged by his treatment, he had given Andrew Morton sensitive information about life with the Beckhams. 'She's got a hard streak,' he said about Victoria. Treating her employees unfairly, Victoria should have realised, could rebound upon her.[33]

Loos was replaced by Terry and Jennie Byrne. A friend and a 'good soul', Byrne had been Manchester United's masseur in 1998. He and Beckham had bonded when Byrne comforted the stricken footballer in the dressing room after being shown the red card during the World Cup match against Argentina. Since then, Beckham's trust in Byrne had continued to grow. The Byrnes moved into a rented house in Madrid.

Victoria remained in London.

CHAPTER 11

DARKEST HOUR

In February 2004, the Beckhams had good reason to believe that the worst was behind them, despite the 'nightmare' of seven injuries in recent months. The previous year had also witnessed two difficult international matches against Turkey. In April 2003, Beckham was booked early on, but scored a penalty in injury time to help secure a 2–0 victory in a fixture played at Sunderland's Stadium of Light. It was a game marred by crowd violence. In the return match in Istanbul that October, Beckham missed a first-half penalty and was provocatively poked in the eye by Alpay Özalan. The match ended 0–0. Nonetheless, Beckham told a Spanish newspaper: 'I couldn't be happier than I now am in Madrid.'[1] His earnings in 2003 exceeded £20 million.[2]

One of the highlights was a grovelling apology extracted by his lawyers from the *Sunday Mirror* about the article published on 23 November, 'It's my way or the fucking highway.' Ben Todd and the acting editor Richard Wallace were outraged by the newspaper's surrender, but had been overruled by Piers Morgan, the editor-in-chief. Morgan insisted that Todd's report was wrong. 'You've made it up. They've never been happier,' Morgan told the journalists. One journalist was not convinced: 'He's bewitched by McAteer and deluded by the celebrity Beckhams.'

The apology was fulsome: 'Victoria did not say that their marriage was over or that David should leave Spain. Far from being in ruins, their marriage is very strong and they are as much in love as ever. They have not discussed a trial separation and there has been no row about the children's education. Furthermore, the *Sunday Mirror* did not intend to suggest that David and Victoria had split up.'[3]

To cement the apology, Victoria agreed to meet Richard Wallace for lunch at the Gary Rhodes restaurant in the City. The room, filled entirely by men in suits, came to a standstill. As the only woman

Victoria was the centre of attention. She instructed the journalist about their future relations. Both she and Beckham were convinced that their lawyers, using Britain's libel laws, would protect them from further embarrassment.

There were consequences of the past months' notoriety. To Victoria's fury she was not invited to the Queen's lunch for 200 of Britain's wealthiest and most influential women. Buckingham Palace's Sam Cohen did not rate Victoria to be either outstanding or an icon.[4] Victoria did not help herself by posing as a sixties sex kitten in a revealing swimsuit for *Pop* magazine, or by making an acid observation during the previous November appearance on *Parkinson*, questioning why the Queen carried a handbag in her own home.[5]

Putting aside that disappointment, Fuller was mapping out her new career. In what became their standard method, Fuller and Victoria surveyed the market and decided who and what to copy. Without any original ideas, Victoria decided that her destiny was to jump on the best bandwagon. On this occasion they decided to model Victoria's future on Jennifer Lopez. In 2003, Lopez had earned £100 million from merchandise branded with her name. With Fuller's help Victoria hoped to create a VB brand of clothing, cosmetics and perfume.[6]

In Madrid, Beckham did not change his lifestyle. 'Just lay back,' he texted Loos, 'and think of what I done to you when you was face down.'[7] And Frida, a Swiss girl, told a Swiss newspaper that after Beckham played a match in Basel, she and her friend Lenha had stayed in Beckham's suite until 8 a.m.[8]

Without the evidence that could be presented in court, Coulson, Todd and other journalists could only harass Beckham. Consistently, he denied that his marriage was 'on the rocks', but then he lost the narrative. Victoria, he insisted in an interview, was never meant to come to Madrid. The Spanish paparazzi, he said, would have pursued Brooklyn. And he denied that he had ever fired Loos. 'I wasn't even aware I had a translator,' he said. 'This is a complete fabrication. Why do people have to lie?'[9]

Safe in his make-believe world, Beckham recorded the names of those who 'upset me most'. In his little black book he listed his critics. 'I don't want to name them,' he told *OK!* magazine, 'because I want it to be a surprise when I get them back. I know I will get them someday.' By Christmas 2003 the book was pretty full.[10]

During January and February 2004, Beckham and Loos met occasionally. Stung by her dismissal she felt cheated. 'I can't let go of him,' she told a friend. Worse, she was angry about the hypocrisy of Victoria posing as the happy mother and doting wife. 'We trust each other,' she had said about Beckham.[11]

The turning-point for Loos was realising Beckham's double standards. After a meal for SFX employees at Madrid's Hard Rock Cafe, Beckham did not leave a tip. The following day, the waitress gave Loos a note for Beckham. Explaining that she survived on the tips, she expressed her anger that someone as famous and rich could be so mean. After reading the note, Beckham was alarmed. 'Give her this,' he said handing over a thick wodge of euros.

Reflecting in February about how Beckham had played her and lied to her, Loos was angry. She had lost the career she loved and felt betrayed by a man she had trusted. 'I feel sick,' she told Emma Basden. 'I've lost everything.' The waitress incident exposed Beckham's fear of any damage to his image.

Angered by both the secrecy and the abuse of her loyalty she looked for an opportunity to hurt him. Not least because on their first night in bed he said that she was his first secret relationship. 'I know I will be up against the most powerful family in the world,' she told Basden in late February, 'but people will appreciate the truth.' Contrary to what some would suggest later, she would claim that she was not motivated by greed or attention-seeking but by anger about the way she had been treated.

'You should speak to Max Clifford,' advised Basden.

In the tabloid wars of the era, no newspaper editor could ignore Clifford's telephone calls. As a publicist famous for representing women keen to sell stories to the tabloids about their secret relationships with powerful men, Clifford's brokering skills were unrivalled. After Basden called to reveal that Loos wanted to 'kiss-and-tell', Clifford jumped at the opportunity. In a telephone call to Loos his offer was explicit. 'If you give a nice, honest interview setting out the truth with all the sexual details,' he said, 'they'll pay £1 million.' Loos agreed at once. Her only condition was that she should not be identified as the source. Her revelations should be disclosed by 'a friend'.

Clifford knew that his market was limited. The *Mirror* had just apologised to the Beckhams, and the *Sun* was their cheerleader. That left the *News of the World*. Andy Coulson immediately agreed, but for a sum around £300,000. Neville Thurlbeck, the newspaper's experienced 42-year-old chief reporter, was assigned to record the confession.

Dressed in a well-cut suit, Thurlbeck arrived in Madrid, a city recovering from an Al Qaeda bomb atrocity that had killed 193 and injured 2,050 people. Appearing as a trustworthy English gentleman, Thurlbeck met Loos in a basement bar. His smooth manner dispelled Loos's apprehension. Over the next days, with good humour she unloaded the details of her relationship with Beckham. She showed the journalist Beckham's text messages on her phone. Even Thurlbeck, who would later be imprisoned for telephone hacking, gasped at Loos's revelations: 'He did things to me he wouldn't have dared to ask his wife for. David is an incredible lover. He makes sure a woman is satisfied. And he has the most incredible stamina.' Her exchange of sexy text messages with Beckham, which she had retained, suggested that she was telling the truth.[12]

To confirm the truth of Loos's story Thurlbeck needed a new text exchange or a telephone conversation between Loos and Beckham. For three weeks he waited in Madrid for Beckham to initiate contact. Nothing happened. Beckham was too suspicious to respond to Loos's telephone call. Thurlbeck would claim that his breakthrough was finding among Loos's possessions under her bed a SFX visiting card. In Beckham's handwriting was his name and a mobile telephone number, the same number that Marbeck had used. That evidence, Thurlbeck claimed, convinced Coulson and the *News of the World*'s lawyer that Loos was telling the truth.[13]

Subsequently, Glenn Mulcaire, a *News of the World* employee at the heart of hacking Beckham's mobile phones, would claim that his activities provided the confirmation of the affair. He was jailed for six months.[14] Thurlbeck insisted that his story based on Loos's confessions did not involve hacking Beckham's telephone.

In Beckham's camp, suspicions would arise about SFX's own culpability. Beckham's and Loos's mobile phones were provided by SFX. In paying the bill the agency would receive print-outs of all their telephone calls. And the time of the calls – during the day and particularly night. The footballer's new advisers speculated that after losing Beckham it was possible that a SFX employee had sold the information to the newspaper.

'BECKHAM'S SECRET AFFAIR' was the *News of the World*'s headline on 4 April 2004: 'David Beckham has had a secret torrid affair with an exotic beauty in Madrid, the *News of the World* can reveal.' Under the video shot of them together in September at the Ananda nightclub, the caption exclaimed: 'Beckham took Loos to bed just 90 minutes after this picture of the two of them together was taken.'

To comply with Loos's stipulation, Thurlbeck wrote, 'When we confronted Rebecca, she said 'I am afraid I have no comment for you. Please leave me alone.' At her request he also wrote, 'She wasn't in love with him.' The newspaper's average weekly sale of 3.9 million copies was enhanced by an extra 600,000 copies.

Four women were particularly furious about the story.

Loos was 'horrified'. 'This isn't what I had in mind,' she told Clifford. 'It has awful stuff about me.'

The second woman was Rebekah Brooks, the *Sun*'s editor. Despite being in a long-term relationship with Andy Coulson, he did not tell her about his newspaper's scoop. Rival editors heard about the sensation before she did. 'Obviously I was not pleased about that situation,' she commented.

The third woman was Tina Weaver, the *Sunday Mirror*'s editor. Seven weeks earlier she had apologised to the Beckhams and paid damages, despite publishing what turned out to be the truth about the state of the Beckhams' marriage. 'You're gutless,' Ben Todd screamed at Piers Morgan. 'Why did you believe McAteer and not your journalists?'

The fourth woman mortified before dawn broke on that Sunday was Victoria. 'If David was ever to cheat on me,' she had said, 'I think I would die of a broken heart. I probably would. It would kill me.' The *News of the World* had turned her love to blind fury. She was distraught, hysterically distraught. The eyewitness of her reaction was Abigail Gibson.

Gibson had started to work as a nanny with the Beckhams in August 2003. That Sunday she heard Victoria scream that her marriage was over, shouting at her family that she was calling the lawyers – the same divorce lawyers Princess Diana had used. Her mother Jackie talked her out of divorce. There was too much to lose, said Jackie. 'I hate Spain, I want us to go home,' Gibson heard Posh yell. Amid her rants she knew that she could not survive without Beckham. Eventually, Beckham's spokesman denied Gibson's descriptions of the putrid exchanges between the Beckhams, but their lawyers did not issue a claim for defamation against her.[15]

'You have ruined my birthday,' Victoria told Beckham on the telephone. Many other recriminations followed. Automatically, from Madrid, he protested his innocence. Both agreed to call McAteer. Posh, their publicist said, believed David's denials. On Victoria's orders, McAteer was also to accuse Loos of lying.

The publicist conjured a scenario: Victoria had never trusted Loos and she didn't believe the newspaper had published the truth. For his part, said McAteer, Beckham called the text messages forgeries. 'During the past few months,' he declared, 'I have become accustomed to reading more and more ludicrous stories about my private life. What appeared this morning is just one further example.' He was a happily married man, he added.

'Ludicrous' was not a categorical denial. Nor had Beckham's lawyers threatened or delivered a writ for defamation against the News of the World. Rival newspapers decided to follow Coulson's scoop. Beckham would express his 'shock' that his denials were not believed.[16]

Later that Sunday morning, fighting back tears, and with her hands on her forehead to conceal her tear-swollen eyes, Victoria headed to Heathrow. She was flying to Geneva with her family for a skiing holiday in France.

There was no privacy as she checked on to the BA flight. Amid a scrum of photographers her brother was hit in the face with a lens and hospitalised, her mother went flying and her father sent a Daily Mail snapper sprawling. 'Heavies, heavies, heavies!' shouted Victoria to cue her minders – a battalion of former Royal Protection Squad, army and police officers – to shepherd them towards the plane.

Secluded in the five-bedroom Chalet Atlantique in Courchevel costing £22,230 for the week, Victoria spoke to friends about 'a trial separation'.[17] To her alarm Beckham appeared to agree. She quickly reconsidered. If they divorced, she said, she would restrict his access to the children. Playing the children's card, she knew, was her best bet. The idea of losing them was intolerable to him.[18]

Beckham would describe what followed as 'a whole sorry procession of spiteful stories ... as if people were trying to break up my marriage.' In his mind the media were entirely to blame for causing 'heartache' for himself and his family.[19] But 'friends' feeding information to the *Sunday Mirror* divulged Beckham's admission during a telephone call. 'I made the greatest mistake of my life,' he confessed.[20] 'My life is fucked,' Beckham told another 'friend'. 'I don't know what to do. I love Victoria but she's really upset. I've let everyone down.'[21]

He had two choices. Either he would immediately appear on television, admit the affair, take the flak and hope to recover after one week. Or he would feed the media with denials. To some male friends he would admit 'playing' with Loos but insist that he had 'not gone all the way'.

Too proud to admit her humiliation, Victoria insisted on fighting back. If she stood by Beckham the damage could eventually be limited. McAteer was told to ridicule the accusers. Some would say the two women created the textbook example of turning a drama into a catastrophe.[22] But Victoria calculated that so long as she denied the truth, doubts about Loos's veracity would protect the marriage.

The following day Victoria discovered that she could not count on her media friends. For the first time her aggressive publicists, agents and lawyers could not rely on the usual horse-trading with friendly newspapers. The *Sun* was sympathetic, but Chris Pharo, its news editor, was caught as usual between the paper's sympathy for the Beckhams and the eyewitness reports delivered by journalists and photographers.

Like other newspapers the *Sun* republished Beckham's breathlessly graphic texts to Loos about their sex antics. 'Remember the last time your tongue was all over me. I have never ...' was the most mundane.[23] But in the familiar kick-and-kiss to retain the Beckhams' trust, McAteer persuaded the *Sun* to predict that Beckham, the 'patron saint of the perfect' would not suffer, and Posh would make sure the marriage survived. In exchange McAteer gave the *Sun* a quote from Beckham: 'I'm fine, she's fine, everything's great and we're having a fantastic holiday.' To damn Loos, the *Sun* found a lesbian fitness trainer who said: 'She is the most flirtatious person I ever met.'[24]

The 'semi-literate ball-kicker', as *The Times* suddenly called him, played badly that day. Real Madrid lost 1–3 to Monaco in the Champions League. After the match Beckham flew to Courchevel. Victoria had decided that her survival depended on restoring the illusion of the Posh and Becks perfect marriage. Those she had damned weeks earlier as 'so bloody negative' were summoned to witness their sincere love.[25]

Naturally, Jason Fraser was chosen first to record Posh and Becks smiling, kissing and clinging to each other as they walked through the snowy village. He sold the exclusive pictures to the *Sun* for approximately £20,000. Posh's words were given by McAteer to the *Sun* 'We've been through a lot worse than this, and we're definitely going to get through this.'[26] The paper added, 'Posh has said she's "more unpopular than Saddam Hussein" but she's a hardworking mum who puts her children first. She represents all that's good about Britain.'

Journalists alerted to the photo-call in Courchevel noticed Beckham's trademark serenity. In a bravura performance the couple clung to each other – she with an iron grip on his hand. Then they performed a piggy-back and smiled. Once the show was over they disappeared into their chalet. McAteer filled the void. Loos, she told the journalists, was a wild party lesbian with 'animal instincts', and had bedded three famous tennis players. She was also, said McAteer, a liar.

As everyone drifted off, one journalist looked through the Beckhams' chalet window. Posh was slapping Beckham hard on his face. That was not the first time she had punched his face and drawn blood.[27] Beckham, famous for his 'short fuse', did not retaliate.[28] His behaviour over the following years suggested he felt little pity for Victoria. More likely, he was just irritated by her hysteria. The witness did not hear Victoria threaten, 'It's my way or the highway.'

At that critical moment, no one questioned whether the Beckhams believed in their own image. Did they think they were a happily married couple? And behind his grin, did Beckham feel ashamed, guilty or just angry that he had been caught? Had both become fantasy merchants, purveyors of hype, or simply forgetful? Other than the pursuit of fame and self-enrichment, could they explain to themselves and to others their purpose in life? Did they represent something substantial or, as their harshest critics would say, were they empty vessels performing for grateful voyeurs? Forever playing to their admirers, were the Beckhams merely accomplished creators of myths?

Self-preservation demanded they play the part. Their financial fate depended on maintaining the charade. The aggressive, well-funded publicity machine, personified by 'attack dog' McAteer, was to deny that the family was broken and perpetuated the image of a happy clan. Neither was to express any sense of shame. Possibly McAteer did not know the truth, but paid to speak on the Beckhams' behalf her aggression aggravated some of the tabloid editors' dislike of the couple.

Rav Singh was quite precise about Beckham's telephone call two days later from Madrid. 'I did it. I'm sorry,' he confessed to Victoria.[29] McAteer denied the conversation, yet could not suppress the challenge to Beckham's piety about his 'family values'.

'Posh thinks we're gullible,' wrote Carole Malone. 'She fears everything is lost amid the sleaze. The pose on the slopes is Posh's "togetherness" to save her multi-million-pound advertising contracts, sponsorship deals and marketability. The day was always going to dawn when Victoria's greed, her control-freakery and her power games would come back and bite her on her skinny ass.'[30]

During the days after, Beckham mentioned again that he would take his revenge on those who had caused him embarrassment. Their names, he repeated, had been recorded in his little black book. An assertion he later contradicted.[31] In the media frenzy Loos had been moved to a hotel near Sotogrande, in southern Spain. To prevent rival newspapers getting Loos before the *News of the World* could publish a second bite the following Sunday, Thurlbeck rented a house 400 miles from Madrid. His first task was to pacify the enraged woman.

The tabloids had dubbed Loos 'The Sleazy Senorita' and 'The Man-eater who set out to ensnare the world's most famous footballer.'[32] Casting doubt on Loos's morality encouraged the sceptical public to distrust the media reports. Most readers did not believe that Saintly David had betrayed his wife and family. But their appetite for more sleaze was insatiable.

Loos called Clifford. 'This is not going the way I expected, or what you told me,' she said.

In a fury Clifford screamed: 'Never call me again!'

Clifford, she decided, was an appalling person.

On Coulson's orders, Thurlbeck was persuading Loos to allow the newspaper to write the following week's saga in her voice, not a 'friend's'. Loos resisted, until in order to guarantee receiving her payment she agreed.

Loos's recollections of sex mixed with football, pop music, celebrity and money made the Beckhams' misery a global sensation. Even one week after the exposé, dozens of journalists were scouring Britain and Spain for more revelations. Max Clifford was also indulging in his familiar double-cross. After selling Loos to the *News of the World*, he fed scurrilous information about his client – without her permission – to competing editors. Clifford also offered editors two more women with 'strong evidence' of their affairs with Beckham. The *Mirror* agreed to pay £75,000 for one. In tabloid jargon, Brand Beckham faced its Darkest Hour.

Humiliated and battered, Victoria had a simple choice – combat or capitulation. Encouraged by her parents, McAteer stoked Victoria's hatred of the media. Seedy journalists were blamed for causing her misery. Defiance was etched in her face as she stepped on to a private jet that Saturday with Beckham. Even before the Sunday newspapers had published their latest horrors, she arrived in Madrid.

On Sunday 11 April, Loos's new revelations in the *News of the World* included Beckham's pillow talk. He no longer was attracted to Victoria, he confided. She was too thin. For her own part, Loos admitted that she was bisexual. While dating Beckham she was also having an affair with Emma Basden. To cash in, Basden would sell her story of sex with Loos to the *Sunday Mirror*, describing her affair in detail: 'She is funny, loving, oozing class and very sexy.'[33]

As a throwaway, on the same Sunday the *News of the World* finally published Sarah Marbeck's account of her affair with Beckham, which had been held back for seven months. Headlined 'I'M BECKS LOVER NO. 2', Marbeck described over seven pages Beckham's 'passion' and sexual obsessions during their two-year affair. McAteer dismissed both women's accounts as 'absurd and unsubstantiated'.

Any doubts were dispelled by Delfin Fernandez, Beckham's Cuban bodyguard. 'In the six months I work for him,' said Fernandez on Spanish television, 'I know of no woman who said "No" to David Beckham. I can't give you a number but it would be high.' Among his responsibilities, he said, was to check all the girls for recording equipment before allowing them into Beckham's bedroom.[34]

CHAPTER 12

ALONE

On Sunday night 11 April 2004, Victoria sat in the Bernabéu watching Beckham. He played badly, proof that contrary to his protestations he could not separate his private life from his football. Real Madrid were defeated 3–0 by Osasuna. The club was heading towards the end of a disastrous season, losing their bid for every title. To rub in the embarrassment, the stadium's giant video screens advertised a newspaper's account of Beckham's adultery. In London, the focus was on Victoria Beckham.

The *Sun* gushed the following morning that 'Posh held her head high' watching the game. 'That takes a lot of courage and a lot of steel.' The paper added 'We must support Posh.'[1]

All newspapers – including the *Sun* – published the latest 'racy' text messages between Beckham and Marbeck. Over fifty asterisks were employed to protect readers from Beckham's explicit fantasies, especially the one about having sex on his Ferrari's bonnet. The car was a present from Victoria. McAteer dismissed the revelations as 'absurd'. Fuller's organisation called the texts 'unsubstantiated'.

The couple had flown back to London after the match in a private jet. The Beckhams had combined to orchestrate a special show. Selected journalists were invited to Beckingham Palace to watch from a distance Victoria celebrating her 30th birthday with her children and parents. They saw the family kissing, laughing and racing around their garden on a quad bike. The Beckhams and Adams families proved themselves to be accomplished performers.[2] Inside the house, Tony and Jackie Adams were alternately lambasting their son-in-law and warning him about the consequences of a divorce.

After waiting for two hours the spectators were allowed to witness the smiling couple leave the estate in a silver Bentley. They headed for a celebratory Dom Perignon dinner in Claridge's. After one hour, just as McAteer predicted, they emerged smiling to pose for photographers. Beckham held Victoria tight while she coyly whispered in his ear. No one saw her lips move. 'Victoria and David look blissfully in love,' McAteer announced. Eleven years later, when Beckham would at first decline an offer to act in a Guy Ritchie film, 'I can't act,' he explained. That's not what seasoned photographers outside Claridge's thought that night.

The Beckhams' stunts failed to bury the story. Fuller proposed a new solution. Victoria and David should appear on Michael Parkinson's show again. The BBC interviewer agreed to be the vehicle for their attack on the *News of the World*. The plan was foiled by Loos. She had flown to London to collect her money, about £300,000 after Clifford took his commission. Thurlbeck had also returned, and after claiming the credit for the story he submitted an expenses claim of £45,285.38.

After meeting Clifford, Loos decided to abandon him. To Clifford's dismay, Loos then agreed to be interviewed on Sky TV. Her fee, paid by Rupert Murdoch's corporation, was a record £100,000. Gerrard Tyrrell, the Beckhams' lawyer, attempted to stop the broadcast. He failed.

Appearing as an intelligent and highly educated woman, Loos described Beckham to a record Sky television audience as 'a very generous lover' giving her 'a mind-blowing experience'. That included feeding her strawberries in bed, a treat also enjoyed by Victoria. If Posh sued, continued Loos, she would reveal in court the marks on Beckham's 'most intimate parts which only a woman who has been to bed with him would know.' Insiders suggested that included a freckle.[3]

At the time of the broadcast Beckham was having dinner with his teammates in Spain. Victoria also did not watch the interview. After dashing to Verbier in France she was ostentatiously eating pizza in a bar. One joker conjured up the vision of her ripping out the Sky cables when Loos appeared.[4]

No newspaper or TV editor chose to deny publicly that Loos was telling the truth. On the contrary. Tina Weaver got her revenge on the Beckhams' lawyer Gerrard Tyrrell by publishing over 13 pages of sex and drama from Loos's old boyfriend, who merely repeated Loos's own detailed description to him about her relationship with Beckham. To Clifford's anger he received no commission on the newspaper's

£75,000 payment. Nor did he earn on the payments to Delfin Fernandez, the Cuban bodyguard, or the Beckhams' chef, or all the other former employees of the Beckhams. All were richly rewarded after the publication of their recollections.

In the fall-out the Beckhams looked for crumbs of comfort. To support Victoria the *Sun* condemned Loos and Marbeck for selling their 'tawdry allegations'. Although it was the *Sun*'s stable-mate the *News of the World* that had paid for the scoop, the *Sun* condemned the two women's 'blatant desperation for money and recognition' as 'the worst example of scum-scraping'.[5]

'Has she any morals at all?' Victoria Newton asked about Loos. 'Doesn't she feel guilty? Rebecca Loos must tell the truth about her motives for destroying Beckham's life.'[6]

The *Sun* had good reason to continue backing the Beckhams. Marketing surveys consistently reported that David's family values had won the people's hearts. The public still described him as sensitive and considerate, the loving father, the faithful husband, the all-round family man. They preferred to believe his denials, especially since they were publicly accepted by Victoria.

On the following Saturday night, after being substituted during another inadequate performance against Atletico in the Madrid derby – Real won 2–1 – Beckham flew to London. Victoria had landed earlier in Stansted from France. In Beckham's pocket, McAteer revealed, was a £1 million pink diamond ring. The bigger the guilt, the bigger the gift, some would say.

As the plane landed, Beckham was greeted by another exposé. In the *Sunday People* newspaper Celina Laurie, a Danish 'vicar's daughter', recalled her late night with Beckham in August 2002. Beckham's security guards, she said, had guided her to his hotel room and then delivered some condoms. 'His kisses made me feel wonderful. And he was so sweet. That's not the behaviour of a man who has never cheated on his wife before.'[7] To add to the Beckhams' embarrassment, Laurie mentioned that all his pubic hair had been shaved off. 'He appreciated the fact that I'm a fan of waxing.'

In the fightback, McAteer was deputed to describe the atmosphere inside Beckingham Palace that Sunday morning: 'They appear to be very happy.' Asked whether Beckham had confessed, she replied: 'Why would he confess to something he hasn't done?' Asked for

Victoria's reaction to the three women's revelations, Victoria was 'quoted': 'I will not let that tart ruin my marriage.'[8] The 'tart' appeared the following day on the *Richard & Judy* television show. Her fling with Beckham, said Loos mischievously, had probably improved the Beckhams' marriage. Before Beckham returned to Madrid that night, Victoria reminded him that 'If you leave me, I'll make your life hell.'

Booed later that week at the Bernabéu stadium for his performance, Beckham appeared to have lost the will to win. Victoria's threat to withhold the children if they divorced was terrifying. As were her heartfelt pleas: 'David, don't leave me. If you do I'll starve myself. I won't eat again.'[9]

Three weeks after the first bombshell revelation, Victoria believed that her husband was cowed. He agreed that he would move back to England and play for a London club. She could remain living in their Hertfordshire home, near her parents.

The Beckhams' survival skills were witnessed by Dannielle Heath, a 22-year-old beautician who Victoria had met in a local Essex salon. She was hired by Victoria to regularly visit Beckingham Palace. 'When I got there,' Heath would later say, 'you would never believe there was anything wrong. They were kissing and getting on well. They seemed so calm.'

Victoria knew she had to calm down and take control. She even visited a hypnotherapist to sooth her nerves, before staging a public display of affection to deny her marriage was not a business arrangement but a blissful relationship.

On a warm night, nearly one month after the crisis erupted, the couple drove to London for a party hosted by Fuller at the Royal Albert Hall. Mingling with the guests, they gave a masterful performance. They looked immaculate. She had pulled them out of the swamp.

'I know my David has never cheated on me,' she said. When asked if she knew for a fact that Beckham was faithful, she replied 'Through all of this, I feel really sorry for David because it's his name that's been dragged through it and he's done nothing wrong. I really do believe deep down that I have the most faithful husband I could hope for. He's always faithful and nothing has changed at all.' Pressed again, she admitted feeling hurt and added, 'I know the truth and my family knows the truth. We're just carrying on. David feels the same as me. You just draw a line under it because that's what everybody wants.' Three years later, she did finally admit, 'I'm not going to lie. It was a really tough time.'[10]

The following weekend Peter Kenyon, now Chelsea's chief executive after performing the same role at Manchester United, offered Beckham about £20 million a year if he transferred to the club.

On instructions from Victoria, Beckham encouraged the club's owner, Roman Abramovich, to fly to Madrid for lunch to seal the deal.[11] The Russian oligarch encountered three obstacles. First, Real Madrid demanded 180 million euros for the transfer. Even the billionaire baulked. Another was Beckham's thrill of playing alongside the Brazilian Ronaldo and the great French player Zinedine Zidane. Although his own poor performances on the pitch undermined his faith in Real Madrid's continuing interest, the mood was still positive.

'Is it true,' Beckham asked Florentino Pérez with moist eyes, 'that you want to sell me?' Pérez's reply was emotional. 'David, listen to me. I would sell the stadium – I would sell the Bernabéu – before I sold you.'[12]

Abramovich's third obstacle was money. Not his offer to Beckham but the footballer's future income. Uppermost in Beckham's calculations were his sponsorship deals, his legal tax avoidance schemes and his career after football.

Fuller had already proved himself more skilled than Stephens. Agreeing to give half Beckham's income from any new sponsorship deals to Real Madrid had been foolish. More important, Stephen had offered no vision for the future. Fuller was in little doubt that his client's future was not in Europe but in America. Breaking into that huge market was critical to Beckham's fortune – and his own. McAteer's promotional programme in New York and Los Angeles the previous year had been amateurish.

The box-office popularity of *Bend It Like Beckham* had given them another chance. Thanks to the film, the sales of Police sunglasses modelled by Beckham had soared. The film also persuaded *Vanity Fair* to feature Beckham on its front cover, an accolade sought by thousands of Hollywood 'wannabes'.

While the editorial process to improve the footballer's recognition across America was underway, Fuller proved his worth by saving the

Gillette deal. The contract had been ready for signature just before the Loos saga broke. In the aftermath, Gillette's American executives feared that any association with Beckham would damage the brand. He had certainly broken the 'good behaviour' clause. To their surprise their marketing teams reported that the Loos relationship had improved Beckham's ratings. Men blamed Victoria and admired his luck with good-looking women.

Once the Gillette deal was signed, the next difficult negotiation was to appoint a photographer for the razor's launch. Victoria disapproved of the company's suggestions. She insisted that the black-and-white photo needed to present Beckham as an iconic hero. Eventually, she approved Jason Bell, from Camden Town in north London. Bell produced an alluring masculine image. The photographer had discovered something special about Beckham, as did Gillette's commercial film crew. Easy to photograph because he looked desirable through the lens, he was always upbeat and easy to relate to. The crew also appreciated his invitation afterwards to his house. He cooked them spaghetti Bolognese.

Under the agreement with Gillette, Beckham would be paid £3 million a year over three years, plus a share of any profits linked to his advertisements. The profit share was unusual but it had become a clincher after Nike, a failing brand in the 1980s, beat Adidas to sign up basketball hero Michael Jordan by offering that bonus. Fuller's publicity suggested that the total deal would be worth £40 million. As Beckham would discover, Fuller often exaggerated. But Fuller did link the contract to a Beckham football academy. That clause prevented Real Madrid claiming 50 per cent of the payment.

By 2004, Fuller had established roots for Beckham in America. Through pop music and *American Idol*, Fuller had developed a relationship with Tim Leiweke, the president of the Anschutz Entertainment Group. The American businessman, who was a football enthusiast, spoke on behalf of Philip Anschutz, a publicity-shy billionaire whose fortune was built from oil, telecommunications, railways and entertainment. Like Leiweke, Anschutz was dedicated to developing football as a major sport in America. Both had targeted Beckham as an agent for their ambitions to expand America's fledgling Major League Soccer (MLS) football championship. The MLS, vaguely similar to England's Football Association, was struggling to survive. Leiweke believed he had secured from Fuller a long-term commitment for Beckham eventually to play for LA Galaxy, Anschutz's Los Angeles-based football team.

Leiweke's relationship with Beckham had been sealed during a dinner in 2004 – before the Loos scandal blew up – in Beckingham Palace. Leiweke had set out to Beckham, Fuller and Terry Byrne, Beckham's adviser in Madrid, the glory the footballer could expect if he joined Galaxy.[13] To entice Beckham, Leiweke had offered his giant corporation's support for Beckham's first football academy, situated near AEG's Millennium Dome by the River Thames in Greenwich. AEG would part-finance two full-size pitches in one building for 10,000 children to enjoy during its first year.[14] Leiweke also agreed to build another David Beckham Academy in Los Angeles. It would be sited adjacent to the Home Depot Center, LA Galaxy's home ground. Leiweke also mentioned the tax benefits Beckham would enjoy in America.

Fuller was a master of legally avoiding taxation. He had arranged for the Spice Girls to live for a year in Ireland after September 1997 to avoid paying income tax on money earned outside the UK.[15] After his dismissal from the Spice Girls he had taken a year off to avoid taxes. Legally avoiding taxes appealed to Beckham. As a non-dom in Spain he was not paying British taxes on income earned outside Britain. And he was not paying National Insurance. The genius of it was that no one in Britain realised that Beckham had become a tax exile. Instead the public believed that he was a global success who paid his taxes in Britain. Partly that was due to sightings of him in London. Legally, he could visit Britain 90 days a year and after five years the annual limit would increase to 120 days. For all those reasons, he was persuaded that playing for Chelsea would be expensive and shortsighted. Kenyon was told that Beckham would not move back to Britain.

Beckham's accounts had been taken over by Charles Bradbrook, a partner at Deloitte, a major international firm. Priding himself on caring for his celebrity clients' income and protecting their confidentiality, Bradbrook also sought ways to legitimately minimise Beckham's tax bill.

Among his colleagues at Deloitte had been Patrick McKenna, a rising star who had left to become a film producer and the chief executive of Ingenious Media. In the nature of these close and profitable relationships, McKenna had been an early investor in Simon Fuller's company, 19 Management. Subsequently, McKenna offered his former colleagues at Deloitte a scheme to invest in films that purported legally to avoid taxes. Accepting the offer, Bradbrook became a director of one of Ingenious' many film companies. He advised Beckham to invest in a succession of McKenna's companies – Inside Track Productions, Ingenious Film Partners and Ingenious Film Partners 2 – based on a scheme devised by the Chancellor of the Exchequer, Gordon Brown, to finance cinema films. Hundreds of other millionaires did the same. None voiced any concerns about the tax avoidance plan.[16]

CHAPTER 13

LAST CHANCE

Just five weeks after Rebecca Loos's revelations, Victoria left her two children with her parents in England and flew to Los Angeles. Any lingering impression of her humiliation was unacceptable. She demanded to be relaunched. With her popularity in decline in Britain, she could console herself that fans still existed in the Far East. 'Let Your Heart Go' was a No. 1 hit in Thailand.

To prove she could still earn money she had insisted on featuring with Beckham in a video advertisement for India's TBC Unisex Salons. Shot before the Loos revelations, Beckham was shown walking into a bathroom with a basket of footballs. While Victoria lay in the bath he dropped the balls into the water. The last shot showed the two Beckhams in the bath saying to camera: 'Just Beauty TBC.' Fortunately, the tacky advert, filmed in Britain, was not shown either there or in America.

Fuller had arranged to release Victoria's disc 'My Love is For Real' in America. He knew that promoting Victoria's relaunch of her singing career was a challenge. Her first stop was to appear on *American Idol*.[1] Simon Cowell, the star of the show, had tried in 1995 to sign up the Spice Girls as their manager. He had been beaten by Fuller.

Nine years later, on the eve of leaving *Idol* to start his rival show *The X Factor*, Cowell was not minded to support Fuller. He disliked Fuller's obsession to get a knighthood, to rank high in the *Sunday Times Rich List*, and worst of all, seek unreasonable advantages in their contracts. Moreover, in the battle of publicity, Cowell would oppose anyone and anything promoted by Fuller's publicist, Julian Henry.

At the end of the *Idol* show Simon Cowell told Victoria to give up her pop career, or at least find a good songwriter. In his judgement she could not really sing. 'I don't know why you're chasing these dreams,' he told her.[2] Cowell's honesty infuriated Fuller. After a pause, the acerbic judge agreed to say publicly, 'She's one of the nicest people I've met. She laughed at herself and didn't take herself too seriously.' In private, he argued that her only hope was to move to America and get invited on to TV shows.[3]

Even Victoria Newton ridiculed Victoria's solo career. 'Posh is threatening to release yet another rubbish single, even though her previous attempts were laughable,' she wrote. Bowing to the inevitable, Victoria conceded that her singing career was over. 'I'm happy to take a back seat from now on,' she volunteered.[4] She was not to know of the Spice Girl reunions to come.

Fuller delayed the launch of her record. To rehabilitate his client he organised a trip to Lima in Peru. Adopting the usual formula, Victoria would pose as a charity ambassador. On what was described as a 'top-secret' mission for Sports Relief, she flew from Los Angeles to spend three days meeting the poorest families living in shacks surrounded by mountains of rubbish. The moment the BBC TV film crew and director decided there was sufficient material she got into her air-conditioned SUV and drove to the five-star El Prado hotel.[5] No one judged the visit a success. 'Posh's problem', said an eyewitness, 'is that she doesn't get on with normal people.' At the end of the trip she was told by one of her managers, 'Move to Madrid and eat more.'

Reluctantly, Victoria agreed to live permanently in Madrid. Her mother Jackie might be furious with Beckham – she had ignored him at his 29th birthday party in his Hertfordshire house – but both of the Adams knew Victoria's future depended on him. Saving Brand Beckham was her best option.

In her absence, Beckham had earned his second red card of the season. Sent off after abusing a linesman as the 'son of a whore' in Spanish. His impetuous outburst – he knew what he had said – cost Real Madrid the match. Tired, frustrated and angry, he had only himself to blame for his miserable game.[6]

Back in his Hertfordshire home while Victoria was still in Peru, he summoned Dannielle Heath, the beautician Victoria had met in an Essex beauty salon. He asked for a tan. To Beckham, Heath was similar to the girls he had known at school. In Heath's recollection, he began flirting with her.[7]

Beckham also summoned Louis Molloy, a tattooist and owner of the Middleton Tattoo Studio in Manchester. He had first visited Molloy after Brooklyn was born. His father Ted had a few tattoos, and Beckham decided to have his own after speaking to the Afro-Dutch actor Jimmy Gulzar, briefly married to Mel B.[8] Each tattoo was to represent his family or express a mood in his life. In autumn 2004, Beckham asked Molloy for 'something that means something to me'. Over three hours, Molloy inked a 4-inch by 6-inch flying cross on his back. Molloy had persuaded Beckham not to have it on his neck. 'He's as tough as teak,' said Molloy. 'On a pain scale of one to ten, his tattoo was a 9.9. He didn't flinch. There's no one on earth who can say a tattoo doesn't hurt and I take my hat off to David. There was no wincing or anything.'

'I actually enjoy the pain,' said Beckham about tattoos. 'They are addictive.'[9]

Paid £200 as usual for his work, Molloy had good reason to gripe. A Japanese tattooist offered Molloy £500,000 for the copyright of his flying cross design. On being told about the proposal, Beckham's representative threatened to sue Molloy if he sold anything associated with Beckham. In compensation they suggested a copyright fee. 'What they offered was derisory, an insult,' Molloy complained.[10] He was not the last to discover Beckham's limited generosity. But that did not damage their relationship.

Simon Fuller made out that he was also angry. Tattoos in America were associated with rednecks and trailer trash. Gillette had removed all Beckham's tattoos in their latest bare-chested advert for M3 Power razors.[11] Fuller recruited Paul Bloch, a publicist, to protect Beckham's launch in America. Even Victoria had urged Beckham to stop his habit. 'You're an Essex yob!' she shouted when he refused. A wodge of banknotes to an informer close to the Beckhams had once again produced that gem.[12]

Reading the tabloids' endless toxic stories about the Beckhams, Fuller decided that the brand would permanently suffer unless he changed the messengers and their message. McAteer, alias the 'Rottweiler', was his first target. Her fierce denials about the Loos affair had destroyed her credibility. She was fired. Taken by surprise, the faithful attack-dog was stricken. After devoting her reputation to the Beckhams for over five years she did not anticipate such disloyalty. Working tirelessly for the Beckhams had earned her no gratitude.

The Beckhams' publicity was split. Simon Oliveira was confirmed as David's spokesman, and the task of promoting Victoria was given to both Julian Henry and Charlotte Hickson under Fuller's control. To reset their relationship with the tabloids, the new team began entertaining the Beckhams' critics in London's Charlotte Street hotel.

The new publicists' task was complicated by Beckham's refusal to believe he had done anything wrong. Defiantly, he blamed the media – who he had compulsively exploited to build his fortune – for reporting the facts. 'The way I and my family have been treated,' he told a pack of football journalists, 'is a disgrace. I'm a nice person and loving husband and father. We've been hurt by all the bad press coverage.' [13]

On the eve of the Euro finals in Portugal in June 2004, his audience knew that the captain's 'hurt' was serious. His performances in Madrid were underwhelming. Although some remained loyal, England's supporters also wondered whether he could actually tell the truth.

'I've never felt so fit,' Beckham told Neil Custis, the *Sun*'s Beckham specialist based in Manchester. 'I am totally in control.'[14]

Custis and all the other football journalists at England's training ground in Sardinia knew that England's captain was in fact wholly unfit. They also knew that Sven-Göran Eriksson was aware that Beckham could not match the pace of many of his rivals. But Eriksson refused to consider dropping him.

In the weeks before the Euro 2004 championship, England's newspapers had naturally fed their readers' conviction that their team would win the cup. In such an unpredictable game as football, even the cynics clung to hope and dreams. The sad truth about England's team and its captain was barely mentioned as everyone headed to Sardinia to watch the team train before flying to Lisbon.

Beckham's supporters believed that his decline was offset by his dedication, charm and personality. All those qualities were essential to bond the disparate players into a team. Others, the sceptical witnesses of England's players, scoffed that Eriksson and the FA's executives were simply hooked to Beckham's celebrity. As the dignity and spirit of playing for England had drained away over the recent years, the FA's executives were relying on Beckham to generate glamour and profits for the organisation.

Few in Sardinia, other than Beckham and the FA's executives, trusted Eriksson. Although paid £5 million per annum – much more than any other international team manager – his disloyalty was breathtaking. Unknown to the FA he had secretly sought jobs at Premier League clubs, including Chelsea. Once exposed, the FA was under pressure to fire him. His cheerleader was Beckham. The captain pleaded for Eriksson to stay as England's manager: 'He's the best chance we've got to win a major trophy.'[15]

Eriksson was also disloyal to his girlfriends. While living with his fiery Italian girlfriend Nancy Dell'Olio during the Euro 2004 tournament, he had secretly invited his assistant, Faria Alam, to come to Lisbon. Neither woman knew that he was also in a relationship with Ulrika Jonsson, the Swedish-British television presenter and model, who later described their sex-life 'as exciting as assembling an IKEA bookcase'. Jonsson's scathing denunciation showed no sympathy for Eriksson's skulduggery. He was understandably exhausted from managing three women. Yet while Eriksson clandestinely dashed between Dell'Olio and Alam in Lisbon, he was unaware that Alam was also dating the FA's chief executive, Mark Palios.

The combination of Geoff Thompson, the FA's inept chairman, and Palios, its unimpressive chief executive, blinded the two well-paid executives to the dire state of England's team. Neither was willing to grasp why the Italians called Eriksson *perdente di successo* – 'The Successful Loser'. The journalists watching England's squad train in Sardinia understood the jibe. Eriksson's methods and strategy were utterly incomprehensible. Nothing he did made sense. They did, however, understand the chemistry bonding the manager with Beckham: secrecy, disloyalty and delusion.

Neither Eriksson nor Beckham grasped the issue of the England team's lack of unity. At mealtimes and after training, the players only socialised with members of their own club. As captain, Beckham's task was to break the tribalism and create a spirit to drive the team forward. Leadership meant spreading his influence across the match. But Beckham, the *Sun*'s chief football writer Steven Howard noticed, 'was failing to create the right atmosphere. He wasn't the magician to make it work.'

Beckham's inadequacy as captain was aggravated by his unresolved tense relationship with Victoria. She had many good reasons to resist going to Sardinia. For a start, she would face the sniggering mockery from the WAGs – the Wives and Girlfriends of the other players. Glammed up, their heavily lipsticked mouths would whisper malicious comments about Rebecca Loos and more. Her solution was to rent a villa. Beckham was furious. As England's captain he must live with the team – and so must she.

Victoria had another good reason to stay away from the team hotel. From bitter experience, she knew that the WAGs and the team staff would be given wodges of cash by prowling tabloid journalists to reveal any secrets. The hotel's personnel would be just as greedy. Doormen, bouncers, barmen, waiters, chambermaids and drivers would be all on Fleet Street's payroll. And she was right. Within a day of the Beckhams arriving at the team's hotel outside Lisbon the couple were heard having 'blazing rows'. The eavesdropper outside their door reported to the *Mirror* that Victoria screamed, 'I'm bored with you, bored with football and don't want to spend the rest of my life in your shadow.'[16]

In public Victoria tried to be the perfect wife. On the eve of England's first match against France, she hosted a dinner for about 15 WAGs. Wearing a Dolce & Gabbana dress, a diamond-studded watch and her £80,000 engagement ring, she plucked at strawberries and drank mineral water. She could not help being accused of behaving like the Queen Bee. She was the Queen Bee. None of her guests, including those she ignored, were allowed to forget that the former Spice Girl had pocketed £1 million for her wedding.[17] Unlike the others, she intimated, her fame was won through sheer talent.

On the morning of England's first match against France, the newspapers naturally flattered the team's chances of winning to please the fans. Even before half-time, their private predictions were proved right. Inexplicably, Eriksson took his most likely goalscorer Wayne Rooney off the pitch, and then Beckham's penalty shot was saved. After being 1–0 up after 90 minutes, England lost 1–2 in injury time. 'Beckham needs to play much better,' the *Sunday Mirror* commented. 'Recently he's been falling over rather than playing.'[18] Choking with tears about England's traumatic defeat, the captain had failed to lead. 'It's a low point of my career,' he told the *Sun*. Faced with unrelenting pressure – either a hero or a villain – he pledged to rise again. 'There is no other way. If you're knocked down you come straight back up again.'

Ten days later, after goals from Wayne Rooney and Frank Lampard had delivered two convincing victories against Switzerland and Croatia, England faced Portugal at the quarter-final knock-out stage. In both games Beckham had been near invisible – unfit and emotionally distracted. A friend reported on the eve of the Portuguese match that 'David is a shattered, broken and beaten man.' Victoria's behaviour had not changed. 'Family values,' Jackie Adams reminded her daughter, but returned to England rather than watch the match. The Adams had been invited to Elton John's White Tie & Tiara Ball in Windsor.

In the stands, England's supporters were optimistic. Eighteen-year-old Rooney had already scored two outstanding goals. Beckham reassured Neil Custis: 'I'm happy with my fitness.'[19] The reality was different.

After an England goal was wrongly disallowed, Rooney twisted an ankle in the 26th minute. Within minutes, England's players collapsed. Their fire was gone. Beckham led a flair-less, defensive game. Spending most of the 90 minutes on the fringes rather than driving everyone forward, he failed to deliver a single notable cross. Almost miraculously, after extra-time it was tied at 2–2, thanks to Owen and Lampard's goals. Down to a penalty shoot-out, Beckham took the first one and badly missed the goal, replicating his previous penalty blunders against France and Turkey. England were defeated 6–5. 'A shadow of his former brilliance,' concluded the *Sun*'s commentator Derek McGregor. 'There's never been a spark and he looked weary.'[20]

In the post-match interviews Beckham was indignant. 'I can still look at myself in the mirror and believe I've done my best. And that's good enough for me.' Giving himself 7/10 'for effort' in the tournament, he said: 'If that's not good enough for some people, so be it. But I believe in my own ability. I won't have any regrets.' Asked whether he should resign as captain he replied, 'I find questions like that offensive. People don't always realise just how strong I am as a person. If they want to write me off, then I'll keep coming back at them until I have won.'[21]

The football writers were outraged. Their reports were unforgiving about England's 'nightmare' and Beckham's 'pitiful' performance. Described as a liability, Beckham was accused of self-delusion. Ever since his equalising goal against Greece in 2001, his game had declined.[22]

That night Victoria sat in the hotel bar smoking a cigar, drinking champagne and tequilas. Accused by others of being moody and rude, she was in no state to disguise her personal misery. Not about England's defeat. She had heard from Fuller that the American launch of 'My Love is For Real' had been abandoned and her appearance with Beckham on Jay Leno's show in New York was cancelled.[23]

After reading the damning media reports the following day, Beckham was advised by his new publicist Simon Oliveira to modify his defiance. 'I just don't feel properly fit,' he admitted. He blamed the lax training regime at Real Madrid.[24] In Madrid, the club's managers instantly scoffed, 'Beckham always makes excuses.' Instead of training, he had repeatedly flown back to England to save his marriage.[25] Embarrassed by that accusation, Beckham next blamed his 'intolerable' living conditions in Madrid. Constantly harassed when he went out, he said he had devoted excessive time 'to protect my children' from being photographed in the school playground. Until then, his sons had been mostly at school in England. Incredibly, he told the *Sunday Mirror*, 'I would never do photoshoots with my children.'

Then he let slip a secret of his survival. After leaving Portugal, he told a journalist he would forget the humiliating defeat. Unless asked to re-enact a moment of unhappiness – as he would about the Loos affair for his Netflix series in 2023 – Beckham's vain glory protected him from any self-recrimination. Unlike other players who crumbled under pressure, Beckham's disciplined self-control withstood the critics. The grit made him special.

Proving their disdain for their critics, the Beckhams were next sighted posing as the loving couple in the south of France with Elton John. Days later they were on a yacht with the interior designer Kelly Hoppen. Some fans were furious. England's captain had denied leading a showbiz life. And worse, he was not mourning the defeat. Their anger was aggravated by David Davies, the FA's executive director. 'We are lucky', Davies said, 'to have Sven and we're immensely proud of Becks.'[26]

In the search for a culprit, no one was more vulnerable than Eriksson. Blamed for being overrated and overpaid, the Swede was blamed for taking orders from Beckham.[27] To prove that he was also oversexed, the *News of the World* now began probing Eriksson's affair with 38-year-old Faria Alam.

Uninterested in the furore surrounding England's football team, Victoria decided to achieve another resurrection. During the summer she had persuaded Beckham to buy a 19th-century villa in Bargemon, near Nice. Set in over 150 acres of rolling hills, the 6,500-square-foot house cost $1.9 million.[28] An estimated $6 million was spent on renovations, supervised by her father Tony. She also persuaded Beckham that on their fifth wedding anniversary – 4 July 2004 – they should renew their wedding vows in Marrakesh in Morocco.[29]

After a tip-off, the *Sun*'s Neil Syson was dispatched to Marrakesh. Despite visiting every boutique hotel in the town he could not find the couple. They had checked into the luxurious Amanjena but remained unseen. Four days later, Victoria Newton described the 'secret surprise' by the hotel pool.

The couple, she wrote, 'acting like a pair of love-struck teenagers, repeatedly embraced, and exchanged tender kisses and shared intimate jokes'. Newton's account of the garden ceremony to repair a year of 'scandal and heartache' included Victoria embracing David and then feeding bread to sparrows while the bodyguards, waiters and staff 'giggled'. The hotel manager was quoted, 'From the way they are acting, David and Victoria are truly in love.' To prove her close relationship with the Beckhams, Newton added that the couple were trying for another baby. And, equally important, England's fans should thank Posh for rescuing David from self-destruction: 'I can't go on,' he had colourfully told his wife after Portugal. 'I'm retiring. I'm finished.' But 'amazing' Victoria, Newton wrote, 'thankfully managed to change his mind'. Posh said to Becks, 'I'm proud of you. You go back out there and show people what you're made of.'[30]

'Neil Syson in Marrakesh' was added to the report's byline. Readers might have assumed that Syson spoke to the hotel's staff. But Syson had not contributed even a comma to the article. He never found the Beckhams' hotel, let alone interviewed anyone. The whole page and its entire contents had been dictated by the Beckhams' publicist. The renewal of the marriage vows appeared to be a stunt. The Beckhams would later say that the actual ceremony to renew their vows had been abandoned after the 'leak' to the *Sun*.[31]

Victoria returned to London determined to save her marriage. Still angry about Beckham's affairs, she finally arranged to move permanently to Spain.[32] Her father, Tony Adams, was tasked with overseeing the renovation of their new home, a £5 million Andalusian-style house set in two acres in La Moraleja, a Madrid suburb.

Beckham had flown directly from Morocco back to Madrid. Hours after he landed, José Antonio Camacho, Real Madrid's new manager, warned that if his performance failed to improve, then his place in the team was uncertain.[33]

CHAPTER 14

SEX SCANDAL

As Beckham's star dimmed, Eriksson's future was threatened. In mid-July, Nancy Dell'Olio stormed out of Eriksson's life, screaming she would 'kill him' if the rumours about his relationship with Faria Alam were true. Instantly, Alam's lawyers sent threatening letters to newspapers warning that the allegations of an affair were totally false and a breach of her privacy.[1] Protected by her lawyers' threats, Alam went to Max Clifford. He sold her story to the *News of the World* for £400,000. 'I BEDDED SVEN AND HIS BOSS' was the newspaper's 'Svengate' headline on 25 July 2004. Despite her fury, Dell'Olio begged Sven to return.

And then up popped Ulrika Jonsson, ready to sell the story of her stormy affair with Sweden's 'Love Rat'. Finally, in early August, Fleet Street was awash with Faria's confessions. Her sexual appetite for a slew of men – especially Football Association employees – was portrayed as 'insatiable'.

Cast as chaotic, sleazy and incompetent the FA's culpability for England's defeat in Portugal was inescapable. Yet instead of removing Eriksson and Beckham, the FA's executives decided to protect them. England's dispirited fans were appalled. Looking for a single hero, they latched on to the still apparently untarnished teenager Wayne Rooney. Photos of his devotion to blissful fiancée Coleen featured in most newspapers. Weeks later, the same newspapers exposed Rooney's relationship with a prostitute, described as 'a brothel slapper'.[2]

Just as English football's sex scandals reached a climax during August, *Vanity Fair*'s major feature about Beckham was published.[3] 'Brand It Like Beckham', illustrated by Annie Leibovitz's macho shots of the celebrity, was a familiar Beckham production. In set-piece interviews he never faltered: Victoria and he would be 'together forever'. As the magazine writer Steven Daly struggled to extract something newsworthy about their marriage, Beckham ridiculed the media accounts of his affairs. But he refused to deny his relationship with Loos.

Unexpectedly, Victoria injected herself into the interview. 'We've got big plans for America – both of us,' Victoria announced. She was echoing Fuller's pitch. Beckham's days in Madrid, the writer failed to realise, were numbered.

The writer could not have known that during those days, Beckham had invited the 22-year-old beauty therapist Dannielle Heath to visit his home in Madrid for a tan. The request to Dannielle was sent by Abigail Gibson, the Beckhams' nanny.

On her second visit at the end of August, Dannielle discovered that Victoria, who had just announced another pregnancy, had returned to England to organise Romeo's second birthday party. Only Beckham was in the house, waiting to play a football match the following day. 'We were lying on sun loungers by the pool chatting,' Dannielle recalled later, 'when David said, "Do you mind if I sunbathe in my pants?" I noticed the whole time that he had an erection.'[4] After he suggested that they go upstairs, they started 'kissing quite passionately' on a sofa. Dannielle flew back to London the following day on a private jet with Beckham.

One week later, the *News of the World* heard about violent arguments between the Beckhams. Relying on a variety of sources, Coulson was fired up about the Beckhams still selling the image of their happy marriage. And then it got worse.

The tension between Beckham and his critics hit a new high after England beat Poland 2–1 on 8 September 2004. Still furious about the media's descriptions of his adultery, Beckham refused the FA's request that the team captain speak to journalists. Security guards were told to keep them away. Coulson now had another reason to expose the real Beckham.

Under the headline 'POSH AND BECKHAM ON ROCKS' the newspaper reported, 'She hates his looks, hates his tattoos all over his body and hates the way he swears and rants all the time.' The couple, stated the newspaper, were planning a trial separation.[5] On Victoria's orders, Beckham sued the *News of the World*. Other newspapers were undeterred, correctly anticipating that Beckham's legal assault would be dropped.[6] Eventually, Beckham surrendered and paid £250,000 towards the newspaper's legal fees.[7]

The *Sunday Mirror* had followed the scent. 'After David had threatened to leave his wife during one particular bitter row,' the newspaper's Ben Todd discovered from an informer, 'Posh begged Beckham to stay.' Todd also heard that 'David has told Victoria "It's over" more than once. He has asked her for a separation. She is very tearful. She switches from diva to hysteria.'[8]

Abigail Gibson, the Beckhams' nanny, confirmed that truth. 'I just don't love Victoria,' Beckham had told her after his brief relationship with Dannielle Heath.[9] After Beckham mistakenly sent Gibson a text intended for Esther Canadas, Gibson texted back, 'Sorry, wrong girl.' 'Oh shit,' replied Beckham. At Dannielle Heath's request Gibson had even shared a bedroom with her in Spain to deter Beckham creeping into the room. Gibson claimed she had watched Victoria search through Beckham's cupboards for evidence of his affairs. To limit the chances of more mischief, Victoria had insisted on accompanying Beckham to Shepperton studies while he filmed a Pepsi advertisement. J-Lo and Beyoncé were also there filming the same ad. Victoria appeared eager to supervise the shoot.[10]

Gibson reported that Victoria, equally fearful of another affair in Madrid, overheard Beckham on the telephone just before midnight making a booking at the Metropolitano hotel to top up his tan. As he set off, Abigail Gibson watched Victoria, despite her pregnancy, jump into his Lamborghini in her pyjamas and follow him. His security guards drove behind in a third car. After arriving, Beckham angrily insisted he would go into the hotel alone. Thirty minutes later he emerged. The couple returned home and, overheard by Gibson, spent the night arguing.[11]

Repairing the damage to the Beckhams' reputation was Simon Oliveira's priority. First, he arranged for *V Man* magazine to interview him. Grateful for the access, the magazine unquestioningly reported Beckham's denial of any marital troubles: 'There's no way in the world we will ever split up.'[12]

More importantly, Oliveira set up the 'Victoria and David Charitable Trust' devoted to help children. First on its publicity-seeking agenda would be Victoria's visit to orphaned children in China. The multi-millionairess revealed that so far the couple had

donated cast-off toys, David's old shirts and £65,000. To save the cost
of the flight, Victoria's visit to China would coincide with a flight to
Japan, the result of Fuller landing a £250,000 contract for her promotion of a new range of Rock & Republic jeans.[13]

Michael Ball, a brash Californian, had rapidly expanded sales of
his high-priced Rock & Republic designer jeans since 2002. Attracted
by his runway shows during Los Angeles Fashion Week, over a thousand stores in 2005 sold his brand to celebrities. Keen to create her
own denim collection, Victoria was introduced by Fuller to Ball as a
potential partner within his brand. Among the ideas she offered, Ball
did incorporate a crown label on the back pocket. In the first year the
Victoria Beckham jeans were sold in London, particularly in Notting
Hill Gate.

The success of her first business venture was highlighted by Oliveira
and Hickson during media appearances that presented the Beckhams
as a happy family. In a series of interviews with Spanish magazines,
Victoria spoke about her new love for Spain as a 'positive country'.
She said that Beckham admired her Spanish omelettes; that Beckham
could not dance; that they spread facial creams on each other; and
they spent many nights together in bed watching trashy TV serials.
And, most newsworthy, that her expected third child was another
boy.[14] 'David told me,' she revealed in yet another interview with the
Sunday Mirror's Ben Todd, 'to be more careful what I say because my
mouth is like a weapon of mass destruction. I say the first thing that
comes into my head.'[15]

All that PR effort crashed one week after Todd's interview. Tina
Weaver, the newspaper's editor, called Beckham's publicist with a
simple announcement. She had paid Dannielle Heath £40,000 for her
revelations about her 'romp' with Beckham' nine weeks earlier.[16]
Beckham had forgotten to obtain Heath's signature on a non-disclosure
agreement. The result was cringe-making.

'We were on the sofa. He said to me, "I want to taste you." He
put his hands down my bikini bottoms and pulled them down and
started fondling me. He was kissing my boobs. He seemed to know
exactly what he was doing and gave me oral sex. I played with him
a bit but was surprised to find he had no hair on his balls. His willy
is big, though – a good eight inches. And for the record, he is not
circumcised.'

'It's not true,' croaked Beckham. Oliveira was stumped. Charlotte Hickson broke the news to Victoria. She was left reeling. 'I'm going to destroy that ugly, lying **** for what she's done to me and my family,' Victoria told the *Sun*. She would sue the *Mirror* and Dannielle. 'I'm sick and tired of people trying to make money out of us.'

Victoria Newton agreed. 'Dannielle,' she wrote, 'has bitten off more than she can chew trying to bring down Britain's No. 1 couple. I can guarantee that Victoria is 100 per cent determined that tarts like Dannielle will not destroy her marriage.'[17]

Once again, Gerrard Tyrrell, the Beckhams' lawyer, telephoned Tina Weaver. In what she described to her chairman as, 'Tyrrell's bully-boy manner,' she reported that the lawyer had denied Heath's story and denied there were any problems in the Beckhams' marriage. The Beckhams did not sue.

'Sandra blamed Posh for being too controlling and telling David what to do,' a 'friend' passed on to the *News of the World*. 'He's stubborn and walked out,' Sandra told her 'friend'.[18] Sandra also blamed Victoria's parents for the problems. The Adams were managing David and Victoria's lives,[19] said Sandra.

Victoria had no choice but sweep aside the mess left by her husband. The alternative would be a difficult future with less money and limited fame. 'If they slag me off,' Victoria had earlier said about the newspapers, 'I don't give a shit.' [20] That had changed.

After the *Sunday Mirror*'s bombshell, Beckham was advised that before any future sexual relationship started he should get the woman to sign a non-disclosure agreement. A stash of blank forms was provided. Before he could use them, the Heath revelations were drowned by another crisis. Beckham's problems got a lot worse.

'England's captain represented,' wrote Steven Howard, the *Sun*'s football commentator in mid-October 2004, 'the morally bankrupt world of professional football.'[21]

England had just beaten Wales 2–0 in a World Cup qualifying match, and Beckham had been booked for fouling the Welsh defender Ben Thatcher. Football journalists watching the game were baffled by Beckham's foul, which followed his spectacular goal.

Few realised the truth. Beckham wanted to wipe the slate clean of a previous yellow card before the next international match. He was due to receive a one-match suspension for the next yellow card he

Victoria Adams was already an internationally famous member of the Spice Girls when she met David Beckham in 1997. They got engaged the following year, when the footballer was hired to relaunch Brylcreem, sparking the birth of Brand Beckham.

After his red card against Argentina in the 1998 World Cup,
Beckham at first struggled to restore his image, presenting
himself as a dutiful father protecting his children from the
media and laughing alongside Victoria when she first 'outed'
him as 'Golden Balls' to Michael Parkinson on his
popular BBC chatshow.

Under the management of Alex Ferguson at Manchester United (*top left*), Beckham became a star across the globe, including China. After their relationship crashed, he was warmly welcomed by Real Madrid fans in 2003 (*below right*).

Ambitious to rebuild her singing career with Damon Dash (*left*) in New York, Victoria delayed moving to Spain. In her absence Beckham was spotted with his personal assistant Rebecca Loos (*below*) in a nightclub in Madrid (*above*), where he would party with Ronaldo (*left*) and other Galacticos.

Intense media scrutiny of the Beckhams' relationship included claims of affairs with Loos and other women, including Sarah Marbeck (*top left*) and Dannielle Heath (*top right*). Beckham's mother Sandra and nanny Abbie Gibson (*above*) supported Victoria under immense media pressure.

England's manager Sven-Göran Eriksson (*top left*) backed his captain despite a series of poor results, including a humbling 1–0 defeat by Northern Ireland in 2005 (*top right*). Hammered during the 2006 World Cup in Germany, England's dismal performance was aggravated by the presence of the WAGs led by Victoria (*right*), but she could always rely on her parents, Jackie and Tony (*above*).

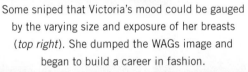

Some sniped that Victoria's mood could be gauged by the varying size and exposure of her breasts (*top right*). She dumped the WAGs image and began to build a career in fashion.

To develop her career in fashion, Victoria urged Beckham to move to Los Angeles, where their phenomenal welcome was matched by the media coverage (*above right*). New celebrity friends included Tom Cruise and Katie Holmes, and Will Smith and Jada Pinkett Smith (*above left*).

received, and he knew this would keep him out of England's next match. Knowing he had just cracked a rib and would be unable to play for a few weeks, he deliberately fouled Thatcher to serve his suspension in a match that he would have had to miss anyway.

All that would have remained largely unknown, but Oliveira had agreed that *The Times*' football journalist Henry Winter could interview Beckham. In the course of their taped conversation Beckham said, 'It was deliberate. I could feel the injury. So I fouled Thatcher. I am sure some people think that I have not got the brains to be that clever, but I do have the brains.'

Beckham has 'brought the country into disrepute,' raged the *Sun*. 'He knows that another bombshell is coming.' The tabloid's front pages and back pages were now aligned. Both ends of the newspaper published negative stories about the Beckhams. 'The role model for young children,' wrote one columnist, 'an ambassador for football and a shining example of the perfect blend of husband, father and sports superstar' had proved to be 'a shaven-headed tattooed thug.'[22]

'I made a mistake. It was wrong,' said Beckham. Shaken by the onslaught, he was not for once in his favourite 'state of Zen' as the hysteria erupted. Fighting in the trenches to suppress two confessions – Dannielle Heath's and his own – the footballer was too proud to further beg for forgiveness, admit any mistakes or appeal to his staff to 'save me'. In yet another of his darkest moments, he relied on the public to accept his values – patriotism, the family and sport.

Beckham's only fear was expulsion from the England team. Eriksson came to the rescue. He could not remain as manager, Eriksson told the FA, without Beckham as captain. The FA's commercial department joined in the chorus. Beckham, they pleaded, was indispensable stardust for the Association's finances. Beckham was saved. 'We refused to believe it was a crime,' said one FA executive. 'He'd done so much good for us. We had to cut him some slack.' The FA's official inquiry concluded: 'There is insufficient evidence to pursue a disciplinary charge.' Although he admitted cheating, England's captain had become a law unto himself.[23]

Beckham's vices infected the England team. 'England were a disgrace,' wrote Steven Howard in the *Sun*, reflecting a commonly shared opinion about their next match against Spain in the Bernabéu. 'A rabble of footballers resembling a battalion of lead soldiers,' concluded Howard. Beckham's 'worst display' – he barely kicked the ball – showed he had 'lost the plot'. Worse was a series of bad fouls by England's players. In the 'cesspit', Rooney proved to be 'an uncouth lout and bully boy who disgusted everyone'. England were defeated 1–0. Eriksson, Howard concluded, was a real threat to the England team's prospects.[24]

Once again the FA recoiled from firing Eriksson or demoting Beckham. 'The squad was thin,' recalled a FA executive. 'The alternatives to Beckham were unattractive.' The only benefit of the yellow card was the swift burial of Dannielle Heath's kiss-and-tell. 'A storm in a teacup,' said Beckham to his adviser.

Four days later, Beckham was damned for his contribution to the Real Madrid side against Barcelona in El Clasico. He was taken off after 54 minutes, and Real Madrid lost 3–0.[25] Beckham's poor performance was repeated against Seville. Real Madrid lost 1–0. A vintage Beckham goal from 30 yards against Levante, a less illustrious team, could not rescue his reputation.[26] Cynics believed he only upped his game because Eriksson was watching. That was Beckham's extraordinary quality. Faced by overwhelming difficulties, he stubbornly defied his critics.

Football experts recognised Beckham's dilemma. After eight years playing at the top, the 29-year-old's brain was still attuned to play as a champion. Nothing gave him more pleasure than performing in a packed stadium. But his ageing legs defied his wishes. They could no longer perform as he wanted. The trajectory had turned downwards. He refused to surrender, but he knew that compared to the Galacticos he was outclassed. He did not delude himself that he was equal to Zidane or Brazil's Ronaldo. Not playing in his usual position as the right-side midfielder, he was just a workhorse showing occasional flair. As an accomplished actor he urged his audience to sing his praises. Forever trying to balance life as a celebrity and a footballer, he was uncomfortably tilting towards the former. That challenged his credibility.

Once again the Beckhams needed to prove their romance was genuine. This time they chose to stage a dinner at the Cipriani restaurant in London. The Beckhams' publicist did not deny they had sat in silence throughout the dinner.[27] Outside the restaurant the summoned photographers were waiting. Victoria grabbed Beckham's hand. She rarely appeared in public with Beckham without clutching his hand. Strangers, she assumed, believed that the gesture signalled their romance.

The stress inside Beckingham Palace was becoming intolerable for John and Nicky Giles-Larkin, the housekeepers since July 2002. Previously employed by the Queen Mother, John Larkin was finding the atmosphere difficult. Posh, he said, kept shouting at him and making unreasonable demands.[28] Although acknowledging Victoria's unacceptable behaviour, Beckham was too malleable to intercede. As always in those crises, he turned a blind eye and walked away. He left Jackie Adams to step in and placate the couple.

Whatever the odds, the Beckhams would not give up. However low they sank, both battled to emerge victorious. Not daunted by humiliation and controversy, they refused to succumb. As merchants of glamour, neither could imagine their blessed lives as other than superior to those of ordinary mortals. Drawing on the talents that secured their original success, they relied on Simon Oliveira to drag them out of the quicksand. The publicist was tasked to rebuild the Beckhams' reputation.

At first, Oliveira relied on a few crumbs. Vodaphone had signed Beckham for a one-year deal. Naturally, the published fee of £6 million was exaggerated, but the deal proved that Beckham's conduct had not harmed his commercial value.[29]

Next, Oliveira revealed that the *Mission: Impossible* star Tom Cruise had visited Beckham in Madrid. After watching a match they had dinner. 'You are my hero,' Cruise apparently told Beckham, and he invited the family to stay with him in Los Angeles. Victoria was quick to tell Cruise that when David retired they would move to Los Angeles.[30] In private she swooned about the worship by a man from another planet. 'He's talking about David all the time,' she said. She never questioned whether there was a reason.

The major coup that Oliveira delivered to restore Beckham's reputation was his appointment as an UNICEF ambassador. UNICEF's Alison Tilbe was thrilled that Beckham would campaign to help children across Africa, and especially in South Africa supporting female AIDS sufferers.[31] As head of the Goodwill Ambassador's programme, Tilbe believed that Beckham's strength would be the sincerity of his appeal to the rich to donate money through him. Perhaps fearing that they might one day find themselves short of cash, this gave the impression that they were becoming 'tight'. Allowing Beckham to protect his reputation, sponsors would be asked to pay UNICEF directly.

Simultaneously, Victoria was relaunched – again. Hickson announced they would follow on from the success of *The Real Beckhams* and produce a television series about their daily lives. Viewers would see 'ordinary people' much in love. Editorial control would be retained by the Beckhams. At the same time, Damon Dash was persuaded not to edit the video he had recorded for a documentary about his relationship with Victoria.[32]

In the relaunch, Victoria revealed a fundamental shift in her career. Having abandoned singing she would become a fashion designer. Describing fashion as her 'passion', she did not reveal that Fuller was organising the creation of her workshop, financed by Beckham. 'For the first time I am using my brain and enjoying it,' she said.[33]

'Oh really?' commented Mark Bolland, alias 'Blackadder', in the *News of the World*. 'The bony ex-Spice Girl has only two looks – tatty and tarty. Her hair and breasts are false and she rarely smiles. Who wants to look like that? Stick to what you do best, Posh. Though I'm not sure what that is.'[34]

The mockery did not help the atmosphere in Sawbridgeworth. Jackie and Tony Adams had been invited for Christmas Day, but Ted and Sandra were not present.[35] In compensation, Beckham gave his father a £20,000 second hand S-type Jaguar sports car. Previously he had bought Tony Adams a new Range Rover and a Porsche costing £125,000.[36] But Ted had been allowed to take six-year-old Brooklyn fishing, and out for the day in London.

Knowing that his father still spent hours watching old tapes of his young son playing, Beckham gave Ted a ticket to watch the Madrid match on 22 December.[37] Ted flew by easyJet to Spain and returned in his son's private jet that night to be present the following day at Romeo's christening party.

One hundred and twenty guests were invited to the extravaganza, but it was the tipping-point for John and Nicky Giles-Larkin. Overcome by the stress of living with the warring Beckhams and Victoria's demands they had left the house, even before the £500,000 celebration commenced.[38] Larkin would later deny that he was writing his memoirs about his experiences, not least because of the Beckhams' draconian non-disclosure agreements.[39]

Abigail Gibson, their nanny, witnessed the Beckhams arguing throughout the week before Christmas. At 2 a.m. she heard Beckham shout at Posh: 'Fucking bitch!' and threaten to leave her. 'He knows how to work her,' recalled Gibson. 'How to make her feel it's her fault that things are going wrong.'

Gibson heard Victoria call a friend, 'I'm worried David doesn't love me anymore. I think he's going to leave me.' The following morning, Victoria needed to speak to someone. She turned to Gibson: 'I don't know what to do. He's on about splitting up. I don't know if he loves me anymore. I have to make sure I don't trigger another argument. I asked him to stay until the baby is born. I'm so worried about losing him.'[40]

The truth was disguised from guests at the christening party on 23 December. Determined to prove Brand Beckham was thriving, Victoria saw the christening as a key event. It had been organised at the suggestion of Jackie and Tony Adams. Surrounded by flowers apparently costing £75,000, Victoria recounted how 'David and I are stronger than we've ever been. I want to let the world know that in 2005.' The beleaguered Beckham emotionally pledged to his guests that in 2005 he would 'stay on the straight and narrow'. Referring to 2004, Victoria told her friends, 'I can't wait to see the back of it.'

The tension between the Adams and Beckham parents was aggravated by the necessity, following their acrimonious divorce in 2002, of keeping Ted and Sandra apart. Other casualties included Mel B – she refused to come because Geri was present – and in turn Geri argued with Mel C.

In contrast Simon Fuller was smirking. He was on the verge of selling 19 Entertainment, the owner of *American Idol*, to CKX, later Sony Entertainment, for an estimated £50 million. He also met Geri, Mel C and Victoria for the first time since he had been fired by the Spice Girls in 1997. Putting aside his anger that the strong-willed young women had stood up to him, he could afford to smile. 'Fuller is unbearably smug now,' noted one observer.[41] All five women had inveigled their way back to him hoping he could relaunch their careers.

Romeo's only godparents, Elton John and Liz Hurley, watched the disharmony. Hurley added to the tension by obeying Victoria's request for women to be dressed in white and cream, but anticipating that Victoria would choose to stand out – she had chosen a black Dolce & Gabbana dress – Hurley's choice had a noticeably plunging neckline. To outdo Hurley, Victoria flashed a new £1 million diamond ring, the latest present from Beckham. The party, she pronounced at the end, 'really paid dividends'. Including, she thought, reuniting the Spice Girls. No one mentioned that Romeo, the star of the day, threw a tantrum while the vicar was trying to bless him.[42]

Victoria's bid to draw a line under the horror of 2004 was an anti-climax, a relief in the circumstances.

CHAPTER 15

SHAME

Max Clifford's description of Victoria as 'widely disliked by the British public' caused Simon Fuller to abandon some earlier tactics. After surveying the wreckage of Dannielle Heath's kiss-and-tell and anticipating the possibility of more 'confessions' sold by Clifford, Fuller decided that fighting the tabloids had been catastrophic.

The threats and writs issued against newspaper editors by the Beckham's lawyer Gerrard Tyrrell had not stopped the deluge of damaging revelations. Equally, offering access to the Beckhams to journalists in exchange for uncritical coverage had not worked. The publicists' threat of denying the journalists any information if they disobeyed the Beckhams' demands had not stopped the tabloids from publishing a succession of embarrassing stories. The solution, Fuller decided, was to forge a new Faustian pact.

Schmoozing the media, Fuller hoped, would win sympathy. The first casualty was Charlotte Hickson, Victoria's publicist. Chewed up by Victoria and lampooned by journalists, she departed. She was replaced by Jo Milloy, who had been formerly engaged to Andy Coulson. Calm and intelligent, 34-year-old Milloy had learned her trade at Channel 4 and with Fuller on *Pop Idol*. Resolving not to lie or threaten, she introduced herself as the opposite of McAteer. 'I will be more open and honest,' she told *PR Week*.[1] Given responsibility for the Beckhams' family media, her brief was to neutralise the poison and befriend the press. She would be assisted by 'strategy and brand consultant' Natalie Lewis for Victoria's 'personal profile' and fashion PR.

Milloy's priority was to rescue Victoria. After flying to Madrid she found her client sitting on the floor of her renovated house crying, sewing plastic labels on to her trousers. Opening a bottle of champagne and dropping down beside the distraught woman, Milloy heard

Victoria, now eight months pregnant, wailing, 'Everyone hates me and I love him. I'm the one hurt. And I'm about to give birth.'

Amid tight security Cruz Beckham was born on 20 February 2005 at Madrid's Ruber International Hospital. Fearing leaks to the press, the caesarean had been brought forward. Her third son was named after Tom Cruise.[2]

The Adams family gathered at the hospital the following day. While Beckham ate cheese and bacon sandwiches and drank Coca-Cola – despite being paid to promote Pepsi – the Adams family listened to Victoria complain about her unhappiness. 'I can't live here,' she said. Without friends and no work in Madrid she wanted to return to her family in England. Seven days later Beckham told an interviewer, 'We're very happy in Spain.'[3]

Beckham's prestige had recovered a few weeks earlier. In a match against Numancia he had scored a trademark goal from a free kick. The improvement in his game, he said, owed much to new stability at Real Madrid. Over the previous two years the club's coach had changed three times. The last one, Mariano García Remón, had been fired and replaced by former Brazil boss Vanderlei Luxemburgo. The new leader, said Beckham, had improved his performance.

Real Madrid's president Sánchez agreed. Not only was Beckham's game getting better but the club's merchandising profits had soared. Sales had increased by £29 million in his first year and had since risen another 23 per cent. Four out of five Real Madrid shirt sales were his number 23. Thanks to Beckham, Adidas had extended its contract with Real Madrid to 2012. 'He's an icon of modern football,' said Sánchez. Beckham's attraction was huge. The proof was Real Madrid's contract to tour America, Japan and China. The contracts worth £14 million would be reduced by 50 per cent if Beckham didn't play.[4]

Although Beckham's contract with Real Madrid expired in two years, he was offered a new four-year deal worth £11.6 million per annum – £4.6 million salary plus £7 million from shirt sales. With his usual exaggeration, Fuller estimated the contract's total value was £100 million.[5]

Expecting that windfall, Beckham's financial advisers in 2005 were changed. Not for more expertise but for window-dressing. While Charles Bradbrook at Deloitte remained his accountant, the legal approval or audit of the accounts for HMRC was transferred to Lakin

Rose, a small firm in Cambridge created by a former Deloitte partner. That removed the perception of a conflict of interest, and was probably related to Beckham's partnership with Ingenious Films. Family partnerships like Lakin Rose did not normally manage unusually complicated accounts.

By being permanently resident in Spain, had Beckham taken advantage of not being obliged to pay tax in Britain on his British income? His accountants had also shortened Footwork's 2003 tax year to eight months, therefore legally reducing his income from Footwork Productions Ltd before he left Britain, something his advisers say was merely to align Footwork's tax year with the tax year in Spain. Beckham also increased his negative reserves from £27,000 to £3.2 million. The cause of the loss remains unclear.

Purposefully, they also changed Footwork's accounting policy regarding the company's income. That allowed them to defer the profits of £3,181,000, which saved Beckham £954,000 in UK corporation tax.

In 2004, the tax year was once again changed – with the effect of reducing turnover and increasing his income in Spain. The accounts made clear that he was not paying British taxes on income from playing, and that he was employed by Footwork Productions Spain SL, a Spanish company. His principal Spanish trading company benefited from the 'Beckham law' that reduced income tax to 24 per cent for foreign stars resident in Spain.

For tax reasons the Spanish Footwork company charged the British Footwork company £821,000 in fees 'for the provision of David Beckham's services'. The money was taken out of Britain, avoiding the payment of British taxes at higher rates. His Footwork income in 2004 was £17.3 million, with a massive increase in cash deposits from £134,000 to £12,798,000. As a non-dom living in Spain he paid no British taxes on money retained by the Spanish company, nor did he pay British income tax.

His accounts cast a smokescreen over the taxation of his £7.9 million salary and £1.25 million in dividends for the eight months to 31 December 2003. The National Insurance contribution was just £157,000 rather than £1,014,000 if he had continued to be resident in Britain after June 2003.

Beckham paid huge fees for all that work. Deloitte's non-audit fees for Footwork Productions Ltd was £203,000, plus £543,000 in legal fees to Lee & Thompson. There was also a provision of £324,000 in disallowed expenses. One result of all that advice was the unexplained change in Footwork's accounting policy in 2004.

In 2005 the accounts became more opaque. Footwork's turnover was £15.5 million, down from £17.3 million in the previous year. But the administrative expenses, or 'operating charge', soared to £23 million compared to £3.9 million in 2004. The result was hugely beneficial. The company earned nothing and paid no British taxes. And claimed a tax refund of £2.1 million. Unusually, Beckham was now paid a salary rather than dividends. No less than £19.5 million. No explanation was offered in his accounts about Beckham's terms of employment with each of his companies.

To benefit from the special tax arrangements in Spain, the money was not paid to Beckham in Britain. Instead the money owed to Beckham was described in the British company accounts as a debt owed to a 'Related Party'.

In 2006, Footwork earned £11.1 million but after paying £11.8 million to Beckham, plus other expenses, declared an operating loss of £2.2 million. Again, the tax effect benefited Beckham. Footwork was owed £5.6 million in corporation tax refunds from HMRC. Unusually, although the company had incurred this loss it still paid Beckham a £1.75 million dividend. Remarkably, the company paid Beckham that dividend even though it was more money than in Footwork's reserves. That arose because of an unusual accounting entry. The company received £4 million from HMRC as a refunded corporation tax, but did not use that money to repay a £5.6 million debt. Technically, Footwork appeared insolvent. His advisers disagree. Footwork, they contend, was 'trading with active long-term contracts and income that had been deferred and so was profitable in the following period'. A cynic would say that such an ostensibly poor commercial decision, by leaving the company in a deficit, would likely only have occurred if there was a positive tax planning benefit.

No one in Britain scrutinised Beckham's accounts. The media described the world's highest-paid footballer solely in complimentary terms. As Britain's hero he was universally applauded. At the launch party of Beckham's Soccer Academy in Los Angeles, Simon Oliveira persuaded journalists that Beckham's troubles were over. 'I want to finish my career at Real Madrid,' the player said. Despite his slightly receding hairline he insisted, 'I'm still Golden Balls, not Oldenballs.'[6]

The only handicap was Victoria. Despite her promise to live in Madrid she had returned with Cruz to live with her parents and in Beckingham Palace in Sawbridgeworth. Even when Beckham played in Newcastle for England and scored a superb goal against Azerbaijan, she did not watch the game. She remained at home while he flew back to Madrid with his two elder sons. And then she blundered.[7]

On a Saturday night her sister Louise spotted Abigail Gibson, their nanny, chatting with Dannielle Heath at Club 195, a dance club in Epping in Essex. Outraged, Victoria screamed at Gibson for being disloyal. The nanny, dissatisfied that she was not paid more for the additional work with Cruz, resigned. She had been employed for two years.[8] Soon afterwards she headed to Max Clifford. He negotiated a £125,000 fee from the *News of the World*.

Tipped off by a friendly journalist about the imminent bombshell, Victoria's publicist arranged for photographers to gather outside the Ritz in Paris on 17 April, the occasion of Victoria's 31st birthday. Gripping Beckham's hand, Victoria had interrupted their 'romantic birthday trip' to emerge into the Place Vendôme to parade their happiness.[9]

A rapidly organised publicity flood followed. In a 10-page spread in *OK!* magazine, headlined 'HOW HAPPY WE ARE', Beckham asserted, 'I was always brought up to treat women with respect.'[10] Simultaneously, 'friends' told the *Sun* that the Beckhams' love was 'back on track' after Cruz's birth. 'After the hard time they have been through, and overwhelmed by Beckham's commitment to her in Paris, they both love each other. They are not about to split.'[11] The Beckhams next flew to Venice to celebrate his 30th birthday – in front of a posse of photographers. During the visit Victoria announced she would host a £500,000 birthday party for Beckham at Madrid's Buddha Bar. Once again the guest-list starred Elton John and Liz Hurley.[12] All that activity created a smokescreen for an ugly battle.

Throughout that week the Beckhams' lawyers were in the High Court trying to prevent the *News of the World* publishing Gibson's description of the Beckhams' arguments and his adultery. Not only, argued their lawyers, would their privacy be breached but also because Gibson had signed a non-disclosure agreement she was barred from speaking. During the hearing the Beckhams' lawyer admitted that David had threatened, during an argument, to leave Victoria but, he explained, that was 'in the heat of the moment'. The couple, he said, were 'happily married'.[13]

The *News of the World*'s lawyer replied that the Beckhams were only together 'cynically and hypocritically trying to convince the public they continue to enjoy a happy marriage' for financial reasons.[14]

The judge refused an injunction to stop the publication. In his succinct judgement he referred to the Beckhams' self-portrayal in their autobiographies and during their recent television TV series as a devoted couple. Gibson's exposure of their hypocrisy, agreed the judge, was in the public interest.[15]

Spokesmen for the Beckhams would claim that the judge, an expert in land law, failed to understand media laws. The following week, after the first instalment was published, the Beckhams returned to the court and argued their case to a different judge. The Beckhams pleaded that Gibson should not be allowed to make more disclosures from her detailed diary. This time the Beckhams won. The court silenced Gibson. Four years later, she apologised to the Beckhams for breaking the four non-disclosure agreements she had signed.[16]

Fearing more embarrassment and in order to present a united front, Victoria flew to Madrid. On the eve of publication of the *News of the World*, Beckham did not accuse Gibson of lying. 'I've been brought up to treat women well and respect them,' was all he could say again, adding about Gibson's betrayal of their trust, 'I find it amazing, quite unbelievable.'[17]

The *News of the World*'s banner headline was 'BECKS IS SIMPLY A LIAR AND A CHEAT – "Nannygate exclusive"'; Abbie hits back after love rat says he respects women.' Gibson told the journalist Jane Atkinson that Beckham was having sex with Dannielle Heath in the house while she and Sandra were downstairs: 'David believes in his own self-importance and that he can get away with everything by using people. While living with them I was living a lie for him and feeling guilt-stricken. David is a liar. He showed no respect to me when he tried to get me to help cover up what he did.'

And, said Gibson, after cheating on pregnant Posh he called her 'a fucking bitch'. After their arguments they slept in separate bedrooms.

Piling on the embarrassment, Gibson also handed the newspaper the sex-text message Beckham had sent Esther Canadas in 2003, which he had mistakenly sent to Gibson.

'Devastated' by Gibson's disloyalty, Victoria told a friend, 'I made Abbie the best-dressed nanny in the world.' Gibson was later accused in other circumstances of being unreliable.[18]

To protect the Beckhams from the photographers waiting outside their house, Sandra flew to Madrid to care for the children. The Beckhams stayed inside. To mislead the media, a publicist 'leaked' that 'Posh was taking Beckham on a two-day villa break to escape their week from hell.' The posse on the street outside did not leave.

Another tactic was tried. A friendly photographer was tipped off that Victoria would be playing with two-year-old Romeo in a Madrid park. As arranged, he found them. With lashings of make-up, perfect hair and wearing designer clothes, her message was clear: their marriage was solid and she did not need a nanny. The photographer was next invited to capture the couple in the house. Their pose became familiar. Clinging to her husband with both arms draped over his shoulders, Beckham's smile reflected indifference to his pouting wife.

Most newspapers enjoyed repeating Gibson's colourful revelations – except the *Sun*. The columnist Jane Moore accused Gibson and the *News of the World* of 'a callous disregard' for the Beckhams' feelings. The Beckhams, lamented Moore, were the latest victims of the 'constant drip-drip of high-profile betrayals'. In Moore's version the Beckhams were 'remarkable' for surviving the pressure. To his credit, Beckham had shown his love by 'whisking Posh off to Venice', and 'only last week scattered rose petals across her bed' in Paris. 'Isn't it time', Moore concluded, 'they were cut a little slack?'[19]

Others were less charitable. The Beckhams had 'shamelessly used the press,' wrote columnist Lorraine Kelly, to sell the fairytale of a blissful marriage. Now, their fame had become a nightmare.[20]

For their part, the Beckhams were so exhausted by the torrent of revelations that the latest – radio presenter Gaynor Morgan's description of her encounter with Beckham at a Christmas party in 2001 – was ignored. 'Beckham slid his hand up my thigh saying, "I've fancied you for ages",' recalled Morgan. She continued, 'What followed next will always remain our secret.' Even Max Clifford's announcement that another two women had emerged to sell their memories of an affair with Beckham was brushed aside, not only by the Beckhams but also by newspaper editors. Their readers' appetite appeared to be exhausted,[21] especially after Beckham's sister Joanna was exposed for having an affair with a friend's partner. He turned out to be the father of Joanna's baby daughter.[22]

Stories of adultery, deception and divorce in the Beckham family daunted their publicists. At least Gibson had been legally prevented from publishing her diary. Ironically, while she profited from disclosing the Beckham's secrets she would be paid £15,000 by the *Mirror* for hacking her phone.[23]

To keep up appearances, Beckham's birthday party in Madrid went ahead, albeit the cost was allegedly reduced to £250,000. Elton John didn't come, but model Elle Macpherson did. Few newspapers bothered to publish the hundreds of photographs offered.[24]

Humiliatingly, Victoria was declared by a magazine poll to have been voted 'the most pointless celebrity'.[25] There was only one solution. At last she moved permanently to Spain and admitted over seven pages of *OK!* magazine, 'All I want to do is stay in the shadows and look after my kids.'[26] She would also stop haranguing Beckham and acknowledge some unpleasant realities about his needs and habits.

'It hasn't been easy,' she admitted to a magazine, 'but I don't want anyone's sympathy. Our marriage is stronger than ever.' On cue she added, 'I'm so proud of David. He's still Golden Balls. Look at him – he's so bloody perfect.' She also insisted: 'I'm not jealous of other women. When people look at him, I think it's because he's very good.'[27] Obligingly, Beckham agreed. 'Our marriage is stronger than ever,' he said, portraying himself as the victim of the British media. 'They put you up there and then try to knock you down. And when you're down, they try to knock you down again.'[28]

To seduce the media, Milloy and Oliveira decided the time was right to invite key journalists and their wives on a trip to Madrid to meet the happy Beckhams. Dinner in Madrid's best restaurant disarmed even the most cynical. Beckham's entry into the restaurant, they noticed, changed the temperature. After saying a few words in Spanish, his audience was convinced that he spoke the language fluently. That was his way: his soft-spoken natural charm concealed his iron will and self-belief. He performed to convince his guests that he was special – and a survivor. He rarely revealed he was down.

His guests in Madrid knew that, despite the serial embarrassments, millions still hailed the self-made East Londoner as their outstanding favourite. Many football fans were still entranced, many women fancied him and many of the rest remained intrigued. Across the globe his admirers regarded his adultery as either irrelevant, or to be envied. Few men would have resisted Rebecca Loos or Esther Canadas. A photo of Beckham's shining chest sparked sales of home-waxing kits. Another photo, of a £20,000 bottle of champagne being opened for him in a St Tropez nightclub, sparked admiration.[29] Vodaphone did not renew his sponsorship contract, probably due to his sex-texts, but politicians knew that no other sportsman rivalled his magnetism.

Beckham was not just any footballer. To win Britain's bid to stage the 2012 Olympics, Prime Minister Tony Blair had appointed him as an ambassador. His presence in Singapore for the deciding vote in July 2005 may have tipped the balance in Britain's favour. All the lies he had told about his private life were forgiven, forgotten or just believed and ignored.

Even when he slipped away to the restaurant's lavatory, he was followed by admirers. 'I had to use a cubicle,' he laughed on his return. Briefly, the mood changed after his eyes fixated on a beautiful girl as she passed the table, walking towards the lavatory. Victoria kicked him. 'She was wearing a pair of your jeans,' he said. 'Funny how you noticed that. Keep your eyes off.' Not reported by the visiting journalists was Victoria's drinking and swearing. 'Leather trousers,' she remarked, 'makes your cunt stink.' Among the weekend's perks were jeans handed out by Victoria to the journalists' wives.

To bring peace and calm to their newly decorated Madrid house (with a garage hosting a Ferrari, Bentley, Aston Martin, Range Rover, Mercedes and Lamborghini), the Beckhams paid £350,000 for a *feng shui* makeover. The atmosphere also improved with the presence of his friend and adviser Terry Byrne and his wife as housekeepers. In order to enshrine the couple's new understanding, Louis Molloy arrived in Madrid to carve the same tattoo – 'May 8' – in Roman numerals on the Beckhams' wrists – the date in 1997 they first had sex. Molloy also tattooed an angel resting on clouds on Beckham's shoulder.[30]

Molloy left Madrid content that there was still 20 per cent of Beckham's body without tattoos.

During the summer of 2005 the rottenness of English football manifested itself. In anticipation of the World Cup in Germany the following year, the fans' excitement about England's chances of winning the tournament surged because of Eriksson's and Beckham's optimism.

In advance of a 'friendly' match against Denmark, Eriksson pronounced his team as the 'best' he had ever known. Beckham echoed Eriksson. Indisputably, he said, the players being trialled for Germany were the most outstanding group since 1966.

England were defeated 1–4 by Denmark. The horrendous result was made worse by the Danes scoring three goals in just seven minutes. 'We lost our way a bit,' admitted Beckham afterwards. Fans ridiculed England's captain and damned the team's manager as a clown.[31] Clearly, Eriksson and Beckham lacked the qualities to forge a united squad. Neither had tried to break up the team's tribal cliques linked to club loyalties. Even at mealtimes, they failed to persuade everyone to sit together.

One month later England's plight worsened. Playing Northern Ireland, who ranked 116 in the world, England were defeated 0–1, for the first time since 1927. Beckham was blamed outright. Before the match he was seen having a manicure. Critics ridiculed a diva among a team of pampered multi-millionaires.[32] During the match his desultory shots all missed the target, and as captain he failed once again to rally the team. 'I've full confidence in the manager,' said Beckham after the match. They had, Beckham continued, followed Eriksson's orders.

The shame of defeat was apportioned to both men, but the reason was disputed. Some said the bungling Eriksson was too scared to drop the immobile Beckham. Others accused Beckham, an astute operator, of manipulating the starry-eyed manager.

One month later, it got even worse. At the end of a shocking match against Austria, ranked by FIFA around 30th in the world, England scraped a 1–0 win but Beckham was given a red card. It was the first

time an England captain had been sent off, and the first time a player
had been sent off twice while playing for England. Eriksson called the
result 'brilliant'. Asked about the previous four defeats he replied
'They were a big, big good step in the right direction.'[33] Eriksson, in
the words of one FA realist, was 'certainly not a Churchill'.

At Real Madrid, Beckham was performing equally poorly. Awarded
yellow and red cards, his aggression contributed to Real Madrid's
failure in his third season to win any trophies for the first time since
1954. After Real Madrid was beaten by Arsenal in the Champions
League, Florentino Perez was forced to resign. Many merely laughed
when Beckham blamed his 'sore back'. Because one leg was shorter
than the other, he said, he needed injections to alleviate the pain
caused by kicking the ball.

He then amazed everyone in a familiar way. He scored a stunning
goal against Cadiz and two goals against Seville – one from a 35-yard
free kick that sailed straight into the net. Sánchez's interest in negotiating the renewal of Beckham's contract was reignited.

Just as few believed English football could slump further, a *News
of the World* sting exposed Eriksson's true colours. Flown to Dubai he
was offered a huge sum if he abandoned England before the World
Cup and became Aston Villa's manager. Not realising his Arab host
was the 'Fake Sheikh', an undercover newspaper reporter, Eriksson
accepted the offer and promised that Beckham would leave Real
Madrid for Aston Villa. After disparaging individually each of his
players, he described English football as corrupted by managers
taking bungs.[34]

Eriksson's treachery, recorded by the 'Fake Sheikh', shattered the
last myths about the England team and the FA's probity. Yet Geoff
Thompson and his board ignored Eriksson's avarice. Instead they
expressed their confidence in the manager. 'We need to stick together
and forget what's happened,' Beckham chimed. 'It's time to forget the
past and concentrate on winning the World Cup.'[35]

Burying the past was also Victoria's priority. Crushed by Beckham's
disloyalty her future depended once again on trying to restore the
image of the happy wife and mother. But that was not enough.
Psychologically, her survival depended on asserting her independence.
She needed to prove her success in her own right. In the search for
salvation Fuller arranged her introduction into serious fashion.

In an industry stuffed with insufferable egotists, smooth self-publicists, flamboyant narcissists, smiling traitors, breathtaking insincerity and stunning beauty, success was granted to those few blessed with originality, genius, hard work and deep reservoirs of cash. For Victoria, always bleating about insecurity, the challenge was to overcome her deficits. Never the prettiest, never the most talented and never the best, she discovered her ability to persuade fashion's power-brokers to align themselves to her interests. Partly because the mass-market celebrity from Essex posed no threat.

Roberto Cavalli, a fading 65-year-old Italian designer, was her first catch. Fashion, Cavalli preached, was not just about clothes but also a public statement, a reflection of culture to impress the world. To one seasoned fashion expert, Cavalli was not outstanding but just one of many more famous for chasing girls than making waves.

An approach was made. Flattered, Cavalli snatched an opportunity for publicity alongside a Beckham. He provided the stage for Victoria to be launched. Escorted by Cavalli, she arrived at the October Monte Carlo show dressed in a stunning gown. 'Victoria Beckham had crowds gasping last night,' wrote the *Sun*, 'as she swept into the Fashion Rocks charity show.'[36] Cavalli hailed his Monte Carlo show a success. Three months later a newspaper reported, 'The mum of three looked sensational' modelling a pleated white silk gown for Cavalli in Milan. Soon after this, she modelled for Chanel in Paris.[37] 'Feel that you're the most beautiful woman in the room and walk in with that in mind,' Victoria advised her fans.

Natalie Lewis, Victoria's PR, worked overtime to build Victoria's image as a fashion icon. She leaked to the media that Asprey had asked Victoria to design a range of jewellery; that Victoria would design sunglasses; and that her 'Rock & Republic jeans have flown off the shelves'.[38] To reinvent herself as a cult, Victoria decided to copy fashion's high priestess Anna Wintour. As skinny as ever, and with the usual pout, she too adopted sunglasses as her trademark.

To reap publicity in the wider media, *Glamour* magazine's editor Jo Elvin was enticed to shower praise on Victoria. Elvin welcomed the opportunity to associate her magazine with a star. Like other editors of celebrity and fashion magazines, Elvin never troubled herself about the Beckhams' controversies. Focused on sales, she bowed to secure Victoria's face on her magazine's front cover.

The angle of the story was Victoria's '10 Style Commandments'. They included such gems as 'shop the world', cover your face with 'sunnies', and do not reveal too much flesh.[39] The article was not illustrated by any of the hundreds of photographs showing Victoria skimpily clad.

The next step was to give Victoria credibility as a fashionista. Simon Fuller hired the *Guardian* journalist Hadley Freeman to ghost-write Victoria's own fashion book. She was given a blistering six-week timetable. Fuller also negotiated to sell fragrances in Victoria's name.[40]

Unlike Elvin, few others accepted Victoria's rebranding as a fashion icon. Shaking off her past was proving difficult. The media were more interested in her marriage, her compulsive spending and her appearance. Photographers, she complained, had become her enemy. At Los Angeles airport they noticed that her breasts had become 'wonky raspberries' pointing in different directions. At the Cipriani restaurant in London they ridiculed her pink dress with 'chocolate, champagne and alcohol' emblazoned on the back. Another tipster reported that Victoria had verbally attacked a Spanish TV presenter, Ana Obregon, for seeking a relationship with Beckham. 'You're too old,' screeched Victoria, safe behind a screen of bodyguards.[41]

Disregarding the humiliation, her publicists were ordered to keep plugging away. Milloy called tabloid writers to reveal that Victoria had been on a shopping spree in New York, spending £60,000 on jewellery at Jacob & Co, including a £43,000 watch with 18-carat white diamonds. That was followed by more shopping in Paris, and then her gift of a £300,000 Rolls-Royce Phantom for David. That was a curtain-raiser for her own 32nd birthday in Madrid. For that day, the tabloids were told, Beckham had spent thousands of pounds on flowers – and had specially handpicked 32 white roses. He also paid her favourite restaurant Nobu to send food from London for 100 guests costing £200 per person.[42]

The publicists never suggested that spending so much money had created happiness. Everyone knew that both Beckhams were struggling. To control the publicity, Beckham occasionally abused photographers in the street and even ordered Brooklyn's school to blank out his son's face from the school photograph. But he continued to share with Jason Fraser the profits from photographs, including those from pictures of his children wearing Chanel and Dior sunglasses while skiing.[43] He failed to appreciate the downside of courting publicity.

Spotted buying women's underwear he was asked if they were a present for Victoria. 'They are now,' he replied angrily.[44]

CHAPTER 16

DOWNFALL

Sheltering from a rainstorm in May 2006, 300 guests were huddled under a marquee in Beckingham Palace for another pre-World Cup party. Dotted around were the feted 'Golden Generation' of England's players. Each guest had paid £2,000 for a ticket, a fundraiser for UNICEF. Beckham served warm German Liebfraumilch. The same white wine was sold by Tesco at £2.99 a bottle.[1] Cynics would later equate the warm wine, sodden garden and fetid air with the decay of the England football team.

England's fate in Germany depended on Sven-Göran Eriksson. He was standing in the marquee with Nancy Dell'Olio. Few could understand the relationship between the bed-hopping Swede and Beckham. Over the previous months the footballer's indifferent performances should have excluded him from the team, but the star-struck manager stayed loyal.

The unreality of the English team's expectations was matched by the pretensions of the fake celebrities.

Wayne Rooney's publicists told journalists that his fiancée Coleen was wearing a £200,000 necklace. Not to be outdone, Victoria's publicists revealed that she would wear a £1 million diamond necklace – loaned by Asprey. Their rivalry reflected the corrosive excesses Brand Beckham had introduced into football. Playing for England was Beckham's passion, but rather than focusing entirely on winning games, international football had become critical for sustaining his sponsorships.

Appropriately, Simon Fuller snatched at the opportunity to consolidate another victory. Thanks to a slick presentation he had wrested a four-year contract with the FA to represent the England team's commercial interests. His fortunes depended on England's success in Germany. The long-established contractor who had been ousted by

Fuller blamed his loss on Fuller's relationship with Beckham. However, Fuller's hope of a windfall was doomed. He did not realise that each player owned his own commercial rights. Even if England won the cup his profits would be limited.

Several invited guests had snubbed the Beckhams. Among those who failed to arrive were the Tory leader David Cameron, Sarah Ferguson, Princes Harry and William, Liz Hurley and Elton John.[2]

Ted Beckham was deliberately not invited. Without his son's knowledge Ted had written an illustrated book about Beckham's career. 'I was up to 4 a.m. reading it,' Ted had said. 'I'm really chuffed with it.'[3] Victoria was outraged. How could anyone dare – without her permission – to make money from their fame? Her father-in-law, primarily responsible for Beckham's success, was punished for his pride in his son. In his absence his son told his guests, 'We honestly believe that when we come back next month, we will have the World Cup with us.' The FA was already planning a victory parade. Two million people were expected by the organisers to flood London's streets.[4]

The hubris encouraged Victoria to dispense advice at her party to Arsenal's 17-year-old Theo Walcott. Chosen for the squad by Eriksson, the manager had never seen Walcott play in a Premier League match – because Walcott had never been selected for a Premier League game. 'Don't let the glamour go to your head,' Victoria told Walcott. 'Be humble.' To his teenage girlfriend Victoria said, according to her publicist, 'Glam up, look the part and ignore the gossip.'[5]

Forty thousand England fans arrived in Germany convinced by Eriksson's promise of victory. 'England is ready for glory,' said the manager. 'It's finally England's time.' Beckham agreed. He repeated what he had said two years earlier in Portugal, about the same players: 'It's the best England squad since 1966.' Heading for Frankfurt, the fans were naturally delighted that their country had been lucky with a comparatively soft draw for the first three matches.

Cosseted at the team's hotel in the Black Forest mountains, the heroes emerged on 10 June for their first match against Paraguay, who were ranked 33rd in the world. After Beckham's free kick, which led to Paraguay scoring an own goal in the third minute of the match, England failed to keep possession and they plodded to a 1–0 victory.

The team's lacklustre performance did not inhibit the team's wives and girlfriends, the WAGs. Staying in the Brenners Park, a hotel in picturesque Baden-Baden near to the players, their parties began soon after lunch by the pool.

Silver trays carrying dozens of sugar-frosted champagne flutes followed by endless spirits and beers fuelled the screeching women and their singing until they left for a nightclub to dance on tables and drink more champagne. In their imagination the WAGs would carry home the cup, probably held aloft by their own Queen Victoria. Lurking on the streets outside, the media circus sensed bacchanalian debauchery.

An army of photographers recorded the WAGs' descent on local shops, spending thousands of pounds on designer labels, shoes and sunglasses, and then returning to the hotel for manicures, facials and massages. The loud claque of bling women scouring through conservative Baden-Baden also prompted the German media to question in lurid headlines whether the WAGs were members of the human race. Initially, Victoria did not join the WAGs in the nightclubs.

Victoria had arrived by private jet from Madrid. She was spotted at the hotel's swimming pool wearing five-inch heels, her face always made up with a camera-ready look. She and her family were sitting targets for hostile journalists. A snatched photograph published by the *Bild* newspaper showed her cellulite thighs. Another German tabloid scoffed that Beckham's mother Sandra looked like a 'peasant', Beckham's sister Joanna was 'lardy', and the three Beckham children around the pool were labelled 'dwarfs'.

Britain's football writers grew uneasy. Germany's journalists had spotted that England's players were spending excessive time with the WAGs – shopping, swimming and sleeping – rather than training.

Beckham-mania took a trashing during England's second match against Trinidad and Tobago, who were ranked 91st by FIFA. Playing like a rabble, England's lions nevertheless secured a victory with two late goals, one thanks to an unseen foul. Beckham was criticised for not being visible. No one could explain why Eriksson had failed to substitute Beckham. Had the Swede, they wondered, been told by the FA that Beckham was untouchable? Eriksson's riposte fuelled their suspicions. 'I'm not married to David Beckham,' he exclaimed.[6]

As the myth of a Golden Generation crumbled, attention switched from Beckham's lacklustre performance to Victoria, who was assumed to be the leader of the pack.

Victoria was determined to assert her place in the spotlight. She could not resist the role of master of the circus. In advance of leaving the hotel, Victoria organised the WAGs to leave in order of importance. Naturally, she was last. Everyone was delayed while her make-up team and her hairdressers in the lobby completed their final tweaks. The waiting photographers needed to record 'perfection'. Her reward was sniggers in the next day's newspapers about her matchstick legs and oversized sunglasses.[7] Sol Campbell's girlfriend, Fiona Barratt, was among those irritated. Posh, Barratt fumed, was 'a nightmare, acting as a prima donna'.

While Brooklyn was allowed by his bodyguard to kick a football around the Brenners Park hotel's reception area, his mother found the pressure of living among bubbling younger women – many better looking than her – intolerable. Seeking an escape before the next match against Sweden, she flew to Canada on a turnaround trip to visit a denim manufacturer.

Victoria's relationship with Michael Ball's Rock & Republic had crashed. After she had contributed ideas and overseen a new range of denim designs, Ball had featured just one pair of Victoria's jeans in his latest Los Angeles runway show. Victoria was furious. She ended her relationship with the ego-driven businessman, who would become notorious for quipping during an economic downturn, 'Recession? I've got five girlfriends now, instead of two.' Victoria launched a $100 million lawsuit against Ball for unpaid royalties. 'We don't owe Victoria anything,' said the company's chief executive. 'This is ridiculous.' Eventually, Victoria retreated with not one penny.[8]

In the aftermath, in early 2006, she had wandered through Kitson, an expensive fashion shop in Los Angeles's Robertson Boulevard. 'This is exactly what I like,' she told Fraser Ross, the owner. Holding a pair of jeans, she asked: 'Who makes these 1921s?' The answer was Michael Silver in Winnipeg. Two weeks later, she met Silver over lunch at Los Angeles's Bel Air hotel.

Ignoring her plate of steamed vegetables, Victoria explained that she wanted Silver to manufacture her own brand of silhouette jeans under the brand name dVb. 'We don't make celebrity jeans,' replied Silver. 'We like volume.' His family-owned business made about 7 million pairs of jeans a year. 'Celebrity jeans is too limited for us. We work for profit.' Victoria would not take 'No' for an answer.

After the lunch Victoria had called Silver urging that they forge a partnership. Finally he relented.

A few samples of her ultra-skinny jeans had been made. She could have flown to Winnipeg at any time to see the samples, but chose to make the complicated trip during the World Cup. She disliked football, disliked the WAGs, and did not want to appear once again in Beckham's shadow. The media would notice her absence. Flying to the Canadian city to do a business deal, she believed, gave her credibility.

'This is not what I want,' she told Silver after a 16-hour flight. Holding a pair of specially made jeans, she listed her demands for 'art' jeans cut to suit her size. Silver listened politely and said tactfully, 'Very few have your figure. So narrow is not comfortable.' No, she replied, Hollywood stars and other fashionistas were equally thin. Elite women, she insisted, would copy her. Stubbornly, she demanded Silver make the jeans her way, for skinny women. Victoria, Silver realised, had no idea how jeans were made and certainly did not understand how to earn a profit. Making jeans just for the 'elite' was a sure recipe for losing money. Yet reluctantly he agreed with what he called the 'stick-in-the-mud'. He was persuaded by her own conviction that, like Jennifer Lopez, she was a cult personality with a huge following. Triumphant, Victoria flew back to Germany. She had missed England's third game against Sweden.

In her absence Beckham had made no contribution to England's half-time 2–0 advantage against Sweden. Immobile in the second half, he watched as England fell apart following injuries. Ninety minutes was physically too much for an ill-disciplined team, dubbed by one writer 'The Valium XI'. The manager was also unmasked. Eriksson's muddled tactics exposed his original bizarre selection. Theo Walcott was destined not to play even once in Germany. At the end, England were lucky to limit the damage to a 2–2 draw.[9]

The crisis in England's football was matched by Victoria's personal emergency. On her return to Germany she saw a photograph of herself published in Canada exposing a bald patch, possibly the result of her extreme diet. Her solution was dramatic. She immediately booked on to a Ryanair flight to Stansted. She needed a five-hour session at Connect Hair System in Chalk Farm in north London. For £1,500 a trusted specialist, Angelo Georghiou, wove in a new set of hair extensions.[10]

In her absence the WAGs had enjoyed another night of partying, with 19 bottles of champagne for the 19 WAGs as their introduction to another raucous drinking marathon ending at 4 a.m.[11] Victoria landed back in Germany just in time to watch England play against Ecuador. England needed to win to qualify for the knock-out stage.

Thirty-one million Britons were tuned in for England playing against a team ranked 23rd in the world by FIFA. They watched another soporific display. In the 60th minute, Beckham saved the day with a trademark bending free kick. His goal defied the bookies' 14–1 odds that he would not score the first goal. The fans roared after his first international goal in 15 months. And then he vomited on the pitch, a graphic sign of the high tension he was suffering. England were through to the quarter-finals against Portugal. With Beckham's strike, wrote Simon Barnes in *The Times*, 'England goes lurching on, like the clowns' car at the circus, with elliptical wheels, lopsided frame and a tendency to shed bits of itself with loud explosions and keep going.' Henry Winter praised Beckham's masterly free kick – 'a weapon some believed mothballed'.

Eriksson and Beckham faced their moment of truth one week later, on 1 July in Gelsenkirchen. 'Trust me, we'll win,' said Eriksson.[12]

Against a weak Portuguese team, England's miskicks – wide, high or into the goalkeeper's waiting arms – wasted England's opportunities. Beckham sent a free kick into the wall, leaving the keeper untroubled. Then Rooney was sent off by the Argentinian referee for an apparent stamp on defender Ricardo Carvalho. Tellingly, Beckham's disappearance in the 52nd minute because of a ruptured Achilles tendon passed largely unnoticed until the very end. After extra-time the match was a goalless draw. England faced a penalty shoot-out yet again. Eriksson's manifest failures were revealed during those fatal minutes. The team's training for that exact situation had been woeful. Eriksson's management obituary was written as England crashed out in ignominy, 1–3. 'The passive, blinking nonentity glued to the bench watched his miscast team,' reported an eyewitness.[13]

'I won't quit,' Beckham tearfully told the *News of the World*'s Dave Harrison, his obliging mouthpiece, immediately after the match.[14] But the newspaper's opinion was damning: 'Beckham's been living on borrowed time. And now his time is up. He's Dead Balls. The only person cheering in the stands was Posh.'

Beckham could no longer deny the statistics. His midfielder contemporary Frank Lampard would score 29 goals for England and 268 goals during his career. Beckham scored rather fewer, only 17 goals for England in 115 internationals despite taking most of the free kicks and penalties. He would score a club career total of 127 goals, and his total number of goals of 144 would include 65 from direct free kicks.

At the post-match press conference, Eriksson said sorry nine times for the shambles. 'It was the biggest delusion,' he admitted about his fantasy that England would win the World Cup.[15] Others were less charitable. Steven Howard in the *Sun* was outraged about the doddering catastrophe who had pocketed £25 million: 'Sven pulled wool over everyone's eyes during a feeble and uninspiring reign' leaving the 'wreckage of another major tournament disaster.' Jeff Powell of the *Daily Mail* wrote for the majority: 'The most disgracefully unprepared team in England's World Cup history was managed by a money-grabbing charlatan and captained by a narcissist so obsessed with himself that when the inevitable humiliation came he cried for himself, not his country.'[16]

The process to appoint Eriksson's successor exposed the FA executives' shortcomings. Candidates were helicoptered to a country house with blacked-out windows. The favoured candidate was Felipao ('Big Phil') Scolari, who had managed the World Cup-winning Brazil team in 2002, but he was appalled by the farce conjured up by the FA and withdrew. That left Steve McClaren, Eriksson's deputy.

Beckham took Steve McClaren's call on Monday 7 August. The message was blunt. There was no place for Beckham in McClaren's bid to rescue the team from the wilderness at the Euro 2008 Championship. Beckham was stripped of the captaincy and would not be chosen for the team. Beckham pleaded to stay to get his 100 caps. McClaren refused. Dropping Beckham, McClaren believed, made him look his own man. It would be a clean break from the Eriksson era. 'I hadn't seen it coming,' Beckham admitted afterwards. 'It was a horrible feeling, absolutely gut-wrenching. There's that helpless feeling because there's nothing you can do.'[17]

The following day Beckham's version of events changed. The world was told that Beckham had nobly chosen to resign. Oliveira described how, with Victoria giving advice on the phone, he had written his resignation speech during the night. 'I cried before and after stepping down,' Beckham would say.[18]

In this new darkest hour Beckham tearfully complained to Terry Byrne that he had been made a scapegoat. 'There was nothing wrong with my game,' he repeated. McClaren had fired him to conceal his own and Eriksson's mistakes. Byrne worked hard to keep his employer sane and out of sight.

In his more temperate moments Beckham hoped that after playing 95 games for England, and as captain 58 times, the totality of his achievement would be praised. Steven Howard was one who crushed that illusion. Beckham, he wrote, never lived up to his billing. 'At the end of the Beckham era, he ground to a halt with feet of clay that stumbled in and out of the tournament.'

As the old power in his legs began to diminish, he took penalties without the probability of scoring from them. Only the FA would miss him – and his ability to generate cash.[19] Beckham crafted his own testimony. 'The reason England didn't do very well,' he explained, 'is because they didn't play well enough.'[20] The PRs moved in to mount his defence.

'The whole family are devastated for David,' Milloy told Victoria Newton. 'Victoria is shocked and upset.'[21] Knowing that their fortune depended on him continuing to be a superstar, the Beckhams were fearful. For the moment, both were reassured by Fuller that the money would still pour in. There were the sponsorships with Pepsi, Gillette and Adidas, and Fuller had concluded a new three-year deal worth £7.5 million with Motorola. Only the £1 million Police sunglasses contract was not renewed. Beckham's voice and Mohican hairstyle lacked the sex appeal of his successor, George Clooney.[22]

In a covert move to edge Beckham away from Spain, Fuller also told Fabio Capello, Real Madrid's new manager, that the player would only sign a new three-year contract if he could keep 80 per cent of his new sponsorship deals and only with global brands. Fuller was unconcerned if that was a deal-breaker. Beckham's wealth, he believed, would be guaranteed if he headed for America.[23]

Moving to America was not Beckham's game-plan. He loved playing top-class international football and a proposed sign-up with LA Galaxy would be akin to retirement. 'The player is not ready for the England scrapheap,' Beckham told the *Sun*'s Eric Beauchamp in mid-August 2006 while he was playing for Real Madrid in America. 'Write that I will find a new lease of life fuelled by anger.' Beauchamp concluded that the 31-year-old player was determined 'to bounce back just like he always does'. Beckham, he was told, would sign a three-year contract when he returned to Madrid.[24]

A familiar conundrum about Beckham resurfaced. The world was divided about his ability. Some, especially the nostalgists, classed him as an outstanding player, others as a talented chancer. Amid the hope and despair of England fans his value was fiercely debated. The unflinching realist was Fabio Capello.

Returning late once again to Madrid from London – he was fined £1,500 by the club – his reception from Capello was cool. Known to be a hard taskmaster, Capello had told a player, 'I'd kick you in the arse if I didn't know how much you'd enjoy it.' Like Ferguson, Capello recognised that Beckham was mentally and physically unfit. Caught up in marital problems, endless sponsorship photoshoots, and depressed by his ostracism from England's team, Beckham was now something of a liability on the pitch. Just as he had struggled to play for England, he could not keep pace at Real Madrid. Not only did the club reject Fuller's contractual demands but Capello also left Beckham on the bench for six consecutive games – and the manager refused to guarantee selecting him again.

'Every day I feel sad and frustrated,' Beckham admitted, 'not playing for my club or country.'[25] Although he blamed his poor game on the constant change of the club's managers and chairmen, moving home three times and the paparazzi hounding himself and his children, no one sympathised with a player who had boasted that his celebrity life never interfered with his game.[26]

'I feel unhappy every day,' he repeated. When asked by his sons why he wasn't playing, he was evasive. 'I want to spend more time with you.'[27]

Beckham, Capello agreed, was suffering psychologically from being dropped. To put pressure on Capello, Eric Beauchamp was encouraged by Beckham's publicist to write that Beckham could leave Real Madrid as a free agent at the end of the season and move to LA Galaxy.[28] But at that moment Victoria told British television viewers that 'David is happy with his football in Madrid.'[29] Her own fate, she knew, depended on Fuller's plans in America.

Walking down London's Bond Street on her new six-inch heels and with an open blouse, 32-year-old Victoria was anxious to be photographed despite saying, 'I look in the mirror and hate the way I look. I've got no bum at all. Saggy skin on my stomach. I look really awful naked.'[30] It was time, she decided, to visit Madrid's leading plastic surgeon, Dr José Maria Diaz Torres.

Despite his work, she still seemed dissatisfied and even confused. To one person she said, 'Do I wish I could be anonymous? Of course. I don't need to feed my ego that way anymore.' And told another, 'Neither David nor I have allowed ourselves to be carried away by our fame. I sincerely believe we are authentic and genuine people.' And to a third interviewer, she said she didn't like being photographed.[31] 'When I got married,' she told a Spanish magazine, 'I stopped singing in order to be a mother.'[32] She forgot that to promote her singing career in 2003 she had left her children in London and her husband in Madrid and flown to New York. Self-awareness was not Victoria's strength. Her answers also begged the question whether she understood ordinary, 'authentic and genuine' people.

Her life in Madrid was lonely and unhappy. Although she had everything money could buy she was isolated. With few friends, she was unwilling to learn Spanish. Her diet, rigorous exercise and chain-smoking reflected her anxieties. The scars of Beckham's affairs were raw. Even in front of her at celebrity dinners he acted flirtatiously, and rubbed the backs of beautiful women. 'He's always trying it on,' a 'friend' reported. One actress noticed that despite Victoria draping herself over him during a dinner, Beckham's eyes were fixed on her. To the actress's surprise, when she emerged from a lavatory cubicle Beckham was standing there. She brushed him aside.

Victoria railed that the tabloids always mentioned his affairs, but never even hinted that she was desirable to another man. Fame as a Spice Girl had made her happy, yet now she was famous only for being skinny and someone's wife. She could not win.

In her competition with Beckham to be on the tabloids' front pages, her publicist had called the *Mirror*'s news desk. 'Send a snapper to Notting Hill Gate,' Milloy said. 'Vic has a new look.' Fifteen minutes later she called again. 'Where is he?' Milloy asked angrily. 'Victoria's getting impatient.' She made the front page with her hair restyled as a bob. Some whispered that the new look was organised to distract from her latest nose job.

Victoria's relaxation was endless shopping at Prada, Gucci, Versace and every other luxury boutique, usually alone. As a reward for wearing their clothes, Gucci gave her a 30 per cent discount.[33] Back home she gazed at the clothes in her cupboards, many delivered by Net-a-Porter. Despite Milloy repeating that 'Victoria's family mean absolutely everything to her,' she had nannies and her parents to help while she rattled around her house.[34] The only person offering her an escape and a future was Fuller.

Thanks to him she launched 'Intimately', her own brand of fragrance manufactured by Coty. Featuring a photoshopped picture of herself pouting, she stood beside a sultry Beckham promoting 'Instinct', his aftershave. Both assumed the launch in Venice was successful, but they were decisively beaten by competitors. 'Everyone loves Kylie's "Darling" fragrance,' said Superdrug's buyer in New York.[35] Victoria would inaccurately claim that their co-operation with Coty was 'one of the first-ever celebrity fragrances'.[36]

Her mistakes were encouraged by Fuller. He also suggested that Victoria had received 'dozens of offers from US networks over the past two years'. He embellished the make-believe by describing his client as 'a fashion expert now who, when she walks into a room in the fashion world, knows as much if not more than anyone'. She was about to star, Fuller said, in her own American fashion reality show.[37] If the show was produced, it has now disappeared.

In reality she had only just entered the fashion business. With Fuller's help she had met Marc Jacobs, an adored New York designer. At his fashion show she had modelled three of his outfits in three hours.[38] Fashion queen Anna Wintour approved of size 6 Victoria. Her self-mockery won Wintour's approval, but subject to her accepting some firm advice. Boob jobs and hotpants were definitely Essex and not East Side. To rebrand her image, her breast implants needed to be fixed.

'I'm done with music,' she said. 'I'm not a WAG.' Fashion would be her new career. 'I've always been the girl next door who got lucky,' she laughed, but she knew that success was difficult. Becoming 'Lady Beckham', she admitted, would be 'fabulous'.[39]

To establish Victoria as a fashion expert, the book ghosted by Hadley Freeman titled *That Extra Half an Inch* was launched by

Victoria at Selfridges. Everyone assumed that Victoria had not read her 'own' book before publication. Indeed, to give Victoria – who had never been known to read a serious book – an idea of the requirements, a reader had been hired to recite, page by page, a published fashion book to her. But the result was successful. Eight hundred books were sold in the store on the first day and thousands more during her nine-day promotion tour across Britain.[40]

Her inspiration, she explained, were three women: Grace Kelly, Jackie Kennedy and Audrey Hepburn. Yet none of them were fashion designers. It was their elegance she admired.

Victoria could not understand that original design is the product of a deep understanding of the modern era. Aspiring designers closely study Coco Chanel, Karl Lagerfeld, Christian Dior and dozens of other giants of fashion. Their emotional intelligence, fed by intellectual curiosity, anticipated how they could shape the future consciousness of women. While Chanel and Lagerfeld's originality produced emotional resonance and distinctive styles inspired by the study of fashion textbooks, Victoria's vision was limited by her own taste. She could not imagine anything beyond her own horizon. 'I don't want to copy anything that anyone is doing,' she said. 'I want to be true to me and very organic.'[41]

Those flaws were irrelevant to Fuller. His priority was to keep the Beckhams together. Launching Victoria's new career served that purpose. Organising her workshop, said Fuller, would only happen once the family moved to America.

Encouraged by Fuller, Victoria flew in early December to Los Angeles. Newspapers were told that she was 'house-hunting'. On her return to London she was 'seen' one afternoon at Claridge's sharing eight bottles of Krug champagne with a group of women. Before dinner a *Sun* photographer snapped her stumbling out of the hotel into her chauffeured car and driven to Sawbridgeworth.[42]

Fuller had sent a message to Real Madrid. The Beckhams would be a lot better off in America.

CHAPTER 17

SALVAGE

'This is the worst time in my career – but I will tough it out,' Beckham admitted while Victoria was on another trip to Los Angeles. Left on the bench for most of the season, he played in seven of the last 25 matches. He had failed to regain Capello's confidence. 'Thinking I'd never play for Madrid again was hurting me a lot,' he admitted. 'I'm working hard and I'll be back.' Although he did score from a free kick against Seville, that was not enough.[1]

One of the happier interludes was flying to Rome for Tom Cruise's wedding to Katie Holmes. The 150 guests included Brooke Shields, Jennifer Lopez and Will Smith. Although Beckham had a knee injury and would be unable to play that weekend, Capello insisted that he return to Madrid for the Saturday match. After enjoying the combined stag and hen party at the Villa Aureli, he flew to Madrid, leaving Victoria to enjoy the wedding in the 15th-century Odescalchi Castle in Bracciano. Thousands of spectators watched the celebrities arrive, including Victoria who was wearing a revealing black Valentino dress. At the end of the Scientology ceremony, there were few refreshments. Some guests returned to Rome unexpectedly hungry. Pizzas were delivered to their hotel rooms. On reflection most realised that since Cruise's best man was the Scientology leader David Miscavige, the wedding had been a publicity stunt for the cult.[2]

Tom Cruise was naturally attracted to Beckham. Not only because of his outstanding looks, but because he too enjoyed fast cars and motorbikes. Some also believed that Cruise's friendship was an attempt to entice Beckham's support for Scientology. Getting Victoria to pose for a photographer in a Los Angeles shop 'reading' the Scientologist's book *Assists for Illnesses and Injuries* was astute. Cruise's error was to misunderstand the Beckhams' attitude towards money. The Church of Scientology expected devotees to hand over a large slice of their income and assets – and the Beckhams clung on to theirs. Beckham's generosity did, however, extend to giving each member of the team in the Real Madrid dressing room a bottle of 'Instinct', his latest aftershave. The reaction was not uniformly euphoric.[3]

Over Christmas, Fuller pressed the case to Beckham to transfer to LA Galaxy when his Real Madrid contract expired in the summer of 2007. The deciding argument in Beckham's mind was his exclusion from both the England and Real Madrid teams. The inevitable consequence, said Fuller, would be for Beckham's brand to lose impact. And Victoria's image would suffer unless she shed her reputation as a WAG. For the sake of the Beckham brand, urged Fuller, both needed to rebuild their careers in Los Angeles. The Beckhams' saviour, said Fuller, would be Philip Anschutz, one of America's richest investors.

As the godfather of Major League Soccer (MLS), Anschutz was passionately dedicated to developing football as a significant sport in America. Signing Beckham for the Galaxy, he believed, would be a turning point. To secure the world's most famous footballer to play in the MLS, Anschutz was prepared to change the rules, spend a fortune and break the MLS's financial restrictions.

As the rumour mill leaked that Beckham was considering a switch to America, English football managers and pundits bewailed his plan. Moving to a footballers' retirement home, they chanted, would be the beginning of the end for the 32 year old. Why, they asked, would he head for a backwater rather than finish his career at the top? By playing lower-grade football he would permanently exclude himself from England's team. Several Premier League clubs including Spurs and West Ham offered him a transfer.

Fuller again argued his case. Going to America, he repeated, would not only increase sponsorship deals. The tax arrangements would also be beneficial. Living in America, Beckham could continue his non-dom status in Britain and pay even less tax than in Spain. With his keen interest in money, Beckham had good reason to reject all the offers from Premier League clubs. There were no European offers. 'We are simply not interested in Beckham,' said an Inter Milan executive.[4]

During the first days of January 2007, as the deadline for Beckham to start unilateral transfer negotiations officially passed, Real Madrid's sporting director Predrag Mijatović said that Beckham's agents had not approached him. A two-year contract was available, but he could not keep 80 per cent of his sponsorship deals. Mijatović appeared to dismiss Real Madrid's $1.2 billion windfall from additional merchandise sales that were partly thanks to Beckham.[5] After meeting Beckham's adviser Terry Byrne on 10 January, Mijatović announced on television that Beckham's contract with Real Madrid would not be renewed. In the summer he would be axed.[6] The following day, Beckham signed with LA Galaxy.

Huge billboards sprang up across America announcing Beckham's arrival. Basking in his own spotlight, Fuller unveiled what he described as an astonishing deal. Besides a weekly salary of £100,000 for five years, the footballer would keep 100 per cent of his annual commercial endorsements, worth at least £17 million, plus performance bonuses, a share of all the club's merchandising and TV deals, and a cut of the ticket sales. The least Beckham would earn over five years, Fuller said, was $250 million (£128 million) but it was more likely to be $500 million (£250 million). Infinitely more than Real Madrid had offered. 'I always wanted to create history with the biggest sports deal ever,' said Fuller, 'and David Beckham is the only athlete in the world who could have made this happen.' Except that the deal had not been negotiated solely by Fuller but largely by Jeff Frasco, a 'pit bull' at Creative Artists Agency (CAA).

The actual deal was worth substantially less for Beckham. His contract with LA Galaxy was worth $32.5 million (£17 million) over five years – $6.5 million (£3.25 million) per annum. He would also earn commissions from tickets and shirts. Irrefutably he was the world's best-paid footballer, but even he would be stretched to earn £128 million ($250 million) over five years.[7]

Beckham's publicists devised the narrative for him. 'People will say I'm only going out there for the money, but I'm not,' said Beckham. 'I have to move on. I need another challenge. I'm going to play football and make a difference.' Few were convinced. The only reason for a celebrity not to play among Europe's giants would be money. Long conversations with Victoria about the wonders of Hollywood, and with Tom Cruise – who also believed in reincarnation – resolved any doubts.

The 'obituaries' about Beckham's career were unsentimental. In the *Mirror*, Oliver Holt gave credit to a poser who had changed the image of footballers and of men. But in his declining years, wrote Holt, he had lost his supremacy as the best crosser of the ball and the best taker of a free kick: 'Those days are gone now. His England career is over.' The statistics of his demise were stark: from Manchester United's Theatre of Dreams, capacity 74,000, and Bernabéu's 81,000, he was heading to LA Galaxy's Home Depot with a 27,000 capacity.[8]

Real Madrid's fans were not sad. Beckham was written off as a failure on the pitch, though good for autographs and selfies. In the club's boardroom there was anger that Fuller had started negotiations with LA Galaxy before the legal date. Beckham, they griped, had been similarly untrustworthy.[9] The unresolved question was his fate during the last six months of his contract. LA Galaxy was expecting him in April, two months before his Madrid contract expired.

'He'll never play for me again,' said manager Fabio Capello. 'He will rot on the stands for the rest of the season.' After refusing to speak to Beckham the Italian wanted him out as fast as possible. 'He's a free-kick flop,' he sniped.[10] The club's president Ramon Calderon joined in. Branding Beckham 'second rate' he swore that at the 'end of his football career' he would leave without any ceremony or thanks. Eric Beauchamp's reports of those damnations annoyed Simon Oliveira. 'We're disappointed in you,' he told the journalist.

Beckham refused to leave unless Real Madrid paid his remaining £2 million salary plus £3 million in bonuses. Furious about his portrayal as a shabby money-grabber he claimed that he wanted to win a trophy before he left.[11] Calderon didn't believe a word. Beckham, he said, was 'just another average cinema actor living in Hollywood,' only good for Real Madrid selling 2 million shirts in his first season.[12] After all, which other footballer would summon his sister on the phone during an awards ceremony in London to come immediately and do his hair, which looked 'too flat'?[13] 'You are liars,' Beckham snapped back at the Spanish critics. 'You have shown me a lack of respect.' That was Beckham's fallback. Critics were unfair. 'My confidence was knocked out of me,' he complained about the hurt.[14]

Calderon's irritation was reignited by the frenzy in Los Angeles as Victoria arrived the day after Beckham signed the contract. Galaxy's publicists went into overdrive about the stars – including Tom Cruise, Steven Spielberg, Rod Stewart and Jennifer Lopez – who had bought tickets for the next season's games. They all paid £50 a ticket instead of the normal £20. Simultaneously, Victoria's publicists described her house-hunting protected by three armed bodyguards, and listed a packed diary to meet Hollywood's celebrities.[15] And then she rushed back to Europe.

Loving the positive publicity, Victoria posed with Katie Holmes at a fashion show in Paris – on her way, she said, to meet Karl Lagerfeld and executives from Coty, the manufacturer of her fragrance. 'Posh looked a million dollars as she left her hotel,' reported the *Sun*.[16] Jason Fraser shot the photographs. He had previously supplied pictures of Beckham on his bike, the Beckhams at Silverstone before the annual Formula One race, and Posh wearing a range of stand-out clothes. Fraser's photos were a testimony to the Beckhams' appetite for publicity. Everyone knew that the intellectual workaholic and bibliophile Karl Lagerfeld was charming to those who posed no threat.

Impatient to leave Madrid, Victoria dreamed of California restoring her self-esteem. 'We can leave the negative stuff from four years in Spain behind,' she said.[17] She did not care about the cynics who wrote, 'He was dragged to La La Land by his starry-eyed wife who wanted to rub shoulders with the Hollywood A-listers and kick-start her career.'[18]

To prove Victoria's value, Fuller had secured a $10 million contract with NBC for a television series about her. 'This show is really something different,' she predicted. 'I think it's going to surprise a lot of people.'[19] The only frustration was David's delayed departure from Madrid.

Soft-spoken, apparently sweet-natured and sensitive, Beckham challenged his critics at Real Madrid to demonise him as a lame duck. His stubborn self-discipline, and avoidance of a slanging match, overcame Capello's anger. Under pressure after poor results, Capello was forced on 10 February to bring back Beckham against Real Sociedad. With one of his classic free kicks Beckham scored, giving Real Madrid a 2–1 victory.[20]

Ten days later he set up the three goals in Real Madrid's 3–2 victory against Bayern Munich. Capello and others were puzzled. Were his targeted long-range free kicks a freak, or a result of natural brilliance? Either way, his place in the team was restored.

At the same time, Steve McClaren's veto of Beckham was fraying. After England's 0–2 defeat by Croatia in October 2006, the team was damned by the *Sun* as 'a bunch of drunks, yobs and lazy wasters parading as professional English footballers'. The 'appalling' second-raters earning £100,000 a week had 'gone catastrophically off the rails'. Picking on John Terry and Rio Ferdinand in particular, the newspaper declared that 'If these players showed more pride in their work and less pride in getting hammered and showing off to tarts, there might be some excuse for their surrender in Croatia.'[21]

In early February 2007, after England had lost four games and scored just one goal, they were in danger of failing to qualify for the Euro 2008 tournament. McClaren was classified across the media as 'a useless manager'. Ahead of the decisive match against Israel, McClaren was desperate. In the national debate, even Tony Blair in the dying days of his premiership advised the manager to recall Beckham. Not wanting to look weak, McClaren hesitated. First, he said he 'had no plans' to watch Beckham, but then he watched the tapes of Beckham playing against Bayern Munich. Finally, he decided to watch Beckham play in three more games before he had to make a decision. In the interim, Beckham summoned the *Sun*'s Neil Custis.

'People think my England career is over. I want to show it isn't. When people doubt me, I want to prove them wrong. I've got three or four years playing at a high level. There's a disappointment every time a squad is announced and I'm not picked.'[22]

At the end of March, England beat Andorra 3–0. FIFA ranked Andorra 175th in the world. Embarrassed by the inadequate score-line, McClaren fled his press conference 115 seconds after arriving. Soon afterwards, England drew with Israel, who were ranked 28th by FIFA. England were ranked 11th.

At the end of May, ten months after dropping Beckham, McClaren faced a make-or-break Euros match against Estonia, ranked 100th by FIFA. He would be fired if England lost. The manager decided to save his neck – Beckham was recalled. 'This isn't a panic measure,' said McClaren. Asked to justify his somersault, he replied: 'To help me win the game – end of story.'[23]

'If Steve McClaren genuinely believes his England team are incapable of winning against Estonia without David Beckham,' commented columnist Martin Samuel, 'only one conclusion remains: he is not the man for the job.' By 'opening the door to the past,' McClaren had taken a 'panicky, short-term move to end them all'.[24]

Oliver Holt, a fierce critic of Beckham four months earlier, dramatically changed his tune once again. Beckham, he wrote, has 'the habit of confounding the cynicism of others'. After watching Beckham's outstanding performance for Real Madrid against Deportivo La Coruna, Holt declared that 'his passing was breathtaking' and that he had contributed to Real Madrid's 3–1 victory. It was 'absurd, laughable', Holt urged, not to admit that Beckham deserved to be recalled. Shambolic England needed his class and experience. Holt ignored the Beckham efforts that had missed two goal opportunities.[25]

Holt's flip-flop, his rivals suspected, had been influenced by his editor, Piers Morgan. The Beckhams' move to Hollywood had galvanised Morgan to challenge the *Sun*'s close relationship with the couple. Eager to get the Beckhams onside, Morgan plotted further changes.

Beckham's 25-yard free kick during an England 'friendly' against Brazil justified Morgan and McClaren's support. Performing his trademark wipe of his hands on the back of his shorts, Beckham looked at the Brazilian wall and sent over a dangerous cross to John Terry, who headed the ball in. 'I brought Beckham back to get us winning matches,' said McClaren, thankful for the nostalgic cheers at Wembley when Beckham's name was mentioned. 'It gave me goosebumps,' said Beckham. 'I was very close to tears.'[26] The recall was a glorious vindication. He felt enormous pride that he had proved everyone wrong.

Victoria didn't wait to see the tears. At the end of the match, after checking her manicure, she dashed straight to Heathrow. She was presenting the MTV movie awards in Los Angeles. She would quickly return to London to be Jo Elvin's guest of honour at *Glamour*'s Women of the Year awards. The imminent move to America had electrified her own relationship with the tabloids.[27]

The trick to beat the *Sun* and win access to the Beckhams, was to publish only fawning reports. Piers Morgan had sent Caroline Hedley to Los Angeles to ingratiate herself with Victoria.

Hedley kicked off by glorifying Victoria. 'Her fashion projects are going great guns in Europe,' she quoted publicists Milloy and Lewis. Victoria's shoes and handbags, Hedley predicted, would soon be selling across America. 'Victoria's A-list pals,' she added, 'will be seen wearing her designs.' Hedley's report was as imaginative as the *Sunday Mirror*'s report of Victoria's 'huge' sales of fragrance and sunglasses in Canada, and claims that her branded accessories in Japan had become 'very, very successful very quickly' and 'very, very lucrative'. Hedley's hype was unswerving: 'To have landed such a major US deal before she and her family have even moved here is amazing.'[28]

Victoria's 'major US deal' was Michael Silver's manufacture of her branded dVb jeans in Winnipeg. Seduced by Victoria's celebrity, Silver had overcome his better judgement. After a series of arguments with Victoria, 200,000 skinny jeans, priced at $250 were being distributed in America, Britain and Japan. Silver's reputation secured their prominence in America's best shops. Success depended on celebrities and American fashionistas wanting to be dressed like Victoria. Silver relied on Victoria's self-promotion. Getting her name plastered across the media was essential.

Mixing with Hollywood's royalty was Victoria's dream. To please her the *Mirror* puffed an appearance wearing $1 million of diamonds at Elton John's Oscar party. 'She looks every inch as if she was made for Hollywood,' gushed Hedley. Welcomed by the elite – Madonna, Meryl Streep, Nicole Kidman, John Travolta and Daniel Craig – Victoria was 'nervous but turned heads'. Thrilled when Tom Hanks welcomed her and said he would buy a ticket for LA Galaxy, Victoria chortled, 'He knows who I am.'[29] Name-dropping bestowed credibility on herself, she believed. 'Penelope's such a sweetie, a real girl's girl,' she mentioned after playing dominoes with Penelope Cruz.

Advised that self-denigration and downplaying her celebrity won sympathy, she said, 'I don't get out much, really. I'm usually with David and the boys. The children aren't spoiled. We live a relatively simple life at home.' She knew that mentioning her husband guaranteed more attention. So she admitted that she cried uncontrollably when he was away from home. But when he returned they spent their evenings watching TV reality shows. They especially liked *Prison Break*.[30] Any gimmick, peddled through Milloy, was usually guaranteed to get free publicity.

On the eve of returning to London she told Hedley that her London hair stylist Ben Cooke had been flown to Los Angeles to make her a blonde to 'drive David wild'.[31] As she stepped from the plane at Heathrow she called Victoria Newton to reveal again that her hair was indeed blonde, that she had crossed the Atlantic with Spiderman Tobey Maguire and she would be relaunching her fragrances. One hour later she was panicking. Virgin Atlantic had lost all her luggage. Left in the rain in New York her clothes were ruined by the water. 'Victoria is absolutely gutted,' Milloy confirmed.[32]

The stress was worse because, as she reported in her running commentary, finding a home in Los Angeles was a 'nightmare' aggravated by the 'bloody hard' search for schools. On each school visit, 'I had to promise to make cupcakes, paint the new playing field and lunch with the mothers. I was on trial.'[33] One of her few successes was a contrived snap of her reading *Skinny Bitch*, a 'tough-love guide for savvy girls', at a fashion show. The book shot up the Amazon charts from 77,939 to 209.[34] Her own good fortune was that Beckham now seemed to be focused on his career rather than other women.

As a surprise 33rd birthday present Beckham had flown Victoria on a private jet to Paris. Their suite at the Ritz was filled with roses. Throughout the day he bought her designer clothes and Louboutin shoes to add to the 200 pairs already in her cupboards at home.[35] Finally, she was on a roll.

From Paris she flew to New York to launch her dVb jeans in Saks Fifth Avenue. Wearing a white pair of jeans with a large star stitched to the back pocket, she beamed towards an army of photographers, cameramen and journalists. Dozens of fans waited to buy signed copies of her fashion book. Naturally, she ignored the experts' carping: 'I think it's easy for these celebs to launch their own labels, which ride comfortably on the strength of their popularity. However, the real test comes within a year of the launch when the publicity dies down a little and the jeans have to perform.' Frank Griffin of the paparazzi agency Bauer-Griffin was blunter: 'The trouble is, nobody gives a bollocks. She's not going to be afforded the celebrity status she thinks she deserves. She'll be torn apart.'[36]

Dissenting voices were irrelevant to the Beckhams. They were back. He too was basking in a rebirth.

Three days after the Brazil match, Beckham produced two perfect crosses for goals in England's 3–0 victory against Estonia. 'I believe I can play for many, many years to come,' he said.[37] Beating Estonia relieved the pressure on McClaren, although his team was identical to that which had left Germany in disgrace during the World Cup.

Beckham returned to Madrid with an ankle injury sustained during the Estonia match. He found Fabio Capello facing a dilemma. On the eve of the decisive match against Real Mallorca to win La Liga, the Spanish league, which had not been won by Real Madrid since 2003, he needed a good midfielder. He selected Beckham for the final game. Until then, Capello had not explained his negative attitude towards Beckham. But after the Estonian match he admitted, 'It's a real pity we allowed Beckham to leave. We made a mistake.' His regret was echoed by Predrag Mijatović: 'We made a mistake not negotiating with Beckham the two-year extension.'[38]

The atmosphere at the match on 17 June was electric. The stakes on Real Madrid winning against Real Mallorca and beating Barcelona to the title were stratospherically high. Tom Cruise was in the stands with 81,000 fans when Beckham came on to the pitch. Against all the odds he was starting in Real Madrid's most critical match. But his free kick hit the post and his passes were wasted. After three injections in his left ankle he was substituted for José Antonio Reyes. Only 24 minutes of the match – a 1–1 draw – remained. Watching from the bench, Beckham saw Reyes score the two decisive goals, the second 'an absolute screamer'.

The British media hailed Beckham for defying expectations, but he had contributed almost nothing towards the 3–1 victory. On an extraordinary day he had played for the winning team without caring that the damage to his ankle had got worse. Ecstatic at the end of the match, he returned with a photographer to the pitch in the empty stadium. Wrapped in the flag of St George he emotionally kissed the turf. 'It's been the toughest season of my career, on and off the field,' he said. 'I've gone through things I never thought possible.'[39]

He had scored 20 goals in 158 matches for Real Madrid. During the same period, Brazil's Ronaldo – admittedly a striker – had scored 104 goals in 177 games.

José Sánchez, Real Madrid's former president, didn't count the goals. His pleasure was that Beckham had generated about £315 million to the sales of merchandise. Paying him a £270,000 bonus for winning La Liga was chickenfeed. Sánchez did not host a farewell party for Beckham. That was left to a handful of players at Los

Molinos, a restaurant outside Madrid. 'You'll Never Walk Alone' was iced on a chocolate cake. Tearfully he told them, 'I'll never forget you.'

That sentiment irritated Victoria. Getting out of Madrid was her salvation. She did not care about the unexpected twists that had revived his career for Madrid and England.[40] Although Beckham repeatedly said during those days that he could have played for three more seasons at Real Madrid – and that was most unlikely – he had no serious regrets about leaving for America. The money promised by Fuller eclipsed any emotions. So long as he maintained his global profile and continued playing for England, he could reap the tax benefits and much more in sponsorships.

'Travelling from Los Angeles is not going to be a problem,' he said about rejoining the England squad. He would have to fly across the Atlantic on commercial flights. The reality was harsh. By playing in America and Europe over the following three months he was committed to 115 hours in the air covering 57,678 miles. The damaging effect on his body, especially his ankle, muscles and tendons, was inevitable. 'I'm top fitness,' he said.[41] Many were not convinced, either about his physical fitness or by his ability to persuade Americans to fall in love with professional soccer.

Fuller was unconcerned by suggestions that Beckham was privately having second thoughts about the move to Los Angeles. He had scored a double-whammy. During a meeting with all five Spice Girls in his Sussex home, he outlined his plan for a revival tour. Persuading them to relaunch their careers had required astute diplomacy. Since their break-up, all five had argued. But now they succumbed to his flattery. The world, he said, had forgotten their triumph. All five, he continued, deserved applause for changing the pop scene – a revolution that broke down barriers. Now was the moment to overcome their feuds, not least to resolve their personal problems.

Needy Geri, plagued by eating disorders and loneliness, was going nowhere despite hit singles in 1999 and 2001. Mel B's last album had sold just 670 copies in its first week, reaching number 453 in the charts. Initially, Mel C had done much better solo, and yet her recent single had crashed. Baby Spice had carefully saved her earnings, but her third album had bombed. And, as everyone knew, Posh's bid for solo stardom had crashed too. She wanted to restore her own celebrity rather than just be Beckham's wife.[42]

As well as guaranteeing them renewed fame, Fuller lured them with money. Each was promised £10 million. 'But do not talk about the money,' Fuller told the women. His advice was ignored.[43] Their 11-date world tour would start in December. The five were publicly reunited over breakfast at the Four Seasons hotel in Docklands. Fuller gave each girl a necklace, and Geri gave them a gold ring.

Fuller's success had been recognised at Beckham's 32nd birthday party at London's Cipriani restaurant. Beckham thanked Fuller for introducing him to Victoria and he thanked her for an 'incredible day'. All the Spice Girls turned up. Determined to disprove the cynics that the Spice Women – all over-thirty mums with boob jobs – should not be renamed The Geriatrics, they drunkenly danced on the tables through the night. 'It's a bit like being divorced and getting back together with our ex,' joked Victoria.[44]

At the end of June, Fuller choreographed over 400 journalists to the official launch at the Dome in Greenwich. The master of publicity claimed that 2 million fans had registered to see the shows and 14 more venues would be added to the tour.[45]

'I just want my kids to see me up on stage,' Victoria told the world, 'because it's always been Daddy who has been the hero.'

She was unaware of her image. Weighing less than eight stone, Brazil-nut body butter covered her skin with a fake-tan. She was dressed in a corset. The effect, a *Mirror* cynic wrote, was her 'eye-catching bazookas'.[46] She would be back on stage performing. Irresistible. Bliss to be the centre of attention.

For David Beckham, money was at the heart of his departure from Spain. The move to America provoked some unusual activity by his auditors, Lakin Rose. The Beckhams' business needed to be realigned to reap the financial advantages.

In the previous year, 2005/6, Footwork had paid Beckham £19 million plus £6 million from Real Madrid and his income from Brand Beckham.[47] But during the year he left Spain, 2006/7, the auditors approved accounts showing that Beckham had earned no income. Yet Footwork's turnover was £11.1 million and Brand Beckham had earned £5.1 million gross profits. While the auditors recorded £10.1 million as Brand Beckham's income, a £13.3 million 'operating charge' wiped it out. Seemingly for tax reasons, he took a one-year loan of £5 million.

Accordingly, Beckham's British company earned nothing in 2006/7 and he paid no British tax on his UK income. What income and tax was paid in Spain cannot at this time be established. It is unclear whether he paid any Spanish taxes, since his Spanish company was closed down after he stopped playing there. But the sale of their house La Moraleja was postponed. Property prices in Spain had crashed. The sale for $5.2 million would not be finalised until eight years later. There were other hiccups.

After Beckham had played poorly in the Euro 2008 tournament and been dropped as England's captain, Gillette ruled against renewing the same contract. In what a Gillette executive called 'a pretty short conversation', Beckham was offered to share the spotlight in 'The Champions Campaign' with Thierry Henry, Tiger Woods and Roger Federer. Fuller refused and demanded a new profit-sharing deal. 'Dream on,' replied the Gillette executive.[48]

That still left Beckham with Pepsi, Motorola, Volkswagen and Adidas, and the hope of finding new sponsors. Fuller's next introduction was risky.

In 2007, Beckham became associated with two wealthy social-climbing Norwegian brothers, Geir and Torben Frantzen. Both had arrived in London to make their fortunes. Geir, already labelled by the tabloids as a jet-setting playboy, had latched on to Sarah Ferguson, the Duchess of York. In 2005 he bought her a Bentley Continental for £150,000. 'She's simply a family friend,' explained Ferguson's spokeswoman while she dated Torben.

In 2006, Geir Frantzen had invested $8 million with others in Hartmoor, a New York company principally owned by Ferguson. Hartmoor's purpose was to turn the Duchess into a household brand by licensing her name across products ranging from dietaries and clothing to monogrammed candles and jewellery. Her earnings from television appearances, speaking events and books would also be channelled into Hartmoor. By mid-2007 the company was sinking. With huge overheads, little income and large debts, it was wound up. Ferguson plunged towards the brink of bankruptcy. Short of cash, she would eventually sell the Bentley.[49]

Despite that dubious legacy Beckham became involved with the Frantzens. Geir had bought Findus, the fish fingers manufacturer. To get close to Beckham, Geir had also become a sponsor of Beckham's football academy in Greenwich. Separately, he asked Beckham to promote Findus's fish fingers and a new Omega-3 supplement to improve the diet of young footballers. To avoid British tax, Omega-3 was registered by Frantzen in Guernsey.[50] Their agreement was negotiated by Fuller's team assisted by Rogers & Cowan, a Los Angeles publicity agency appointed by Fuller.

Under the slogan 'Success on a plate for you', Frantzen's first £2 million video campaign showed Beckham playing football with children in Hawaii. The promotion linked Beckham with Findus's range of 12 healthy meals and the company's investment in community sports and team kits.[51] As a child, announced the advertisers, Beckham had eaten fish fingers. That was disputable. Neither Beckham nor his mother had ever mentioned him eating that particular food.

Beckham's relationship with Geir Frantzen quickly became fraught. Sales of fish fingers were falling and Findus hit financial difficulties. During a Findus promotional trip to Grimsby Town football club, Beckham was dissatisfied with the entire arrangements. 'Next time I'll read the small print,' he said, referring to the contract. While the owners of Omega-3 boasted that 'the product has exceeded all expectations in its first six weeks', sales of Findus and Omega-3 were struggling and the company debts were growing towards £700 million.

At the same time as Geir began negotiating to sell his interest, and Beckham was attracted to the lifestyle offered by the playboy brothers,[52] Fuller was focused on the Beckhams' new careers.

CHAPTER 18

PHONY

'They need to arrive in Los Angeles like stars,' ordered Simon Fuller. 'We have to create a special moment in time. Like a Big Bang to capture the town.'

In Fuller's publicity, Beckham's $32.5 million five-year contract with LA Galaxy was escalated to be worth $250 million. 'I always wanted to create history,' said Fuller, 'with the biggest sports deal ever.' Laying the foundations for the big moment had started before the Beckhams arrived.

In a quarry a hundred kilometres from Madrid, Victoria was bursting to make herself look breathtakingly sexy. Dignity was junked and excess was exaggerated. 'I was quite shy and reserved,' she once said. Not anymore.[1]

Scantily dressed and oiled up, and wearing high leather boots, she was lying – in some shots with her enhanced breasts spilling out and her legs open – on the bonnet of a 1980s Oldsmobile. Towering over her, bare-chested David Beckham's muscles glinted with thick oil. The metrosexual gay icon was ready for action. 'We like to lock the doors and wander around naked,' Beckham had said.[2] The image of narcissistic celebrities always ready to experiment was critical to Fuller's launch of the Beckhams before they arrived in the Galaxy's stadium.

The couple were being photographed for *W*, a magazine popular in Hollywood and Manhattan. Curiously, at the same time Beckham told a journalist, 'It's important to have as normal a life as possible because mine and Victoria's are so blown up.'[3] Simon Oliveira had negotiated not only the *W* cover story, but also a major feature in *Sports Illustrated*. Football rarely featured in America's biggest sports magazine with its 3.1 million circulation. The headline was, 'David Beckham: Will He Change the Fate of American Soccer'. This was the first time an MLS footballer had appeared on the magazine's cover.

Oliveira congratulated himself on achieving that coup. In addition, Fuller had negotiated with the TV sports channel ESPN a $4.5 million payment to produce a TV documentary called *New Beginnings* under Beckham's editorial control.

The quarry photoshoot was being filmed for NBC's six-part $10 million docu-series about Victoria's arrival in America. Authenticity was a challenge during the filming of the *W* interview.

'We're not out to be the most famous people in America,' Victoria told James Reginato, the magazine's writer. 'We're not looking at the move as boosting the brand.' Forgetting what she had just said, she then explained her ambitions Stateside: 'I'm launching a jeans line, a collection of sunglasses and two fragrances.' They would be sold at Saks Fifth Avenue and other stores. 'In short,' the writer concluded, 'the Beckham brand is poised to invade America.'

Not surprisingly, Reginato also did not quote the judgement of American fashion expert Robert de Keyser about Victoria's new brand of jeans as, 'seriously overpriced for a line made out of a cheap fabric'.[4]

Why, she was asked, did she always scowl at photographers? 'When you're out there, they're trying to get pictures up your shirt, down your top.' She overlooked how often she wore dresses for photographers – tipped-off by her publicists – that revealed her breasts and were split to her crotch. At the *Glamour* Awards in London's Berkeley Square, she chose tiny sequined black hot-pants and a low-cut bustier. As Victoria pouted for the cameras, her publicist revealed that she had abandoned hair extensions to avoid looking like a WAG.[5]

During the interview Victoria described to Reginato how she was 'embarrassingly' stopped by a Los Angeles policeman for making an illegal turn in her car. In his profile Reginato described how Victoria had been unable to produce a valid Californian driving licence after she was pulled over. 'The policeman was gorgeous,' Victoria cooed. 'And he loved my shoes.' Later her publicists told Reginato, 'It's all a bit embarrassing, luckily no charges were brought against her.'[6] Victoria forgot to mention that the policeman was an actor hired by Fuller's film production company for a sequence in the NBC series. The 'driving licence' sequence was entirely fake.

Filming for the six-part fly-on-the wall reality show *Victoria Beckham: Coming to America* started in early May 2007. The schedule for the $10 million project, masterminded by Simon Fuller and directed by his brother Kim, was for a 32-day shoot around Los Angeles. Among Fuller's ambitions was to bring all the Beckhams together during the filming.

To maintain security Victoria Beckham's name was not mentioned on the call sheets. Instead, it was 'MT' – Major Talent. Filming was scheduled to start at 9 a.m., but on the first day the 40-plus crew and production staff discovered that Victoria rose only at 10 a.m. By the time the hairdresser and make-up artists were finished, filming started after midday.

Her driving sequence – filmed on the first day – had required exhaustive arrangements. The storyline, with a policeman stopping Victoria Beckham as she made an illegal turn and then discovered that she had an invalid Spanish driving licence, became difficult to film. The camera would follow her while she got a licence reissued in a government office. Except that Victoria refused to drive the car rigged up with cameras. 'She's quixotic,' complained a production staffer. 'A law unto herself.' Another SUV was produced and the sequence inside the licence office was, on her insistence, rejigged. 'It's hard work being fabulous,' she said as a fly-on-the wall aside. The scripted sequence was reshot several times.

During the second day the production crew's patience was tested further. Kitson, the boutique on Robertson Boulevard, had been chosen for Victoria to visit. The owner, Fraser Ross, recalled that Victoria had discovered Michael Silver's 1921 jeans in his shop. Once the dVb brand was manufactured, Ross had stocked the jeans priced between $290 and $486, but sales were derisory. Nevertheless, always eager for publicity, Ross agreed to re-stock his shop window with her jeans in return for appearing in the documentary.

Victoria's visit sparked an argument. Ross complained that Victoria had failed to promote her own brand. 'No one in Los Angeles has heard of you,' he said as the cameras rolled. At the end Victoria angrily demanded that the crew also film her visit to Lisa Kline, a rival boutique on the other side of the road. Ross was 'absolutely livid' and took her denims out of the window.[7]

Victoria's decision also 'super pissed off' the TV production crew. Robertson Boulevard divided two areas – Los Angeles and Beverly Hills. A different filming permit was needed for Lisa Kline. 'She's putting the kybosh on things,' said a producer watching 'the MT' spend her time drinking champagne and eating edamame. 'Her capricious behaviour is wasting a lot of effort and money,' agreed another producer. 'She just does what she wants. She must always be surrounded by yes-men and women.'

Victoria's problems were more fundamental. She did not appear to understand any of the costs involved in making a documentary. Many filming ideas agreed by her before leaving Europe had been set up, only to be ditched by her at the last moment. 'On a human level,' complained a producer, 'she didn't seem concerned about all our wasted work and effort.'

On the third day of filming, after sunbathing in high heels with 'my friends' – Marie-Louise her make-up artist and Ben her hairdresser – Victoria was filmed hiring Renee, her new PA. Accompanied for the series everywhere by Renee, the PA was recorded taking the butt of her demands and humour – except that Renee was an *Ugly Betty* look-alike comedy actress from Chicago. And their lines had been scripted by 'top buck' writers.

The filming in her 'new home' in Beverly Ranch Road, rented for one week, included Victoria's 'discovery' of an earthquake survival kit. As directed, she looked 'flummoxed'. Enough food was stored for two people for 72 hours. 'That would keep Victoria going for two months,' sniped a soundman.

Speaking on the phone to David and Brooklyn in Madrid, she told the camera, 'He's just kissed a new girlfriend.' She failed to explain whether that was David or Brooklyn. Although the series was planned to show all the Beckhams relocating to America, Beckham had refused to participate and insisted that the children would be also excluded. At that moment, Beckham appears to have had second thoughts about co-operating to salvage Victoria's career.

During the following day's filming Victoria rejected the scripted visit to a beautician for her pedicure. 'My nails have been done,' she announced, dismissive of the money and time wasted – and was driven directly to a barbecue arranged at her 'new house'. Since Victoria had failed to get any Hollywood A-listers on to her programme the production crew had invited 20 friends to pose as celebrities, including the hip-hop group Three 6 Mafia. Two Porsches and other expensive sports cars had been hired for the forecourt and

$1,000 of food was spread across the tables. Minutes after she arrived she surveyed the scene and pronounced: 'No.' Without explanation the party was cancelled. The food was dumped and the guests told to leave. Victoria was clear that she did not want to be seen with the hip-hop group. Standing in front of Victoria the frustrated crew sang the Spice Girls' song, 'Tell me what you want, what you really, really want.' She smiled, raised her champagne glass and uttered a graphic insult.

Security paranoia took over. Not only was all the production paperwork methodically shredded but the garbage bags were ordered to be stored – in case they were stolen by prowling journalists. By the fourth day the offices were packed with garbage bags. 'This is extreme and bizarre,' sighed a production manager.

The script next required Victoria to visit a sex shop. 'I wish I could move without being chased by the paparazzi,' she repeated from the script. 'I need to come up with a plan.' In a convoluted plot she bought a life-sized doll to sit in an open-topped car for the paparazzi to follow while she escaped. 'The paparazzi followed the doll all day,' she chortled. In truth, the 'hordes' of snappers were tuning in to the producers' 'walkie' radios. 'If you want to avoid the paps,' scowled a cameraman, 'don't phone them.' As Victoria would later admit, 'In Los Angeles, the paparazzi leave us alone. No one's that interested in us.' 'That explained why she comes to London', said a British critic.[8]

On 1 June the NBC executive who signed the deal with Simon Fuller was fired. Half the production crew was also 'released'. Left behind was Simon's brother Kim, the show's director. 'It's "Grab what you can footage",' Kim was told. Haplessly he agreed: 'Her life's so boring we'll have to fabricate it.' On the same day the NBC's new executive ordered that the six-part series was hacked down to merely one hour. *Victoria Comes to America* was billed as a 'highlight of NBC's autumn schedule'. The edit was difficult.

The *Mirror*'s Caroline Hedley launched the promotion of the documentary by quoting NBC's president of Entertainment Kevin Reilly: 'The series will give viewers a glimpse into what makes Victoria so popular and admired as one of the most glamorous women in the world.'[9]

NBC's publicity continued, 'Victoria's every move is documented by the paparazzi but only our cameras have been allowed inside the world of what being Victoria Beckham is really like.' Quoting Simon Fuller, the promotion added, 'Funny is the key word. There was huge public demand to see Victoria's real life. After much thought, we have finally decided to do it. She has conquered the world but now faces her greatest challenge yet, moving to Los Angeles.' The final words were Victoria's, 'I think people will get to see what I'm really like.'

In a flyer for the British tabloids about the 'sensational fly-on-the-wall documentary', Victoria said, 'It's all about me. This show is really something different. It's pushing the boundaries.'[10]

Although the *Mirror*'s TV section revealed that 'No preview tapes were available', Hedley puffed as a news report that NBC 'has had such glowing reviews prior to its screening tonight ... NBC is pleading with her to sign up for more.' Hedley quoted Victoria, 'It's so flattering' and reported: 'Celebs queue around the block to snap up Victoria's denim designs from her sought-after dVb line.'[11] Hedley's enthusiasm was exceptional.

'Some scenes created for dramatic effect' read the caption before Victoria's opening line: 'People always say, "David is so good-looking and so gorgeous and she's so funny." Basically, that means I'm a pig with a good sense of humour.' At the end of the hour her self-mockery had rebounded.

'An orgy of self-indulgence,' judged the *New York Post*, awarding the film zero stars. The *New York Times* described Victoria as 'vapid and condescending. She has tea with a group of golden-haired, Botoxed and bosomy matrons and fits right in.' On transmission it was fourth in the ratings, eclipsed by a repeat of *Wife Swap*. 'Lock that skinny rump inside that 32,000-square-foot house and leave us all alone,' concluded one American commentator.

'The most over-hyped couple on the planet,' was the final stinger, reducing Victoria to tears. Seen drinking at a hotel that night she had learnt something about the reality of life in Los Angeles.[12]

In Britain the reception was even more acidic. 'A charm offensive without any charm,' reported the *Sun*. Her intention of offering a 'tongue-in-cheek, ironic portrait of her celebrity life' was 'drained of irony, honesty and humour'.[13] The *News of the World* compared Victoria's flashing breasts to the routine of 'an ageing lap-dancer'. The *Sunday Mirror* condemned a show 'full of fakery' which should be renamed *Victoria Beckham Conning America*.[14] The *Guardian* was no better: 'The programme and its subject were utter, utter crap – boring, mendacious and requiring the invention of a new vocabulary to describe its unreserved vapidity.'[15]

New Beginnings, Simon Fuller's parallel hour-long television profile of David Beckham, was not panned as badly: 'I am quite a man's man,' he told viewers, 'but I also like to look after myself. I like to use creams, facial creams and body creams.' Among his disclosures were 'I'm always going to the toilet'; and 'It's nice to be married to Victoria because she has everything. When people say, "Victoria wears the trousers", I'm happy with that.' While his bathroom was always perfectly tidy, hers was permanently messy: 'She leaves the drawers open and leaves the toothpaste top off too. It's her mess, though.'[16]

Victoria was distressed by the bad reviews. She hit back: 'Negative comments don't bother me. If they did, I'd have slit my wrists years ago. I'm not here to break into America. I'm ugly. I'm not pretty. I'm not a model.'[17]

As the Beckham family flew across the Atlantic, occupying the whole of BA's first-class cabin, Victoria could not get over the 'hurt' of the reviews. 'It may be bit crazy when we first get there,' she said, 'but people will realise I'm quite boring.' To those who mocked her for only shopping and pouting she replied, 'It's the way my face falls.'[18] Addicted to the media but with nothing new to say she repeated, 'The fact is, David and I are very boring people.'

Fearing that she was only famous for being famous, she could not help craving for attention. In a call to the *Sun* before the plane took off, she had conjured a sex scene: during the *W* magazine shoot in Spain she and David got 'so steamed up they had to take a break and slip away for a romp'.[19] The *Sun* published her 'confession'. In all her self-conscious confusion, she underestimated David's celebrity.

Long before their plane landed, ecstatic fans had brought Los Angeles's International Terminal to a standstill. Old hands compared the bedlam to Beatlemania in 1964. Amid screams and mayhem, over a hundred media journalists recorded the couple, dressed in black, walking out of the terminal building on a hot July afternoon. Standing on the pavement Victoria gave a regal wave. Her large sunglasses firmly hid her expression. Beckham smiled. Hailed as the 'saviour of

US soccer' Beckham's swollen ankle had been troubling him through-out the flight. But ever the actor he concealed the injury and told waiting journalists, 'I'm 32 now and as fit as I was when I was 22.' Coming to America, he said, was 'my dream come true'. He added, 'I'm moving to America for the soccer. It's not the big brand thing.'[20] He was word perfect, repeating the prepared script.

Naturally, Victoria wanted to be heard. 'I love America. What better place to bring up children,' she said, suggesting they would spend the rest of their lives in Los Angeles because 'the weather's better for a start. The people smile more.'

Hovering helicopters followed their police-escorted motorcade to Beverly Hills. Beckham would be seeing his new home in San Ysidro Drive for the first time. The six-bedroom, 11,000-square-foot house with a 1.25-acre garden had cost £9.1 million, about £2 million less than the asking price. 'We wanted something cosy,' Victoria said, explaining why she had rejected a sprawling mansion. The 'modest' house, alternatively described as 'Spanish style' and 'Italian style', had been redecorated by Kelly Hoppen with beige walls and cream carpets.[21] Several of the Beckhams' cars, shipped from Madrid, were already in the garage, including his Cadillac and her cabriolet Bentley with VB etched into the alloy wheels. Soon afterwards, Victoria acquired a white Porsche with the VB trademark on the wheels. For commuting, Beckham bought a massive black Escalade SUV.[22]

Waiting for them in the house were Victoria's parents and two nannies, each hired at $6,000 a month. Drawing a salary from his son-in-law, Tony Adams had supervised installing security around the property. Within weeks, they would be employing more than ten staff.[23]

The following day, after parading their three sons in front of an army of photographers at Toys 'R' Us, they had dinner at Chateau Marmont, one of Los Angeles's most famous hotels. Given the best table they sat with Fuller until 2 a.m., 10 a.m. London time. Pertinently, the restaurant soon tired of Victoria's visits because she tipped off photographers about her arrival.[24] Six hours later, David and Victoria were driving to his debut in the Home Depot stadium, just two miles down freeway 405.

CHAPTER 19

AGONY

Tickertape, fireworks, music and wild cheers greeted the Beckhams as they entered the stadium. Limping into the spotlight Beckham was emotionally overwhelmed. Introduced as an indestructible athlete taking over the world, he appeared to be taken aback by the chants of 'Beckham'. In response to the ecstatic cheers from fans wearing T-shirts emblazoned with 'Bend It Like Goldenballs', he held up his number 23 shirt. In 90-degree sun, Beckham waved to over 500 journalists and 65 television cameras. In a skin-tight pink dress and perched on five-inch Balenciaga heels, Posh shouted: 'I had no idea I was so popular.'

The promoters claimed that 11,000 fans were in the 27,000-seater stadium. Some journalists reported that the number of cheering fans was closer to 8,600. The following day the *New York Times*' columnist reported it was 2,500 people: 'He's showing up not as an athlete but as a celebrity. But I get the feeling that Los Angeles doesn't care.'[1]

The *Los Angeles Times* joined the chorus. Over one week the newspaper had devoted two pages every day to the Beckhams. Even some nurses employed in the Whipps Cross Hospital maternity ward in Leytonstone where he was born in 1975 were interviewed, although none of them had been an eyewitness.

Other newspapers interviewed women in Hollywood. 'He's simply gorgeous and loaded,' said one *Playboy* model. 'He'll be a target. Girls know how to play the game. They will just slip him their telephone number, even if he's standing next to Posh.'[2]

Tim Leiweke, the chief executive of the Anschutz Entertainment Group, and Alexi Lalas, the football club's president, were ecstatic but for different reasons. Morale at the club was rock bottom. Just 5,000 spectators had watched the team's latest defeat by the Richmond Kickers. The club's TV audience was next to zero. Interest in Beckham, said Lalas, 'exceeds everything else. The US will never have dealt with an athlete who has had this kind of international impact.'[3] The proof was the sold-out match at Home Depot against Chelsea. Lalas and Leiweke were just as excited by the potential commercial profits. Throughout the welcoming ceremony in the stadium, Lalas urged fans to buy Beckham's number 23 shirt for $80 (the equivalent of £40 at that point). In advance 250,000 had been manufactured. And the television rights to Galaxy's games had been sold in a hundred countries. 'Beckham's not joining Galaxy as an athlete,' the *Los Angeles Times* journalist Bill Plaschke observed, 'but as an advertising campaign. A walking Super Bowl commercial, a big-haired billboard.'

To counter that impression, Beckham told the cheering fans, 'I'm as hungry as I ever was to take football to a new stage in America.' Walking down the long line of cameras in the stadium to give each TV station a soundbite, he recited the line, 'It feels like my first day at school again' and added once more, 'I'm as fit as I was when I was 22.'

Tom Cruise hosted a 'little welcoming party' at the Museum of Contemporary Art. Billed by the *Los Angeles Times* as 'Hollywood aristocracy clamours to rub shoulders with the Beckhams', 600 guests including Will Smith, Demi Moore, Bruce Willis, Jennifer Lopez, Jada Pinkett Smith, Eva Longoria and Stevie Wonder were welcomed by Cruise and Katie Holmes to the £500,000 reception. Cruise had returned from filming in Germany solely for the party. It helped that Creative Artists Agency, Hollywood's most powerful influencers, encouraged their clients to accept Cruise's invitation and organised the event. 'This is the hardest party to get into,' said Beckham's Los Angeles publicist, Rogers & Cowan. 'It's A-list only. And no press.' Unspoken, few doubted that Cruise hoped to recruit the Beckhams to Scientology. Politely, Beckham dismissed the suggestion. Tinseltown, he wanted to believe, was feting a global footballer.

Standing close by, Victoria accepted all the invitations for television interviews. 'They are honestly such nice, genuine people,' she told NBC about the Cruises, their new neighbours. She confided to Jay Leno about the crowds at the airport, 'We were absolutely shocked that anyone even knew we were coming.' In another interview she described how David brought the looks to the marriage while she brought the comedy.[4] 'We're private people,' she couldn't help saying in another interview and then namedropped that 'we were at Demi Moore's house for dinner with Ashton Kutcher and Penelope Cruz.'[5]

Leading the welcome in LA Galaxy's changing room was the team captain, 25-year-old Landon Donovan. Rated as a world-class footballer and the top American goalscorer, Donovan earned annually $900,00 (£450,000) but the four lowest-paid players in the room earned just $12,900 per year, which was half of Beckham's daily pay cheque.

Although Beckham was seven years older than Donovan, they had much in common. Both came from modest backgrounds, both were reared by ambitious fathers and both were famous footballers in their own countries. In 2002 both had reached the quarter-finals of the World Cup. Their personalities, however, were sharply different. Unlike Beckham's overwhelming, thick-skinned self-confidence, Donovan was self-critical and occasionally insecure.

After standing in the spotlight at LA Galaxy, Donovan was inevitably edged aside by Beckham. More serious, his adviser Terry Byrne told Lalas that Beckham expected to replace Donovan as captain. Neither American was pleased.[6] Adding to the changing room's irritation, Beckham was visibly appalled by the unhealthy food served in the team's dusty canteen. 'It's a shock to his system,' Byrne reported. The ramshackle facilities reflected the MLS's dire finances. Badly managed, the MLS had survived only through regular infusions of millions of dollars by the clubs' billionaire owners. LA Galaxy was a pauper-show compared to Real Madrid.

Only 5,000 fans turned up for Beckham's first match against Tigras. They were shocked to see Beckham hobbling into the executive box with Lalas. For the next two hours Terry Byrne held ice-packs on the ankle of the team's highest-paid player. Beckham watched grimly as Galaxy's hillbillies failed to tackle, kick properly or move in formation. Defeated 0–3 the Galaxy team were booed off. 'A miserable performance,' Lalas admitted. British journalists were less charitable. LA Galaxy, wrote the *Mirror*, was 'no better than a Sunday afternoon pub team'.[7]

Three days later, the sell-out match against Chelsea attracted the unlikely quintet of Arnold Schwarzenegger, Ray Winstone, John Hurt, and Ant and Dec. Generously, the fans whooped as Beckham came on to the pitch in the 78th minute. Chelsea won 1–0. 'Amazing, incredible,' Beckham said about the torrent of publicity. *Sports Illustrated* called his appearance 'rated off the charts in electricity and excitement'.[8] Although the ESPN TV audience was unusually high it was still less than 1 million, not even a 1.0 rating.

Although flying would aggravate his ankle injury, Beckham travelled with the team on a 2,100-mile round trip to Denver but did not play. Soon afterwards he flew to Dallas. Jeering fans waved a placard: 'David, welcome to America where people like you are paid to do nothing.' Five days later, fans in Toronto booed when Beckham appeared on the screen but not on the pitch. 'Beckham bent and broken' proclaimed one placard. Four weeks after his wild welcome, some intensive therapy finally worked. He played for 63 minutes and scored a goal from a free kick. That was followed by triumph at the New York Giants' stadium. A crowd of 66,237 – six times bigger than usual – paid to watch the revered footballer. His passes helped create three goals, although Galaxy were defeated 4–5 by the Red Bulls.[9]

Hours after the match Beckham flew to London for a 'friendly' match against Germany in the new Wembley stadium. Since he had not played in a top-class football match since the final Spanish game of the season two months earlier, Beckham was not fit for an international. But McClaren was desperate. Germany won 2–1.

After failing to help McClaren, Beckham flew back to Los Angeles. Five days after playing in New York he creaked on to the pitch to play against local rivals Chivas USA. Chivas won 3–0. Beckham was exhausted and virtually crippled. During the following game against Colorado he suffered a knee ligament injury. Limping from the pitch, he sat on the bench with his head in his hands, hearing the fans boo. Beckham was declared unfit to play for at least six weeks. He was automatically excluded from England's critical Euro 2008 qualifiers against Israel and Russia. His invincibility was tarnished. Adding to his woes, Victoria was heard complaining that he was too often away from home.[10]

In his first Galaxy season Beckham played five times and missed 12 matches. LA Galaxy was at the bottom of the MLS table and had failed to make the play-offs. Their season abruptly ended in October.[11] 'It's hard to figure out what is going on with Galaxy,' commented Chivas player (and future Leeds United manager) Jesse Marsch about

Beckham. The player himself was robust about being in America: 'It's been great so far, very positive and smooth. Apart from the season.'[12]

Beckham baffled Donovan the captain and his teammates. At team dinners, Beckham's stinginess kicked in. The owner of a Rolls-Royce Phantom refused to pick up the bill. He expected every player, including the four earning just $12,900 a year, to pay the same as himself.[13] Donovan's unease was silenced by the sudden introduction of free five-star hotels, high-class restaurants and chartered flights for all the team. Beckham had opened a new world for LA Galaxy. But there was no friendship. The Beckhams never invited his teammates to a barbecue at their house. 'They're such a different breed,' said Donovan about a couple who kept themselves quite separate.[14] Life with Beckham was discomforting. Wherever he went with the team, the media circus followed. When he disappeared because of his injuries, normality resumed.

Tim Leiweke denied that there was any friction. He was delighted that attendances at LA Galaxy's matches were over 50 per cent higher and the sales of shirts had exceeded 300,000 – 700 times more than Galaxy had sold in 2006. But even Beckham at the end of the season admitted, 'It was a nightmare, to be honest.'[15] He was speaking about football, not his social life. Late into the night, he was often seen in Los Angeles clubs with Hollywood stars and their girlfriends. Victoria and his publicists believed his explanation that he was bonding with his Galaxy teammates.[16]

At the Wolseley restaurant in London, Jo Milloy was enjoying a raucous dinner in honour of a tabloid journalist. As the bottles were replaced, Milloy's guard fell and she admitted that Beckham was forging close relations with Victoria's new friends and others in Los Angeles. He was easily tempted by Hollywood's stars. Names were mentioned and the journalist's eyes lit up. But the chance of publishing any kiss-and-tell confessions was, as Milloy and the journalist knew, zero. Even if the stories were true, Britain's new privacy laws made repetition of Rebecca Loos-style revelations by newspapers difficult.

Just as David Beckham suffered from mixed publicity, Victoria's fortunes rose, thanks to the misfortune of a talented French fashion designer. Over the previous year, Roland Mouret had been feted across New York and Hollywood for his figure-hugging Galaxy dress, which was a well-cut hit with film stars. But at the end of 2006 the 46-year-old's career nosedived. After breaking with his backers he was ousted from his own business.

Over the previous year, Fuller had been searching for an entry into the fashion business. Like many successful pop promoters and actors, he spoke about 'cross-media platforms'. Fuller's girlfriend Natalie wore Mouret's designs. The Frenchman was a natural partner. With Victoria in mind Simon Fuller financed Mouret's new label, 19RM. The deal was basic: while Mouret rebuilt his business with Fuller's help he would simultaneously introduce Victoria to a team of fashion stylists and teach her the essentials of design. 'I was her mentor,' Mouret later said. The finance – initially about £2 million – would be provided by David Beckham. Some of those involved in his business suspected that Beckham was unaware of his subsidy. They also wondered whether Beckham properly understood that Fuller had increased his commission from 10 per cent to 30 per cent. In Fuller's opinion, he had explained that nothing was a straight deal anymore. He was more like a partner than a commission agent.

Hidden away in New York's Wall Street, a backwater for fashion design compared to Paris and Milan, the Frenchman created a workshop. Victoria began to learn from Mouret how clothes were cut and shaped and where to source the materials to produce a well-finished garment.

Competing with over 30 experienced designers on the runway, she had entered a crowded market. To persuade celebrities accustomed to Dior, Chanel, Versace and Valentino to be dressed by a former singer rather than choosing world-famous couturiers was a challenge. Victoria's pink dress, which she had worn for her arrival at LA Galaxy's stadium, had been created by Mouret in 2005. It had been hailed by Germaine Greer as 'a work of genius'. Some fashion experts were less convinced by Greer's description of Posh as 'a lone champion of elegance for working girls'.[17]

The public's mistake was to imagine Victoria toiling away to learn her craft. Reluctant to sit long hours behind a desk concentrated on a task, she preferred to criss-cross America, dash to Japan and stop over in London to promote her nascent brand. One appearance in New York's 2007 Fashion Week produced a gushing tribute from the *Mirror*'s Amber Morales: 'Posh is putting the wow factor into New

York Fashion Week.' She continued: 'All eyes were on Victoria at the Marc Jacobs show and she knew it.' An 'expert' told the *Mirror* that she just stole the show.'[18] Insiders knew another version. Victoria was damned as a 'trend killer', derided by Alexander McQueen, banned by John Galliano from his shows, and shunned by Kate Moss.

Constant travelling was expensive and took its toll. Two nannies caring for her three children walked out, blaming her arrogance and her mother Jackie's demands. The tipping-point apparently occurred when a nanny used one of the children's toilets. 'Working for Posh,' one said, was a 'nightmare'.[19]

That complaint was echoed by June and Eric Emmett, the house-keepers at Beckingham Palace. After ten years' employment the relationship ended after both were suddenly arrested by the police on suspicion of theft. The allegations were fallacious and dropped. Neither received an apology from the Beckhams.[20]

The couple's hectic pace was partly to blame. An additional complication occurred at the end of September when Ted Beckham suffered a major heart attack. He blamed the stress of working extra shifts to pay his bills. Both Beckhams flew to London to be at his bedside – Victoria from the Far East and Beckham from America. During their reconciliation at the hospital, an eyewitness reported that Victoria refused a cup of hospital coffee because it wasn't made with bottled water.[21]

Skinny as ever and photographed with her forehead covered by acne, she flew from London via Los Angeles (to see her children) and on to Paris for a fashion shoot. Abandoning her blonde bob, she had agreed to wear 'outrageous costumes' in exchange for free publicity in *Elle* magazine. While staying at the Ritz in Paris she seized an unexpected opportunity. Photographers, she heard, were waiting outside the hotel in the Place Vendôme. They were there to film the English jury and lawyers in the Diana inquest leaving the building to inspect the route of their car and the scene of the fatal crash in 1997. Instead of slipping out at the back, Victoria chose to be seen. In a choreographed exit she walked into the Place Vendôme. Although she was pleased to be photographed, the following day's tabloid headline – 'SPOTTY SPICE'[22] – was an unfortunate consequence.

Victoria's success was mirrored by her husband's. Beckham's football career was being revitalised.

In November 2007, Steve McClaren's fate depended on England beating Croatia to qualify for the Euro 2008 tournament. His predicament resembled Britain's beleaguered new Prime Minister. As a depressive prone to violent outbursts, Gordon Brown had fluffed an opportunity to secure his position by calling a snap General Election. Instead, the self-anointed Iron Chancellor was steering the country towards a financial crisis. The similarities of Brown's drift towards doom with McClaren's were striking. Beckham's prospects had seemed equally dire, but unlike the other two he found a way to overcome earlier disappointments.

Discreetly, Terry Byrne spoke to McClaren's officials suggesting that Beckham could be England's salvation. He mentioned that Beckham had been supportive of the derided manager. McClaren unexpectedly summoned Beckham to rejoin the England squad.

In preparation for the Croatia match, England played a 'friendly' game against Austria. Beckham's corner produced a goal. Once again he showed his deadball skills but after one hour he was exhausted. Lacking the necessary stamina, his legs gave the impression to one football writer of 'wading through treacle'.[23] And yet his 98th cap was commercially invaluable. Exposure on the world stage was vital to sustain his income.

To check that Beckham would be fit for the Croatia game, McClaren flew to Los Angeles. Before leaving, McClaren forgot to ask whether LA Galaxy had any fixtures. They did not. 'I wanted to see his lifestyle,' explained McClaren later.[24] Their brief reunion was sufficient for Beckham to win over McClaren, just as he had wooed Eriksson. Weak managers could seldom resist Beckham's charm and professions of loyalty.

Shortly after the meeting Beckham headed with LA Galaxy to Sydney. Seventy-four thousand tickets had been sold by the Telstra Stadium. The profits for Galaxy were guaranteed so long as Beckham played for at least 55 minutes. If he failed to play, the match would be cancelled, a remarkable testament to the player's pulling power.[25]

Except that Beckham flew to Australia via Beijing. After a 13-hour flight, excited Chinese teenagers mobbed him while he launched a new mobile phone. After one day he flew another 12 hours to Sydney. Thousands of fans greeted him at the airport. The match against Sydney started well. Beckham scored a trademark goal from a free-kick. Then disaster. His ankle collapsed. He limped off the field. LA Galaxy lost 5–3 but the profits for both the club and Beckham made it worthwhile. After a third and 22-hour flight he arrived at Heathrow.[26]

The reputation of England's team had sunk to new depths. McClaren had finally realised that his injured captain John Terry had been getting drunk until 4 a.m. in Soho with lap dancers. On one occasion Terry had urinated on the nightclub's floor.[27] The talk of sleaze was the curtain-raiser for England's decisive match against Croatia.

Torrential rain was soaking the Wembley pitch. Beckham was on the bench with an injured ankle. In his place, McClaren selected Shaun Wright-Phillips, who would be substituted at half-time for Beckham, with England already 2–0 down. The goalkeeper was the internationally inexperienced Scott Carson. A Frank Lampard penalty and then a Beckham pass set up an equaliser. The boos turned to cheers – until reality shot back.

As the rain bucketed down, McClaren stood on the touchline under an umbrella watching England fall apart, and Croatia scored a third goal. England had failed to qualify for the 2008 Euros. 'The wally with the brolly' was the merciless headline about McClaren, damned as 'a flop, a dismal lightweight, a lame-duck manager' responsible for a 'hapless, hopeless, incompetent mess – a lame-duck team of spoiled millionaires performing like an antiquated shambles'. The obituaries were merciless. 'English football was in the gutter last night after an agonising horror show,' concluded the *Sun*, highlighting Beckham's lack of fitness. 'A soul-destroying embarrassment,' concluded the *Mirror*. 'The whole overpaid team crushingly underperformed. An example of bombast and self-deception.'[28]

After the debacle McClaren refused to resign. He was fired by the FA's board instead. England's leadership, wrote the critics, had appointed McClaren but were incapable of taking responsibility. Strangled in a web of greedy self-interest and incompetence, the FA executives were accused of being the poison that destroyed the team.[29]

Beckham was not deluded. Football fans, he knew, were disappointed that he not rescued England's Euro 2008 hopes. In some fans' judgement, Beckham's football had become a vehicle to make him a rich celebrity. He was the epitome of the failed generation of England's golden hopes. For those deriding Beckham as a role model he now embodied the Boyzilian, a man who has all their hair removed. 'The good news,' concluded the *Mirror*, noting that Beckham's performance dovetailed with England's spectacular failure, 'is that Beckham's England career is over.'[30]

The criticisms fired Beckham's defiance. He was thinking only of his own interests. For his brand he needed his 100th cap. A 'friendly' match was scheduled against Switzerland. He hoped McClaren's successor would be generous. The bookmakers William Hill gave 9–2 odds that Beckham would not make 100 caps.

The Beckham publicity machine kicked in. Weeks after failing on the pitch he appeared as a star guest on Michael Parkinson's final television chat-show. The event was billed as historic. Some were unimpressed. 'Why does crawler Parky believe,' asked Kevin O'Sullivan in the *Sunday Mirror*, 'that interrogating dim, dull David Beckham was a career highlight? Squeaky-voiced Beckham should let his boots do the talking.'[31]

But that was Beckham's genius. His poor football did not inhibit his attractions to his fans. To his good fortune, those who admired his image and his body did not generally care about his performance on the pitch. Most still saw him as a loyal, family-loving but sexy hero. And as a reward, Fuller delivered a three-year £15 million contract for him to promote Armani underwear. He had waited to finalise the deal to avoid giving Real Madrid 50 per cent of the proceeds.

To advertise his success, Beckham talked to ITV in a recorded interview about his underwear preferences: 'It used to be boxers but now it's Y-fronts.' And as usual he was modest. Asked about his life in Los Angeles he replied, 'I'm always starstruck by famous people.'[32] By the broadcast date, Beckham had flown to New Zealand – a 24-hour journey – for another Galaxy promotional match. He arrived with a swollen ankle. During the match, he cracked a rib and dropped out.

After the match Beckham spent 45 minutes at a reception with the son of New Zealand's future Prime Minister John Key. The politician's recollections were uncomplimentary. When Beckham was asked by Key's son whether he was a 'volatile' player he replied, 'Well, I can play in the centre, on the right and occasionally on the left side.' The footballer, said Key, was 'as thick as batshit'.[33]

From New Zealand, Beckham flew 16 hours to Vancouver to watch the opening show of the new Spice Girls world tour. He and Victoria had been apart – in different continents – for over three weeks.[34]

After ten weeks of rehearsals in Los Angeles there had been a trial concert in Hollywood. After a seven-year gap the Spice Girls mimed rather than sang their old tunes for a rehearsal with a thousand guests. Once the show was declared a success, an army of the Spice Girls' children, nannies, minders and technicians flew in Spice Force One to Canada. Fuller claimed that 1 million people had tried to buy tickets for the world tour. They were sold out, he said, within 38 seconds. Puzzlingly, the Spice Girls' new single had sold less than 5,000 copies, and was dropped.[35] Not without coincidence, most of the concert venues were owned by Philip Anschutz's AEG, the owner of LA Galaxy.

In Vancouver, Beckham discovered a grumpy catfight among the group. All five women were arguing and on the verge of moving into separate hotels and rebooking onward flights on different planes. Cynics recalled the Spice Girls' hit song, 'Friendship Never Ends'. Notably, Victoria was asserting herself. Surrounded by a huge entourage, one bodyguard was entrusted to follow her with fruit and a bottle of champagne, while another bodyguard occasionally warned staff not to approach Victoria because she was 'tired'. From the outset, she had been struggling to sing and dance.[36]

Cue an avalanche of publicity to boost Beckham after a succession of football failures. On the first night of the Spice Girls' show his publicists revealed that he had given each woman a £50,000 diamond bracelet. Then Beckham was appointed the tour's official photographer. Next, to keep his name in the media, it was made clear that Beckham had paid Robert Friend, an actor, £25,000 to be Santa on Christmas Eve in Hertfordshire. And that he would be paying thousands of pounds to decorate Beckingham Palace as a winter wonderland.[37] As an extra aside, his publicist hinted that Beckham might buy Posh a £5.5 million Bulgari necklace for Christmas.

Finally, Caroline Hedley was told by a publicist about Beckham's Obsessive Compulsive Disorder (OCD) habits before boarding a private jet. The leather seats had to be rubbed with a selected balm and, before loading, his suitcases had to be laid out in order of size for inspection. Once on board, the newspapers had to be set out in a straight line. For meals, the different-size glasses were set in a special sequence, and the plates, cutlery, and salt and pepper had to be laid out to his stipulated preference. Deliberately omitted from the list was his earlier admission that in succumbing to OCD he bought 30 pairs of Calvin Klein underpants every two weeks.[38]

Even Armani's sales executives were stunned by the public excitement as vast billboard hoardings of Beckham were unveiled in New York and San Francisco in late 2007. Wearing only brief underwear, and with his legs apart, his oiled, waxed body on a silk sheet wowed men and women. For gay men, big spenders on underwear, smouldering Beckham was especially appealing. Since posing for *Attitude*, a gay magazine, he had become their icon and even their screensaver. The closest, a joker commented, they would get to him.

Looking at the hoardings, everyone's attention was drawn to the 'focal point'. Had Beckham 'padded his package?' they asked. Was an airbrush used? What was the real size of his 'package'? Never known to avoid the chance of turning vulgarity into an art form, Victoria's publicists released her chosen words: 'He really does have a huge one. You can see it in the advert. It is all his.' She added, 'I'm proud to see his penis 25 foot tall. It's huge. It's enormous. Massive.' Then another soundbite: 'I'm proud I still have a really good sex life with David.' Delighted that the world was focused on the size of Beckham's manhood – and lapped up every word she uttered – she made the assertion, 'I'm a gay man trying to get out.' And then she claimed, 'All the men that like me are gay.'

Her messages highlighted Beckham's success. Armani announced that sales of the £15 pants had increased by 260 per cent.[39] To the delight of her own fans, Victoria glorified her background. Essex, she said, hailed golden couples 'at it' like rabbits. Her critics mentioned a different explanation why she brazenly spoke about sex.

Beckham's publicists became concerned. To promote herself, Victoria was overplaying her vulgar humour. For some in Beckham's team he risked losing credibility. After she rejected suggestions to tone down her self-promotion, Fuller agreed that Milloy's operations for Victoria should be entirely separate from Oliveira's.

CHAPTER 20

CHEAPSKATE

On Beckham's return to Los Angeles he was faced with a new crisis at LA Galaxy. The club was near the bottom of the league. A radical solution, Tim Leiweke agreed, was necessary. Beckham was convinced he could solve Galaxy's poor performance.

With Leiweke's approval Terry Byrne took over managing the team. Alexi Lalas was relegated to the sidelines. Beckham and Byrne also persuaded Leiweke that the club should recruit the Dutch footballer and former Chelsea manager Ruud Gullit as the senior coach. Byrne, Beckham's *consigliore* and Footwork's manager, conducted the negotiations. On the day of the announcement, Fuller claimed credit for recruiting Gullit. To the American team's amazement, Fuller positioned a 19 Entertainment logo behind the lectern for the media announcement. Fuller, it appeared, had taken over managing the club. Beckham flatly denied influencing Gullit's appointment.[1]

Undoubtedly, Gullit had been a great player in the 1980s and early 1990s, but as a manager and coach he had been a serial failure since leaving Chelsea in early 1998. Soon after his arrival in Los Angeles, Gullit showed why over the past decade he had been fired and eventually not rehired. He was often moody and vindictive, and the players found his decisions at Home Depot were incomprehensible. Acrimony spread among the team. That unhappiness was aggravated in early 2008 by another decision to satisfy Beckham. After some manoeuvring by Fuller and Byrne, the team captain Donovan was ousted. Beckham was appointed Galaxy's captain. He again denied playing any role in the change.

Within weeks Beckham's behaviour reminded England's fans of all the reasons for his inadequacy as their team's captain.[2] He was uncommunicative, isolated and ungenerous. The result was predictable. He led Galaxy's bad-tempered players to a succession of defeats.

LA Galaxy was renamed in a newspaper as Dysfunction Junction. Although his repeated setbacks were glaring, his team saw no indications that he felt any responsibility. If he harboured any anxieties they were alleviated by the promise of money from sponsors. Millions of pounds were dangled in front of Beckham by the Frantzen brothers, Torben and Geir.

Assured by Simon Fuller's business managers that Torben Frantzen was as successful as his brother Geir, Beckham arrived in a private jet on 28 January 2008 in Natal, a small city 1,300 miles north of Rio de Janeiro. Escorted by police motorbikes, Beckham and Torben headed to Cape São Roque, a Brazilian beach resort in a coconut plantation. After dropping Beckham's bags in the Grand Hotel's 164-square-metre presidential suite, Frantzen took his guest on a helicopter ride across 3,500 pristine acres. Over the next three days the Norwegian described his plans to build 1,350 private homes, three luxury hotels, swimming pools and, most importantly, 'David Beckham's World of Sport'. With eight football pitches and a 10,000-seater stadium, Beckham was encouraged to assure local politicians: 'I want to offer a safe space for kids to develop their abilities.' Promised by Frantzen that he would be paid a huge sum, Beckham declared, while standing on a barren building site, 'I intend to have a beach house and bring my wife and my children on vacation. I'm sure they will love it.'

One woman, Fabiana Ferreira Da Costa, a 31-year-old masseuse, was certain Beckham would come back. 'He said in Portuguese', she recalled, 'that he would call me again when he returned to Natal.'

Beckham never returned to Natal. Torben Frantzen's development never materialised. Fuller had sent him off on a dud mission.

Just as Beckham landed in Brazil, Geir Frantzen was launching Omega-3 supplements in America. Beckham's face and signature were on the packet, urging parents to include Omega-3 in their children's diet. Over the next months, sales of the capsules stalled. Beckham was deemed by the company's marketing adviser to be the wrong promoter. 'Omega-3', observed the insider, 'is associated with brain development and concentration but Beckham's known for his sporting prowess rather than his intellectual ability.' Omega's sales revenue fell to just £633 in one month.[3]

Sales of Geir's Findus fish fingers were also faltering. One month after a relaunch, Findus's monthly sales were worth just £150,000.[4]

By the new year Geir Frantzen's business was tottering into bankruptcy. Just as Frantzen's major bank lender, Landsbanki of Iceland, collapsed with huge debts, an unexplained fire destroyed the Findus factory near Newcastle.[5]

Months earlier, Beckham had no idea how his relationship with the Frantzens would end. While playing keepie-uppie with a football on the Cape São Roque beach, he had reflected wistfully on his fate after Fabio Capello was appointed England's new manager. They had not parted amicably in Madrid.

The FA's appointment of Capello for a £6 million per annum salary was made out of fear. 'The media were a nightmare,' admitted an FA executive. 'We wanted to avoid the tabloids' criticism.' Capello's four-and-a-half year contract was worth about three times more than any other European national manager. In that surreal world Terry Byrne negotiated on behalf of England's players their additional remuneration with the FA's commercial executive, Jonathan Hill. Fearing media criticism if they didn't get the players onside, Hill agreed to overly generous payments. The FA's executives hoped this would save them from trouble.

Among the Italian manager's first decisions was not to pick Beckham to play against Switzerland. Even before Beckham left Brazil for London the *Mirror* applauded Capello for putting the 'national team's show-pony out to grass'. 'Caps for the Boys' was over. The newspaper predicted that Beckham had more chance of getting a 100th tattoo than a 100th cap.[6]

In a telephone conversation from a Brazilian beach, Beckham appeared resilient. 'There's no chink of retirement crossing my mind,' he told the *Mirror*'s Oliver Holt. 'I won't get bitter and twisted.' But he admitted that when McClaren had dropped him, 'deep down, I didn't think I would ever play for England again'. During the conversation he sounded reasonable: 'I don't fear a life without playing but I want to carry on playing. I want to be part of the team. I want to play under Capello again.'[7] To win a place he had spent a few weeks training with Arsenal.

Although Beckham sounded reasonable to Holt he was secretly furious. Instead of returning to London to host a children's charity dinner at the Dorchester hotel, he flew to Los Angeles.[8] He burned with resentment. Brand Beckham required that he win more caps and a place in the record books, beating the legendary World Cup-winning duo Bobby Charlton and Bobby Moore. He knew Capello from his Madrid days, and recognised he would never select anyone who had not played in first-class matches for months.

Prickly, and with little English, Capello's task to rebuild England's team would not be easy. Beckham's only hope of selection was if FA executives put pressure on Capello. That was unlikely until fate intervened.

Jack Warner, the Trinidadian FIFA vice-president who controlled three of the 24 votes that would decide the host nation for the 2018 World Cup, had said that he might be minded to support England's bid if Beckham played in a match for them in Trinidad.

In January 2008, Beckham met Gordon Brown in Downing Street. The Prime Minister, forever in historical competition with Tony Blair, was determined to equal his predecessor's success. Blair had won the Olympics for London, so Brown wanted England to stage the 2018 World Cup. Brown believed that Beckham was essential as a national ambassador. Their agreement was straightforward. Beckham would join the FA's bid team and both would endorse each other.

After leaving Downing Street, Beckham said, 'He's a very good man, a man that's looking after our country and he's doing a very good job. I'm very proud to be here tonight.'[9] In return, two days later, Brown visited the David Beckham Academy in Greenwich. Describing Beckham as an 'inspiration to young people', Brown praised Beckham's charitable work and his help towards the government's target of children doing five hours of sport every week. In reply to Brown, Beckham announced plans for football academies to be opened in Manchester, Scotland and the north-east.

Just as arranged, Capello bowed to the FA and the Prime Minister. Beckham was recalled for a 'friendly' match against France. Capello knew that Beckham had nothing to offer. Unfit and unprepared for international football, over the previous months he had only played for LA Galaxy in Hong Kong, Dallas and Sydney. The FA's announcement, noted Steven Howard in the *Sun*, signalled that Beckham's ego had triumphed. Thinking only of himself and the importance for the brand, wrote Howard, Beckham would get his 100th cap in Paris's Stade de France on 26 March.[10]

Depending on who was asked, there was either a 'huge' cheer across the stadium as No. 7 came on to pitch wearing specially made golden boots, or 'polite applause' from the half-empty stands. Victoria, their three sons and Beckham's parents were watching. After two trademark crosses, Beckham was yellow-carded for the 16th time for a foul, making him the most booked player in England's history. After 63 minutes of a 'pitiful game without pace or inspiration' he was exhausted and substituted. Even playing against a second-tier French team England were defeated 1–0. Beckham, concluded the *Sun*, was a 'symbol of the past with an inflated reputation'.[11]

The cap would be presented weeks later by Bobby Charlton before the kick-off in Wembley stadium, where England played in a dismal match against the USA. Once again, Beckham was substituted.

Hours after the match in Paris, Beckham flew to Beijing. Hoping to cash in on his popularity during recent trips to China, the Galaxy had arranged a short tour. To Leiweke's disappointment, only a handful of fans greeted the star. LA Galaxy was not Real Madrid. Beckham's appeal seemed to be fading.[12]

On the team's return to Los Angeles, Galaxy were defeated 4–0 by Colorado Rapids. 'I was maybe not at my sharpest,' admitted Beckham, complaining about the constant air travel.[13] He redeemed himself days later with two goals from a penalty and a free kick against Real Salt Lake, but few were noticeably impressed.[14]

While Beckham junketed around the world with ever-decreasing success, Victoria's bid once again to revive her pop career was in trouble again.

At the end of January a vicious argument between the two Mels sparked the news that their '£100 million' tour would end prematurely at the end of February in Toronto. The global backlash was loud. Over 500,000 had seen the show in Europe and America, but tens of thousands had bought tickets in Asia and South America. Some blamed the schedule. Others claimed that both Mels planned to relaunch their solo careers. The five women protested that they missed their children and husbands.

Amid the rancour over the meltdown, Victoria insisted that it was her refusal to continue that had terminated the tour. She had only agreed to the tour, she said, to show her sons that she used to be a pop star. 'Our kids now need to go back to school,' she said. More truthfully she later admitted, 'I lost the passion after the first week of doing the shows.' The previous excitement for the make-up, hair extensions, buzz and hassle had gone. She was too old for all that. Amid the drudgery, she and Mel C had argued and, they noticed, ticket sales for future shows were falling. She decided the moment was right to quit music for fashion permanently. She predicted that her fashion business would produce profits of £15 million the following year.[15]

As the Spice Girls tour ended in Toronto, Beckham was spotted at 4 a.m. with a girl at the Circle nightclub in Seoul. Her arms were curled around his neck. He was in Korea to promote a hotel chain.[16]

To counter the obvious rumours after both of the Beckhams returned to Los Angeles, an 'eyewitness' spotted them loudly ordering gadgets and clothes at the Pleasure Chest adult sex store in Hollywood. They could leave nothing to chance.[17]

'I trust my husband 100 per cent,' she said. 'It's my job to protect the family. If it's not positive and nice, I don't want to know about it.' While admitting 'my share of heartache' from the Loos affair, she believed much had changed. 'I know some people don't want to believe it, but we really are happy. Everything about my life is good.'[18]

The best news was the decision by Alexandra Shulman, the editor of British *Vogue*, to take an interest in Victoria's ambitions. They had been introduced over lunch by PR Natalie Lewis during the Spice Girls tour in London. Shulman was attracted to Victoria's pitch.

Unlike many in the fashion world, Victoria knew how to make herself appealing to Shulman, not least by self-deprecation and small talk, and asking about Shulman's own family. There were not many in the fashion world willing to admit openly, 'I'm not the easiest person to work with. I'm a complete control-freak. I don't mind making mistakes. I just can't live with anyone else's mistakes.'[19] Even more bizarre was to hear that 'David doesn't like my clothes.' Shulman was impressed by Victoria's clothes that day: 'A tight corseted number that emphasised her waist and bottom, with a little black mink shrug'.

More than anything, Victoria wanted to be accepted by *Vogue*, the fashion bible. She was there to listen and learn, and hire the best people to realise her ambitions. Like Joe McKenna, famed for directing fashion shows. Her clothes, she said, were aimed at women seeking 'a curvaceous fit', looking sexy but conventional, not wanting high fashion but pleased to feel powerful. For a magazine editor as interested in journalism as fashion, Victoria offered something unique – a crossover from celebrity to fashion. By the end of the lunch Shulman decided to feature Victoria on the magazine's front cover.

Her problem was to persuade *Vogue*'s staff, who took fashion seriously, that Victoria was not just an ordinary Essex girl but potentially a cultural phenomenon.

Vogue's stylists agreed that Victoria should be dressed like her favourite actress Audrey Hepburn as Eliza Doolittle in *My Fair Lady*. In addition she would be dripping with Chopard diamonds – presents from Beckham. Celebrity sells. The magazine's circulation increased. In gratitude for securing the seal of approval, Victoria sent bunches of flowers to the editor and staff. Since that was an unusual gesture by a cover story model, she won more kudos. From that moment, featuring again on *Vogue*'s cover became her passion.

Vogue's recognition of Victoria raised her status. Wearing Roland Mouret's clothes during Paris fashion week, the *Mirror* reported that 'Posh is the queen of the catwalk shows.' Effortlessly, wrote the reporter, Victoria had outclassed Claudia Schiffer and the Wonderbra model Dita Von Teese: 'Victoria looked dazzling' while the other two were 'so last season'.[20]

The whirl of fashion shows, parties and celebrities had more than justified Victoria's move to America. Just as hundreds of fans cheered wildly as another giant photograph of Beckham wearing skimpy Armani briefs was unfurled in San Francisco, the two of them were flying on Giorgio Armani's private jet with George Clooney from London to a fashion show at the Metropolitan Museum in New York. 'A superstar friendship forged in heaven,' Milloy puffed. To excite more titillation, Armani's publicist revealed that Beckham wore skimpy briefs when playing for Galaxy. For most Americans, Beckham remained unknown as a soccer star, but he had become famous for modelling underpants.

During the trip with Giorgio Armani, Victoria won her own one-year deal to model his underwear.[21] She was photographed lying on an unmade bed, and Giorgio Armani labelled her a 'stylish, intriguing woman'. In the trade press the digitally manipulated photo of Victoria was classed as 'highly polished, colour-saturated and hyper-real'. Mert Alas, the photographer, said about his art, 'I love making something out of nothing.' Victoria claimed to have been paid £12 million for one year's work, while Beckham received about £8 million for his three-year contract. The family contest passed unnoticed.

Some sniggered about Posh's appearance at the Met Ball – 'over-dressed and over-made up' – but few could ignore how she swooned about the Cristal champagne, described meeting Julia Roberts – 'Incredibly, she knew who David and I were' – and had dinner with Giorgio Armani himself before clubbing at Bungalow 8. Thanks to Fuller the move to America had transformed her life.[22] The curtain was raised for her debut as a fashion designer.

Ten of her dresses were shown in New York's Waldorf hotel to a handful of journalists. All were near identical to Mouret's figure-hugging 'cling' dresses, using his fabrics, seamstresses and pattern-makers.[23]

Lacking the hundreds of million dollars that financed the major fashion houses' marketing campaigns, Victoria relied on free publicity to promote her new label, called 'Victoria Beckham'. Her publicists were tasked to nurture friendly journalists and their editors, feeding them newsworthy titbits and the occasional outrageous confession. As ever, photographers were orchestrated at airports and restaurants to deliver favourable headline images. Magazines were easy to please. Her interview routine rarely changed – recycling 'confessions' of insecurity, being a dedicated mother, love for David, hard work and her tireless keep-fit routine, topped off with a dose of self-deprecating humour. The new brand was not just about her designs but about her. Women, she was certain, would buy a £3,000 dress from a 'girl's girl' from Essex.

In a world so dependent on the approval of fashion journalists and commentators, Victoria's advantage was Anna Wintour's support of a fellow-Brit for her first show in 2007. 'For a start,' wrote *The Times*' Lisa Armstrong, 'it's very good.'[24]

Professional fashionistas were less enthusiastic. 'I thought she would have given up,' commented a senior fashion writer, criticising Victoria's unimaginative designs for lacking identity, mystery, sophistication and romance. 'But she just keeps making the stuff.' Years later Victoria admitted that the professionals were right to be underwhelmed about her first collection. 'I liked the fact that I didn't know a lot,' she said.[25]

Those invited soon afterwards to Marc Jacobs' summer collection noticed a new swagger as Victoria entered. Instead of sitting down, the star stood in a key spot, parading a new Audrey Hepburn hairstyle with a Cuprinol tan. 'It's a very flattering, refreshing, under-styled look,' said her hairdresser. Deliberately, Victoria posed for pictures, feeding what she herself called 'an unhealthy obsession with Posh'.[26]

Simultaneously, Natalie Lewis told friendly journalists that Jennifer Lopez, also at the show, was being 'upstaged' by Posh: 'Poor Jen sat miserably in the shadow of her new Brit pal.'[27] Lewis's variation at another venue was that 'Posh stole the show.' Soon after this, Victoria abandoned the 'bedhead bob' hairstyle and reverted to extensions.[28] Having sought acceptance, she said in an interview after the show, 'I don't really care what people think.'[29]

The same swagger was on display at the launch of Victoria's new denims at Harrods in London. Although sales in America had slumped she made extravagant claims of success. Her dVb jeans, she said, were sold in over a hundred retailers in the US and UK; sales of her sunglasses and handbags were 'booming'; and sales of her fragrances over the previous year had hit $200 million. That exaggeration surprised the Coty executives who were hosting Victoria's £10,000 dinner to launch her 'Signature' scent at Harvey Nichols in Manchester. Similarly, the launch in New York of 'Intimately Beckham', a 'Signature' fragrance endorsed by David, was a damp squib.[30]

Michael Silver knew the truth about the denim sales. His warehouse was full of unsold Victoria Beckham jeans. 'She's a stick in the mud,' he lamented. 'It had to be only her design, to only fit her. She rejected our suggestions.' Victoria, he decided, didn't understand 'profit'. Money was spent like water – but only other people's money. She also did not have a business plan. Other than selling her name stuck on jeans she did not understand how to create business opportunities. Vanity rather than value was her principle motive. 'I don't have the patience to carry on,' he declared in late 2008. Quietly, all the stock was sold off at a discount and the relationship ended. Victoria never acknowledged that setback. The Beckhams rarely allowed failure to be seen to bother them. In public, their cure was always to move on, fuelled by hype.

To Victoria, exaggeration had become natural. Reliant on Beckham's fame and fortune she told a journalist that she was a fashion 'hit because I never flash my tits'. Dreams and reality were expressed by Victoria in three simple sentences. 'I'm a terrible actress,' she said, and then mentioned the offer of several Hollywood parts. 'But I've turned down lots of roles. I can't act.'[31] Undoubtedly she believed that, just as she said with conviction in another interview, 'It never interested me, spending your husband's money.'[32]

Beckham paid for all three of Victoria's 34th birthday parties. The most extravagant was at the Via Veneto in Santa Monica. Among the stardust guests were her 'close friends' Kate Beckinsale, Gwen Stefani, Eva Longoria, Katie Holmes, Tom Cruise, P. Diddy, Will Smith and Elton John. Beckham's birthday present was a Californian vineyard. (The couple got to like good wines in Spain.)[33] Life, it appeared, had rarely been better. Naturally, the guest list and venue were leaked to the *Sun*.

Photographers noticed that she was slightly tipsy as she left the Los Angeles restaurant, stepping into Beckham's new £300,000 Rolls-Royce Phantom Drophead Coupe with 23 embossed on the wheel hubs. In her accompanying interview she once again played the modesty card. 'I'm not the kind of person that stands there and loves the attention,' she said. 'It might look that way but it makes me very, very nervous. I just make the best of what I have. I'm incredibly ordinary.'[34] Not everyone believed her.

'She's rammed down our throats how insanely happy she is,' observed a *Sun* columnist soon after, 'because she's done so incredibly well. But if it wasn't for David she'd be like the other Spice Girls, a fading star. She's rich and has three healthy boys, but shows no humility. So many women hate her.'[35]

Those comments hit Victoria. No one swooned about sexy Victoria, she complained. Especially not an old boyfriend, Corey Haim. 'Posh can't kiss, but gnawed on my lips,' he had said ungallantly.[36] She was increasingly worried that her 'close' girlfriends in Los Angeles were too attracted to Beckham. 'Everybody says, "David's the handsome one and she's so funny",' she had repeated. 'I'm sick of being the funny one.'[37]

Sustaining illusions was necessary for a woman repeatedly pleading about her insecurity, being boring and being bullied at school. 'I've never really told my story about being the underdog at school,' she trotted out. 'I was bullied – a lot.'[38] With nothing new to say about herself or the world, she switched her focus to appearances. Her clothes, shoes, accessories and make-up. It was not clear whether she understood the effect her words had.

Going to bed, she revealed, she covered her body with moisturising cream and then wore gloves and socks. In the mornings she described her dash to the bathroom to paint on eyebrows. 'David has never seen me with natural eyebrows,' she said. 'They were all plucked out years earlier. They're the first thing I do: wake up, put on the brow.'[39]

Even at her boys' school fête she put glamour before comfort. While all the other parents wore, in classic Los Angeles style, jeans and sweatshirts, she was dressed in a £11,500 leather trouser suit, with a £1,000 Chanel handbag, £300 Aviator glasses and five-inch Louboutin heels. On the games fields her Louboutin heels sank into the mud.[40] In another school outing, she led her children to 'daredevil rock climbing' wearing a tight mini-dress and five-inch heels. Unaware of her image, she spoke self-deprecatingly after serving school lunches, cake baking and going on trips with other parents, 'I'd rather go to the school than have dinner at the Ivy.' Her children were proudly introduced as modest angels: 'You don't want to end up with spoilt little sods. I want them to know you have to work hard for things. Brooklyn is a budding footballer.'[41]

The reward for the Beckhams' hard work was reflected in the £24.4 million he earned in 2008. The increasingly complicated structure of Beckham's corporate empire concealed the details from outsiders.[42]

In 2008, Footwork earned £12 million. Beckham's accounts showed that he took £9.9 million in salary offshore on which British tax was not payable. At the same time his accountants entered into circuitous inter-company trading. Beckham Brand sold £0.6 million services to Footwork Productions and paid the company £2.2 million for its services.[43] Next, Beckham Brand sold services to Beckham Ventures for £560,000, leaving Beckham Ventures owing Beckham Brand Ltd £4.2 million. A similar circular exercise to put the profits in the right hole was followed after his earnings in 2009 hit about £30 million, prompting the *Sunday Times Rich List* editor to predict that he would annually earn £50 million by 2015.[44]

Curiously, Beckham Brand's accounts were signed by Fuller, but earlier that year he had resigned as a director from the company. Seeing the error, he was reappointed, but the statutory form AP01 was not filed at Companies House. Technically, Deloitte's accounts were not legally approved. The charitable explanation about the confusion was over-stretch by his advisers. To reduce Beckham's tax bill the accountants and auditors were creatively moving his money between a succession of companies and lost track of their machinations. Their fees were unusually high, but the Beckhams benefited.

CHAPTER 21

MORE CAPS

As an ambassador for Britain, Beckham was unrivalled. Throughout the world he was admired, not least in China. At the Olympic hand-over ceremony in Beijing in August 2008 he was Britain's modest, magical star. For Brand Beckham the billions watching the footballer throwing balls from a moving London double-decker bus in the Beijing stadium was priceless. The cost was his performance as a foot-baller.

From Beijing he flew to Los Angeles to play for LA Galaxy, then to Boston and next to England and on to Barcelona for a World Cup qualifier. Even young players would struggle to stay fit criss-crossing 13 time-zones. Playing for England in Trinidad on 1 June 2008 he struggled to shoot straight, let alone run fast enough.

Fabio Capello denied that he had selected Beckham as England's captain to please Jack Warner. And similarly, Beckham praised Capello for bringing back 'seriousness and passion' to revive the squad. No one was fooled. The match and Beckham's inclusion in it were dictated by the FA to help secure the 2018 World Cup. Those watching the match, including the *Sun*'s Steven Howard, blamed Beckham for hindering the team's speed of play. Compared to the thrilling, fast football displayed by their rivals in Euro 2008, England's players plodded. Beckham's presence, wrote Howard, proved that Capello had still not found a new generation of players capable of attacking.[1]

Hours after England beat Trinidad and Tobago 3–0, and while Beckham was spreading his charm among local boys, Warner openly accused the visiting FA executives of complacency in their bid to host the tournament. Not one of the blinkered FA officials on the trip understood Warner's requirements. None wanted to believe the alle-gations that Warner had illegally resold World Cup tickets in 2006 with a huge price hike. They refused to even suspect Warner's dishonesty. Beckham was similarly myopic.

Focused on playing for England, maximising his sponsorship income and enjoying his colourful social life, Beckham also seemed oblivious about Galaxy heading into another crisis. 'It's going really well. Brilliant,' the captain told the *Sun*'s Charlie Wyett after scoring an extraordinary goal from 70 yards against Kansas City Wizards. LA Galaxy, wrote Wyett – impressed by a famous player who treated a journalist with class – had been transformed thanks to Beckham's 'extraordinary' popularity. The team was destined to win the league title.[2]

The truth was different. After seven consecutive defeats Galaxy were convulsed by disorganisation. The dressing room's atmosphere was toxic. Beckham's promotion of Gullit and Byrne had been destructive. The players blamed the captain for failing to rally the team in tough times, and choosing not to train on optional days. They were outraged by his refusal to pay for even one team meal. Without a blink he ignored their dissatisfaction. The captain remained silent. He did not call a team meeting; he said nothing to Donovan, the team's highest scorer; he did not discuss the possible solutions with Alexi Lalas. Beckham's way was to conceal his emotions and motives. Lalas was perplexed. Was Beckham, he wondered, a 'narcissistic, manipulative person?'[3]

Tim Leiweke had had enough. On 8 August, merely nine months after his shock appointments, he fired Lalas, Gullit resigned and Byrne departed. Fuller was silent about his own culpability. Amid that turmoil Beckham was inscrutable. Not a hint of emotion suggested he even cared. No one, especially Beckham, wanted to take the blame, only the credit for the millions of dollars earned from higher attendances and the additional 350,000 shirt sales.

Gullit's replacement was Bruce Arena, a 57-year-old American star coach. Despite an intensive burst of training, Arena watched the LA Galaxy's next five consecutive defeats. Beckham turned up for the matches, but after repeated transatlantic flights his legs could barely move. On one critical match day he was in London having dinner with Geri Halliwell after another miserable attempt to relaunch Findus and Omega-3. Although he was paid double that of any other player in the MLS league he appeared to feel no obligation to be in

Los Angeles. And as he admitted on his return, 'I'm just a little bit tired.'[4] LA Galaxy was destined to end the season at the bottom of the league. Over two seasons they had won more matches when Beckham did not to play.[5]

Beckham was focused on his selection for England. He expected FA executives to persuade Capello to include him in the England squad for the next four World Cup qualifiers. Regardless of being unfit, his inclusion was non-negotiable if the government and the FA wanted him to lobby for England to host the 2018 World Cup.

In early September he flew from Los Angeles to Barcelona to play against Andorra, now ranked 169th in the world. England had already won 2–0 when he appeared on the pitch for the last ten minutes. Four days later, England seemed transformed in Croatia. Theo Walcott, the Arsenal teenager, took Beckham's place and scored a hat-trick in an astonishing 4–1 victory. Beckham walked on to the turf five minutes before the end. He had flown 13,000 miles to collect two caps.

'I would be happy going home having not even got off the bench,' said Beckham. 'Whether I play is immaterial.' For the brand that was true, but for LA Galaxy it was damaging. Hours after landing back in Los Angeles from Zagreb, exhausted from jet-lag, Beckham stood paralysed on the Home Depot ground watching the Kansas City Wizards win 0–2. Booed by the fans, Beckham's sole contribution one week later in a match against DC United was an argument with the referee. At least after 12 games Galaxy finally won a match, 5–2.[6]

Then back to London for England v Kazakhstan. Coming on in the 79th minute, Beckham's free kick led to one goal, but that made little difference to England's 5–1 victory. Four days later against Belarus in Minsk he walked on to the pitch three minutes before the final whistle for another England victory, 3–1. Asked why he included Beckham in the squad, Capello mumbled in broken English that Beckham was good for morale in the dressing room. No one openly criticised Capello. 'He was God for winning against Croatia,' sighed an FA executive.

Beckham rejected any suggestion that his career had hit the buffers, but he took Capello's advice. He needed to play with a top European team to qualify for the 2010 World Cup. Unwilling to return to Britain and lose his tax advantages, he agreed that Byrne should negotiate a three-month loan contract with AC Milan. Beckham forgot to tell LA Galaxy about the negotiations. Bruce Arena learned from a

European newspaper report that Beckham had triggered an option clause in his Galaxy contract. When American journalists tried to ask Beckham about the news as he emerged from the Galaxy dressing room he ran for his car. Faster than he had run on the pitch for weeks, they all agreed.[7]

Beckham was welcomed to Milan by a huge Armani advertisement of himself and Victoria – him in skimpy white briefs and she wearing a polka-dot push-up bra.

At the end of December he flew with the Italian team to Dubai for ten days' training. Dubai, he discovered, remained an excellent location to legally avoid British taxes. He bought a condo in the world's tallest building, Burj Khalifa, for about $5 million; and he gave a beach villa bought in 2003 to his in-laws.

On his return to Italy, Beckham began 'loving his football again'. In a match against Genoa he shot an 18-yard free kick into the goal from a difficult angle to secure a draw. Bend-It-Like-Beckham was revived. Although he limped off with a hamstring injury, he felt that playing for Galaxy never inspired similar kicks, except for that 70-yard goal against Kansas City Wizards.

Playing in America, he realised, had also damaged his brand in Europe. Much to his surprise, Pepsi ended its £2 million a year sponsorship contract. To limit the humiliation, Beckham claimed that he had ended the Pepsi contract to launch his own brand of water. Nothing materialised.[8]

After scoring another goal for AC Milan he decided that at the age of 33 he would never be reselected for the England team if he returned to Los Angeles. 'I see my future here,' said Galaxy's captain. 'I realise I want to stay at this level. I don't know how Galaxy will take it.'[9]

His lawyers were told to find an escape clause in his Galaxy contract. But there were problems. Victoria refused to move to Milan. America had transformed her life. He could stay alone in Milan, she said. Milan's players, unlike Real Madrid's, she heard, did not indulge themselves in champagne and fast women. Beckham's gift of a £80,000 diamond-studded Birkin Hermes handbag was calculated to calm her anger.

Fuller also opposed his decision. Beckham's financial future, he said, was in America. Significantly, in the original negotiations the MLS's commissioner Dan Garber had granted Beckham a lucrative concession that he could establish his own MLS team if he played to

the end of his contract. Beckham would remain in the football business.[10] 'You'll be a star in America,' said Fuller. But if he stayed in
Milan he risked losing everything. Beckham dismissed Fuller's
protests. All he thought about was playing football. The rest was
irrelevant. If he could legally break his contract with LA Galaxy in
November, it should be done immediately. He was not interested in
owning an MLS club.

Beckham's disloyalty infuriated Tim Leiweke. On the eve of his
arrival 18 months earlier, Leiweke had said of him, 'David Beckham
will have a greater impact on soccer in America than any athlete has
had on any sport globally.' Instead, to Leiweke's embarrassment,
Beckham had paid only lip-service to those words in Los Angeles.
Even Beckham admitted the American dream had turned sour. 'It's
been a success' off the field, he said, but 'a flop' for Galaxy.[11]

Leiweke stipulated that Beckham should return to Los Angeles as
agreed in early March. Beckham refused to take 'No' for an answer.
In reply, LA Galaxy demanded financial compensation. AC Milan's
£3 million offer was dismissed. Leiweke wanted £10 million and a
further £18 million from Beckham. Milan's vice-president Adriano
Galliani refused to increase his offer. Beckham's performances showed
he was not worth more.[12]

Regardless of Beckham's claim that his fitness and technique had
improved, thanks to Milan's manager Carlo Ancelotti, his game for
England against Spain in mid-February was calamitous. Coming on in
the second half for his 108th cap, he was outplayed. After providing
one great cross he chased Spanish shadows and was booked for a
foul. England were defeated 0–2.

The negotiations to stay in Italy became protracted. For AC Milan,
Beckham was just a player but for Galaxy he was a commercial asset.
Beckham, Leiweke repeated, should return to Los Angeles by 9
March. Fuller negotiated a compromise. Beckham would return to LA
Galaxy in July and permanently leave Los Angeles at the end of
October 2009. He would personally pay compensation to Galaxy for
ending his contract. Milan would give him a short contract from
November. The fate of his own MLS football club was to be decided.

Over the following nine months Beckham was planning to fly tens
of thousands of miles to play 44 matches for AC Milan, LA Galaxy
and England.[13] 'It's his last chance to play top-flight football,' said

Simon Oliveira. 'He'll get booed by the fans,' predicted Alexi Lalas from the sidelines. 'Maybe Alexi will be doing the booing,' replied Beckham. He did not care that Landon Donovan was reinstated as Galaxy's captain.

There was good reason for Beckham to feel bullish. Against the odds, playing in Milan had demonstrably improved his game. Brought on after half-time in England's match against Slovakia, he supplied the pass that allowed Rooney to score. England's 4–0 victory confirmed Capello's judgement. England's self-confidence had been restored. Beckham was awarded his 109th cap, a historic first for a midfield player.[14]

He felt he was on a roll. Despite a rail strike in Britain, huge crowds turned up at Wembley to watch him play against Andorra. Many fans had earlier blocked Oxford Street to watch Beckham unveil a huge poster of himself in Armani underpants.

Playing from the beginning of the match, Beckham shone – taking the corner that led to one goal, then the free kick for a second goal, and then making a tackle to prevent an opposition goal. On occasions his energy disappeared, but when he managed a killer pass he was invaluable. The fans roared as England won 6–0. England rose in the FIFA rankings to 6th.[15]

This new self-confidence provoked infighting between Beckham's advisers. Byrne wanted to expand Footwork. Fuller disagreed, not least because he didn't trust Byrne's ambitions. And he objected to Byrne's outrage when Fuller interfered in football issues. Nor, more pertinently, did Fuller like Byrne's counter-accusation that Fuller's 30 per cent commission was excessive. Fuller told Beckham that his friend should be fired.

In the dispute between a trusted companion and the proven money manager, Beckham acknowledged that there could not be two bosses. By siding with Fuller he lost a true ally. Byrne resigned to become a football agent in Britain. His career as a football agent would be mired by controversy. After the bankruptcy of an investment fund, Byrne admitted in 2023 that he owed money to his clients, including the England team manager Gareth Southgate and the former England manager Glenn Hoddle.[16]

As Beckham prepared to return to Los Angeles from Milan in early July 2009, his triumph in Europe was overshadowed by the publication in America of Grant Wahl's book *The Beckham Experiment*. Describing Beckham's first year with LA Galaxy, Wahl challenged his reputation. He was accused of abandoning a sinking ship, and Wahl quoted Landon Donovan's criticism of Beckham as an uncommitted, selfish, untrustworthy 'cheapskate who took the team for granted'. After winning only one game in their last 13 matches, Galaxy's players were united in their dislike of Beckham. Since he had collaborated with Wahl, Beckham had good reason to feel that his searing exposé should have been modified by his media advisers. They had failed. On his first reappearance at the Home Depot Center in July, booing fans held a banner: 'Go Home Fraud'. As usual his publicists waved aside the handful of malcontents, but Beckham was riled. In a fury he challenged a fan in the stadium. He was fined $1,000.

As the temperature cooled, Beckham limited his criticism of Donovan's candour as 'unprofessional' and accepted his apology. Once again he fought back by improving his game. LA Galaxy won 3-1 against the New York Red Bulls. The bad news was that his Los Angeles Football Academy was haemorrhaging money. It was destined, like its London predecessor, to be quietly closed.

Beckham's revival was matched by Victoria's. Soon after celebrating her 35th birthday over lunch in Los Angeles with Eva Longoria, Heidi Klum and Kate Beckinsale, she had flown to Milan for Fashion Week. Despite her business's debts, she glowed as her dresses were paraded in the show. Then she hurried back to New York. Along with Madonna, Kate Moss and Rihanna she was invited to a dinner hosted by Marc Jacobs at the New York Met Gala.[17] Her publicist had also secured 16 pages in *Harper's Bazaar* featuring her designs. No other British start-up designer could boast that coverage. Elle Macpherson and Carol Vorderman, they claimed, wore her dresses.[18] Victoria appeared to have turned a corner.

Celebrating their 10th wedding anniversary in July 2009, the Beckhams congratulated themselves on their worldwide acclaim. Media coverage confirmed that they were the world's favourite couple. To cement publicly their relationship, Victoria agreed to a tattoo in Hebrew on her left wrist – 'Together forever eternally.' Beckham's maternal grandfather was Jewish,[19] and he also had the tattoo. Another tattoo Molloy had recently cut on Beckham's chest read in Mandarin,

'Death and life have their determined appointment – riches and honour depend on Heaven.' No one questioned his addiction to tattoos and the pain. The Beckhams' genius was to disguise so much.

Not everyone was persuaded. The forthright columnist Carole Malone spoke for the non-believers:

'I don't like Posh. Her fake DD boobs, fake insistence that her marriage is fabulous, her life is fabulous and her career is fabulous. I hate her claim that she is just an ordinary mum who wants to stay at home with David and the kids. In reality, her life is geared to parties, razzmatazz, glitz and ignoring his infidelities to keep the show going. She persuades herself that her truth is the truth. During Loos, she smiled and pouted because image is everything. Her limited talent needs Beckham to survive. He has the magic she lacks. Sticking to him showed that Girl Power was phony. In reality she should have walked away. But her lust for fame and money made her stay. She's fake. There's no proof of happiness. Behind the clothes, diamonds and shoes and bags, there's a hard, cold calculating woman.'[20]

Two days after that uncompromising judgement was read by millions of Britons, Victoria was seen at Nice airport. She looked ill and was sick on the plane to London. She was recovering from the removal of her implants, first inserted as 34Ds in 1999. 'No more torpedo bazookas. Gone,' she later told Vogue, keen to realign her image as a svelte fashion executive.[21]

Back in Los Angeles she was depressed. Giving beautifully wrapped gifts to celebrities had not fulfilled her wish for meaningful relationships. Her novelty had petered out. All her doubts, mistrust and paranoia surfaced. Living among the beautiful Hollywood stars always ended with unfavourable comparisons to Beckham. Nothing she said had won applause. Boob jobs, nose jobs, endless face packs, exhausting training – and yet inside the house she still looked like a washed-up WAG. Worse, if she went out with Beckham, his eyes were always searching for beautiful women.

On Fuller's orders, Jo Milloy's task was to protect her client from the truth about her husband and make sure the two stayed together. Placating the two was a full-time chore. Scheduling Victoria's diary was critical to maintain harmony.

Arriving for London's fashion week in September 2009, Victoria pleased Vogue's editor by turning up at her party in a tricolour bubble dress. She did not expect another reaction. Everyone was shocked by her appearance. With a 25-inch waist and the body of a young girl she looked ill. 'I am fine – happy and healthy,' she told inquirers. 'It's untrue to say I do not eat and that I'm unhealthy.' Her low-acidity vegetarian diet, she said, was 'honestly healthy'.

Eight years earlier she had confessed in her autobiography that she had been 'obsessed with her weight ... I just stopped eating. I was shrinking and the excitement of getting thinner took away the hunger.' As a designer reliant on free self-promotion to sell her clothes, a YouGov poll of 2,000 women that asked which star had the most desirable body was disturbing. Kate Winslet topped the poll with 16 per cent. Victoria was bottom with 1 per cent.[22]

To gain more positive reports, Milloy and Lewis, the two publicists, invited London's tabloid editors for dinner with Victoria at Nobu. Following Victoria's example of ordering a basket of steamed mushrooms, all ordered the speciality sushi as a starter. To their surprise, that was it. Victoria refused to order any more food. They emerged into Mayfair starving. None were surprised to hear Milloy's complaint that she received a low salary. Unlike Beckham, who gave his staff £1,000 Apple iPads as Christmas presents, therefore making a distinction between his staff and his Galaxy teammates, Victoria was not as generous in her gifting.

Unsurprisingly, irritated by her meanness, the *Mirror* republished Victoria's admission in her 2001 autobiography: 'Fooling people becomes part of the buzz.'[23]

CHAPTER 22

FOOLED

David Beckham relied on persuasion rather than publicists to secure his prize. After his sluggish performance in three successive England matches, he dug deep. Magically, his play picked up in the fourth game against Belarus. Coming on after half-time for his 115th cap he immediately delivered the pass for the second goal in a 3–0 victory.

The next day he was rewarded. Following a quiet FA executive's nudge, Capello included him in the 2010 World Cup squad. Guaranteed eight months in the global limelight, he celebrated until 3 a.m. with his old friend and adviser Dave Gardner in Bungalow 8. Gardner had become more important in Beckham's life. After Byrne's departure he had assumed more involvement in Beckham's business affairs by managing Footwork. And now that he was finally divorced from former soap actress Davinia Taylor, citing her 'unreasonable behaviour', he looked forward to more partying with his old friend Becks.

Hours after the celebration Beckham jetted off to Los Angeles – and landed with a bump. Customs officers at the airport spent three hours going through his 12 bags. Possibly they were looking for a forbidden import, Cuban Cohiba cigars, which Beckham had started smoking. His complaints were ignored.[1]

Finally, convinced by Fuller that he should stay in America to qualify for an MLS team franchise, Beckham renewed his contract for two years with LA Galaxy. He also signed a short-term contract to play for AC Milan after 28 December.

Over the following weeks Beckham's performances were patchy. His free kicks and trademark passes occasionally produced winning goals – as they did against Barcelona, Chivas USA and the San José Earthquakes – but he could not run much, especially not on an injured ankle. Cortisone injections and long-distance flights reduced his stamina during matches almost to hobbling speed. His wheezes were relieved by an asthma inhaler and energy supplements. His handicap inhibited Galaxy from winning outright against Real Salt Lake in the MLS finals on 23 November. In the penalty shoot-out Beckham scored, but Donovan's kick went over the bar. Galaxy lost 4–5.[2]

And then he was back long-distance flying – arriving in Cape Town via Germany on 4 December 2009 in a private jet. In the FA's desperation to parade Beckham as a key asset in its bid to host the World Cup, it had contributed £100,000 to the jet's cost. Beckham paid £50,000.

Greeted by the FA's chairman David Triesman, Beckham was not aware of the unusual chaos within the organisation. Not only was Triesman, a former Labour politician, openly mocked by the sports media as 'greedy' and not a football expert, but since inheriting the position from Geoff Thompson two years earlier, he had failed to remove from the board those directors accused of being excessively focused on the international gravy train and not specifically on the complex politics of international football.[3]

As a group, the FA executives – and Beckham – misunderstood FIFA's Swiss president, Sepp Blatter. In Blatter's opinion, Britain's FA was steeped in sexual and financial scandals and was unable to control the hooligans among England's fans. Equally irritating to Blatter, the FA boasted about the Premier League's global success, and in their World Cup bid declared that 'Football's Coming Home'. In Blatter's opinion, they forgot that foreign billionaires controlled much of the Premier League. Most pleasing to Blatter was the FA's naivety. The FA seemed unaware that corruption was endemic throughout FIFA. Triesman and his board ignored reports that South Africa had only won the right to host the 2010 World Cup by secretly giving $10 million to Jack Warner in exchange for his three votes. There was an added delicious irony for Blatter. During the last election for FIFA's presidency, the FA withdrew its support for his Swedish opponent – honest Lennart Johansson – because Blatter promised to support England's bid to host a World Cup.

On the eve of the Cape Town meeting, Triesman and his executives failed to draw the obvious conclusion from Blatter's visit the previous week to Vladimir Putin in Moscow. At FIFA's headquarters everyone knew that Russia was the favourite to host the 2018 tournament, despite a US embassy description of Putin's Russia as 'a corrupt, autocratic kleptocracy in which government officials, oligarchs and organised crime are bound together to create a virtual Mafia state'.

Blind to the bonds between Blatter and Putin, Triesman and his board were certain that England's outstanding stadiums and infrastructure would secure victory. They accepted at face value the pledges by Jack Warner and his corrupt co-conspirator, the American Chuck Blazer, to support England's bid. They also believed the 'sincere' advice from South Africa's football chief Danny Jordaan and Warner that England's bid depended on Beckham.

Just three weeks earlier the *Sun* had warned that England's bid was already a disaster created by the FA's 'amateurs'. 'Only Becks can save it,' announced the newspaper. With Beckham on board, all the media fell behind the FA.[4]

'We just can't be arrogant,' Beckham's spokesman read from the script before arriving in Cape Town. 'We must show respect for other countries.' He added on Beckham's behalf, 'We had two or three good meetings with Jack Warner and Sepp Blatter. I like Jack a lot because he is very honest, direct and tells you what he wants.'[5] Beckham sincerely believed those sentiments, and he was undoubtedly the man of the moment.

As he walked into FIFA's hall, heading for England's stand, Beckham's magnetism thrilled the delegates. Everyone rushed to see the hero. Enjoying his stardom as the centre of attention, he quietly presented to his audience England's credentials to win the bid. Among those in the crowd, the Qatari delegates noted his attraction. He was identified as the man to help them in the future.

Blatter played the English delegates. To Triesman's delight, Beckham was chosen to draw out the balls for the first games of the 2010 tournament. On stage with him was the South African actress Charlize Theron. 'The body language between them is electric,' murmured a delegate. In the full glare, the two stars barely took their eyes off each other.

The senior FIFA officials including Blatter, Warner and Chuck Blazer quietly sniggered. The idea that a footballer could trump the influence of protagonists like Putin exposed the calibre of the FA's officials.

As he flew back to Milan, Beckham's spokesman added that the next World Cup in 2010 would be 'Becks's swansong. He wants to go out with a bang. He will spill his guts for his country.'[6]

Back in Italy, Beckham was clearly unfit. While his publicist persuaded the *Mirror* that AC Milan's last three victories owed much to Beckham, the Italian sports newspaper *Gazzetta Dello Sport* reported of the same games that 'he looked like he was in a waxworks museum'. Another Italian reporter judged Beckham to be the worst player in the Milan team, while a third described him as 'confused and confusing'.

AC Milan's two Champions League games against Manchester United were embarrassing for Beckham. During the first home match, Beckham provided one cross and thereafter remained invisible until he was subbed. In the return match on 10 March at Old Trafford the fans cheered, but he was on the bench. Sitting as a spectator until the 64th minute, the forlorn figure watched Paul Scholes and Wayne Rooney play outstandingly well. Eventually, when Milan were 4–0 down, the manager surrendered to the crowd's chants of 'We want Beckham.' Nostalgia was Beckham's ace card. Seven years after leaving Manchester United he resurrected some of his old magic, supplying accurate corners and one powerful volley goal-wards. Milan were beaten 7–2 on aggregate. At the end of the match the crowd roared as their hero wrapped a United scarf around his neck and saluted. Then he disappeared down the tunnel. His record for Milan in 33 appearances was two goals and a few productive crosses.[7]

To some Italians, Beckham had become a figure of fun – a footballer enjoying flashbulbs and fortune. While he promoted Armani in a Milan street, a TV presenter, Elena Di Cioccio, sneaked up from behind him, followed by a live TV camera. Wearing yellow rubber gloves she grabbed Beckham's 'golden balls' in order to judge the veracity of the Armani advertisement. 'I touched it,' she told viewers, 'but it's small, David. It's a trick. What did you use? Cotton-wool?'[8]

In Los Angeles, Simon Cowell was also winding up the Beckhams. After Victoria's lacklustre appearance on Fuller's show *American Idol* – some viewers criticised her as bland and unimaginative – Cowell invited her to appear on his rival *X Factor* show. Furious that Cowell had invaded his turf, Fuller made sure that his offer was rejected, prompting Cowell to describe Fuller as brainy but with 'the personality of a wet weekend in Hastings'. That week, Victoria's fate had become irrelevant compared to Beckham's misery in Italy.[9]

Four days after his humiliation in Manchester, just before the end of Milan's match in the San Siro stadium the ball was at Beckham's feet. He shifted his weight, paused and reached down. He found a 'huge hole' in his Achilles tendon. Struggling to the touchline, he collapsed. 'It's broken, it's broken,' he wailed as he was carried off on a stretcher. His international career was ending in tears. In the dressing room he spoke tearfully to Victoria on the phone, and then flew to Finland for surgery. She joined him there. They were so often apart for the children's and her own birthdays, she wondered if it was the right moment for him to retire. He would not consider it, although the inevitable cost of constant air travel was six months away from the pitch. Tim Leiweke was left with the bill; he was legally committed to pay Beckham's $2.5 million annual salary.

Nine days after his injury, Beckham flew from Heathrow to Los Angeles. On the same day, Victoria landed at Heathrow from Los Angeles and flew on to Moscow. They did not meet. 'There's already a 2,000-strong waiting list for her new designs in Moscow,' said her publicist.[10]

That fiction did not suppress the increasing rumours that the Beckhams' marriage was once again troubled. The sight of Beckham with Charlize Theron at a Lakers basketball match in Los Angeles dressed in similar checked shirts sparked gossip that the two had become more than good friends since their encounter in Cape Town. To keep the show on the road, Victoria's publicists were summoned into action.

The *Sun*'s Richard White was encouraged to write breathless accounts of the Beckhams' exhausting sex life – 'five times a day despite his injured leg' – to satisfy Victoria's demand to be pregnant again. The following week White was told that their sterling efforts were interrupted by Victoria's unscheduled dash from Los Angeles to London. 'David's knackered and was relieved to get a break,' a 'friend' told White. But Victoria was eating fruit to 'fatten up'. Then the 'friend' told White, 'They are getting on better than ever.' On her return to America, said the 'friend', Beckham sent Victoria flowers every day.[11]

In another flurry of publicity, Victoria spent £3,000 on erotic gear for Beckham during a trip to Barneys in New York. Among the packages carried by her assistant was an S&M seductress's £82 mask. 'It's a surprise for David,' she told the saleswoman. Her own publicist added, 'He's one lucky guy. Posh is head over heels in love with David.'[12]

In case that wasn't enough, Milloy described how Posh and Beckham acted in an advert to launch, for the fifth time, another fragrance, 'Beckham Yours'. Naked in a moving lift they seductively groped each other. As the doors reopened, Beckham emerged with dishevelled clothes, wiping lipstick from his smiling mouth. After minimal sales, the latest fragrance evaporated.[13]

To hammer the sex theme for her latest fragrance, Victoria announced that Wednesdays were kept free for sex. 'It's sacred', she insisted. To promote herself she focused entirely on him. Asked about Beckham's high-pitched voice she replied, 'He was sitting at the end of the bed and he had no clothes on. He has all those tattoos, which I love. He hadn't done his hair. He just naturally looks good all the time. So he's sitting there all ripped. And I thought, "You done good, girl." I sure wasn't thinking about his voice.'[14]

The climax of the FA's £15 million campaign to host the World Cup was David Beckham's rehearsed presentation of a 1,700-page dossier to Sepp Blatter in Zurich on 14 May 2010. Standing gratefully next to Beckham, David Triesman echoed the icon's sentiments of England's 'passion' for football.

Less than one week later, Triesman was forced to resign from the FA. In a crude sting operation, a woman recorded Triesman saying that Spain and Russia planned to bribe referees in South Africa. Some suspected dirty tricks to derail England's bid.[15] Triesman's departure foreshadowed England's World Cup campaign in South Africa. Culturally divorced from England's players, Capello housed the team in a remote hotel. Denied beer and bonding, the atmosphere among the players deteriorated. Ferried long distances to different stadiums, they arrived disgruntled and unmotivated.

Beckham sat alongside Capello in the dug-out as England's players delivered shameful performances against both Algeria and the USA. But the soft draws allowed England to scrape through to the knock-out stage against Germany.

England's fans in Bloemfontein were devastated. After a pathetic display of passing the ball backwards and sideways and never storming towards the opponents' goal, the national team was thrashed 4–1, an unprecedented scale of defeat by Germany. Described by the media as 'pampered schoolboys', 'overpaid buffoons', 'bad-mouthed, selfish sociopaths playing a crippled game', their £6 million-a-year manager defended his team's performance as 'tiredness'. Naturally, the Italian looked for scapegoats.

In the fall-out, Capello announced on television that Beckham at 35 was 'probably a bit too old' to be selected again for England. Although he was forewarned the previous night by Capello's right-hand man, Franco Baldini, Beckham reacted to the news as if to an unexpected, almost fatal shock. His scripted line by Oliveira was 'disrespected, disappointed and dismayed' by Capello's axe. Victoria added that she was 'disgusted' by the rude and insensitive manager for his thoughtless treatment of a national hero. Two days later Capello resigned as manager, pocketing a £6 million pay-off.[16]

With no alternative team outside Britain, Beckham agreed to stay with LA Galaxy until his contract ended in 2012. The Californian lifestyle, sunshine and lower taxes had their advantages as his injury finally healed in September. 'I felt like I was dying,' he admitted about his first shots as he resumed playing. By early October, after scoring from a free kick, he had slightly recovered. He still showed little loyalty towards the club. Although he had played only 48 games out of 120 for Galaxy, his latest priority was to be selected for Great Britain's 2012 Olympic team playing in London. 'I would be very proud,' he said. 'Especially as it's in a part of London where I grew up.' He began searching for a European club for training. After Milan's rejection he accepted Spurs' offer for a few weeks and took a pay-cut from LA Galaxy. 'I always try to prove people wrong,' he said to those who assumed his football career was over.[17]

Days later, Beckham snapped up Jack Warner's request for another appearance in England's team playing yet again in Trinidad. To satisfy his sponsors he needed to boost his global profile. But his expectations of a relaxed trip unexpectedly soured. On the eve of the private jet flight from Los Angeles with Brooklyn, he was targeted by *Touch*, a German-owned magazine based in America.

Michelle Lee, the magazine's editor, published the outrageous claims of Nici 'Irma' Nezirovic, a 26-year-old Bosnian prostitute, that she had been paid about £9,400 by Beckham for sex five times in New York and London between August and September 2007. Contrived by the magazine to maliciously damage Beckham and England's bid for the World Cup, *Touch*'s report was utterly untrue. British journalists who interviewed Nezirovic effortlessly exposed her repeated lies. Yet

Touch's editor and her employers, the Bauer Media Group, insisted that their 'scoop' was accurate.

For once, Milloy's description of Victoria's 'rage and humiliation' was justified.[18] Beckham lodged a $25 million claim for damages in Los Angeles. A judge would reject his complaint. Nici and the magazine, ruled the judge, had the constitutional right to free speech about a man of public interest, even if their account was 'sordid lies'. There was no evidence, ruled the judge, that the magazine had 'avoided the truth', even though Bauer provided not a shred of evidence to justify their story. Worse, in order to punish Beckham, he was ordered by the judge to pay Bauer's £170,000 legal bill and cope with *Touch*'s boast to have 'successfully opposed' Beckham's 'unmeritorious complaint'. In the brief post-mortem, some believed that the prostitute's story was delivered to the German publishers by the Russians to discredit England's bid for the World Cup.[19]

None of the English team and FA officials seeing Beckham enter the Trinidad hotel by the back door noticed his distress. He concealed his anger. His only visible upset was the Marks & Spencer suits given to each member of the delegation. 'I'm not wearing that again,' said Beckham. New suits were ordered from Paul Smith.

During dinner with Jack Warner in a Chinese restaurant, Beckham worked hard to charm the Trinidadian. Warner played his own part perfectly. Beckham returned to Los Angeles convinced that Warner's three votes would be cast for England. He spent the weekend with Victoria in Napa Valley, unaware that Warner was already pledged to support Russia's bid.

The curtain rose on 2 December 2010 in Zurich for the FA to make their 30-minute 'Oscar-winning presentation'. Beckham arrived from Los Angeles. Confident that England would secure sufficient votes to get through to the second round and then victory, the FA had persuaded Prime Minister David Cameron and Prince William to join the parade around FIFA's headquarters.

William and Beckham had bonded over football before the 2006 World Cup. Ever since then the Prince, an Aston Villa fan, had enjoyed discussing football with Beckham. Whenever newspapers published stories about Beckham's adultery, William dismissed them as intrusive and untrue. Like Beckham, William could not have anticipated the unfolding disaster.

'I'm sure we can see off Putin,' Beckham told journalists, thrilled that he, Brand Beckham, was ranked equal to the Prince and Prime Minister. The Prince smiled as Jack Warner put his arm around him with the pledge, 'You have my vote.' Because the Russian leader was not coming to Zurich, Cameron was assured that England had won at least six votes in the first round. The three famous Britons seemed unaware that a BBC TV *Panorama* documentary by Andrew Jennings had exposed FIFA's process as wholly corrupt.

The faces of the Englishmen froze as the results of the first round's vote were announced. England were eliminated with just two votes, which included its own. In the aftermath, Andy Anson, the FA's co-ordinator, was seen arguing with a Cypriot delegate for failing to deliver his promised vote. 'We walked into a room,' recalled one FA official with hindsight, 'filled with all the baddies from the James Bond films.' Another lamely recalled, 'We came with squash rackets and didn't realise it was a game of tennis.'

But on that day, when Qatar's improbable victory to host the 2022 tournament was also announced, no one accused FIFA officials of pocketing corrupt payments. Only five days later, after Qatar's successful bid had been priced as $50 million in alleged bribes, did Beckham brand FIFA's corruption as 'disgusting'.[20] Gary Lineker would call for Qatar to be stripped of hosting the competition after an email allegedly showed that Mohammed bin Hammam, a Qatari vice-president of FIFA, had dispensed £3 million in bribes, including £1 million to Jack Warner.[21] The accusations were to rebound.

To humiliate England, FIFA's ethics committee reported in 2014 that the bidding process was free of any corruption – with one exception. England was condemned for handing out Mulberry bags to delegates' wives. In addition, the FA's attempts to forge a close relationship with Warner by sending Beckham and a team to Trinidad was judged to have 'undermined the integrity of the bidding process'.[22]

If ever there was a moment for Beckham to stand on principle, it was the exposure of FIFA's corruption. Had the world's most prominent footballer denounced Blatter and his cronies, Beckham would have been known as more than a glamorous icon. Instead, Beckham quickly withdrew from the controversy. Football was his meal ticket. He could not afford to jeopardise his future income by alienating FIFA. Nor could he risk future sponsorship deals. His reward for silence was an invitation to Prince William's wedding and the BBC's Lifetime Achievement Award.

Back in Los Angeles, Beckham and Tom Cruise drove on their $60,000 Hellcat Combat motorbikes into the California hills. Calling themselves the Midnight Boys Bike Club, they spoke about liberating themselves from celebrity and domestic turmoil. They had much in common.[23]

Katie Holmes was uneasy in her marriage. One year later she fled to New York. 'Suffocated' by Scientology, she described her need to save her daughter Suri from the cult. She doubted that her 'irreconcilable differences' with Tom Cruise could be resolved and filed for a divorce.[24]

Victoria's reaction to her differences with her husband was the opposite. She sent out messages about getting pregnant. Having said she was 'too busy', she pronounced 'I am getting to bed with David Beckham every night, so I am trying. Obviously, I am trying.'[25]

CHAPTER 23

MIXED MESSAGES

Beckham's image was restored during a visit to British troops in Afghanistan's Helmand province over four days in May 2010. All the allegations of sleaze, adultery, petulance, self-promotion, greed and indifferent football performances evaporated as soldiers met a selfless, humble family man.

Arranged on behalf of the British army by Stuart Higgins, a former *Sun* editor, even that professional cynic was amazed by the spectacle unfolding on the rugged terrain. In the midst of battle, hundreds of soldiers in Camp Bastion queued to meet their hero – and each one of them was individually greeted by the visitor. Posing for selfies, signing autographs and exchanging memories of past football glories, Beckham patiently stood on a stage and genuinely engaged with every squaddie. 'I've never seen the same impact of one man on a group of people,' thought Higgins.

The 'squaddies friend', alias the *Sun*'s 9 million readers, were his fans and he always needed more. While he had 3.5 million Facebook friends, Cristiano Ronaldo had 10 million. To build his fan-base as he neared the end of his sporting career, he agreed to appear at the newspaper's annual charity event, Help The Heroes.[1]

Now he was 35, not only was his football career nearing the end. Covered with tattoos, his thinning hair and fading youth were also not so appealing to global brands. In their search for new international champions Beckham was excluded. Asked about his future, Beckham answered, 'I want to be a successful businessman.' By any measure that was a challenge. His huge income was – relatively speaking – static. In 2012 he earned £2.5 million from LA Galaxy and £15.2 million from Footwork, up by £1.7 million. Fuller's team was once again looking for new business opportunities. Recent experience should have made them more discriminatory.

Despite Beckham's earlier failure to promote Omega-3's sales, Findus under their new owners Young's contracted him to relaunch and promote their 'GO3 Superheroes Challenge'. The prize for the young winner was to meet Beckham.

The first hurdle was to agree the photograph of Beckham on the packaging. Findus wanted a large picture, Beckham wanted it to be small. 'There were endless arguments,' recalled an advertising executive. 'It was a real balls-ache getting there. Our designers were practically pulling their hair out with constant reworkings.' Their only success was getting Beckham's authentic signature – a key attraction for young boys. The advertisement plugged that Beckham grew up eating fish fingers. Strangely, in a podcast conversation with the celebrity chef Ruth Rogers in February 2022, Beckham mentioned all his childhood favourites – jellied eels, pie and mash, gammon and chips – but again did not mention fish fingers.[2] The £1 million fee for Beckham failed to deliver results. Sales of Young's fish fingers and Omega-3 that year fell by 20 per cent.[3]

Beckham was also contracted to be the new face of Sainsbury's Active Kids campaign. The £1 million deal would promote sport and combat obesity. That campaign failed too. Both the Beckhams' fragrances – 'Homme' and 'Intimately Yours' – flopped. He was not on a winning streak. Fragrances by Beyoncé, the Rooneys and other celebrities outsold those of the Beckhams.[4]

After losing the Armani contract, Beckham decided to launch his own brand of underwear, favouring 'the pouch to the fly'. Lucy Litwack, a London-based designer, developed the 'global business strategy and the business plan' of David Beckham Bodywear. After completing the design work and contracting a manufacturer in Sri Lanka to match her specifications, Litwack was dumped. Beckham switched to promote his new underwear collection with H&M. The contract, said Fuller, 'marks an important step in the evolution of David's journey from sporting hero to entrepreneur and icon'.[5]

During a low-key promotion party for Beckham's H&M pants in Fuller's Los Angeles office, Victoria announced: 'David designed it all himself. He developed the project in its entirety. David created it, we own it and H&M does the distribution.' Not for the last time, the Beckhams claimed the credit and expunged the earlier involvement of anyone else. The Beckhams' harsh non-disclosure agreement imposed on Litwack silenced any complaints. In the first months, sales of H&M underwear fell by 6 per cent.[6]

Victoria's financial results and sales were even worse. In 2011 she lost £1.6 million. Victoria's publicists told a different story. Since her fashion launch in September 2008 they claimed that her clothes had been 'virtual sell-outs'. Among the buyers, said her publicists, were Jennifer Lopez and Madonna. Anxious to secure further A-list approval she mentioned Kim Kardashian's endorsement: 'One of my favourite designers is Victoria Beckham.'[7] Most discerning rich women did not identify with Kardashian. Coco Chanel would have loathed Kardashian's vulgarity. In an excess of hype Natalie Lewis also announced that 'Gwyneth Paltrow, Charlize Theron and Cameron Diaz are said to be queuing up to wear the Victoria Beckham range on the red carpet at the Oscars.' The detailed reports the following day suggested that possibly only one Beckham dress was worn – and that at an after-party. Briefed by Victoria's publicists, *The Times*' Lisa Armstrong reported that the annual turnover for clothes and accessories was '£200 million'.[8] But the financial report filed by Victoria Beckham Ltd revealed a less flattering truth. Annual sales were poor – just £6.7 million.

In the world of fashion, facts were irrelevant. The prize was to keep Victoria's name in lights. Accordingly, her publicists negotiated that she would win the 2011 British Fashion Awards prize as the Designer Brand of the Year. She beat Stella McCartney. Since there were no other serious competitors, McCartney also won an award.[9] Less famous designers later complained that Victoria's team ensured that they would fail to win any prizes.

Although admired for effort, Victoria was 'not having a jot of influence on the world of fashion,' according to a doyenne of the business. 'Her clothes are not effective for women,' said another expert. 'It's always about her.'[10] Serious fashionistas also criticised her commercial skills. Even Victoria would later admit about her early years that 'there were a lot of raised eyebrows – from those who could raise their eyebrows'.[11]

Fuller was also financially bruised. Few insiders in 2008 had understood his master plan to support Mouret and Victoria. Now his entry into fashion was even less comprehensible. To improve sales, Victoria's workshop was transferred from New York to London. Financed by

Beckham, Victoria proudly presented the mirrored walls and acres of black carpet of her new atelier in Battersea. Unseen in the background, Roland Mouret was still giving advice to a team of about twenty.

In Victoria's mind, although the average woman was size 16, she was the brand leader for women to follow. Since she had not learned how to professionally sketch, her working methods were unusual. 'I stand in my knickers,' said Victoria, and let her staff drape fabric over her size 6 figure. Or, 'I get naked and make the clothes on myself.'

Her staff also adopted other unconventional methods. On one occasion an employee bought a rival's dress at Harvey Nichols in London. After it was returned days later, the designer noticed that his stitching had been removed and replaced. Before that discovery, the store had refunded the purchase money. The designer was too scared to complain.

Hankering after headlines Victoria's publicists looked for whatever publicity they could rustle up. She appeared as sultry as ever on the cover of Turkish *Vogue*. Posing for *Elle* magazine in Coco Chanel's house she was dressed by Karl Lagerfeld. Instead of portraying Chanel's exquisite chic, her pout implied torment. In the accompanying interview, she described how, after her children went to bed, 'I shove on a face-pack and pluck my eyebrows – it's all I'm fit for.'[12] In another interview she complained that accompanying David made her miserable: 'No one ever looks at me. They're here to take David's picture.' In another confession she lamented, 'I don't want to be such a public figure,' but could not help adding, 'Of course, getting into bed with David Beckham every night after having four kids ...' Her vulnerability divided emotions. Some felt pity for a hard-working mother trying to hold together her marriage, while others were irritated by a spoilt multi-millionairess has-been.

Her fourth child, Harper, was born on 10 July 2011. Victoria had publicly wished for a girl. Some speculated that an American fertility clinic had facilitated her choice of gender. Cynics added that at birth Harper was probably heavier than her mother. Within hours of the event Victoria could not resist revealing on social media her £3,000 purchase of 50 bottles of cream to prevent stretch-marks.[13] A few weeks later, working hard to recover her figure, she was seen in a figure-hugging black dress, Louboutin high-heels and heavy eye make-up. 'First time ever I wasn't actually sure I could cope,' she said, repeating that she was a control-freak who found it difficult to trust people.[14]

Among those she suspected was her husband. After publicly thanking her as 'truly an inspiration for me every day', he was seen with Katherine Jenkins and Prince Harry at The Arts Club in London. Shortly afterwards, Jenkins denied having an affair with Beckham. Her long denial was the more remarkable because no one had realised that there was the rumour of an affair in the first place.[15]

Beckham was also indulging in a favourite pastime: having tattoos. His latest was of Harper's name on his neck. That one had followed Mark Mahoney's 12-hour marathon of a chest tattoo showing Christ surrounded by three cherubs, representing his three sons looking after him. That idea, said Beckham, emerged during the night: 'I use them to express how I'm feeling or thoughts or memories.'[16]

Among his other 33 tattoos was a tree; a 2003 pledge on his left arm to Victoria, *Ut amem et foveam*, meaning 'So that I love and cherish'; a 2007 pledge to her, 'Forever by your side'; and other symbols meaning 'Death and life have determined appointments', 'Riches and honour depend upon heaven', 'Death comes to us all and if you lead a good life, you will be rewarded in heaven.'[17]

In that unreal atmosphere, anxious about Victoria's business losses and uncertainty about his own future earnings, Beckham decided to follow the example of the Kardashians, and especially their success on social media. Giving up all pretence of protecting their family's privacy, they posted endless photos of the proud parents with their baby daughter and a video of the whole family playing on Malibu beach. They also issued detailed descriptions of Tony, Jackie and Sandra helping Victoria while renting a house in Malibu.[18] After the closure in July 2011 of the *News of the World* in the midst of the telephone hacking scandal, they assured themselves that the media would become more subject to their control.

That confidence was dented at the launch of the new Range Rover Evoque in China. For some time the Beckhams had enjoyed a close relationship with Land Rover. In exchange for cars and payment, Victoria agreed to support the brand.

The relationship had begun two years earlier in Kensington. Reading from her script Victoria had said, 'I am honoured to be part of the creative team.' Two years later at the launch of the new Range

Rover Evoque in China she forgot the script and said, 'I've designed a car that I want to drive, a car I think David wants to drive.'

Standing nearby, Jaguar Land Rover's design director Gerry McGovern was startled. 'Victoria, that wasn't on the script,' he said. 'You weren't involved in the design.'

'Oh, I didn't realise what I was saying,' she replied.[19]

'It's hard to believe anything she says,' concluded Dean Piper after an interview with Victoria for the *Sunday Mirror*. He spoke to her, downcast and moody, as she flitted between Los Angeles, London and New York accompanied by sleepless baby Harper. Her sons stayed in Los Angeles either with Beckham or her parents and staff.

'Our entire lives are planned around their lives,' she told Piper about her sons. Similarly, while denying that she Googled to see what people wrote about her, in the next breath she referred to the comments about her fashion: 'I'm blown away by the reviews and I read every single one.' But after drawing breath she lashed out at those who wrote, 'I look fucking miserable.'[20]

David Beckham's swansong from LA Galaxy lasted much longer than planned. His five-year contract ended in November 2011. To qualify for England's Olympic team Beckham needed to train and play in Europe. Weeks before his Galaxy contract expired, Fuller negotiated an 18-month contract with Paris Saint-Germain (PSG) for a basic £4 million. Fuller's focus was not on the last gasps of Beckham's football career but the prospect of Beckham owning an MSL club, possibly in Miami.

Qatar was a potential money-rich investor. As the producer of one quarter of the world's liquefied natural gas, money was no object. If the sheikhs were attracted to a prize property, a deal could probably be done. Unaware of Fuller's calculations, the public recalled that only one year earlier Beckham had condemned the Qatari government's bribes to corrupt FIFA officials and secure the 2022 World Cup. Since then the truth about FIFA's decision to give the tournament to a tiny desert kingdom without any football infrastructure and intolerably high temperatures had become well known to Beckham. The global media had exposed the corrupt background to Qatar's $150 billion World Cup plan from mid-2010, months before FIFA's decision and climaxing in Qatar's purchase of PSG in 2011.

After huge property investments in London, Qatar's rulers wanted to imitate Sheikh Mansour of Abu Dhabi by purchasing a sporting trophy like his Manchester City FC. Mansour's fortune was transforming the club into a European Champions League team. Envious of a rival Gulf ruler, Qatar's advisers identified their potential allies to win the bid for the 2022 World Cup.

Among their targets was France's president, Nicolas Sarkozy. Nine days before the 37 members of FIFA's council voted, Qatar's leaders had lunched in the Élysée Palace with Sarkozy. Another guest was the European football (UEFA) chief and French football hero Michel Platini. During that lunch, the Qataris made an offer. If Platini voted for Qatar in Zurich the sheikhs would invest billions of dollars in France, including the purchase of PSG, Sarkozy's favourite but troubled team. After Qatar was named as host of the World Cup, Platini never denied that he had switched his vote because of the agreement over lunch. The promised rewards soon followed.

Since calling FIFA's corruption 'disgusting', not only had all of those facts become known to Beckham but he also knew that Qatar's rulers disregarded human rights, including those of migrant workers, and particularly pursued medieval discrimination against women and homosexuals.

The possibility of millions of pounds flooding into the Miami club persuaded Beckham to change his opinion. Awarding Qatar the World Cup was no longer 'disgusting'.

It fell to Simon Oliveira to mitigate the threat to Beckham's image. Unlike Beckham, Oliveira had no illusions about Qatar's morality. Only months earlier Oliveira had advised Beckham against allowing Qatar to invest in his Miami football team. 'I'm seriously worried that Qatar would have a toxic impact on your brand,' he emailed.[21]

Victoria's refusal to move the family to Paris put an end to that option. She and the children, she said, would not leave Los Angeles. Fuller's deal with PSG collapsed. Rather than play for an English club and pay higher taxes, Beckham signed for one further year with LA Galaxy. Considering that Galaxy claimed to have earned more than $100 million over the previous years, thanks to Beckham, Fuller failed to extract the best deal for his client. Beckham's annual wage would continue at £2.5 million rather than the original £4 million.

Fuller's timing was unfortunate. Just after Beckham signed, Galaxy beat Houston 1-0 and secured the MLS title for the first time. Landon Donovan scored the winning goal after a header from Beckham and a pass from Robbie Keane. Thereafter, Beckham was once again struggling on the pitch.[22]

Stuart Pearce, Great Britain's Olympic football team manager, flew to America to watch him play. He saw Beckham fail to make a critical tackle that led to a goal. He also missed an open goal and was booked for a foul. Pearce refused to include him in the team. 'I'm disappointed,' said Beckham quietly.

However, he then exploded during the following match against the San José Earthquakes. He kicked the ball at a player prostrate on the ground, kicked another ball at the referee, and then burst into anger on the pitch. Banned for a match and fined, he returned to score four goals and set up four more. That was too late for Pearce. He ignored the demands that Britons wanted to see Beckham play. He was wrong, complained the fans, partly because it was Beckham who had helped bring the Olympic flame from Greece to Greenwich. The protests were pointless. Beckham was no longer loved by all of football's leaders.

In Great Britain's 2012 Olympic triumph one big disappointment was football. As is all too common in knock-out tournaments, England were defeated in the quarter-finals on penalties. Beckham might well have made the difference. His absence was highlighted by Victoria's agreement to perform with the Spice Girls in the closing ceremony. After a week of unpaid rehearsal the quintet stood on top of five black cabs singing some of their hit songs as a sensational finale to the super-successful Games.[23]

And that, Victoria decided, truly was the end of singing with the Spice Girls. No more shows. After numerous arguments between the five – Geri ignored Victoria, and Mel C did not forgive Victoria for refusing to lend her a dress for a television show two years earlier, claiming it would lower the tone of the brand[24] – Victoria refused to co-operate in the production of a TV documentary to promote the Spice Girls musical, *Viva Forever*.

On the night of the premiere in London, Victoria arrived late wearing a trench coat. She looked miserable as she posed with her family and sat apart from the other four girls. When the others stood up for the music she sat glued to her seat. There would be no further reunions, she insisted. The show never recovered from terrible reviews.[25] However, she did pocket her share of the merchandising sales.

Five months later, Beckham refused to sign for another year for Galaxy. His family were returning to London. On 2 December he played his last match. Victoria arrived too late to watch the game. LA Galaxy beat the Houston Dynamo 3–1 to win the league, but the stars were Robbie Keane and Landon Donovan. Beckham didn't dare to take the last penalty. 'I've missed a few over the years,' he said after the match. 'Success doesn't come easy. It's hard graft.'[26]

'David has delivered for us,' the MLS commissioner Don Garber asserted, echoing a benevolent opinion that Beckham had improved American football's popularity and image. The raw statistics hardly supported the accolade. Neither the attendances at the stadium nor TV viewers had increased substantially, and the standard of football had hardly improved. On reflection, Alexi Lalas lamented that Galaxy was sacrificed to Brand Beckham. That was unfair. When Beckham arrived Galaxy were among the weakest teams, and they were the champions when he left. The critics' opinion was summarised by the *Mirror*'s Brian Reade: 'Beckham is the ultimate symbol of the Golden Generation in that he promised much, yet delivered little but hype.'[27] Fuller's boast at the outset that Beckham would earn £128 million ($250 million) over five years proved to be an exaggeration. He pocketed an estimated £54 million to retain his rank as the world's highest-paid footballer.[28] In his farewell interviews Beckham talked up American football, not least because – thanks to the original contract – he had the right to own the franchise of an MLS team at the markedly reduced price of $25 million.

And then Beckham's life got better. Unable to extract a contract from AC Milan, in early 2013 he agreed to start training at Arsenal. That option was abruptly abandoned after Dave Gardner delivered a five-month contract with PSG.[29] Unannounced, the Qataris were back as potential investors in Miami. Beckham's £3.3 million deal was shrouded in mystery. 'The money doesn't interest me,' said Beckham after signing the contract with PSG's Qatari chairman Nasser Al-Khelaifi. To a fanfare he announced that his entire income from PSG would be donated to a local French children's hospital charity.

'Big-hearted Beckham,' raved the *Mirror*. 'Here is a good man and we should cherish him,' wrote Tony Parsons. Similarly, Oliver Holt, another former critic, praised Beckham for not 'chasing one last payday' because he has 'chosen one last shot at glory'.[30]

In their snap judgement neither writer grasped either the real purpose of the deal or the tax advantages Beckham had secured. His unpaid contract was structured to avoid France's 75 per cent tax rates; and, more important, to keep his non-dom status and avoid British taxes until the new financial year started in April 2013.

In anticipation of that change, Beckham's finances had become even more complicated. In 2012 he had earned £16.5 million from Footwork and taken £14.1 million salary from his sponsorships, on which he paid no British tax. But in 2013, Footwork paid Beckham no salary. On an income of £14.8 million, he took £7.5 million in lower-taxed dividends, and left the rest of the money in his company. His American income was, as usual, taxed in America.

That was the short-term advantage of his income-free contract with PSG. Over a longer period there was an understanding that Beckham might be employed by PSG's owners, the Qatar state, as an ambassador for the World Cup. Although the final agreement would be signed only in 2018, over the following years he would be paid a retainer, although none of the Qatari payments were especially identified in his established trading companies. The accountants would add what some experts interpreted as a smokescreen to a £10 million payment in the 2016/7 accounts.

Beckham knew he could not avoid questions about Qatar's corruption in his first press conference on 16 February 2013 in the Parc des Princes. Nearly 400 journalists crammed into PSG's underground press-room, which was built for 200 people and normally occupied by a mere 20.

Asked if he could speak French he replied '*Bonjour*'. Then, speaking with unusual fluency in English, he acknowledged that Qatar had bought the Beckham image rather than the footballer. With pride he accepted that he was a tool to spread Qatar's credibility beyond Europe, Asia, Africa and South America. Unhesitatingly he also admitted that his relationship with Qatar would continue after he stopped playing for PSG. But he revealed no details. There was no hint of any self-doubt in associating himself with a virtually absolute monarchy that had not only supported the Taliban's destruction of Afghanistan's fragile liberalism, but also had a notorious human rights record and was the main financial backer of the Islamic Resistance Movement known as Hamas.

Similarly, he was untroubled by what was certainly his last football contract. At the age of 37 he said he felt like a 21 year old: 'I've not lost any pace, because I didn't have any to start with.' He brought to PSG experience and commitment. 'When I play it's never about the biggest contract, the amount of money. It doesn't interest me.' In his first match he came on to the pitch in the 76th minute. And got a yellow card.

Living alone in the Bristol hotel's 3,400-square-foot Imperial suite with three bedrooms and a massive pink marble bathroom – the published tariff was $21,000 a night – Beckham exploited the other advantage of playing for a major club: to promote his brand.[31]

Among his staunchest allies was Dylan Jones, the editor of GQ magazine, who named him in 2013 'the most stylish man of the year'. Jones also obtained an endorsement from Tommy Hilfiger: 'Beckham is the men's fashion icon of today, undoubtedly No. 1.' As a cheerleader, Jones had featured Beckham six times on the magazine's cover and would grant Beckham his 'special award'. He would write about their long relationship and say: 'Beckham was the victim of the media, whereas now he is more in control of it.'[32]

Jones was just part of a constellation of journalists cultivated by Milloy and Oliveira to promote the Beckhams. Close-knit and secretive, they peddled influence through close friendships, usually platonic but occasionally more. Among their recruits over the next months would be Julian Payne of Matthew Freud's international public relations firm. Freud prided himself on getting direct access to an editor on the telephone to kill a story. 'We're going to take over,' Payne told the *Sun*'s Dan Wootton, pleased to join the self-appointed elite of publicists denying journalists the power to publish the truth. Payne would later become Prince Charles's spokesman.

On their advice Beckham resisted interviews. Unless his publicist had total control over the publication he would in future communicate through images rather than words. Admired as a patriot and adoring father, he promoted himself as the man who women want to sleep with and as a man sought by other men as their best friend. Any words he thereafter uttered were scripted.

That partly explained his new friendship with Guy Ritchie. Few became closer to Beckham during those months than Ritchie. Booked to film Beckham for an H&M boxer-shorts advertisement, the director fed the footballer's vanity. Born in 1968 in Hatfield, 20 miles north of London, Ritchie was known as a director of gangster movies – and for being Madonna's husband for eight years. Ambitious and talented like Beckham, he inspired the footballer to share his interests, including wine, beer-making, architecture and shooting.

Ritchie's sizzling H&M advertisement, shot in Los Angeles, glorified Beckham and won his friendship. The camera tracked Beckham, solely wearing his pants, as he vaulted over tall hedges, ran across a tennis court and dived into a pool. 'It was fun playing an action hero for the day,' said the star, adding that he had no ambition to become an actor.[33]

Interviewed on French television, Beckham was asked whether the director had used a body double and if any shots were faked. 'No,' Beckham replied. 'I can say that the crotch is mine and the backside is mine as well. I can confirm that's my bum.' And he added, 'I did all my own stunts.' After the film was examined, his truth unravelled. The right arm bore no tattoos and the bum was not his. Reluctantly, H&M admitted that Ritchie did use a double.[34]

None of those mishaps influenced Beckham's image. Regardless of whatever he said, or failed to do on the pitch, he remained beloved by fans and especially politicians. Even those no longer seeking re-election enjoyed meeting the famous sportsman.

A Los Angeles agent arranged for David and Victoria to visit President Barack Obama and his wife and their daughters in the White House. During their light-hearted chat the celebrity president joked about Beckham modelling his own pants. The next day the footballer sent him a box of his H&M underwear. Michelle Obama, Beckham's publicists briefed, had insisted that her husband wear them. New York's Times Square was later covered with photos of Beckham in his pants.[35]

Despite the publicity, H&M's underwear sales fell by a further 3 per cent and an advertising blitz during the Super Bowl crashed. The company would claim that 600 pieces had been sold, but just three were sold to the public – the rest were hurriedly bought by the company's employees. A technical glitch had ruined the marketing operation.[36]

Brushing aside any misstep, Fuller's team in Battersea grabbed every opportunity to promote the Beckham brand while he still played in Paris. He was employed as a 'face' for the season's Premier League matches on Sky Sports and was contracted by the Chinese Super League to be its ambassador. Flown to China, he shrugged aside the CSL's match-fixing scandals. 'I'm not here to clean up anything,' he said. 'I'm here to educate children and give them a chance to become professional footballers.' He dismissed the same accusations during a second trip to Shanghai. A thousand fans greeted him on his first day to promote football. His fee for the week was about £2 million.[37]

In between he fleetingly visited London to watch ten-year-old Romeo and seven-year-old Cruz start a six-week development programme at Chelsea football club. He also went to see 13-year-old Brooklyn trial for Chelsea in the youth team. 'He impressed his coaches,' said Beckham.[38]

Inevitably, constant travel undermined his own football perfor-mances. Although he once came on to the pitch at the end of a PSG match to set up a winning goal,[39] French football journalists dubbed him 'Le Flop'. The decisive blow came on the eve of his 38th birthday. He gave the ball away to Barcelona's Lionel Messi, who went on to score.[40] Booked for a foul and jeered, Beckham's performance was judged by the sports newspaper L'Equipe as 3 out of 10 and by another newspaper as 'all washed up'. Beckham was so bad, reported one newspaper, that the children's hospital would be justified in returning the donation of his salary. Beckham was never in Messi's orbit – arguably, no one was – and the Argentinian would score over 800 goals before he left Barcelona, but the truth finally dawned.[41]

Asked later when he realised it was time to quit, Beckham would reply: 'Probably when Messi was running past me.' His image-makers quickly refined the message. Oliveira, alias 'a pal', told the Sun that Beckham had rejected PSG's offer of another year's contract as 'it was best for the family'.[42] The Mirror was told by Beckham that after speaking to the owners and manager, 'I know how happy they are with me here.'[43] He was retiring, he said, 'at the top'. Famous for scoring from deadball situations, in his playing career he had scored a creditable 127 goals for his clubs, plus the 17 he had scored for his country.

Generously, the French saluted the 38 year old in his last match against Brest. Appointed captain, and with his whole family watching, the last corner he took was volleyed into the goal and PSG won the league title. 'Merci, David!' shouted the fans. Playing for four clubs, he had won a championship with each one[44] – which of course became part of the 'mythology' surrounding him.

In Britain, the judgement was also positive. Bookmakers suspended taking bets that he would receive a knighthood at the end of the year. Praised by some as a great footballer, a selfless ambassador for sport and an outstanding father, only a few were sceptical. 'The retired show-pony has finally grown bored of parading in his underpants and trying to figure out what his tattoos mean if translated,' wrote one critic. He had never taken England beyond the quarter-finals of a tournament.[45]

Among the eulogies and career obituaries, one statistic was ignored: the extraordinary number of yellow and red cards Beckham received during his career. Playing in the Premier League for Manchester United, he was given 42 yellow cards. Thereafter, he was given 38 yellow cards in his four years at Real Madrid, 27 yellow cards during his sporadic six seasons at LA Galaxy, and six yellow cards at AC Milan. Besides the 113 yellow cards whilst playing in four different domestic leagues, Beckham received another 17 yellow cards in his Champions League career, 20 in various domestic and international Cup competitions, and an unprecedented 19 yellow cards playing for England – an aggregate of 169. That indiscipline was overshadowed by the nine red cards he was shown in his career. To put that figure into some context, the three most red-carded players in the history of the Premier League were each given eight red cards. Significantly, not a single English referee gave Beckham a red card.

That intemperance reflects the real Beckham behind the mask. Rather than the smiling legendary role model, his record of indiscipline and an aggregate of 169 yellow and nine red cards mirrored the same crude anger he expressed in his private communications, a trait which would later be exposed publicly. The public and private Beckham were different characters.

Returning to Hertfordshire after the beginning of a new tax year on 5 April 2013, Victoria understood that their income now totally depended on David Beckham's image.

During a dinner with chef Gordon Ramsay and his wife, Victoria asked, 'David, I wonder how long it would take if I put a pic of us having this dinner on Instagram before it gets on to *Mail Online*?'

'Go on,' Beckham concurred. 'Try.'

Within 15 minutes the photo was published for the world to see. The Beckhams laughed. Fuller's suggestion that they control the media by feeding them Instagram images had worked. Social media trumped the tabloids. Aggressive journalists, they agreed, could henceforth be ignored.

CHAPTER 24

KNIGHTHOOD

'You're a shoe-in,' Beckham's friends assured him. A knighthood was a certainty in the 2013 New Year Honours List. Excited by the resonance of Sir David and Lady Victoria, Beckham knew that Sebastian Coe, who had headed London's successful 2012 Olympics bid, had started the process. 'You've done everything that's been asked of you,' Coe told Beckham. A nomination had been submitted to the government's honours' committee to be endorsed by 'the great and the good'. In Beckham's view, a knighthood would automatically materialise.

Qualifying for a knighthood, Simon Oliveira and Dave Gardner knew, required evidence that Beckham had contributed to society in a broader way. Fortunately, he had already established markers. Visiting British troops in Afghanistan and his various charitable acts, including sending a signed football shirt to a young cancer sufferer, had won substantial credits. To seal the deal, the man-of-the-people needed to confirm his generosity to charities, minimise his wealth and crush any jealousy aroused by those Instagram images displaying his opulent lifestyle. All good ideas offered by his staff would be considered.

Some proposals were eccentric. One publicist, Tess O'Sullivan, suggested that sponsors for Beckham's chosen charities should finance his flight into space. 'He'd stay up in a space station for a few weeks,' she wrote. 'He'd be in the public eye all the time.' In a memo headed 'Planned revenue streams for DB's space adventure,' O'Sullivan speculated that the highest sponsor should pledge $12 million to a charity and others between $3 million and $5 million. Among those to be approached were the dictators of Kazakhstan and Azerbaijan. The charitable angle, admitted Tess, was a fig leaf: 'The approach is not to bring in revenue but to find a legitimate reason and purpose behind DB's journey that attracts paying sponsors and supporters.' By this reasoning Beckham would not be backing a great cause, but rather staging a stunt to promote himself. 'You must be kidding!' Beckham exclaimed. 'Up in space? Nah!'[1]

The more important initiative to secure a knighthood was Beckham's support of UNICEF. Building on the existing relationship with the charity that had been established during Beckham's period at Manchester United, Oliveira suggested that he make some substantial donations. Beckham did not reply. Instead, to prove his commitment, in November 2013 he volunteered to head to the Philippines in the aftermath of Typhoon Haiyan. About 6,300 people had died across the devastated islands. 'I want to make a difference,' Beckham said.

His charitable image was blended by his publicists with snippets about the 'normal bloke' who had played an important role in getting the Olympics and bidding for the World Cup. Among his stream of posts, Beckham was shown to enjoy drinking in local pubs, eating jellied eels and a pie in his favourite East End café, building Lego, especially the 4,287-piece Tower Bridge, and expressing his devotion to the Queen. On some mornings the 'normal bloke' walked down the hill from his newly rented home in London's Holland Park to Paul, the local patisserie, for a croissant and coffee. Paul's female employees had compiled a rota so that each served him in turn.

Encouraged by his publicists, the tabloids reported that the charitable efforts by the man-of-the-people was 'certain' to secure his knighthood in the New Year's list.[2]

Simultaneously, Victoria attempted to dilute her image as a multi-millionairess dressed in diamonds and couture clothes who cavorted in private jets between countless houses and Ritz hotels. In an interview with *Vogue* she described herself as an average mum shopping every week at the local Waitrose: 'Harper balancing on one hip, Brooklyn hanging on the trolley' while she yelled at the other children, 'No, you can't have that.' To flatter herself, she continued: 'People look at me in awe like I'm from the circus, but it doesn't bother me.' While the Waitrose scene might have occurred once, she was invariably accompanied by helpful bodyguards and a driver. Her description of watching her husband play football was similarly fanciful. 'We stood cheering on the terraces,' she said. She always sat in the directors' box.[3] To prove her own commitment to charity she tweeted a photograph of her donation to raise cash for victims of Typhoon

Haiyan. The photo was a shoe mountain with hundreds of pairs of her own shoes. It suggested that she still owned hundreds of other unused shoes.[4]

After establishing the positives, Beckham's campaign managers sought to neutralise any negative stories. The most high-profile danger was the publication of Alex Ferguson's autobiography. In anticipation of Ferguson's criticisms of his former protégé, Beckham published a new version of his own autobiography. Although there were no new revelations it joined Ferguson's on the bestseller charts. Astutely, at his press conference, Beckham did not respond to Ferguson's criticism of him: 'He lost the chance to become an absolute top-dog player.' He also refused to attack Ferguson personally. Everything seemed set for the arrival in early December of the formal letter offering a knight-hood.

Neither he nor his advisers appear to have reflected that since 1949 only 16 football personalities had received knighthoods, and only six of those were former players, including Pele, Bobby Charlton and Stanley Matthews. Beckham obviously believed that he ranked with those giants of the sport.

The routine of the Honours Committee in considering awards was to request adverse information on every candidate from the police, the security agencies and the Inland Revenue, or HMRC. In Beckham's case, HMRC automatically flagged up that Beckham had quite legally registered as a non-dom but they were puzzled by the complexity of his companies' accounts. Moreover, Fuller had stated that Beckham would earn £25 million a year from LA Galaxy alone. That money was missing from the British companies. For the tax inspector, Beckham's audited returns did not make complete sense.

Equally important, he had joined a supposedly legal tax avoidance scheme organised by Ingenious Films. Hundreds of famous Britons had signed up to the scheme. The average saving for each of the 697 members of the scheme in the first year had been about £200,000. The biggest investor had pocketed £19 million by avoiding taxes. In HMRC's opinion, Ingenious' investors were involved in 'aggressive tax avoidance' which should in retrospect be outlawed. Beckham was one of their targets for recovering those taxes. HMRC's demands, Charles Bradbrook emailed, were 'a nightmare'.[5] Beckham's partner-ship in Ingenious Media's tax structures classified him as a tax dodger.

The combination of Beckham's aggressive self-promotion and tax avoidance through his non-dom status and the Ingenious schemes did not persuade Bob Kerslake, a former head of the civil service and the chairman of the Honours Committee, to be sympathetic. To Beckham's misfortune, Kerslake wanted that year to reward the nominations from the voluntary sector and the champions of diversity. Beckham's opulent lifestyle grated upon Kerslake's left-wing political inclinations.

Beckham's wealth had allowed him to keep his Los Angeles house and buy a seven-bedroom house in London's Holland Park for about £21.4 million ($37.9 million). The masterly renovations supervised by star interior designer Rose Uniacke, including a house on adjoining land for Brooklyn and an indoor pool, would cost an estimated £8 million. While the work was completed, the family rented a similar house opposite. The family house in Hertfordshire was sold for £12 million and their house in France was sold for $2.9 million. They had kept the Los Angeles house, whose value had fallen to £4 million, for summer holidays.[6] That would leave them with a total of five homes: in London, the Cotswolds, Dubai, Los Angeles and Victoria's apartment on New York's Upper East Side. All of them had been bought with loans.

The notion of 'Lady' Victoria irritated Kerslake. To make her life tolerable, Victoria had admitted that she employed five permanent staff including a nanny, a chef and two housekeepers, plus security staff. In reality, the payroll across their five homes consisted of more than 20 people. Yet despite that wealth some habits were ingrained. At the Pizza Express in Loughton in Essex, Victoria paid the £115 bill for Sandra and six children in cash, but left no tip. 'She never does,' said the manageress. 'But she does say "Thank you".' At least Victoria's self-description as a 'tight-arse' was honest.[7]

Unimpressed by the Beckhams and their charitable work, Kerslake believed it was 'too soon'. Beckham's bid for a knighthood was rejected.

By mid-December the Beckhams suspected the bad news. The discreet letter asking whether he would accept an honour had not arrived. 'What have I done wrong?' he asked. Coe mentioned HMRC's black mark but did not know the details.

On 13 December, Beckham appeared on Jonathan Ross's television show. With a mischievous smile the interviewer asked Beckham whether 'they haven't tipped you a wink?' The master performer grinned and mentioned his OBE: 'I'm very honoured and lucky to have what I already have. I'm very proud of it.' As agreed before the programme, Ross then said: 'I am convinced you're going to get it. I don't see how they could possibly pass you over.' Beckham and Ross laughed and the audience clapped. End of the show.[8]

Soon after the list was published on New Year's Eve, Jo Milloy admitted that Victoria was 'gutted' not to be Lady Beckham.[9] Oliveira said nothing publicly, not least because Beckham's reaction had been unfortunate.

The honours committee, Beckham emailed Oliveira, were 'unappreciative cunts'. In his splenetic diatribe he dismissed the possibility of a CBE – 'Unless it's a knighthood, fuck off. They're a bunch of cunts. I expected nothing less.'

After helping to get the Olympics and acting as a UNICEF Goodwill Ambassador since 2005, he had been snubbed: 'It's a disgrace, to be honest, and if I was an American I would of [sic] got something like this 10 years ago.' What made it worse was the singer Katherine Jenkins receiving an OBE: 'Katherine Jenkins OBE for what? Singing at the rugby and going to see the troops plus taking coke. Fucking joke.' Jenkins would be furious that Beckham never apologised for writing that email.[10]

Oliveira refused to be defeated. 'You aim for the highest honour, you should not give up so quickly,' he emailed Beckham. 'This gives us even more reason to work for UNICEF, the armed forces, other charity commitments etc. this year.'

In early 2014, Beckham could at least celebrate Fuller's latest success. Against the odds he had concluded a new multi-million-pound contract. In addition to Coty, Adidas, H&M and several Asian companies, Beckham was contracted by Diageo, the global spirits manufacturer, to be the 'face' of Haig Club Scotch, a 100 per cent grain whisky to be sold at £60 per bottle.

The unexpected success of George Clooney's campaign to sell Casamigos Tequila, created in 2013, proved the value of celebrity endorsement. In an attempt to attract young people to whisky, Diageo sought a celebrity and landed on Beckham. Their marketing team decided that Beckham, famed as a 'modern sportsman and business-man', represented all the right values for Diageo. Sold in a blue bottle with the strapline 'Make Your Own Rules', the challenge was to persuade young people, especially women, that Beckham liked whisky. The only downside was Beckham's reputation as a teetotaller. And was he really a notorious rule-breaker? Perhaps adultery counted! Excited by Fuller's claim to have secured a share of the profits, the bonus for Beckham was filming commercials in foreign locations. Dave Gardner, Guy Ritchie and other friends would be invited.[11]

Now that Brand Beckham was earning more than ever, Dave Gardner and Oliveira calculated that Beckham could afford more money to prove his devotion to charity. That, they were certain, would help to manoeuvre a knighthood during 2014.

UNICEF's relations manager for high-profile ambassadors, Chloe Edwards, agreed that Beckham should become the lead sponsor of his own '7 Fund' dedicated to help children at risk from violence, abuse or disease. His name would encourage the rich across the world to contribute to UNICEF's work through his fund.

The 7 Fund, Beckham announced in 2014, was his 'Number 1 priority'. The reality was different. After the fund's launch, Beckham's relationship with Edwards became fraught. Asked by her to donate £1 million immediately and then match the highest bidders at the fund's imminent New York charity auction, he emailed Oliveira and Gardner. 'Chloe asked me outright which I was pissed off about. I don't want to do it and won't do it with my own money.'[12]

Beckham's refusal to contribute the first £1 million put Oliveira under pressure from Edwards. The £1 million, he was told, was 'desperately needed'. Oliveira emailed Beckham that he should personally 'deliver some money before the end of the year'. Oliveira warned that if he failed his image would suffer. Beckham's German lawyer came to the rescue. His client, he told Oliveira, had already contributed 'a seven-figure pound amount'. That was doubtful, not least because Edwards had not received any money.

Flustered by Beckham's stubbornness, Dave Gardner emailed Oliveira that 'UNICEF is crucial to his brand' but Beckham treated it 'like a burden'. The reality emerged in the aftermath of another Philippines typhoon in February 2014.

Beckham's two-day visit to the destitute Filipino children was beamed across the world. He was flawless. With charm and sympathy he greeted the victims, played games with the children and listened with interest to UNICEF's officials. The countless photographs, wrote Gardner, had produced a 'halo effect' for Beckham's charitable work.

Unseen by the public, but familiar to Gardner, was Beckham's irritation about the trip and the cost. Beckham flew to the Philippines in a private jet paid by the hotel group Sands and Diageo. In return, Beckham would promote their brands in the region. But Beckham was dissatisfied with that arrangement. Since UNICEF had saved his fare, he wanted them to reimburse him £6,685 for the business-class tickets. 'To be honest, there's no way it should be costing me anything,' Beckham emailed Oliveira.[13]

Gardner understood the downside of Beckham's approach to money. 'UNICEF is crucial to the brand and his life,' he emailed Oliveira. 'All you and me have tried to do is ... create things that he must do for charity so he looks good and people see the great work instead constantly reading how much money he makes or what the brand is worth.'

For Beckham the priority appeared to be keeping his own money. 'There is no way it should cost me anything,' he retorted as another financial demand was made. Asked to donate £1 million to UNICEF for a prize-giving dinner in Shanghai, he replied: 'I don't want to put my personal money into this cause. To pour this million into the fund is like putting my own money in. If there was no fund, the money would be for me. The fucking money is mine.' Beckham's refusal to contribute to UNICEF contradicted his spokesman's insistence of his personal donations at that time. The public and politicians could recall his 2012 assertion about his wealth: 'I never thought about the money, the fame. It never interested me.' In 2014, he would earn £50 million.[14]

Not surprisingly, Beckham enjoyed spending his money on luxuries, but the media reports of his excesses were unlikely to impress Bob Kerslake.

His purchase of a £50,000 diamond bracelet for Victoria's 40th birthday was akin to his pocket money. The gift, along with Victoria's celebration of her birthday in Los Angeles with Ken Paves, her hairdresser, and Eva Longoria followed by dinner with Gordon Ramsay, was topped by stories of a wild birthday party at the London Arts Club. Everyone, including all the Spice Girls, drank champagne until nearly dawn. Not included in the celebrations was Kate Beckinsale, formerly Victoria's 'great friend', who was now suspected of getting too close to David, although no evidence ever emerged.

Soon afterwards, Dave Gardner moaned about Beckham's image as a 'man of the people' taking another hit.[15] In an Instagram post to his 32.6 million followers, Beckham included a shot of a gold-plated laptop. 'First one in the world. Great present,' he captioned.

'Nice,' Oliveira emailed to his employer soon after the post appeared. 'Will keep that one off social media, as then the idiots will say we're being showy like Lewis Hamilton private planes etc.' Oliveira added, 'You and VB need to be careful about that one, as you've always handled that one well. You're the man of the people.'[16] Resenting that mild putdown Beckham replied, 'I like to be in control of pics that go up and also the way some of it is written. I'd like to be able to post.'

After reading that reply, Oliveira emailed Gardner, 'This is when things go to pot. Celebs think they know best but because they don't live in the real world like you and I, they make mistakes.'

A new 90-minute television documentary produced by Fuller and bought by BBC TV was another self-inflicted mistake. *David Beckham Into The Unknown* followed Beckham and some friends on an expedition into the Brazilian rainforest. His quest, as described in Fuller's proposal, was to find one 'native' in the remotest jungle who had never heard of David Beckham.

'What are you going to do about your hair?' asked Victoria before he left. 'I'll wear a hat,' replied Beckham. 'Make sure you do,' advised Mrs Beckham sternly. The film was memorable for his perfectly styled hair and Beckham's much-repeated line, 'I love my kids.' Eventually, one native was 'found' who did not recognise Beckham. Apparently, the native was also not surprised by the large film crew.

The film cost £1.25 million to make, including £322,000 for travel, £79,000 for 'sundries' and a £50,000 fee to Fuller. The final accounts show that the concoction lost £491,000. Mocked by viewers, BBC TV rejected Beckham's next proposed documentary *For the Love of the Game*. Fuller offered to film Beckham playing football in seven continents. Fuller's company, DBrazil TV, eventually ceased trading with losses of £536,000.[17]

Oliveira's only good-news message was Beckham's nomination for Spain's highest sporting award. Beckham was unimpressed: 'If it's not a knighthood – forget it.' Oliveira emailed back, 'Then we might need the ghost of Christmas future [as] the ghost of Christmas past hasn't worked.'[18]

In the summer of 2014, Oliveira was as ever looking for new opportunities to land the knighthood. Unexpectedly the Prime Minister, David Cameron, asked for Beckham's support in the Scottish independence referendum. Making public his opposition to Scottish independence in the last weeks of the campaign, Oliveira advised Beckham, was certain to be rewarded. 'I also think your support will play well with the Establishment and in turn help your knighthood.'

'OK, let's do it,' Beckham replied. On the eve of the vote Oliveira released Beckham's statement, 'What unites us is greater than what divides us. Let's stay together.'[19]

With that box ticked, Oliveira once again urged Beckham to donate money to UNICEF. His employer refused. 'He doesn't care if he gets a knighthood or not,' concluded another employee. Intending to cling on to his own money, Beckham revealed his priorities during a UNICEF visit to Cambodia. The trip was combined with his opening of an H&M store in Macao. The private jet was paid for by H&M, and UNICEF was not asked to reimburse the commercial fare, but UNICEF's reservation in the five-star Sofitel in Angkor Wat was rejected. Beckham wanted to stay in the more luxurious Amansara resort hotel. Instead of Beckham just paying for those three nights, UNICEF was asked to contribute their Sofitel rates to his bill at the Amansara.[20] He refused to contribute his personal money to UNICEF. Beckham appears to have thought that giving his reputation and time was a sufficiently generous donation for the charity. No further personal financial costs could properly be expected.

Increasingly, Beckham's company accounts raised questions. In 2014, marking his return to Britain, his salary drawn from Footwork was merely £25,000. That small sum minimised any National Insurance contribution. From the profits of £12.4 million he took a dividend of £6.5 million, on which dividend tax would have been payable. The cash left in the company soared from £6.9 million to £16.8 million. Such high cash levels left in the company suggested that his advisers might be considering he resume life outside Britain as a non-dom.

With money uppermost in his mind, Fuller once again recommended that Qatar should be encouraged to invest in the Miami football club. Oliveira opposed the idea, in part because it would be another reason for the honours committee to reject Beckham's nomination.

'Don't give a fuck anymore,' interjected Beckham. 'I'll decide who my investors are, not these cunts. They are fucking cunts.' He continued, 'I pay taxes and always have done so. They have no right to do this ... Cunts.'[21]

CHAPTER 25

FASHION FOLLIES

Charity, Beckham believed, started and mostly stayed at home. By 2014, Victoria's six-year-old fashion business had racked up debts of £3.4 million owed to her husband and the bank. Away from the sunshine and easy lifestyle in Los Angeles, her ambition in London demanded more money. Millions of pounds more.[1] To her good fortune, Beckham was not worried. Keeping Victoria happy was his priority and he trusted Charles Bradbrook, his accountant, to care of his finances.

To be taken seriously in London a fashion brand needed a show-case. Choosing a narrow shop in Dover Street off Piccadilly, Victoria paid a record annual rent of £650,000, to be guaranteed by Beckham Brand Ltd. Neighbouring shop-owners were infuriated after the land-lord demanded matching rent increases.

The shop's interior featured a polished concrete staircase, green-glass changing rooms, American walnut cupboards (all made from the same tree – 'That's really, really expensive', volunteered Victoria) and a stream of scent projected from Diptyque's 'Feu de Bois' candles. The cost was about £3 million. She hung a Damien Hirst artwork taken from their private collection.[2]

To her irritation she missed the shop's showbiz opening in September 2014. She was in New York to address the United Nations as a newly appointed international goodwill ambassador for AIDS. Just as she was telling delegates in anticipation of her first trip to Ethiopia that 'It has taken me until 40 to realise I have a responsibility,' David opened the Mayfair store and posed for selfies. Scrutinising the shop's two clothes' racks, fashionistas discovered that no dress was bigger than a size 10, a sequined skirt cost £3,750, T-shirts were £700, a handbag sold for £18,000 and the price tag on a VB key ring was £165. Over the following days, staff revealed that hundreds of women had walked through the store, but only three items were sold in one day.[3]

Three months later, Milloy told the *Sun* that Victoria had earned £1.3 million profits by doubling the 2013 sales to £30.39 million. 'Posh is sitting on so much cash,' said Milloy.[4] The accounts told a different story. The company's debts in 2015 had risen to £4.5 million. Yet the editor of *Management Today*, a small circulation magazine, named Victoria the UK's 'Entrepreneur of the Year'.[5] The award for her 'finely based business acumen' to create a 'wildly successful' company was based on the research of *Sunday Times Rich List* editor Philip Beresford. Over five years, Beresford calculated, the number of employees had grown by 3,233 per cent and her sales had risen 2,900 per cent. Putting Victoria on the front cover produced record sales – for the magazine.

Seven years earlier, Michael Silver had identified her lack of management skills. 'You always say that your dad was a businessman, but you don't seem to understand profit,' he had told her when he ended their relationship. She did not realise that her company was overpaying suppliers and factories, and employed too many people.[6] Repeatedly she recited that she was 'blessed with my team'. She regularly thanked Ken Paves, her hairdresser, and Sarah Creal, her make-up artist. But without trained managers and unable to draw, cut or sew – let alone sketch a design – she relied on Beckham's money to limit the remorseless slide into debt. Also thanks to him, Anna Wintour was prepared to sit in the front row with both Beckhams at Victoria's 2015 New York fashion show.

In public, Wintour never revealed whether she believed that Victoria's clinging designs appealed to A-listers seeking exceptional glamour. But even being named Designer Brand of the Year at the British Fashion Awards did not convince enough women to wear Victoria's designs. Her principal showcase in America were Neiman Marcus stores. That was a weakness highlighted by her uncomplimentary competitors. Undermining her pretensions as a fashion designer, Dolce & Gabbana's spokesman compared her clothes to H&M and other high-street brands.[7] There had not even been a boost after her visit to the White House. Despite sending her clothes as a gift to Michelle Obama she admitted, 'I haven't seen her photographed in anything.'

Without a publicity budget Victoria relied on stunts and interviews to get attention. In one interview she finally admitted having had breast implants: 'I don't have them anymore. I think I may have purchased them.' In another she revealed the laser treatment for her legs, and repeated that being bullied at school was 'horrible'. Without any other original disclosures, she resorted to being photographed wearing an apron entitled 'Too posh to wash' and unveiled a £8.39 M&S football cake bought for Beckham.[8]

'My job,' admitted Victoria's publicist Natalie Lewis, 'is the art of smoke and mirrors.'[9] Lewis presented her client as a down-to-earth, hard-working mother blessed with unique talent. Victoria offered sincerity to those she needed, especially the fashion writers. Few of them left her company without a good word. Accordingly, in the eyes of Joely Chilcott, Victoria's indifferent New York show 'proved to be a hit and won rave reviews'. With remarkable enthusiasm, Chilcott predicted it was 'only a matter of time before her A-list pals are seen wearing her statement pieces'.[10]

Jo Milloy's friend, *Mirror* journalist Clemmie Moodie, was similarly happy to plug the brand. Victoria is 'one of the world's most sought-after fashion designers,' she wrote. 'Since 2009, a Becks frock was what everyone wanted to wear on the red carpet.'[11] Even the *Guardian*'s Jess Cartner-Morley was charmed: 'Victoria Beckham is one of the most compelling characters in the fashion industry today. Everyone, everywhere is fascinated by her, and how she pulled off the coup of the century transforming herself in five years from Spice Girls Wag to designer.'[12]

Beneath the froth Victoria worked long hours, starting with an early morning workout in the gym, doing a combination of weights, running on the treadmill, yoga and stretching.[13] Then she juggled her business, her children, supervising the renovation of her new London house, and catching up with her husband.

To her misfortune, as a retired footballer Beckham no longer needed to spend as many hours training. After an hour in the gym he was free. Looking for a new purpose he spent his days socialising in London. Regularly, he was spotted in pubs in Notting Hill Gate and Primrose Hill, no longer the teetotaller, eating dinner at the Chiltern Firehouse, or jetting around the world to promote his sponsors and party with friends.

Inevitably some thought their relationship was again strained. The tension between the Beckhams was noted after Victoria refused in July 2015 to go to Guy Ritchie's three-day wedding extravaganza to his long-term girlfriend Jacqui Ainsley. She claimed that Harper was ill. Others said that Victoria didn't like Beckham's new social circle.

Ritchie appeared to be smitten by Beckham. Ever since they had filmed the underwear commercial, Ritchie had spoken about casting Beckham in his next film, *The Man from U.N.C.L.E.* While Beckham denied any ambition to become an actor he had befriended several actors including Henry Cavill and Charlize Theron and the model Rosie Huntington-Whiteley. Posh blamed Ritchie and Dave Gardner for introducing him to that stream of glamorous women. Some assumed that she did not want to be in the same room as Rosie Huntington-Whiteley. With undisguised suspicion of Gardner she also failed to show up at his engagement party in New York to actress Liv Tyler.[14]

An unexpected tell-tale sign of tension between them were their tattoos. Just as Beckham appeared with 'Buster', a new tattoo adjacent to 'Pretty Lady' on his neck, Victoria was having laser surgery to remove her tattoos. 'I was just a bit sick of the tattoo,' she said about the Hebrew inscriptions down her neck, 'I am my beloved's' and 'My beloved is mine'. A tattooed pledge of her love for David on her wrist was also fading.

After Ritchie's wedding, Beckham flew back to Los Angeles while at the very same time Posh flew out of Los Angeles. They did not meet at the airport.[15] Soon afterwards, Beckham was persuaded by Ritchie to appear in his film about the Knights of the Round Table. His performance, in the opinion of actor Freddie Fox, was 'great'.[16]

Throughout those months the fate of their four children was being recast.

Back in February 2013, Victoria was invited by the Prime Minister's wife Samantha Cameron to a British Fashion Week reception in Downing Street. Normally, Victoria would have made a grand entrance, posing like the other celebrities by the front door. Instead she arrived late and left after 30 minutes by the back door. Her excuse was that she needed to look after her children.[17]

Over the following months she decided that the children should be part of the Beckham brand. Just like the successful Kardashians. In February 2014 all four children appeared on the front row in the New

York Fashion Show, alongside Anna Wintour.[18] Two of them apparently had been taken early out of their London schools.

Since then, 12-year-old Romeo had modelled Burberry clothes, on one occasion with Cara Delevingne. He earned about £45,000 for each shoot. Simultaneously, helped by his parents' connections, Brooklyn earned a similar fee modelling for the covers of New York's *Man About Town*, *Reserved*, *Rollercoaster* and *Miss Vogue* magazines. Both sons, their parents agreed, were 'keen to become a public face'. With Beckham's help, Romeo walked on to the Wembley pitch alongside Wayne Rooney as an England mascot before a match against Switzerland. Brooklyn, with a passing ambition to be an actor, had been seen at a football match in a private box completely fixated on his phone. Recently, he had spent a weekend in Paris with a girlfriend after a three-day trip to Kenya with Victoria.[19]

'Our kids aren't spoilt,' Victoria had insisted three years earlier. 'They aren't kids who find everything super-super-easy. They really have to work at it.'[20] Brooklyn's 5 million Instagram followers noticed that he now modelled with an earring. Watched by his parents and Romeo, his ear had been pierced for £45 at west London's Westfield shopping centre.

Their sons' glamorous lifestyle caused the Beckhams some disappointment. Since Brooklyn's birth Beckham had wanted his eldest son to become a professional footballer.[21] During 2014 the family had mentioned Brooklyn's trials with Chelsea, Manchester United, QPR and Fulham. Finally, after posting pictures of Brooklyn posing in an Arsenal kit in the Emirates stadium changing room, Beckham told 'friends' about the praise from the club's staff about his son's performance. That abruptly ended in January 2015. Brooklyn was let go by Arsenal. The shock was followed by Romeo's decision not to become a footballer. 'Part of me was devastated,' said Beckham.[22]

Some wondered why Beckham was surprised. His children enjoyed a luxurious lifestyle, tagging on to their father's foreign trips including an Arabian banquet for his 40th birthday party at the Amanjena hotel in Marrakesh. Golden balls hung from the ceiling as 90 friends danced until dawn. The guest list included Guy Ritchie, Liv Tyler, Gordon Ramsay, Simon Fuller and three Spice Girls.

Mel B had refused the invitation to Marrakesh after Victoria had rejected Fuller's latest attempt to stage a Spice Girls reunion tour. Mel

B called Victoria a snob and stopped following her on Twitter. Without Posh, Mel C also refused to take part in the tour. 'The other two bitches didn't want to do it,' cursed Mel B.

Also absent from the party was the boyfriend of Beckham's sister Joanne, Adrian Taylor. He was about to be charged with fraud. Victoria's sister Louise had also arrived without her husband Darren Flood, who had not been invited. After his business collapsed, police were investigating a £1.5 million fraud. Flood had falsely told people that the Beckhams had invested in his diamonds and gold business. He would be convicted and sentenced to 30 months; so too Taylor, who was convicted and sentenced to six years.[23]

Since Beckham's birthday party was partly financed with his anticipated income from Qatar, it was a fitting coincidence that while they were celebrating in Morocco, the Swiss police raided FIFA's headquarters. Fourteen FIFA officials were indicted by the FBI on corruption charges linked to taking bribes for awarding the World Cup to Russia and Qatar. The arrests also coincided with Sepp Blatter's re-election for a fifth term. Shortly after this he was forced to resign because of the allegations of corruption. Beckham was undisturbed by those events. Having taken the Qatari's money to play for PSG in Paris he supported FIFA's decision to hold the World Cup in Qatar in 2022. 'Whether it's corrupt or not,' he said, 'those countries have been chosen. People need to get behind that.'[24]

After his Marrakesh party Beckham flew to Mexico for filming while Victoria headed to New York and on to London. In their criss-cross schedule, he gave a speech at the UN in New York on a Thursday while she returned to New York on the following Sunday. They were not seen together. She then flew to Ethiopia to promote UNAIDS, posing with children and politicians. He celebrated his 10-year relationship with UNICEF and the 7 Fund by opening a stadium at the Africa Cup of Nations in Libreville in Gabon, and then presenting UNICEF awards in Shanghai. But Oliveira's attempts to extract a donation from Beckham for his own 7 Fund was proving difficult. To encourage him Oliveira had found two sponsors who each agreed to match $1 million if he contributed. 'Let's think about this as neither sounds great,' Beckham replied before again rejecting Oliveira's entreaties.[25]

Although the Beckhams could not hide their separate lives, they stuck together to support the Brand. In a display of unity in September

2015, Victoria summoned Beckham and Brooklyn to the front row at New York's 2016 spring collection. Beckham forgot his mantra 'I never go to the shows because she gets unbelievably stressed, so I stay out of the way.' Once again, Anna Wintour sat behind dark glasses. The reception was mixed. *The Times*' Anna Murphy praised her classic fitted dresses, which 'hang loose to be sombre but sexy'. Other commentators ignored her designs and critically focused on her use of teenage size-zero models.[26] They reflected Victoria. She was eating spinach 'with a touch of salt'.

After the show Beckham was seen eating alone in Manhattan. The following day he went with a friend to the US Open Tennis tournament. A day later he was in Miami promoting Haig Club whisky while Victoria remained in New York to appear on *Good Morning America*. 'There's a lot of love in that marriage,' she announced. 'We work together, we share the business.' Beckham, she said, was 'the best business partner that anybody could have'. But with 'busy' lives, she agreed they were rarely in the same country and didn't spend enough time together.[27]

One week later, during London Fashion Week, she asked Beckham to return to London for a dinner in her Dover Street shop. By the end of the celebration she must have wished he had stayed in America. Morosely, he sat staring at her guests. Some whispered that the two had been embroiled earlier in a foul-mouthed row. At the end of the evening, a grim-faced Beckham appeared to drag his wife by the wrist out of the shop towards a waiting car. As she stumbled, photographers snapped a wet patch on her black trousers. Later that evening Beckham was seen at Heathrow taking a late flight to New York. He flew on to Dubai to promote Adidas.[28]

Once again Victoria swung into action. Regardless of Beckham's moods and his other relationships, no one dumped a husband crowned 'The Sexiest Man Alive'. Never underestimating the importance of their 16-year-old marriage to her business, life and stability, she gave a series of interviews to restore the image of solid happiness.[29]

'David and I have nothing to prove,' she told one interviewer. 'We love each other.' To the question about the Dover Street argument she replied: 'My husband constantly inspires me and guides me.' To those speculating about their separate lives, she said, 'I am blessed to have a wonderful husband.' In solidarity with a beleaguered woman,

Beckham's patchy performances with LA Galaxy were criticised by Landon Donovan, the club's star American player (*top left*), and his teammates were also puzzled by Beckham's promotion of Armani underwear and fragrances. Victoria snubbed the critics (*top right*).

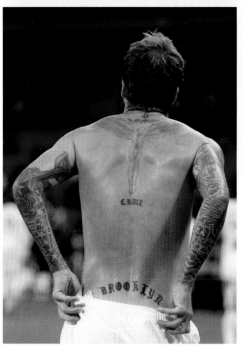

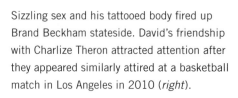

Sizzling sex and his tattooed body fired up Brand Beckham stateside. David's friendship with Charlize Theron attracted attention after they appeared similarly attired at a basketball match in Los Angeles in 2010 (*right*).

As his global popularity soared, Beckham was deemed essential to accompany the then Prince of Wales and Prime Minister David Cameron (*top left*) for England's doomed bid to host the 2018 World Cup, presided over by FIFA's Trinidadian Vice President Jack Warner and President Sepp Blatter (*below, both flanking Beckham*).

Simon Fuller (*top left*) and Dave Gardner (*top right*) were Beckham's key managers in helping build his fortune and develop a Miami football club with Marcelo Claure (*above, centre*) and Jorge Mas (*above, left*). Beckham partied with Poppy Delevingne (*above right*) in Los Angeles on the night European newspapers published his hacked emails. One highlight of his hectic trip to Glastonbury in 2017 was partying with Lady Mary Charteris (*far right*).

Beckham's career owed much to his parents Sandra and Ted (*top*), while Victoria's fashion ambitions were aided by Vogue editor-in-chief Anna Wintour (*middle*). Victoria's business was supported by her husband's money, including the millions of pounds Qatar paid for his controversial endorsement of the 2022 World Cup staged there.

Brand Beckham promoted the
image of a close family plus
girlfriends, one that was dented
by their publicly rocky relationship
with Brooklyn's wife Nicola Peltz
(*above, far right, and centre right*).

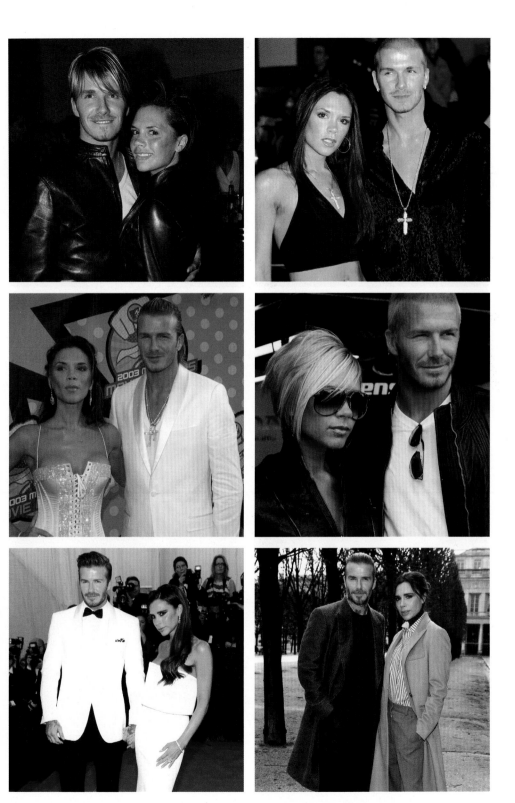

Keeping themselves in the public eye despite repeated questions about their relationship, the Beckhams have successfully maintained their 'golden couple' persona.

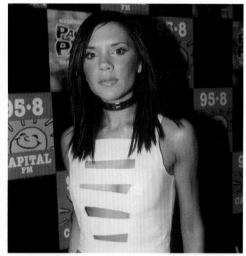

Ever since she founded her own label in 2008,
Victoria has tried to become a global fashionista.

Grazia's editor Hattie Brett praised Posh as 'the queen of reinvention. She's constantly doing new things.'[30]

Glamour magazine also offered support. Victoria's publicists negotiated that she would be Woman of the Year at *Glamour*'s 25th anniversary. Accompanied by 16-year-old Brooklyn at the New York ceremony, she did not mention publicly that David was in Argentina.[31] Jo Elvin's potted biography was selective: 'After the Spice Girls – amicably – went their separate ways, Victoria Beckham had a brief solo career but decided to devote most of her time to being a mom.' Writer Louise Gannon exaggerated the success of her $57 million 'fashion empire': 'Every celeb in Hollywood has a Victoria Beckham dress in her closet – from Oprah to Jennifer Lawrence.' Naturally referring to Anna Wintour's endorsement, Gannon echoed Victoria's sales pitch: 'Women respond to her clothes because she lives a life they understand ... She's making clothes for women who are working, travelling, balancing, juggling all sorts of things at the same time.'[32]

Inevitably, Victoria could not resist embellishing that story. Only journalists who did not question the fiction were invited to her Holland Park house. Victoria Moss was persuaded to praise the 150 people on the payroll of her 'impressively successful business' and rewrite history. Roland Mouret was 'firmly dismissed' by Victoria of any 'involvement' in her business. 'He's never had anything to do with the collections,' said Victoria. 'He wasn't involved in the designs.' She also told Moss, 'I never watch TV.' Not so long before, she had told Dominic Mohan that 'a perfect night would be in a tracky with my dogs and David watching *Blind Date*.'[33]

Another collaborator to dispel the rumours was Janicza Bravo, the producer of a television documentary about Victoria. With apparent sincerity Bravo reported her glowing impression of the blissful Beckham family gathered in good spirits for dinner at the end of the day in Holland Park. In Bravo's judgement, nothing had been arranged for her cameras.[34]

As a last resort the Beckhams announced that they would spend a happy family Christmas in the Maldives. On New Year's Eve they posted a photograph of themselves kissing.[35] There was no evidence that they were in the Maldives, or that the photo had been taken that day. Probably the photograph was genuine, but everything about the Beckhams was open to question.

CHAPTER 26

COUNTDOWN

At the beginning of 2016 the gossip got worse. With both Beckhams appearing in different countries throughout January, and their four children in London, some assumed that the couple were reconciled to a distant business relationship. Once again Victoria's publicists summoned photographers.

On the eve of the New York Fashion Show in early February, they arrived together, dressed in identical white suits, for a dinner with Anna Wintour. 'They are very much in love,' said Jo Milloy. Their marriage, she insisted, was not in trouble.[1]

The following day they parted. Victoria headed for Italy and France and finally to Hong Kong to open a shop. Beckham took the children back to London and flew on to Miami and Los Angeles. 'Happy Birthday to the most amazing husband,' Victoria posted to her 11.2 million instagram followers, with a picture of her present: a special motorcycle helmet she had designed. He could use it on his forays into the hills around Los Angeles with friends.[2]

OK! magazine decided to expose a charade. '£1 BILLION DIVORCE SHOCKER' was the sensational front-cover headline. The magazine reported that the Beckhams, living for half a year apart, were to divorce and split their fortune. Newspapers repeated the story and the magazine's sales rocketed. The Beckhams protested. The suggestion of marital troubles, said their lawyers, was untrue. Their marriage, the Beckhams insisted, was perfect. The newspapers agreed to publish an apology and correction.[3]

The *Sun*'s picture editor knew a different story. Splash, the photo agency, had offered the picture editor a long-range shot of Beckham with Gardner on a boat in the Mediterranean. A beautiful unnamed blonde was sitting on Beckham's lap. Publishing the photo became difficult once Beckham's lawyers claimed that their client's privacy was infringed. After an inconclusive legal argument the picture's copyright was bought by an unknown person and was no longer available.

After a crisis meeting of the family's army of publicists, a dinner party was arranged in a Los Angeles restaurant. The star of the family photo was Brooklyn's latest girlfriend, the young actress Chloe Grace Moretz, and her mother. Jo Molloy assigned the exclusive 'sighting' to the *Sun*'s Dan Wootton. 'Chloe and Brooklyn are very much a couple,' the 'eyewitness' wrote at his desk in East London's Wapping. 'Chloe kept stroking Brooklyn's hair and putting her head on his shoulder. Victoria was making a huge effort with Chloe too.' With 8 million Instagram followers, Brooklyn had become an essential ingredient of Brand Beckham.[4]

On the eve of his 17th birthday Brooklyn had effectively given up school. Regularly seen with his mother in New York and Los Angeles he liked walking down the red carpet at Hollywood premieres, and was spotted with Chloe at Disneyland. On the eve of his school exams he was seen drinking at record company parties in London during the Brit Awards. Soon after his birthday he was learning to drive in a £38,000 Mercedes, a birthday present. After featuring in a Huawei advert selling a mobile phone – allegedly being paid £100,000 – Brooklyn told friends that he aimed to become a rapper after recording an album with The Vamps. By the summer his by now 10.3 million Instagram followers were assured by a profile in the *Mirror* that their hero was 'an exemplary young man – fit, healthy, gorgeous and studies hard with a genuine passion for photography'. With the support of the Beckham machine, Brooklyn said that he 'turns down 95 per cent of job offers'. By the end of that year Brooklyn and Moretz had parted – she was deemed by him to be 'clingy' – and Brooklyn, after passing his driving test, was collecting parking tickets.[5]

Encouraged by Victoria to include the other three children in the brand, more publicists were hired. One showcased five-year-old Harper's special talents, including her 'love to play with make-up'. Another publicist claimed that at Beckham's suggestion Cruz's talent for guitar and singing had tempted Justin Bieber's manager to mastermind his son's road to stardom. Reportedly, Fuller's offer of help was rejected despite his achievements as a music agent. After the release of Cruz's record 'If Every Day Was Christmas', Piers Morgan slammed his parents for reaching 'a new low – cynically pimping out their 11-year-old son to the pop world'.[6]

Victoria could not resist joining the Brooklyn, Harper and Cruz bandwagon. 'Posh wants to stay in the limelight,' said her publicist. A flurry of posts showed her laughing and doing 'crazy' acts across the world: like hanging on a clothes rail with a bag over her head in London, dancing with a fashion dummy in Hong Kong, sitting astride a bull in Las Vegas, and sprawled across a piano in Los Angeles. 'I like to poke fun at myself,' she explained.[7]

She also repeated once again her teenage horrors. In a 'Letter' to teens published by *Vogue* she described her victimhood – 'crippled by insecurities' – the 'complete hell' as a target of school bullies who taunted her acne, fat and ugly face. As a teenager, she wrote, she never bonded, didn't fit in and was rejected at auditions. But, she told her readers, despite the humiliation and feeling 'a complete wreck', she hung on. 'And yes. Love at first sight does exist.' Her one resolution, she concluded, was to learn more about football. On her own admission she failed.[8]

Those sympathetic to Victoria's bruised innocence would understand her self-description as a shy, control-freak workaholic. She dreaded New York's Fashion Week as a 'tempestuous place at the mercy of tyrannical egos'. Her admirers could identify with her fears of the spotlight: 'I just can't wait to get down the red carpet and be done with it. I can't wait till I'm off it.' She had forgotten a telling admission in her autobiography: 'The only time I feel comfortable is when I'm on stage performing.'[9]

Perhaps that explained why, with Anna Wintour once again sitting nearby, she asked Beckham and their four children to fly from London during their school term to sit alongside her as the autumn 2016 designs were unveiled. *The Times*' Anna Murphy was not overwhelmed by the reappearance of her 'fitted bustier tops' and bubble skirts. 'I am a minimalist,' Victoria told Murphy. The writer generously concluded that 'she pulled it off'.[10] Six months later, Murphy was more enthusiastic. Victoria's floral pleated skirt, she wrote, was paper-thin leather. 'Beckham's game has changed,' she wrote. 'It's clever. It's contemporary.'[11]

The *Guardian*'s Jess Cartner-Morley was similarly enthusiastic about that show. Yet for a designer who had built her reputation, like

Mouret, on 'cling', her descriptions of 'oversized, louchely loose clothes for the busy woman' were unlikely to appeal to A-listers. Her language was challenging: 'Asymmetrically panelled skirts and loose-slung trousers were balanced by pretty botanical prints and flashes of skin at the ribs and spine. A crushed velvet dress in peppermint green was an instant stand-out.'[12] Murphy praised her designs as 'clever and contemporary'.[13]

Favourable publicity did not solve Victoria's financial problems. The stagnant £34 million turnover and latest £3.8 million loss in 2016 forced her to concede that 'I made big mistakes.' She relied on a further £5.2 million loan from Beckham. Although that hardly dented his own £45 million earnings, their commercial enterprises were legally split.[14] He had resigned as a director from Victoria's business in 2014 and she was no longer a director of many of his companies.

The Beckhams' finances had become unusually complex for a small private business owned by two individuals. At the top of the pyramid the parent company Beckham Brand Holdings Ltd (BBH) combined a number of associated companies and partnerships. Over the years the ownership of those companies – Footwork Productions, David Beckham Ventures, Victoria Beckham Ltd and many subsidiaries – and their inter-company trading had puzzled even a diligent forensic accountant about the businesses.

The companies' memorandum and articles of association were also changed, no less than five times over nine years. As an added compli-cation, the companies were audited by different firms of accountants, each listing different criteria for their audit. Those discrepancies appeared to allow the auditors to ignore the effect of Victoria's grow-ing debts on Beckham's finances. All that work was richly rewarded. Beckham's new auditors, SRLV, a boutique firm specialising in media and marketing companies which Charles Bradbrook would join from Deloitte, charged BBH alone up to £437,000 for a year's work. 'A very strong fee,' according to the profession.

Despite the high fees, some accounts were regularly filed months late at Companies House. In 2016, Beckham's holding company BBH filed so late that it was threatened with being 'struck off'. Part of the reason appears to have been the accountants' indecision about 'adjust-ments' to Beckham's finances. The result was a series of errors. In 2015 and 2016 a dividend was paid without sufficient funds.

Technically that was 'illegal'. The same would occur in 2017. Equally surprising, every year the previous year's accounts were substantially 'adjusted'.[15] Drily described as 'revisiting the accounting treatment', the repeated mistake was failing to include additional large payments. On one occasion the additional income was relegated to a sub-note rather than more prominently declared. In 2017, after approving the accounts, the Beckham Brand auditor missed 'material errors' after 'complex adjustments'. That year, Beckham took £5.7 million in dividends from Footwork.

Beckham's spokesman said that the complexity in BBH's accounts resulted from 'accounting for 7 Global and [the] adjustments needed due to late invoices, [the] complex nature of the structure ... all standard accounting practice'.

Paying Britain's high taxes and conscious of Fuller's constant reminder that America was the source of his future fortune, Beckham began to despair, especially about establishing a football team in Miami. The prized project was spluttering.

'It was my vision to have a team in Miami,' Beckham would say in 2023.[16] That is not the recollection of those at LA Galaxy or the MLS negotiating the original contract in 2007. The only people involved were Jeff Frasco of Creative Artists Agency, Simon Fuller and Terry Byrne. The exceptional concession for Beckham to own a club was inserted into the contract, possibly with Beckham's subsequent knowledge but not on his initiative. Tim Leiweke would also claim credit for suggesting that idea. Pertinently, in 2013 Beckham told CNN that Fuller was responsible for inserting the key concession into his contract.[17]

Nothing formally had been agreed until the MLS commissioner Dan Garber asked Beckham and Fuller in 2013 whether they would like to trigger the option for a club. Initially Garber had suggested that Beckham build a club somewhere in the outback. Anywhere except Miami, New York and Los Angeles. Only after discussions did Garber finally agree that Miami was the best location, but he cautioned that several attempts to build a club there had failed. Not least because Garber insisted that the stadium had to be built within the city.[18] That stipulation was not changed. The putative club was registered in Delaware as Miami Beckham United LLC. The state of Delaware has tax advantages. It does not impose corporate tax on interest and investment income, and allows companies to operate in some secrecy. Shortly after, Beckham Brand Ltd based in Britain bought 100 per cent of the club for £1.89 million. The following year, Beckham sold 10 per cent of the club for £6 million, earning a £5.8 million profit.

Beckham's announcement in 2013 that his team would be ready to play within three years in Miami had proved optimistic. The difficulty was finding a suitable site and sufficient finance for a stadium. Beckham's criteria were unusual. Lacking the necessary money, he wanted the land for free and a partner to build the stadium. The attraction for an investor was that his 2007 option gave him an MLS team for £17.7 million ($25 million) rather than £106.5 million ($150 million), the commercial rate in 2013. That made Beckham's concession particularly valuable to an investor. Any partner had to accept that Beckham's sole investment was £1.89 million in the club's holding company, Miami Beckham United.

To Fuller's frustration, Qatar had been vetoed by the MSL directors. The Qataris were labelled as enemies of Israel and financiers of Hamas, the terrorist organisation dedicated to the destruction of Israel. His good fortune was to have met in 2009 Marcelo Claure, the chief executive of Sprint communications, at a party hosted by Jennifer Lopez in Los Angeles. Born in Guatemala and raised in Bolivia, 43-year-old Claure was an alpha male employed by the Japanese billionaire Masayoshi Son, the founder of SoftBank. As a football enthusiast, Claure owned a club in Bolivia, had close relations with FC Barcelona, and had unsuccessfully tried to launch an MLS football team in Miami. At Lopez's party, Fuller had explained that after Beckham retired from football he would launch an MLS team. Claure suggested he choose Miami.

After Beckham retired and decided to trigger his option, the MLS's commissioner, Dan Garber, encouraged Fuller to hold a beauty parade for rich investors. Garber believed that MLS teams needed to be financed by billionaires rather than multi-millionaires. After discarding private equity groups, Fuller turned to Claure, a dynamic and commercially successful multi-millionaire managing one of the world's largest mobile telephone distribution companies, who had a passion to build an MLS team – with the support of Masayoshi Son. Claure instantly embraced the idea of being Beckham's partner. Nothing pleased that breed of self-promoting businessmen more than walking into a Miami restaurant with a mega-celebrity.

In February 2014, Beckham Brand sold 10 per cent of its 100 per cent ownership to Claure for £6 million. Beckham invested £2.6 million back into the club. Claure gradually increased his stake to 37.5 per cent. Relying on Marcelo Claure's financial assurances, Fuller triggered the $25 million option.

The first bid to build a 25,000-seater stadium on 36 acres of publicly owned land on Dodge Island for free was rejected after opposition from the port director. The second attempt to build a 20,000-seater stadium in the Museum Park area was opposed by residents. 'Would London's mayor agree to a stadium in Hyde Park?' asked a protestor. 'It's an abomination.' After a passing interest in a 73-acre golf course was also fiercely opposed, Beckham's third bid for Marlin's Park, a site near Little Havana, was rejected.

After those disappointments, Beckham and Fuller acknowledged they lacked close connections with Miami's property and political powerbrokers to overcome the city's murky relationships. Even Claure, it appeared, was an outsider. With a tight deadline, the trio were told they had just one more attempt to get the franchise. They bid for a downtown site in Overtown.[19] The omens were mixed. The bad news was that Overtown was not an ideal site. The good news was that Brand Beckham appeared to be on the verge of delivering serious money.

Mercurial and aggressive, entrepreneur Bruce Rockowitz's attraction to Simon Fuller and Beckham had been understandable. Based in Hong Kong, the fitness fanatic had said, 'I like brands.'

Introduced to him by fashion designer Tommy Hilfiger, Fuller was impressed by Rockowitz's recent achievements as the chief executive of the Global Brands Group, a subsidiary company of the Hong Kong conglomerate Li & Fung. Included in Rockowitz's stable was the manufacture and sale of products for Calvin Klein, Disney and Kate Spade. For his part Rockowitz was attracted by the Beckhams' mix of sport, celebrity and fashion.

Keen to monetise Beckham's brand and pocket some cash, Fuller focused on Asia, a region destined for huge growth. Two-thirds of the world's population lived in Asia and the growing middle class was buying luxury goods. The region was natural territory for Beckham's commercial expansion.

Fuller's enthusiasm to seal a deal with Rockowitz in 2014 ought to have been tempered by the scepticism among some Hong Kong analysts about Global Brands. Rockowitz had previously failed to provide sufficient financial data. But, like others, Fuller and Beckham were impressed by his glitzy relaunch. At Hong Kong's Grand Hyatt hotel the showman announced that Global Brands' net profits in 2014 had jumped by 36.6 per cent. Annual growth, he predicted, would continue at 30 per cent. The company's share price recovered and since Rockowitz was also associated with the Creative Artists Agency, Fuller labelled him a winner. Unknown to Beckham, Fuller misunderstood Global's business and failed to take into account the analysts' scepticism. Nor did he apparently realise that Rockowitz had deliberately focused 85 per cent of sales in the United States and not in Asia.[20]

Beckham liked Rockowitz and his wife, Coco Lee, a famous Chinese singer, and he trusted Fuller's judgement. So did Victoria. Eager for the injection of more money into her business, she encouraged Beckham to back Fuller's deal with Rockowitz. In 2015, Fuller predicted, Beckham's companies would hit record profits of about £65 million.[21] Similar profits were anticipated in 2016. Those profits were not achieved. Beckham's publicists also spoke about 'long-term deals' including H&M, which 'will continue'.[22] They did not reveal that the H&M sponsorship was coming to an end. On the basis of those revenues, Fuller's sale in 2015, of a 51 per cent stake in Beckham Brand Holdings to Rockowitz's Global Brands for about $36.7 million plus a deferred $36.7 million over the following six years, was cheap.

At the heart of the deal, Rockowitz's Global Brands and Beckham owned respectively 51 per cent and 49 per cent of the shares in the specially established Seven Global Holding Company (SGHCL) and its subsidiary Global Seven. Their apparel business would develop the David Beckham brand not just for football boots and clothes but also insurance, travel, moisturisers and other consumer products.[23] Jason Weisenfeld, formerly employed to shape Victoria's enterprise, was appointed Global Seven's president with an annual sales target of

$1.5 billion by 2020. No one appeared to question that enormous figure, roughly half of Rockowitz's total projected sales.

'I'm going to learn a lot,' Beckham said after the deal was announced. 'It's a venture which hasn't really been done before. This is a partnership which is special.'[24]

Among the first results of the new partnership in autumn 2015 was the relaunch of the British heritage menswear label Kent & Curwen. Claiming to own 113 stores in 51 cities worldwide, Rockowitz told Beckham that his fortune would be earned by branding that label. Beckham's new company, Seven Global, was meant to earn 5 per cent of Kent & Curwen's net retail sales and 10 per cent of its wholesale sales.

Kent & Curwen's first-year earnings for Beckham were £5.5 million. He earned a further £3.5 million from Luneng, a local estate company among several Chinese companies contracted to feature Beckham in their promotion. Seven Global's net profits in 2016 were $17.2 million, a long way from the projected $1.5 billion sales target for 2020 but contributing that year to DB Ventures' total £44 million earnings.[25]

The apparent success of the partnership with Rockowitz was offset by Victoria's increasing losses. During 2016, after losing £4.6 million, her company's debt to the bank was £8.4 million and she owed Beckham £6.7 million. Profligacy aggravated her losses. She was employing a huge staff of 141 costing £7.8 million per year. She appeared oblivious to the increasing debt. Instead, she was upbeat after being told that her work for the United Nations and the fashion industry had been rewarded by an OBE.

Beckham awaited his own letter. Encouraged by Oliveira, he had not given up hope.

GQ's editor Dylan Jones was always a reliable ally. His magazine's cover story 'Retirement, Family Life and Protecting His Kids' was a tribute to his hero. Jones described 'the Sun God' as 'a cultural phenomenon'. The profile of Beckham written by Michael Paterniti was unashamedly glutinous. 'He's a billboard and an icon in the imagistic sense who, with time and a few rugged wrinkles at 40, has begun to accumulate 3-D substance.' In approval of his modesty Paterniti quoted Beckham, 'I've never seen myself as a celebrity.' Even those who called him the Sexiest Man Alive, wrote Paterniti, needed to grasp that Beckham was 'a different ideal of manhood – the softer, metrosexual father – a lover, supportive spouse and style icon'. Devoting space to Beckham's own eulogy about his 'amazing kids, wife, parents, in-laws and friends who I trust,' Beckham was quoted: 'I'm secure as a person, as a husband and as a dad. It doesn't matter what people say.' His critics, Beckham insisted, were ignored. All that mattered was his work with UNICEF. The charity, he said, is 'my number-one priority'.[26]

His devotion to UNICEF was uppermost on his agenda when he was given the accolade of appearing on the 75th anniversary edition of BBC Radio 4's *Desert Island Discs*. Introducing him as 'footballer, global brand and humanitarian', the host Kirsty Young continued, 'He's as at home at the United Nations making a speech on child welfare as gracing billboards in those designer pants.'

Tracks by Elton John, Ella Fitzgerald and Michael Jackson, jazz musician Sidney Bechet and the Rolling Stones' 'Wild Horses' were among his favourite discs. No Spice Girls track was chosen. Twenty years earlier Posh Spice had revealed that her boyfriend didn't like her music. 'I asked him if he was a fan the other day,' she had said. 'He said: "I'm a fan of you but not the others!".'[27] But, he told Kirsty Young, after 19 years of marriage they were a 'strong family unit'. He denied they stayed together for Brand Beckham. 'We stay together because we love each other.' He took with him to the desert island an England cap and a cookbook called *Fire*.

One condition of his appearance, the BBC accepted, was to allow Beckham to promote his 'passion' for UNICEF. 'More than anything ... one of the most important things in my life at the moment is my charity work,' he said. 'That is what gives me the most pleasure of what I do.' His motive, he said, was 'not for vanity'.[28]

The programme was widely praised. The BBC's audience was unaware at the end of January 2017 of the threat Beckham's lawyers were struggling to suppress.

CHAPTER 27

THE STORM

On Wednesday 1 February 2017, Beckham was partying with actress Poppy Delevingne at The Friend, a West Hollywood cocktail bar.[1] By the time a dishevelled-looking Beckham and Delevingne had departed, it was daybreak in Hamburg. The first copies of the weekly German magazine *Der Spiegel* were being printed. Woken by his London lawyers early on Thursday morning, the shock was considerable but not unexpected.

Simon Oliveira had discovered in late 2016 that his emails had been hacked, including not only many personal messages but also his traffic with Beckham. After refusing to pay the hackers a bribe to protect his privacy, Oliveira discovered that the emails had been shared among several European newspapers, making it impossible to prevent their publication.

The hacker, codenamed 'John' and based in Portugal, justified his crime to *Der Spiegel*'s Rafael Buschmann. Oliveira's emails, said John, had been hacked on behalf of football fans. All were victims of 'an extremely corrupt system that is only in it for itself. I hate how officials and players are abusing fans' trust so badly, just because of their greed.'[2]

John's haul contained Beckham's emails to Oliveira describing the honours committee as 'unappreciative cunts', his calculated opposition to Scottish independence just to be rewarded with a knighthood, his ridicule of Katherine Jenkins, and the 'toxic impact' of his lucrative deal with Qatar. Worst of all, the emails exposed his refusal to give his own money to UNICEF. In his own words, the credibility of his cultivated image as a generous, honest bloke was blown apart.

To prevent publication of the emails in the London *Sunday Times* his lawyers successfully obtained a High Court injunction. But the British judges could not stop publication of the emails in Germany and across the world. Beckham was furious. The purpose of Brand Beckham was to be personally liked. That risked crashing into ruins.

After dashing to Los Angeles airport, Beckham flew first-class with American rapper and songwriter will.i.am to London. Just after he landed on Friday at 11 a.m., the world was reading *Der Spiegel*'s considered assessment of the Englishman. Beckham, wrote the Germans, was 'never a world footballer, never a champion, just one of many'. In the magazine's opinion, while 'outwardly Beckham always appears as Flawless, Mr Perfect', in truth he was simply the highest-paid ex-footballer who always placed his image way above the 'minor matter' of football. He was the creator of a dreamworld feeding his fans' fantasies. *Der Spiegel*'s verdict was that the real Beckham was 'stingy, ordinary, bad-tempered and freaking choleric'. At the *Sunday Times* he would be described as a miserly, foul-mouthed hypocrite.

That weekend the lawyers of every British newspaper were wondering how to overcome the High Court's injunction. Although the *Sunday Times* was barred from reproducing the emails, no judge would dare to injunct British newspapers once *Der Spiegel*'s revelations had been reproduced across the globe. The *Sun*'s new editor, Tony Gallagher, formerly on the *Daily Mail* and *Daily Telegraph*, was chaffing to publish the emails. Unlike his predecessors he refused unequivocally to play the Beckhams' game. 'He hates showbiz and hates the Beckhams,' was the buzz along the *Sun*'s editorial floor. 'If an atomic bomb goes off,' Gallagher was heard to joke, 'it would be best if it was over Soho Farmhouse.' The Beckhams were frequent visitors to the Oxfordshire country club and had bought a home nearby.

Gallagher's more nuanced approach was that he loved showbiz and front-page stories about the Beckhams because that sold newspapers, but he refused to hide the truth. He rejected Oliveira's entreaties. He would not cut a shoddy deal to suppress the emails in return for access to the Beckhams.

On Monday morning the *Sun* reproduced some of *Der Spiegel*'s revelations alongside a column by Piers Morgan. Beckham, wrote Morgan, was 'repulsive' and 'a fraud'. Morgan added, 'Oh. My. God. RIP Brand Beckham. No one will be envious of David Beckham by tomorrow. They will be sickened by him.'[3]

As Brand Beckham's formerly trustworthy reputation apparently collapsed, his spokesman offered excuses. The newspapers, Oliveira claimed, had 'doctored the emails, giving a deliberately inaccurate picture'. And contrary to the impression of not giving any money to UNICEF, he had donated £1 million. Some assumed that was a reference to the $1 million to be paid by Global Brands over the next five years to UNICEF, not £1 million from his personal fortune.[4] In reality it was a £750,000 payment due to Beckham in a sponsorship deal that was paid directly by the company to UNICEF. Getting Beckham's agreement for the payment, Gardner told a friend, followed some discussions. But Beckham was told he had to bite the bullet.

To show that he didn't care what the newspapers reported, Beckham posted a new video of himself reading a bedtime story to Harper. The following morning photographers were told where he would be watching Brooklyn skateboarding in London. At that moment, furious about her husband's self-destructive emails, Victoria was flying to New York for yet another Fashion Week.

In private, Beckham was enraged. Not about himself but with the media. Lacking a scintilla of remorse, he felt no reason to apologise for his honest opinions. Star footballers do not tend to repent. Wayne Rooney could be caught speeding with a young woman in a car while his wife and three children were on holiday, and Jamie and Louise Redknapp could endure a public crisis, but football fans did not expect contrition. 'No one wants to fail,' Beckham said later, 'but it happens. It's how you deal with it.' And his advisers dealt with 'it' by doing nothing. To his satisfaction, not a single one of his sponsors had made any comment. 'We all have to be optimistic and positive,' Victoria said in New York after she was joined by Beckham and the four children. At the end of the New York show the Beckhams kept silent, invisible and separate. For once, the email scandal diverted attention from the tailspin of their fractured relationship.[5]

Out of the blue, Fuller's spokesman Julian Henry called the *Sun*'s showbiz editor Dan Wootton. Lay-off the Beckhams and their marriage, suggested Henry. 'Simon's spoken to David and Posh and advised them how to save their marriage.' Wootton was expected to comply with Henry's suggestion. With Gallagher's support, he refused. Instead he noted an unexpectedly muted twist in the Beckhams' life.

Brooklyn celebrated his 18th birthday with his father and Victoria's mother in Britain. On the same day, Victoria was seen shopping in New York.

Few in the Beckham household were smiling. Even Victoria's appearance at Buckingham Palace to receive her OBE, eight weeks after the email scandal broke, was played down. The Beckhams arrived at the Palace separately. Black sheets covered both cars' windows. Unusually, no one saw Victoria's face or her clothes for that special occasion. After the ceremony the family left by a side entrance. 'I want to empower women,' was Victoria's only comment. No mention was made of their disappointment that once again there was no knighthood for David.[6] No official photo was released and there was no grand party. Just Beckham's Instagram photo of a family dinner with his plug, 'Haig Club Clubman kind of night.'

Within three weeks the storm had passed. It was business as usual. Brand Beckham had survived. Wearing a white T-shirt, Beckham arrived with Brooklyn at the London premiere of Guy Ritchie's film *King Arthur: Legend of the Sword*. Father and son partied late into the night with model and television presenter Alexa Chung and Poppy Delevingne. Reportedly, Victoria refused to come. She missed the 13 lines delivered in the film by Beckham. He did not underestimate his own efforts. 'I practised a huge amount,' he volunteered. The reviews were not flattering. Even the ultra-loyal football club director Karren Brady was merciless. 'Beckham's delivery is as wooden as a door,' she wrote. Remarkably, the East Londoner could not even assume a proper Cockney accent. The *Hollywood Reporter* was equally scathing: 'King Arthur is a paint-by-numbers disaster.' Unabashed, Beckham headed for the Cannes film festival. He was seen enjoying himself with singer Rita Ora. Four weeks later, he met socialite Lady Mary Charteris at Glastonbury.[7]

Victoria faced a testing challenge. Her husband appeared to be unfaithful; her business was in debt; and endless global travel was damaging her health. Excusing her use of 'a bucketload' of make-up and sunglasses to hide the bags under her eyes because 'I'm up all night looking after the children,' she flew from New York to Hong Kong to promote 'aspirational glamour' with Estée Lauder.[8]

Five months after the email revelations, the couple's publicists agreed that the Brand needed a boost. The spotlight was to be directly focused on to the children.

All the children's names, including five-year-old Harper's, had been registered as trademarks. Brooklyn was already a star. Given his own driver and a bodyguard called Bobby, Brooklyn was tattooed for the first time in Los Angeles by Mark Mahoney with a Native American design. Beckham was watching. By the end of the year Brooklyn had another eight tattoos. Beckham had also added four more – a horse, a woman playing a flute, 'Dadda', and birds flying up his neck – bringing his total to about 50 carvings.

Brooklyn's next career move was agreed. He would move in September to New York and enrol in Parson's School of Design. By coincidence, Global Seven's chief executive, Jason Weisenfeld, was a board member of Parsons. To celebrate Brooklyn's stardom his parents arranged a launch party for *What I See*, his collection of around 300 photographs. It would be held on 27 June at Christie's in London's St James's. In the introduction the reader was told, 'This stylish and beautifully designed edition will be comprised of fan favourites as well as new and exclusive images from his personal archive, offering a rare and intimate glimpse of the world through his eyes.' Among the photos was a fuzzy picture titled 'Elephants in Kenya'. Brooklyn's caption read, 'So hard to photograph but incredible to see.'

Three weeks later, Harper was the family's media focus. For her sixth birthday the Beckhams had arranged with Prince Andrew's former wife Sarah Ferguson that Harper could have a princess-themed tea party in Buckingham Palace. With the Queen absent in Balmoral, Harper was escorted to Prince Andrew's private suite. The Instagram photos posted by the Beckhams showed Harper dressed as Cinderella. There was a series of other pictures of Harper having a manicure and pedicure, wearing £240 Gucci boots, a £695 monogrammed cashmere Burberry coat, a £1,525 Versace gown, and holding a £1,200 Goyard leather mini-bag.[9]

Other children at the party included Stella McCartney's daughter Bailey. McCartney was not pleased that the photos of her child were posted. Unlike the Beckhams, she claimed to protect her children's privacy – although she did subsequently pose with her children for a *Vogue* front cover. Relations between Victoria and Stella were already tricky, but got worse after Victoria hired Stella's nanny with the offer of a higher salary. Next, Victoria hired a key member of McCartney's design team. She was disinvited from McCartney's social group and then ignored. Victoria appeared to believe that grovelling apologies would excuse her behaviour.

Equally, no one questioned Victoria's outrage about a Ralph Lauren press release boasting that Brooklyn and Romeo had worn Ralph Lauren blazers at the christening of Geri's daughter. 'Victoria and David are fiercely protective of their three sons,' Jo Milloy explained, 'and went apoplectic when they discovered what Ralph Lauren had done.'

Strangely, neither parent was apparently disturbed that Brooklyn had posted a photo of himself waving a gun and pointing it at the camera, as they made no public comment on it. His 10.8 million followers revelled in his cool.[10]

'I love the development process and the packaging,' Victoria said in autumn 2017 about her fashion business on its 10th anniversary. 'David thinks I'm so boring talking about boxes and stuff.' David was not bored. He was startled. Victoria's losses, reported his accountants, were worse than anticipated – and unsustainable.[11]

During 2017 her losses increased from £4.8 million to £8.5 million. Sales were stagnant at £36.4 million. She had borrowed that year £6.7 million from Beckham. An extra £38.3 million had been invested in the company and the accumulated debt had risen to £16.4 million. Curiously, the auditors of BBH had agreed a strange ruse. They had bought from Victoria Beckham her intellectual property rights for £1.5 million. That was an odd transaction because BBH had been using Victoria's brand name for years. Moreover, there had been no royalty payments between Victoria's two companies, yet without explanation Victoria's non-income producing company suddenly owned an asset worth £1.5 million. The implications of that trade between the Beckham entities were not set out, but the tax saved for BBH by that single transaction was in excess of £525,000.[12]

Compared to Louis Vuitton's £15 billion annual turnover, Chanel's £9 billion (rising to £17 billion in 2022) and Dior's £60 billion revenues, Victoria's £36 million turnover classed her as minuscule. While the French giants bought pages of glossy magazine and television advertising, she relied on puff pieces in the *Guardian*, a left-leaning newspaper not known for its love of wealthy followers of fashion.

'The image she presented was of bullet-proof serenity,' commented the newspaper's fashion writer.[13] Anna Murphy in *The Times* praised her 'stealth of gorgeousness', especially her 'blush sheath dress layered over graph-paper check cotton shirting and slips'.[14]

Insulating herself as ever from reality, Victoria was puzzled why her long hours failed to deliver financial success. The truth was that despite saying that she was running the business in Battersea, she attended only the quarterly board meetings, avoided day-to-day management and paid herself £700,000 a year. Understanding balance sheets, market trends and sophisticated promotion were not her strength. And then, Beckham's publicists firmly told journalists that Beckham was financing Posh.[15]

Part of the reason for the unprecedented briefing was the unexpected fall in 2016 of Beckham's own income. His accountants had prepared tax returns showing that Footwork Productions' turnover had dropped from £14.3 million to £8.02 million. Footwork's profits fell from £11.4 million to £7.2 million. The accountants wrote down the company's assets from £21 million to £263,000. To pay his bills he took £12.7 million from the company's reserves, accumulated in 2015 and 2016, as a dividend.

The following year, the fiscal 2016/7, showed that Footwork's revenues, calculated in dollars, were $72.4 million, producing a profit of $16 million. That was a drop of 20 per cent from 2015. Nevertheless, Footwork paid out £19 million in dividends, up from £10.2 million in 2016.

Beckham took comfort from Rockowitz's bullish prediction in September 2017 that within six years Global would be worth $10 billion. 'Our double-digit growth is huge,' Rockowitz said.[16] The accounts did not reveal Global Brands' seriously bad news. Kent & Curwen had lost £10.7 million. Beckham seemed to be unaware of the lurking danger.

During a lunch of pie and mash and sticky toffee pudding in a London restaurant to promote Kent & Curwen's expansion, Beckham confidently told his guests, 'Having the relationship in Asia that I have, the popularity that I have, it helps.'[17]

But during the following year, 2018, Kent & Curwen's losses increased to £18 million. Apparently unknown to Beckham, who had no accounting experience, while he flew around the world promoting the brands his profits were being paid into Global's 'reserves' and not his bank account. Within one year he was owed over £10 million. Excuses were offered about depositing the income in the 'reserves', but, unseen by Beckham, Global Brands' income fell by two-thirds. By the year's end, the company lost $886 million. Rockowitz resigned as an executive director.

Fuller's deal began to feel like a dud. Beckham's brand had not only been sold too cheap but the wrong partner had been chosen.[18] Beckham's accounts for Seven Global that year revealed that $11.3 million of income – half the expected profits – was lost. Rockowitz's Global Brands was sliding towards bankruptcy. Beckham decided to follow Rockowitz and get out. His problem was to find an escape route and recover the ownership of his own brand.

At the same time, David and Victoria were searching for a way to reverse her losses. Once again, they focused on fragrances.

Although the $48 billion global beauty business was growing, sales of celebrity fragrances were falling. Only the rich were buying a 30ml bottle for £100. For the rest of the public, the celebrities' over-priced scents were no longer aspirational.[19] Coty's managing director, Bernd Beetz, was the creator of the world's biggest celebrities' perfume business. He had discovered that sex and seduction were no longer selling points. Young people wanted scents that enhanced their sense of individuality and identity. Success depended on creating 'culturally relevant brands' reflecting their communities.[20]

Beetz's wisdom was lost on Victoria. She was selling only herself and her values to the punters. For that, she relied entirely on personal appearances on YouTube and Instagram. In September, as part of her make-up tips promoting an Estée Lauder product, she had posted pictures to 16 million followers showing her peeling off aluminium foil from her face. Swiftly her site was inundated by critical comments. Estée Lauder's product cost £348 while Boots sold a similar foil for £125.[21]

David Beckham's cosmetic promotions experienced an even worse fate. Fronted by Beckham, 'House 99' was L'Oréal's collection of 21 'grooming' creams. Great hopes rested on his brand during the launch of the creams in the Knightsbridge store Harvey Nichols, and then rolled out in 19 countries across Asia. The range was a flop.[22] Next, L'Oréal attempted to launch Beckham's 'collection' of four fragrances.

The four, called 'Refined Woods', 'Amber Breeze', 'Intimate Acqua' and 'Aromatic Greens', were said to represent aspects of Beckham's personal life. Pitched during a personal appearance by him at money-conscious shoppers at JCPenney in New York's Garden City, he plugged the different smells in his life – cedar wood, the Pacific Ocean, the open road and nightclubs. That campaign also crashed. Both Posh and Becks were failing to master the fragrance business. The result worried Fuller. Their combined income was stagnant and Victoria's debts were rising.[23]

Fuller's solution was to hire Paolo Riva as Victoria's chief executive. Billed as 'a fast-rising management star', the New York consultant had previously been a marketing supremo at Valentino and Ferragamo. Employed to save Victoria's business, Riva pledged that 'we continue to develop a pioneering consumer-led business'. He joined a new chairman, Ralph Toledano, who had been employed six years earlier by Chloe.[24] Praising Riva as a 'smart, strategic and a great leader', Toledano said he was committed to turn Victoria's debt-laden enterprise into a 'modern luxury group'.

Within months, both were overseeing chaos. The board of directors and Riva could not prevent a logistics crisis. Supplies were poorly sourced and overpriced, orders were dispatched to the wrong addresses and the staff were confused. Riva left after ten months. Thereafter his CV did not mention his employment by Victoria Beckham.

As the losses increased, Fuller sought a new investor to bring professional management to the business. At the end of November 2017, Toledano introduced NEO Investment Partners, a private equity group led by David Belhassen, to invest £30 million in return for a 28 per cent stake. That left the Beckhams with 48.4 per cent of the company, Fuller with 23.6 per cent, and Toledano as chairman. NEO's investment flatteringly valued the business at £100 million. The announcement was accompanied by Victoria's remarkably candid confession. 'We have been crying out for a leader who can guide us all and I can learn from.' She needed, she added, the right 'infrastructure around me to turn my ideas into reality'.[25]

To stop the ship sinking, Toledano ordered Victoria to fire over 50 employees. She was not in the office when the announcement was made. 'The staff are raging,' the Daily Mail's Katie Hind was told.

'She doesn't know what she's doing. She's blaming the consultants, rather than thinking it's her fault.'[26] David Beckham, whispered one of his staff, had warned that he would not lend more money to Victoria.[27]

The hiatus clearly confused Victoria. She urged Beckham to pose with her in Paris dressed in Louis Vuitton clothes and carrying a £2,000 Vuitton bag and a £797 suit carrier, and wearing Vuitton £750 trainers.[28] Even though they were paid to promote a competitor, their decision was odd but reflected her predicament. She had to abandon New York. 'I want to celebrate my 10-year anniversary at home,' was the quotation conjured up by Milloy to conceal her difficulties.[29]

Other news in New York was also depressing. After one term Brooklyn abandoned his photography course at Parsons. Fellow students scoffed that he was incapable of the most simple task.[30] The following day, after a reconciliation, he was seen celebrating Chloe Grace Moretz's 21st birthday in Los Angeles. Victoria arranged that he would return to New York to start an internship with photographer Conor McDonnell. 'Brooklyn's photography career is going from strength to strength,' said a spokeswoman.[31] There was some truth in that. Victoria had arranged for Brooklyn to be the official photographer for a Burberry range and BMW's Z4 sports car.[32]

Twelve-year-old Romeo, her second son, was also unsettled. After a game of tennis with Andy Murray he decided to become a professional player. Neither parent appeared to appreciate that tennis professionals usually start their career from the age of about five years old. To help Romeo train with top coaches, Beckham built a £30,000 tennis court in their newly converted nine-bedroom Oxfordshire house adjacent to the Soho Farmhouse country club. The house had been bought in December 2016 for over £6 million and was registered only in David Beckham's name. He regularly strolled across to the club to play table tennis, swim and meet glamorous fellow members. In the school holidays, many mothers stayed with their children during the week. Most were married and would be discreet about their conversations with Beckham. Regularly, he asked for his dinner to be delivered from the club's kitchen. Victoria discovered that Dave Gardner had bought a smaller house nearby, financed, some assumed, by his commission on the Qatar deal.

The need for money enticed Victoria to engage seriously in Fuller's latest attempt to reunite the Spice Girls for another tour, the first since 2012. Fuller knew that all five women needed the money badly. Each had spent the £38 million they had earned as Spice Girls. Promises of £5 million or even £10 million individually for the new tour were murmured. And Victoria was assured she would not need to sing. Their first meeting since the *Viva* musical flop was held on 2 February 2018 in Geri's north London home. That evening, after a sushi dinner Victoria posted a reunion snap with the caption 'Love my girls'. Within one week they were arguing. Victoria, Geri and Mel B could not agree about the group's leadership and whether they should tour, appear in a few 'epic' shows or just record an album. One month later Victoria abandoned the idea. Mel B was blamed.[33]

Arguing with the Spice Girls was a major distraction. Once again Victoria needed to reinvent herself. The best praise she received for her February show in New York was 'Beckham may not define the fashion moment but she is adept at the follow-through.'[34] Unsure of her destination, she would soon return to her old 'cling' style because it was all about herself and the clothes she wanted to wear.[35]

In a *Vogue* video she appeared in a black dress in a make-up room: 'We're here to celebrate one of the most enduring style icons of all time – me, Victoria Beckham.' The endorsement of 'Victoria Beckham – a decade of elegance' by the magazine's editor Edward Enninful was generous, but jarred with the launch of another new image six weeks later.[36]

As the master controller of the Beckham empire, Simon Fuller was conscious of managing their two businesses but also their marriage. Brand Beckham would only survive if Victoria was seen to be 'successful' and that depended on their relationship continuing. To boost her income, Fuller and Victoria had agreed to associate her business with Reebok, owned by Adidas. Junking her tag 'Simple, pure chic, elegant', Victoria hyped her collaboration with Reebok sportswear to sell 'Health and Youth'.

The launch was set for April 2018 in West Hollywood. At an Art Deco house, a nervous group of her employees hovered in the corridors whispering 'VB is coming' into their mobile phones as she moved between interviews and a photo-call.

Promoting fashion with a health tag was astute, but a thin woman who survived on apple cider vinegar, bee pollen, spinach and occasionally plain fish challenged the image of the fitness market. Her choice of birthday cake made of watermelon and berries was certainly eccentric. Although she had moved on from her assertion in 2008 that 'I can't concentrate in flats' and no longer watched her children play football in five-inch heels, she needed to convince young women to wear a T-shirt from a collection embossed with the slogan 'A dark but happy place'. That was brave for a woman who was repeatedly made-up, re-dressed four times a day and was always seen wearing sunglasses.

'This,' said Reebok's chief executive Matthew O'Toole, standing by a long table covered with food, 'is one of the most incredible nights in the history of Reebok.' Among his small audience were Victoria's stylist Rachel Zoe, her hairdresser Ken Paves and her ubiquitous friend Eva Longoria, as well as three Beckham children dressed in hoodies. Plus Simon Fuller. 'I wear sunglasses a lot,' said Victoria in the dark room, 'so it's always dark in my world, but I'm happy really'.[37]

Victoria was unlikely to have been happy for long. The news from Paris was that Beckham had watched PSG play Real Madrid sitting next to model Bella Hadid.[38] Nor did she like the reports of her husband meeting glamorous guests at Soho Farmhouse. Worst of all were the rumours across all the social media platforms that Harper had been moved from Pembridge Hall school to Glendower in South Kensington because of a friendship between Beckham and a teacher. 'Total fiction,' vehemently claimed one of Beckham's spokesmen.

Amid all that swirling gossip and speculation, Beckham moved to Miami. Some of his staff believed he wanted to live separately from Victoria. Others insisted that he was rescuing his football club.

Although Victoria had said in January, 'We can't wait to be spending much more time in Miami as a family,' she resisted moving to Florida. Financial necessity – regularly flying between London, New York and around Asia – left no alternative but to live separate lives. Despite Victoria remaining behind in London with three children, both paid lip-service to one mantra. In interviews Beckham said, 'We teach our children that they must work hard for success.' Victoria echoed that, saying how she devoted her time to caring for her children. No one openly challenged that image.

There were good commercial reasons for Beckham to move to Miami: the fate of his football club was in doubt. Under the MLS's original conditions in 2014, Beckham's discounted franchise for a

Miami football club would be withdrawn if the team failed to start playing in 2020. Over the following four years Beckham had floundered. With a tight deadline, the fate of the club and stadium was precarious. 'There were many times we were at death's door,' admitted the MLS Commissioner Don Garber, as he looked back to December 2015 and the fourth attempt to build a stadium in Overtown.

Miami's council had sided with Beckham's bid for Overtown, not least because he promised to build a state-of-the-art football academy for local children. Conditional permission was given for a stadium to be built on a nine-acre site. 'This is a city built on dreams,' said Beckham emotionally after hearing the good news, 'and today you've made my dreams come true.' After the Bolivian multi-millionaire Marcelo Claure spent $19 million on one part of the site, the local authority of Miami-Dade offered to sell an adjacent six-acre area, a former truck depot, for a 25,000-seater stadium for £6.5 million ($9 million).

The final hurdles faced by Beckham and Claure were legal challenges by disgruntled neighbours. One complained that he had been prevented from bidding for the site, while local groups demanded that the land be used for housing. By the end of 2017 their objections had been overruled, but other uncertainties surfaced. The earliest a new stadium could be built would be 2021. A temporary stadium was found at Fort Lauderdale. It would need $100 million to transform the dilapidated building. Then new problems emerged.

The Overtown site was too small to justify the $300 million cost of a permanent stadium, especially because there was no space for car parking. Garber's insistence that the stadium should be built within the city made no commercial sense. By then, a succession of potential investors had joined and left the project.

Then, over breakfast, Marcelo Claure told Beckham, 'I'm calling it a day.' The Bolivian realised that he lacked the close political relationships that were critical for obtaining the city permits for building. Without those friends in the mayor's office, he could not raise sufficient money. Although Claure did not quit, Beckham was left without a properly funded partner. Both he and Fuller were out of their depth. As Beckham had said in 2013, 'Management is something that does not float my boat.'[39] The absence of billionaire shareholders, observed

Garber, now jeopardised the project. Tim Leiweke thought Beckham's prospective club was dead in the water.[40]

Garber offered Beckham $50 million to surrender the franchise. Fuller advised Beckham to accept. Beckham was on the verge of abandoning the project when Claure offered a solution.

Over previous weeks, Jorge Mas, a Miami-based billionaire, had been messaging Claure that he and his brother José were keen to invest in the potential football club. The sons of a penniless Cuban refugee who became a leader of the exiles against Fidel Castro after the 1960s, the brothers had by 2017 developed their father's telecommunications business into a $7 billion empire. As a Real Madrid supporter who had previously sought to buy an MLS club, Jorge Mas was a natural investor. Claure knew the Mas brothers as customers. By then, he had saved Sprint, a giant telecommunications company, from bankruptcy and transformed the corporation into a profitable success. Over a dinner in an Italian restaurant in Manhattan with the Mas brothers and Garber, Claure agreed in principle that the Cuban-Americans could become minority partners.

During a second dinner in an Italian restaurant in New Jersey with Beckham invited, the division of the share ownership was agreed. The Mas brothers would have 37.5 per cent, Beckham would have 10 per cent and Claure would have a majority stake of 52.5 per cent – of which Claure had 37.5 per cent and Masayoshi Son of Japan's SoftBank took 15 per cent. 'They're a lifeline,' Beckham admitted in August 2018 about the Mas brothers after the deal was signed.[41]

Beckham had no choice. Without serious money, no business ability to raise the necessary funds and no relationships in Miami, he had to rely on others.[42] He was relegated to play as a part-manager and front man. 'It's been painful at times,' he conceded.[43]

'That's the final piece of the puzzle,' said Garber about the settlement. Claure was satisfied. In his mind, he was the owner of the new team. He gave it a name – Club Internacional de Futbal Miami, alias Inter Miami – designed its logo, and agreed that they search for a new site for the stadium.

Unwilling to be outshone by the Mas brothers, Claure suggested that he run the club for the first three years, and then the brothers for the following three years. Mas rejected the idea. Claure's ego was bruised but he stayed on board. Involved in managing many giant corporations as a SoftBank director, he agreed that Jorge Mas should become the leading executive.

Jorge Mas proposed building the stadium on a 131-acre golf course adjacent to Miami international airport. Sidelining Beckham, Mas began negotiating with the city council to build a $1 billion complex of homes, offices and hotels around a 25,000-seater stadium. With his political and commercial pedigree in the community, Mas never doubted that an agreement with Miami's mayor Francis Suarez to create the Miami Freedom Park would eventually be signed. It would take four years.

Keeping Beckham as the figurehead, Mas let the footballer stand in the spotlight at a glitzy fanfare on 29 January 2018 announcing the birth of his own football club, Inter Miami. Asked about recruiting top European players, Beckham replied 'I've had calls from top players saying "I'm in." I'm not going to say who.'

His presentation included video goodwill messages from Olympic champion sprinter Usain Bolt, the Brazilian footballer Neymar and the Argentinian Lionel Messi. 'Who knows,' joked the world's greatest footballer, 'maybe in a few years you will give me a call.' Few outsiders took Messi's message seriously, but Mas knew that the 31-year-old player and his wife Antonela eventually wanted to live in Miami. Keeping alive the hope of Messi joining Inter Miami was slender, but there was a better chance of it happening than the recruitment of Cristiano Ronaldo.

Signing up top foreign players was essential. LA Galaxy, the 2014 champions, had slumped to the bottom of the league. Without Beckham and the former Ireland international Robbie Keane, Galaxy's driving force had evaporated. The priority was finding a manager to build a club from scratch. On the spot, Beckham ruled out his friend Gary Neville. 'He talks too much,' he said. After prevarication and delay, Beckham named Paul McDonough, a former player and agent, as the sporting director, and after several rejections he chose the Uruguayan Diego Alonso as the coach. Alonso failed to fit McDonough's job description as 'proactive' and, worse, Alonso had managed six clubs in rapid succession since 2011. Mas gave the impression that he had not interfered.[44]

With that settled, Beckham assumed he had no further chores at the club. He needed to earn his income from his sponsors. From

Miami he sped around Asia – Tokyo, Jakarta, Macao and Shanghai – opening a new hotel, appearing at events and acting as the British Fashion Council's ambassador. Beckham's staff had been sniffy about the unpaid ambassadorship but it allowed *GQ*'s Dylan Jones, who had arranged it, to claim that it would rebuild Beckham's public reputation after the publication of the emails. Publicity about the Fashion Council was preferable to photos of Beckham posing with a young woman at a hotel reception.[45]

On his return to Miami, Beckham socialised with new friends. He and Victoria met only once in Miami before he returned to London for his 43rd birthday. A video of the celebration posted on social media showed Harper in a restaurant giving her father a £4,950 Louis Vuitton wine-case. Brooklyn made a surprise entrance.[46]

The countdown had begun for the Beckhams' live reunion at the wedding on 19 May in St George's Chapel, Windsor Castle, of Prince Harry and the Californian actress Meghan Markle.

CHAPTER 28

WARFARE

Over previous years Beckham had met Prince Harry at celebrity functions and also socially. As neighbours in Oxfordshire – Harry had rented a converted barn on the Great Tew estate near the Beckhams' house – the laddish prince enjoyed joshing with the famous footballer in a restaurant or a pub. As celebrities it would appear they had much in common.

However, 37-year-old Meghan had, an observer noticed, 'put on airs'. As a Californian she felt little in common with Victoria. Yet as a fashionista, Meghan might have been sympathetic to Victoria's attempts to build a business.[1]

In an attempt to advance the relationship between the two couples, soon after Meghan moved into Kensington Palace a member of Victoria's staff offered Harry's fiancée advice on the best facials and hairdressing in London. Meghan also asked Victoria to supply free clothes and handbags. Her request was vetoed by the Palace for being against their rules. Despite that, and unknown to the public, when Meghan privately returned to Los Angeles she had stayed in the Beckhams' house in Beverly Hills. Her excuse was to avoid the paparazzi. At no cost, all her needs were secretly provided for by the Beckhams' staff. If there was a hint that Meghan was taking advantage of her new status, the Beckhams pushed their gripes aside. Only after the *Sun* reported how Victoria had given Meghan make-up advice did the relationship between the two ambitious women crash.

Sensitive to the media's probing into her unusual past, Meghan was outraged by the *Sun*'s report. This was the latest of a series of nasty revelations by London's newspapers. Harry was ordered to complain to David Beckham. The telephone conversation was difficult. Beckham was embarrassed, but after speaking to his wife he denied that she had leaked any information. A beautician was blamed, although the culprit was probably a boastful publicist employed by Beckham. That was the beginning of a bigger problem.

In Meghan's celebrity world, ranking depended on wealth and fame. As a seasoned operator, Meghan deluded herself that her status in the Royal Family placed her above Victoria in the social pecking order. She was irritated to discover that the Beckhams had considerably more wealth than herself. They owned five homes, had constant access to private jets, invitations to sail on yachts and much more money. And she was soon to be a duchess.

Then a new issue arose. Meghan and Harry were irritated by Beckham's friendship with Prince William. Ever since the World Cup bid in 2010, the two had enjoyed a good relationship. For the Sussexes, who were already complaining about their unequal status and wealth compared to the Cambridges, the sight of Becks with William was annoying.

Meghan appeared to want to punish the Beckhams. Television pictures of the couple arriving at St George's Chapel for the wedding showed Victoria stony-faced and David chewing gum. Meghan had not invited them to the wedding dinner. Her veto was an insult. After all, many guests such as George Clooney and other Hollywood stars invited that evening did not even know Meghan.

Victoria's sour expression also reflected her anger about David's behaviour at a Soho House party the previous night. He had been buying drinks for a brunette while Victoria sat silently thunderous nearby. Worse still, that very morning the woman had posted photos of herself and Beckham on the web.

At the end of the wedding service the Beckhams met Prince Charles at the sunlit reception in the garden. Twenty years earlier they had met at the Old Trafford football stadium. As he drove away, Charles had said to his aide, 'Why do these people never wear socks?' On that afternoon, Charles encountered a member of the People's Royalty and he was wearing socks! Moving on, Beckham congratulated Harry. During their conversation the Prince asked Beckham to join him in October in Sydney for the Invictus Games competition for injured servicemen. He instantly agreed. His staff were tasked to find a sponsor to pay for his fares. He planned to take Victoria and his four children.

Days later, Beckham flew to Miami and on to Japan and finally China for a football summit. With the couple once again apart, gossip about their imminent divorce began to trend on Twitter. 'It's embarrassing and laughable,' said Beckham's spokesman. 'This is just fake social media news,' said Milloy. To the Beckhams' fury, bookmakers were refusing to take any more bets on their separation.[2] Beckham's return to Miami did not end the rumours. Victoria was still flitting across the globe promoting her business. Her love message on Instagram – 'Morning cuddles x So much love' – did not halt the rumours that their marriage was falling apart.[3]

Photographs of the couple at London's Fashion Week fuelled more gossip. After arriving separately – he flew in from Miami – they sat on either side of *Vogue*'s Edward Enninful. The message she posted afterwards was simply: 'We're stronger together.' There was no mention of love.[4]

'I'm trying to be the best wife I can be,' she told a *Forbes* Women's Summit in New York a few days later. 'And I try to be the best mum. I try to be the best professional. I mean, I'm trying. It's a juggling act and it's not easy.' She tried hard to be positive.[5]

In the battle of Instagrams and Tweets she praised Beckham: 'I'm so lucky that I have the support of an incredible husband.' Followers noticed that his reply to Victoria's reference to her 'amazing' husband mentioned her as a mother and businesswoman, but rarely as a beloved wife.[6] To give herself 'positive energy' she carried a white Howlite crystal in her bag. That could not prevent the oncoming explosion.

The couple's dependence on their image-makers, Simon Oliveira for Beckham and Jo Milloy for Victoria, had run into unusual problems. Reflecting the acrimony between the Beckhams, the two publicists began to compete rather than collaborate to promote their own client. Both fed negative stories about the other side to their favourite tabloid journalists. Milloy was especially close to the *Sun*'s Clemmie Moodie and the *Daily Mail*'s Katie Hind. In June 2018, after a drink with a publicist, Moodie reported to her editor Dan Wootton that Milloy was drafting a statement announcing the Beckhams' separation. After Milloy's vigorous denials, Wootton did not publish the story. He simply noted that the Beckhams were working hard to present a happy image before they set off for

Australia. Everyone knew that Victoria put great value on a forth-coming *Vogue* cover story.

Natalie Lewis had agreed with Edward Enninful that *Vogue* would celebrate the 10th anniversary of Victoria's fashion label with a cover photo, an interview and photographs of the whole family. For the cover, Victoria agreed to pose in various outfits to recreate the Spice Girls' look.

At London's Fashion Week, Victoria agreed with Enninful that the interview would not be just about fashion but also feature her marriage. That would be an ideal platform to crush rumours of a split.[7] The interview would be accompanied with photographs of the Happy Beckham Family. Beckham had returned to London for the photoshoot.

The challenge for *Vogue*'s staff during the run-up to the photoshoot was dealing with the Beckhams' publicists. Making endless demands, the four separate squads – one for Beckham, one for the children and two for Victoria (Lewis for fashion and Milloy for personal) – were 'all over' *Vogue*'s team.

The scenario devised by the magazine's artistic director was of an idyll. The entire Beckham family was to be photographed sitting as a harmonious group in a wooden rowing boat on a pond, which was to be shot as if it were a lake. The image would illustrate Victoria's homily in her interview with *Vogue*'s Claudia Croft: 'We're stronger together than we are as individuals. Would either of us be in the position that we are in now had we not met and been together all those years ago?' She added that both of them were 'pretty used to ignoring the nonsense' that they were divorcing. 'People have been making things up about our relationship for 20 years. But these things have a wider effect on the people around us, and that's unfair.' Yet, she admitted, her children needed repeated reassurance that their parents' marriage was solid. 'It's all about the family unit,' she insisted.

Naturally, she did not want to admit the reality of her marital problems. Nor did she want to acknowledge the conflict between being a protective parent, a loyal wife and her ambition to remain fabulously famous in her own right. But she failed to say that she loved David.

Claudia Croft followed the agreed rules of the interview. She did not mention that Brooklyn had dropped out of Parsons, or that 'tennis-obsessed' Romeo could not hack it, and that Cruz was not, as spoon-fed by the publicists, a 'talented musician ... the new Justin Bieber'. Instead, Croft repeated the publicists' standard line that Victoria had shown the fashion industry a 'new way to sell' clothes. She did not mention her business's small static turnover and growing debts. There was not even a hint of sarcasm in the article when Victoria was quoted about the difficulties of living amid a deluge of publicity. 'I wasn't courting it,' she told Croft. Her publicists' regular summons to the paparazzi was unmentioned. Without irony, Croft quoted Victoria: 'Everything I'm doing is very honest.' Following that agenda, Croft ignored the revelations during the day's photo-shoot.[8]

Oliveira announced that Beckham would not appear with Victoria in a family photo. The tabloids, he knew, would highlight the obvious. 'David feels it's going back,' Oliveira told *Vogue*'s editors. 'It's like the old *OK!* magazine stuff. We're not on safe ground with the glossy family image. We can't control it. We don't need it.' Not mentioned was Beckham's new opinion that his children should not be exploited for the brand.[9] Unspoken was his apparent fury with Victoria's endless self-promotion campaigns.

On Victoria's behalf, Lewis and Milloy fretted that Victoria must get her way. 'We'll lose the cover if you don't do it,' Beckham was told. His co-operation was vital. Milloy asked why was Beckham denying the Brand the opportunity to pose as Britain's most famous family? The wrangling was followed by an outburst between Beckham and Victoria. Beckham relented.

Finally, the family was shuffled on to the boat. Unexpectedly, once the six were afloat, Beckham insisted that his cocker spaniel Olive should feature in the shot too. The dog had 71,000 Instagram followers. Gingerly, the boat was pushed from the shore. Suddenly, Olive jumped into the water. Beckham was about to follow and rescue his pet. Screaming 'No', worried that his clothes would get soaked, several assistants plunged into the water to grab the dog. Victoria's face turned to thunder. Another argument blew up. A sulk descended. Plans for the family photo were ditched. Victoria posed only with the children and the spaniel. In the aftermath, Beckham and Victoria posed as a twosome, separate and looking rather severe. But they were, as ever, consummate actors. No one looking at the perfect images could have imagined the dramas over the preceding hours.[10] The cover photograph would be of Victoria, and only with her four children. Later it was called, the 'ultimate pornography of celebrity and the genteel savagery in compelling their children to pose to conceal reality'.

Long before the magazine was printed, Beckham dispatched Izzy May, a publicist, to Vogue House. 'He's off to Miami and wants to read the magazine during the journey,' said May, standing at reception. She was told that the section had not yet been vetted by Enninful before being printed. May was insistent. 'David demands that he approve it before it's printed.' Reluctantly, she left the building empty-handed. 'Shoddy behaviour by May,' complained *Vogue*'s staff.

Warfare resumed in the run-up to publication. After looking through *Vogue*'s press release, Beckham's publicists objected to highlighting Victoria's quote, 'We're better together than apart.' In the ensuing 'huge explosion', Oliveira demanded, 'Remove the quote.' Beckham wanted no mention of their marital problems. 'It's in the magazine,' he was told. Milloy insisted that it remain. 'HANDBAGS AT DAWN' was the *Mail on Sunday*'s headline about the three-way argument between the two Beckham publicists and Enninful about the quotation.[11] In the end it was belatedly removed from the publicity but published in the magazine.

To celebrate the cover, Enninful hosted a dinner at Mark's Club in Mayfair. The rival Beckham publicists co-ordinated the separate arrival of Beckham and Victoria. Professional as ever, they posed holding hands with inscrutable smiles and entered the club. Unknown to the photographers, after ten minutes Beckham left through a rear entrance. Victoria remained, drinking red wine until, amid cheers, she stood on a couch to sing the Spice Girls' big hit 'Wannabe'. No official party photographs, Natalie Lewis ordered, would be distributed.

Throughout, Enninful sat bemused. Previously unaware of the Beckhams' torrid relationship, he accepted that making both the Beckhams happy would be impossible. He was working against bizarre forces. But Enninful felt triumphant. Under his editorship, celebrity was all that counted. Unconcerned whether *Vogue*'s article offered original insights or exposed genuinely new talent, Enninful was always searching for impact. Trivia could be precious if uttered by a celebrity. That was the Beckhams' value

Vogue's Victoria Beckham cover was a triumph. The magazine's sales rocketed. At Victoria's request, in order to stop the rumours of divorce spreading, the magazine promoted an online subscriber edition featuring Victoria and Beckham on the cover. They were sitting apart.[12] 'This potentially superlative piece of PR collapsed,' concluded the *Daily Mail*, 'into a widely ridiculed publicity misfire, which may be the final blow to the already reeling Brand Beckham.'[13]

As hard as Victoria tried, the genie refused to go back into the bottle. When she took Brooklyn to Elton John's 25th AIDS Foundation party in Windsor, some wondered why Beckham was missing.[14] And after they staged a 19th wedding anniversary celebration at the Bristol hotel in Paris, and one publicist posted pictures of their dinner with a £1,544 bottle of Chateau Lafite Rothschild 1990 with the accompanying message, 'I love you so much', a rival publicist poured scorn. However much the public still wished to believe the best about the Beckhams, the surprises kept coming.

In July 2018, Milloy mentioned to Clemmie Moodie an extraordinary exchange that had occurred during the Beckhams' summer holidays. 'Daddy's not a cheat,' Victoria had apparently told her four children. Reading the newspaper report, Beckham raged that Milloy and Victoria were waging a media war against him.[15] In reality, he was doing a good job of self-inflicted harm.

At the end of September, Beckham was due in court in Wimbledon charged with driving his loaned £200,000 Bentley at 59 mph on the A40, contrary to the 40 mph speed limit. The journalists and public crammed into the crowded courtroom were disappointed that the accused was absent, although he had just posted a picture of himself to his 51 million followers looking relaxed and happy in his Bentley. He captioned his photo: 'Angry. London traffic.' His humour was justified. His lawyer, Nick 'Mr Loophole' Freeman, was certain that he would escape conviction on a technicality. The official letter notifying him of the offence had arrived one day too late in the post. Beckham expected praise for his skill in once again dodging justice.

In 1999 'Mr Loophole' had successfully engineered Beckham's escape from a similar speeding charge. 'Petrified' Beckham, he claimed, was escaping at 76 mph in his Ferrari from a well-known 'maniac photographer' in a white Fiesta – a defence which was later undermined, because on that day the photographer was in Canada.[16]

He was not convicted. Nineteen years later in Wimbledon, Freeman again succeeded.

'I am very relieved with the verdict,' Beckham posted. 'Very happy with my legal team.' Beckham was on a private jet flying to Paris to promote a Vietnamese car firm, VinFast. For £1 million he agreed to endorse their luxury cars. 'It's incredible,' Beckham said four times in a perfunctory outburst in the showroom. And then for the next two hours he fell silent. One irony was lost on Beckham's frustrated hosts and paymaster. *GQ*'s editor Dylan Jones had just acclaimed his hero's eloquence: 'Nowadays Beckham talks like a statesman. These days he talks in perfect paragraphs.'[17] Not in Paris for £1 million it seemed. For the unfortunate Vietnamese, the media were focused on Beckham's acquittal rather than his staccato eulogy for their car. And for that matter, the media were distracted by Beckham's hair transplant to conceal a bald patch.[18]

Victoria was also in Paris. She posted a picture of the £1,300 bottle of Burgundy wine that she and Beckham had drunk in celebration of his speeding acquittal. That was followed by pictures of the snails and steak David had eaten. Their publicists were appalled. Neither seemed to have considered the impression they had created – of grubby chancers. Warned of the danger, and to minimise the damage, Victoria sought to present an image of normality over the following days. A stream of photos showed them enjoying their holiday in Bordeaux with Gordon Ramsay and Eva Longoria.[19] Two weeks later her efforts unravelled.

To pay for their first-class flights to Sydney for the Invictus Games, Beckham's office had arranged with AIA, an Asian insurance company, that he would promote his sponsor in Australia while he was there. As part of the advertising campaign, Beckham agreed to record before leaving London an interview for Australian TV's show the *Sunday Project*. As requested, the interviewer, Lisa Wilkinson, explicitly mentioned AIA during the interview.

But then, unexpectedly, she also asked him about his marital problems. 'To have been married the amount of time we have,' he told Wilkinson, 'it's always hard work.' After repeating how 'hard' marriage was he added that life had 'become a little more complicated'. Pushed about his marriage he admitted, 'I feel I'm doing OK but it's a struggle.' His priority, he said, was to 'protect our children' from media intrusion. He was not asked why he refused to appear with Victoria and his family on the *Vogue* front cover.

The Australian TV channel posted the interview clips of Beckham's confessions to his combined 74.7 million Instagram followers ahead of the Sunday broadcast.[20] Beckham's admission that his marriage was troubled was juxtaposed in the post with an old soundbite by Victoria: 'People have been making things up about our relationship for 20 years, so David and I are pretty used to ignoring the nonsense and just carrying on as normal.' Not warned in advance, Victoria watched Beckham's clip and her contradiction on her mobile with disbelief.

'It was like a nuclear bomb had gone off,' Milloy told Moodie.[21] Milloy's surprise was trumped by Victoria's tearful hysteria. Her husband's disloyalty baffled her. His truthfulness had destroyed her efforts to conjure up an image of happy families. Why, she sobbed, would David embarrass her? Worse still, why could he not understand the consequence of his own stupidity?

Why, she wailed, had he become the enemy of her ambition? Without any answers, she fled to a Baden-Baden spa hotel for two days. The trip was to recover her 'emotional balance' but she was overwhelmed by rage and recrimination.

Even as she cried for herself her steely sense of survival took control. On the eve of returning to London for the flight to Australia she posted a selfie of herself hiking, #wellness. Asked about her marriage she replied, 'It can get quite frustrating but I leave it to my PR team. I don't get involved.'[22]

Her PR team duly briefed Moodie. 'Things with him and Victoria aren't great at the moment – and nobody can predict the future.' However, Moodie believed that as 'consummate professionals' the Beckhams planned to 'put on a united front and smile for the camera'.[23]

Victoria got off the plane in Sydney with three children – Romeo, Cruz and Harper – looking downcast. During the flight the Australian TV station refused the publicists' requests to delete Beckham's references to their 'complicated' marriage.

To deflect the media's attention a publicist released CCTV footage showing an attempt by masked burglars to break into the Beckhams' country home in Great Tew. Victoria's tears, the spokesman suggested, were provoked by the burglary and not the interview. Convinced that the Beckhams were seeking to manipulate the world, some newspapers questioned whether there had actually been a break-in. The police, they reported, said there was no evidence of a burglary, or even an attempt at one. The Beckhams insisted they were telling the truth.[24]

After the family settled into their spacious rented house on North Shore near Sydney harbour, Victoria posted a photo of a beer bottle labelled 'Victoria Bitter'. She also allowed herself to be photographed on Bondi Beach with Cruz putting a protective arm around her. Beckham walked alone, behind.

Beckham also found himself alone at the Invictus Games stadium. Arriving on the agreed day to meet Prince Harry he was perplexed why officials were playing a dance to keep him happy, but away from Harry. 'Where is he?' Beckham asked the Games' officials as he waited. 'When will I meet him?' he kept asking. Beckham was unaware that the Prince had ordered that under no circumstances was the footballer to be allowed near him. Photographs of the two together were forbidden. The royal snub was brutal. David Beckham was puzzled. Why did the Prince refuse to meet him?

The exclusion order, it later transpired, was issued by Meghan. She did not want any competition in the media from Beckham, and especially not from his wife Victoria.

Meghan's visit to Australia, her first foreign royal tour, was a huge success. Meeting cheering crowds of admirers convinced Meghan that she was the Royal Family's new Diana. The added excitement was Meghan's announcement of her pregnancy.

But inside the Sussexes' headquarters in Sydney the atmosphere was less positive. Outraged that in the royal hierarchy she was subservient to Catherine, Duchess of Cambridge and the future Queen, Meghan shouted at her staff and allegedly threw a cup of tea into the air.[25] Few insiders were surprised. She had been formally accused in London of bullying her staff. In her bad mood, both she and Harry were constantly searching the internet for critical comments about themselves. She was not happy to read anything flattering in the media about the Beckhams.

At the Beckham's rented house in North Shore, Harry's snub was barely mentioned. 'A bit strange,' Beckham said, but he did not call

Harry. Nor did he return to the stadium. At that moment the couple were more concerned about their marriage, their brand and Victoria's faltering self-confidence.

'I feel I am standing naked in a room full of people saying, "What do you think?"' she had told a radio audience shortly before they flew to Australia. 'None of this has just been given to me. I work really, really hard. What I have achieved is great.'[26]

Success was not the impression reported by the experts at Fashion Week on her return to London. Victoria's latest designs were modelled in a modest Mayfair art gallery by 47-year-old Stella Tennant. Later, at a major event at the Royal Albert Hall, leading designers were asked to name their favourite creations. Giorgio Armani, Donatella Versace and Vivienne Westwood gave detailed descriptions of revolutionary designs and fabrics. Victoria named a 'dove-grey dress' and added, 'I wasn't trying to prove anything to anyone but myself.' She won no prize that night. Beckham arrived at the event with his friend Dave Gardner. He left without Victoria.[27]

After thinking about the past weeks she realised that, for her own self-esteem and to save their marriage, she needed to stop relying on Beckham's loans. Her 2018 results suggested the problems were worsening. On slightly increased sales she had lost a further £12.2 million, increasing her debts to £39 million. Beckham and his advisers agreed to rethink the brand's finances.[28]

Hours after the news about her recent losses was revealed, Victoria and her parents went with Beckham to the private club Annabel's in Mayfair for a pre-Christmas dinner. While Victoria plucked at nuts and berries, all four looked miserable. Two years earlier she had said, 'I would never be in a nightclub, ever – not any more.'[29]

Their Instagram messages over the Christmas holidays were illustrated with pictures of the children, but not of David and Victoria together. David realised he needed to get a grip and resolve the crisis. Asserting control over his family and his business became his priority.

CHAPTER 29

A NEW YEAR

'It's going to be brilliant,' David Beckham's spokesman predicted about the planned New Year's Eve party they were hosting in Great Tew. No one asked about the knighthood.

Brooklyn, now 20, arrived with 22-year-old Yorkshire model Hana Cross. 'Me and My Girl,' Brooklyn had earlier posted of the two of them at the Eiffel Tower. 'Luckiest Man in the World.' Hana and Victoria, the publicist disclosed, were 'getting on famously', not least because Hana wore Victoria's designs.[1]

According to the *Sunday Times Rich List*, Brooklyn was worth £6.5 million and had 11.5 million Instagram followers. His parents were less pleased to discover that he was also having an affair with singer Rita Ora, eight years older than him. Beckham ordered his son to end the relationship and return to New York to continue his internship with Conor McDonnell. He obeyed.[2] Beckham's more important decision was to take control of his own future. As an adviser said, 'David had looked behind the curtains and discovered a spider's web.'

The more he thought about it he realised that brand fatigue was a growing danger. H&M had dropped him after five years and recruited a younger face. As he was no longer a footballer and as he grew older, the younger generation was certain to follow new heroes. During his conversations with Dave Gardner, the prospect of Fuller securing new lucrative contracts with major corporations seemed less likely. Fearing a downward spiral as his income from sponsorships fell – in 2018 the revenues of Beckham Brand Holdings had dropped by 18 per cent, registering a £1.6 million loss[3] – he doubted whether Fuller had the vision to re-energise his brand. Too much of his focus was on money and not Beckham's future. Fuller struggled to define what the brand would represent. He did not appear to understand that there was a limit to the public's fascination with two aspiring people from Essex.

The brand risked becoming superficial. Since Beckham's contribution to UNICEF was petering out to an annual appearance at Soccer Aid for children, he needed to be more than just a face. Beckham wanted to revitalise his image. The best strategy would be to focus on being an entrepreneur at the Inter Miami football club.

Fuller knew little about football and, over the last five years, his relationship with Beckham had deteriorated. Living in Los Angeles and rarely flying to London, Fuller delegated a lot to his employees. His control had weakened. In his absence, Beckham resented Fuller pocketing 30 per cent commission on his income.

The nub of his anger was the bad deal Fuller had concluded with Rockowitz and Global Brands. Not only had Fuller undervalued the Beckham Brand's value but Beckham was only earning two-thirds of the 50 per cent he still owned. Fuller was pocketing the remaining one-third of the profits. And it was Beckham who flew around the world, doing all the work, while Fuller enjoyed his Californian vineyard. To cap it all, Rockowitz's prediction of sales worth $1.5 billion in 2020 had proved to be a fantasy. The company's executives were misleading Beckham's staff about the company's future. Their reassuring predictions were contradicted by the sharp decline of payments to Beckham as the company quietly headed towards declaring bankruptcy.

Beckham was persuaded by Gardner not to allow gratitude or nostalgia for the past 12 years influence his future. They could manage without Fuller. Gardner and Nicola Howson, the feisty in-house publicity chief, had just pulled off a major coup. They had finalised a multi-million-pound deal with Nasser Al-Khelaifi, the chairman of Qatar Sports Investments, for Beckham to appear as the face of the 2022 World Cup. The Qatari money – an estimated £15 million annually and a seven-year contract with David Beckham Ventures – would buy his freedom. With his future focused on Inter Miami, there was every reason to remove Fuller from the potential goldmine.

In their conversations Fuller insisted that he had invented Brand Beckham. 'Not true,' replied Beckham, mindful that Fuller always claimed to have invented the Spice Girls. Beckham ignored Fuller's boasts. His mask of modesty hid his stubborn selfishness. By the end of the discussions their relationship had broken down. There was no sentimentality or gratitude in the lawyer's letter to Fuller. 'It's the end of the gravy train,' said a close aide. Not quite.[4]

Beckham Brand Holdings paid £30,875,000 (or $40 million) for Fuller's shares in the company. Beckham funded the transaction by paying half from his own assets and borrowing £15.5 million from a bank. To minimise his taxes Fuller structured the payment as a dividend from the reserves to his own company.[5] Over the following two years the description and amount of Beckham's loans were changed, introducing more confusion for anyone trying to understand his finances.[6] Beckham was helped to write the short explanatory script.

'After a while with Simon Fuller I thought I can do this myself. Management never interested me. Personally, I never felt that was something I would be good at. Now that has changed.' He wanted to be 'able to actually control everything that was going on in my world'.[7]

The deal gave Beckham full control of Beckham Brand Holdings, which included his 10 per cent stake in Inter Miami FC as well as Seven Global. Automatically he also took complete control of David Beckham Ventures (DBV), a subsidiary owning his brand name and partnerships with businesses including Adidas and L'Oréal. His friend Dave Gardner became his managing director. Fuller's riposte through his publicist was blunt: 'He no longer needs David in his stable.'[8]

Beckham's new headquarters and small staff were housed on one floor in London's Great Portland Street. Among those promoted was Nicola Howson, converted into a true believer of the Beckhams, who he had met through Gordon Ramsay. With a profitable portfolio, the hunt for a new investor and partner began.

One legacy from the past remained. Beckham could not extricate Fuller from Victoria's indebted fashion business on any advantageous terms. The XIX Entertainment group retained its 33 per cent stake as a partner with David Belhassen's NEO Investment Partners and with Victoria.[9]

Once the divorce was completed, Fuller was removed from Beckham's biography. Another mentor had been written out of the script. When asked about the 'Miami clause' in his original 2007 Galaxy contract, Beckham replied, 'I asked for that clause. I went with my gut.'[10] Others involved in concluding that agreement recalled the option was devised by Fuller, CAA's Jeff Frasco and Terry Byrne. Beckham, the eyewitnesses said, was unaware of that bonus until Fuller later explained their achievement.

After the turmoil Beckham's memory continued to be unreliable. 'There are a lot of responsibilities that come with having the kind of profile that I do,' he reminisced at a crucial moment in 2019.[11] 'When you're young, you're allowed to make mistakes, but it's how you behave after that that counts ... I've always stood up for myself. I've always admitted the mistakes that I made.' Those recalling his original, somewhat circumspect statements about his relationship with Rebecca Loos had different recollections of his reaction to 'mistakes'.

Everything was a matter of interpretation. Just as he spoke about his 'obsession' for his children to learn to 'work hard', he also described his abiding credo as 'Work hard, be passionate, take care of your family.' But independent observers recalled his global junketing over recent years. Any expressions of loyalty to Victoria raised questions. His contradictions were understandable once he explained that his models were David Bowie and the actor Steve McQueen: 'I look up to people who do things differently but do it with style.'[12]

Hype, he knew, was critical to showbiz success. And so he claimed in 2019 that Inter Miami was 'already the third most popular team in the MLS' and that his academy offered kids huge potential. That was another Beckham fantasy. The football team did not yet exist. The deadline to build the stadium would be missed and no academy had been created. But the seeds of success had been sewn. Beckham, Oliveira and Gardner had formed Kin, a footballer's agency with Lionel Messi's manager, Rodrigo Messi.[13] Simultaneously, he had created OTRO, a digital platform, with Lionel Messi and Zinedine Zidane to promote commercial endorsements for sports heroes. Both ventures were unsuccessful, but they paved the foundation for Beckham's relationship with Lionel Messi's managers.[14]

Expanding his own commercial organisation in Great Portland Street, Beckham prioritised a remedy to Oliveira's decision to gradually break away from him, and the exit of Fuller's PR operation. In order to control totally Beckham's image as the creator and owner of his brand and his reputation, and benefit from the tax advantages offered to film producers, Nicola Howson launched Studio 99. The company would make all the documentaries and the advertisements about Beckham. Their first success was to finalise a £16 million contract with Netflix to produce an autobiographical series for transmission in 2023. Beckham retained full editorial control over the proposed content – which was to be wholly uncritical but entertaining self-promotion.

Media interviews, they decided, were best avoided. There was nothing to gain from conversations that could not be controlled. Only a handful of trusted allies should have access to him. Leading that small band was *GQ*'s editor, Dylan Jones. He could always be relied upon.

In March 2019, Jones recalled a 2002 photoshoot in a warehouse. Almost naked except for 'snug' Dolce & Gabbana trunks, Beckham's body glistened with baby oil. His fingernails were painted black. Jones put the rhetoric into Beckham's mouth: 'My style? It's from another planet.' Beckham was candid about his lifelong lust for publicity: 'There is literally no photoshoot I regret. They were all great opportunities to actually do something different. And I wasn't scared to do it.' Beckham, wrote Jones, had spent 20 years building a brand. 'The next five years is all about building an empire.'

Unashamedly, Jones and Beckham assumed their readers had no memory. 'At the heart of Beckham's world,' wrote Jones, 'and reflected throughout his office is his 20-year relationship with UNICEF. It's a point of passion for Beckham: "I am passionate about it. So that really is our number-one focus in this office".'[15] The facts were different. Beckham had reluctantly contributed £750,000 from his own fortune towards UNICEF, and the number of his engagements for the organisation was declining.

His real focus was to earn more money and build his reputation in America. Although he won passing fame for the Armani advertisements he was still relatively unknown, because comparatively few Americans were football fans. One step towards wider recognition was seeing a statue of himself erected outside LA Galaxy's stadium.

The club had commissioned a fitting statue, but there was a twist. Unknown to Beckham, the *Late Late Show* host James Corden had commissioned a spoof statue that grotesquely distorted Beckham's face and body. Unaware of the plot, but knowing that he was ostensibly being filmed by LA Galaxy during a private preview in a hangar, he reacted to the statue with expletives. Viewers saw a man under pressure: vain and assertive, puzzled yet polite, incandescent but self-controlled. As he left the hangar in disgust, Corden revealed himself. Beckham reacted as a generous good sport. The nine-minute TV segment would be watched 44 million times on YouTube.[16]

Just as Beckham's image was being rebuilt, Victoria's remained troubled. With familiar resilience she was convinced that, as a universally admired star, everyone would want her clothes. 'I don't feel I have anything to prove now in the way I dress,' she said. 'I don't want the brand to be predictable – but it still has to be believably "me".'[17]

However, Britain's tabloids and magazines had tired of her self-promotion. Countless interviewers had tried to find a hidden meaning to her life – a hint of imagination, creativity and originality – but their tapes always recorded identical fables and reminiscences. Victoria was not famous for her mystery or eloquence. She did not understand the strength of silence and posed as enviably cool.

Nevertheless, the *Guardian*'s Jess Cartner-Morley responded to the promotion of her Reebok T-shirt, which was blazoned with her logo and priced at £225. An identical shirt without her logo was sold in high streets for £25.

Invited to a New York warehouse, Cartner-Morley described Victoria as dressed immaculately during a Reebok fashion shoot. Sipping San Pellegrino through a straw to avoid smudging her lipstick, she explained that she always had to look perfect because the paparazzi were forever waiting to pounce. Being hunted by publicity seekers, she sighed, was so tiresome. Without a blush she added, 'People are not interested in my private life,' and then she reeled off her usual self-deprecating lines: her dedication as a working mother, reliant on her beloved husband and modern father to care for the children in her absence.

'I'm ready to put my foot on the gas,' she said. In return for the access Jess Cartner-Morley cast Victoria as 'an industry leader' and added, 'The public fascination with Victoria is the heartbeat of her brand.'[18]

The Reebok campaign backfired. Seeking the consumers' pity had been an odd pitch. Her luminous socks cost £30 a pair in her shop, while Reebok charged £15 for three pairs of the same socks. A newspaper investigation showed that her £380 shirts were being made in China by workers paid less than £2 an hour.[19] Victoria refused to comment. Reebok, responsible for manufacturing the shirts, explained that they paid 'fair wages' and the shirts' high cost was down to Victoria demanding the best materials. A range of cosmetics remained the elusive prize.

The problem was that Victoria seemed to have no original ideas. The best she could do was to copy Gwyneth Paltrow's success. Paltrow had earned huge profits by selling a product that promised eternal youth. By injecting a special blood once a week into the gluteal muscle, she promised women would 'reduce auto-immunity, strengthen the immune system, and detoxify'.

To join the bandwagon, Victoria promoted Sturm moisturiser, a face-cream that stimulated the production of collagen. Her YouTube promotion described the product as one made from a special serum, although some tabloids mistakenly described her moisturiser as made from her own blood. The launch price was £1,200. She also posted a video of herself removing a £118 Sturm facemask in the morning.[20] When sales did not materialise she launched a new Victoria Beckham cell-rejuvenating Chamomile face serum manufactured by Augustinus Bader. Convinced that she enjoyed 'cult status' among women, her serum was sold for £180. Her detractors identified a similar Nivea product selling for £10. Bader's sales never took off.

Next, Victoria launched The Chair, a series of self-mocking videos posted on YouTube for fashion fans.[21] Among her notable items was her appearance in an untidy hotel room. 'David would have a panic attack if he saw this,' she had told her audience.[22] No one, even her long-serving staff, dared to tell Victoria that she was not a subject of widespread fascination. She was making a fool of herself.

By February 2019 her business bore a hint of desperation. At the London Fashion Show at Tate Britain, the Beckham family sat on the front row. Seven-year-old Harper was the star. Her hair was cut and styled just like Anna Wintour's. As part of the gimmick, the child and the fashion czarina sat next to each other. Harper, Victoria said, loved putting on make-up and walking around the house in high-heeled shoes. Shortly before this, Victoria had said about her daughter: 'I don't like her to focus too much on her appearance.'[23]

Naturally, the Beckhams posted the shot of Harper and Wintour on Instagram and glowed as the image spread across the internet. Victoria's designs were headlined: 'Unleash her naughty side.'[24] The sales remained static.

Her latest designs did, however, appeal to Meghan Markle. Forgetting the insults and swallowing her pride, Victoria agreed to provide a coat, dress, boots and a handbag worth £6,000 to Meghan for the Royal Family's traditional Christmas Day parade in Sandringham. Later, Meghan wore a Beckham custom-made pregnancy outfit and a white coat and dress for a service in Westminster Abbey. Victoria's style also attracted Melania Trump. She wore a Victoria Beckham dress during the president's official visit to London.[25]

But the financial benefit was nil. The only success in 2019 was a £1,400 handbag that had been displayed by Meghan. Victoria's Instagram video prompted the sales. The disappointment was reflected in the increased losses – £10.2 million in 2018 on static sales of £42.5 million. 'Big mistakes,' she admitted to the *Financial Times*, had bedevilled her business from the outset.[26] Beckham Brands Holdings lost £1.6 million in 2018, compared to £12.3 million profits in 2017. DB Ventures' profits halved from £23.2 million in 2017 to £11.5 million in 2018.

The 2018 report for Beckham Brand Holdings Ltd (BBH), the main company, showed that the group's pre-tax profits were just £1.7 million, down from £15.7 million, after an 18 per cent fall in turnover to £45.8 million. BBH's value had fallen from £43.7 million to £31 million. Part of the reason was Victoria's £12.2 million losses, but there was also the payment of two dividends. The first dividend paid to the Beckhams and Fuller in 2018 was £11.1 million and the second dividend was £18.7 million. To complete the break with Fuller, a £27 million dividend was paid in 2019.

In turn, Fuller invested £13.5 million in Victoria's business (VBL) to keep it afloat.[27] The combination of loans and investment in Victoria's business from Beckham, Fuller and NEO Investments had exceeded £100 million. To maintain their standard of living, Beckham had plunged into the company's reserves. The financial problems were exacerbated by a flurry of embarrassing headlines.

Beckham admitted in court using his mobile phone while driving. Photographed by a pedestrian and confirmed by CCTV, he claimed to have 'no recollection' of the offence. He was disqualified from driving for six months.[28] Next, the model Helena Christensen posted photos of herself with Beckham at a Miami party. Beckham's hand was on her back. Other photos Christensen released showed the two at another party. There were also pictures of Beckham partying with another model, Bella Hadid, in Japan and Miami.[29] Capping all that, Victoria was immersed once more in an acrimonious dispute with the Spice Girls.

Lured by money, the other Spice Girls had agreed in October 2018 to start another tour the following May. Modest Management's Richard Griffiths had replaced Fuller as their manager, but the tour would generate less income for them than before – just over £4 million for each of the five. As usual, Victoria had annoyed Mel B. Not only had she had used Spice Girls costumes for the *Vogue* shoot but then, after a disagreement, threatened legal proceedings to stop the tour.

'Fuck off, you bitch,' Mel B told Victoria during a meeting. She wore a Posh mask for Halloween.[30]

One month later, without Victoria agreeing to participate, the tour was announced and the £70 tickets at Wembley were sold out within minutes. Touts were offering the tickets for over £1,000.[31] By March 2019, chaos threatened the tour. On television Mel B admitted to having an affair with Geri, Mel C threatened to pull out, Geri was outraged and Victoria refused to go to the opening show in Dublin. 'Victoria is likely to be away on business for the duration of the tour,' said Milloy.

On the first day of a 13-show schedule, Victoria entered a £5,000 per week sanatorium in Germany. Just as Geri quipped, 'I'm really happy. Everyone's happy. We're having a blast,' Victoria was detoxifying and re-energising her body and spirit. During the hours of a full moon she drank special bottled water and applied moisturiser made from her own blood. On the eve of the Spice Girls' triumphant finale at Wembley, Victoria flew to America. 'I expected her to come and just say "Hi" at least,' said Mel B. 'I was upset.' Even more annoying for the others was that, as a director of Spice Girls Ltd, Victoria earned about £800,000 from the licensing deals generated by merchandise sales during the three-week tour.[32] Her earnings from singing appear to have been deposited in a company called Moody Productions Ltd. In recent years, Moody Productions had earned roughly annual profits of £500,000 from Victoria's singing career. Unnoticed, Victoria was using her annual income to borrow millions of pounds for her business.

Emerging from the clinic, Victoria began to commute between London, Los Angeles and New York. At the same time, Beckham flew between Miami, Macao and then on a fishing holiday in Iceland. When they finally emerged from their first-class cabins and private jets, they were confronted by negative reports of Brooklyn's behaviour.

As an influencer with 11.5 million followers, Brooklyn earned a substantial income for organising shoots for *Wonderland* magazine, Sir David Attenborough and Burberry.[33] But he had failed to excel at his latest internship with Rankin, the celebrated photographer. Although enthusiastic, he was once again dismissed by his co-workers at the studio for lacking basic photographic skills. Some carped that he could not be trusted even to make a cup of tea.

More worrying for his parents were his public arguments with his girlfriend, Hana Cross. There had been an unpleasant dispute during Victoria's 45th birthday party in April 2019 in an Italian restaurant in Santa Monica. Fearing Cross might walk away and sign a kiss-and-tell deal with the media after their relationship ended, the Beckhams had asked Brooklyn to persuade her to sign their customary non-disclosure agreement. Brooklyn refused. By the time the couple reached the Cannes Film Festival in May on a private jet, his parents' fears were justified.

Sitting on their hotel terrace – the £3,000 per night Martinez – Brooklyn and Cross engaged in what startled onlookers called 'a vicious brawl'. Spectators reported that the couple ignored the hotel's security officials' pleas to stop screaming. After another public argument later on in Colorado, the Beckhams wondered how Brooklyn's problems were reaching the tabloids, especially Clemmie Moodie at the *Sun*.[34]

Victoria tried to repair the damage. 'I know everybody thinks their kids are angels,' she said, 'but my kids are genuinely very kind. And they're all very humble kids – they really are.'[35]

To rebuild their 'loving family' image, the Beckhams kissed while dancing at Glastonbury, posted family pictures of their holiday in Florence and organised the sale of photographs of the family holidaying with Elton John on his yacht. Elton would later complain that the 'Takums' had forgotten the customary courtesy of tipping the crew. A sum of about £25,000 was expected for one week. Once again, Dylan Jones came to the rescue, anointing Beckham as *GQ*'s Man of the

Year. 'Well done, Dave,' wrote Piers Morgan. 'You've had another great year. Not sure what you've been doing.'[36]

Thankfully, Beckham had been earning enough money to fund Victoria's taste for a £2,000 bottle of Romanée-St-Vivant Grand Cru. She posted a photo of herself drinking the wine in a Paris restaurant.[37] She gave the impression of being totally unconcerned that few high-rollers were buying the £1,000 dresses and £890 gold sandals in her shop. Very few women had even taken her £500 dresses off the rail. They knew that very similar designs were being sold on the High Street for considerably less.[38]

Cosmetics, insisted Ralph Toledano her chairman, would be the brand's saviour. Victoria once again set out to follow the leaders. Cosmetics were comparatively cheap to make. Dior, Chanel and all the major fashion houses earned enormous profits from the 'wellness' industry. Hollywood celebrities had copied the majors by marketing themselves to match the mood of their potential buyers by age and background.

The roll-call of success made Victoria envious. Gwyneth Paltrow's Goop had earned profits of $250 million selling a vagina-scented candle; Rihanna's 'Fenty Beauty' range, after selling £51 million worth of products in its first month in 2017, was allegedly worth £2 billion; Kylie Jenner's lipstick was reportedly sold to Coty for £865 million; and Kim Kardashian's make-up, launched in 2017, was estimated to be worth £723 million. Other celebrities, including Madonna, Katie Holmes, Cindy Crawford and Lady Gaga, were all pocketing millions from beauty products.

As usual, Victoria believed that her personality and lifestyle enjoyed cult status among her 27.7 million followers. 'It's important to embrace who I am and what I have,' she said as she launched Victoria Beckham Beauty – 'clean, real and authentic' make-up products – on her YouTube channel. 'I'm no supermodel', she admitted. Rather, she presented herself as the representative of 'inclusivity', being 'proud of my community' and being 'kind to the planet'. Above all, she said, she pursued a healthy lifestyle. She made that statement posing with a bottle of £120 Don Julio Tequila – 'which I take everywhere,' she said in all seriousness. That image, she continued, was symbolic of her, 'Empowering women through beauty and fashion to be the best version of yourself.'

'Looking after myself,' she told her audience, involved taking a list of vitamins, a daily two-hour workout and wearing a series of face masks. The latest masks were made from porcelain flower biopeptides, Moroccan argan oil and Tom Ford's lava clay. She also advocated using LED lights to transmit ten minutes of light to energise her skin-cells by improving blood circulation, a Tuxedo eye palette and a new product made from blood serum. Promoting her own serum became complicated while shooting the video. She struggled to pronounce her latest brand-name. 'Sherry,' she said. Corrected, she said 'Cherry'. After more corrections, she finally uttered, 'Cherie'.

'David is a big fan of Victoria Beckham Beauty,' said Sarah Creal, the newly appointed chief executive of the beauty business. 'Victoria says he's obsessed and uses her make-up too. He steals it.'[39] To boost sales, David was recruited to pose on Instagram with a skin specialist. Victoria's rejuvenating serum, he said, removed his wrinkles. 'Don't do it very often,' read the caption, 'but had the most amazing facial. Don't I look fresh?' The 30ml bottle cost £180.

Any hint of mystery was firmly buried. Her hair stylist Ken Paves was scripted to reveal that Victoria, after applying her serums, swallowing her vitamins, rubbing in her mask and working out, 'then makes breakfast for everyone'. Into that mix she plugged a special brand of bread called Ezekiel 4:9 costing £6 plus Amazon's £3 delivery charge. That replaced her previous favourite, pumpkin seeds soaked in liquid aminos.

The only complaint was heard from Tom Ford, the fashion designer. His staff wanted no association with Victoria Beckham. 'Get her out of our clothes,' was the order.[40] She bought his clothes in shops, he was told.

None of the other 46 fashion houses used similar images as Victoria to advertise themselves during September's London Fashion Week. Parisian Marie LeBlanc, an experienced designer, had been employed by Victoria to develop a new range.[41] Their new inspirations to copy were Donna Karan and Celine. The star model was 74-year-old Helen Mirren, the celebrated actor. Eight-year-old Harper, wearing a £438 patterned dress and with her hair in a topknot, was again seated next to Anna Wintour. Her collection, Victoria said, was about 'Twisting our codes. That is what I call my gentle rebellion.' That phrase was meant to explain why she carried a £16,000 black Hermes Birkin crocodile handbag. Many assumed she had received a 'gift' to break her pledge to be '100 per cent cruelty free'.[42]

Her credibility slipped as the losses became unsustainable.

During 2019 the £38 million invested two years earlier by Ralph Toledano disappeared. In the 11th year of operating losses, Victoria's sales slid by 16 per cent to £35 million. Victoria Beckham Ltd's losses in 2018 grew by 20 per cent to £12.2 million. With accumulated debts of £49 million, HSBC announced that her company was failing to meet the terms of the bank's loan. Despite Beckham's guarantee, including a £16.9 million bail-out, the bank was not satisfied.

Undoubtedly that assessment was based on the bewildering accounts of Beckham's own businesses approved by his auditors. Despite all the millions he earned from sponsors, Footwork Productions was running at a loss, and Footwork Management's accounts managed by Gardner and Howson were more unusual than Footwork Productions'. At the beginning of the year the company recorded accumulated losses of £353,000 but there was £185,000 in cash in the bank. At the end of 2021, the company owed over £1 million but had £1.1 million in cash in the bank. Commercial sense was being challenged.

There were no hidden financial details in Victoria's business. After 11 years the harsh truth was that she had failed the basic test of a budding entrepreneur. Namely, she had not created the opportunities or realistic ambitions to achieve financial success. She had not benefited from the luck of receiving investment of over £100 million. Simply saying, 'I'm here. Buy me' had led her to the edge.

To save Victoria's business at the end of 2019, Ralph Toledano ordered her to dismiss more employees – one-third of her staff would be gone. Among the casualties were the two senior publicists, Jo Milloy and Natalie Lewis. He also ordered that she cut prices by 60 per cent. A £1,495 dress was to be sold for £598. Describing the business as 'a sinking ship', Clemmie Moodie quoted a departing insider, 'It's a body blow for Victoria. She's been unable to persuade some of her most valued members to stay put.' Victoria was also told to ditch her YouTube channel. With just 109,000 subscribers it was earning only £25 a day from a handful of viewers. In a sign of desperation, her office was moved from Battersea to Hammersmith. All the potted plants were thrown out. Even Victoria's chauffeur was fired. She was told to use taxis.

The Beckhams' genius – amid the departure of long-serving publicists – was to hide the chaos. For that, Victoria resorted to a familiar ruse. She talked about David.

'I tend to wear nothing in bed,' she said. 'But David bought me these little sets from Agents Provocateur. I'm proud I still have a really good sex life with David. He is very much in proportion.' Asked about the Armani advertisements which had appeared 13 years earlier, she said, 'I was thrilled to see his penis 25 foot tall. It's huge. It's enormous. Massive. He does have a huge one. He does. You can see it in the advert. It is all his. It is like a tractor exhaust pipe.'[43]

CHAPTER 30

MIAMI

Playing with the lads had become Beckham's way of life. Among his closest mates was film director Guy Ritchie. As joint owners of the Walmer Castle, a pub in Notting Hill, Beckham had followed Ritchie into field sports. He began wild fishing, and shooting on Ritchie's Wiltshire estate, Ashcombe. He also had shooting lessons at the nearby Rushmore estate. After his first miserable shots, his teacher said, 'Imagine you're passing the ball. You aim to place it just ahead of the player. Swing the gun the same way, just where you want to shoot the bird.' He became a good shot.

Flying to Iceland with Ritchie on 20 June 2020 was just another junket to enjoy fishing and good food. The two were guests of Thor Bjorgolfsson, a 53-year-old Icelandic businessman they had met in a gym. Famous for leading his bank Landsbanki into bankruptcy in 2008, Bjorgolfsson's depositors included 300,000 British savers who had potentially lost £4 billion. Eventually, they were compensated. By 2020, Bjorgolfsson had restored his fortunes and was worth an estimated £2 billion.

'It's not about falling, it's about how quickly you can get back up,' Bjorgolfsson explained in his autobiography *Billions to Bust – and Back*. 'You must not focus on the past, but on the future. You have to know that you will get back up, whatever it takes to do so.'[1] He was the type Beckham admired. Like the Frantzen brothers, he paid all Beckham's expenses.

Arriving on Bjorgolfsson's private jet, the three men spent the night in a fishing lodge in Haffjarðará. In the early hours of the second night, Beckham heard raised voices in a neighbouring bedroom. The hotel owner described an argument between Bjorgolfsson and a girl, which Beckham settled. At daybreak Beckham and Ritchie flew out, leaving Bjorgolfsson behind to resolve the dispute. Social media photos of the three men fishing were deleted. The *Sun* and other tabloids decided not to report on the Icelandic trip, nor comment the following year when the three men watched together the England v Denmark match at Wembley. Some said that was because editor Tony Gallagher, a critic of Beckham, had been moved in February 2020 from the *Sun* to *The Times*. His successor as editor, Victoria Newton, admired the Beckhams. Clemmie Moodie at the *Sun*, who had previously written critical pieces about the Beckhams, re-emerged as the couple's cheerleader.[2]

Miami had become the centre of Beckham's focus. To make life comfortable in the city, he bought a £14 million ($19.8 million) five-bedroom penthouse at the top of a 62-storey block with spectacular views over South Beach and the ocean. The 10,335-square-foot apartment in One Thousand Museum on Biscayne Boulevard had its own high-speed lift and a convenient helipad. Beckham Brand Ltd financed the purchase with loans. He took a 30-year $12.6 million mortgage at 2.5 per cent, and the remainder was borrowed from his other companies. For accounting reasons, the apartment – the Beckhams' fifth home – was described as a 'freehold' rather than a 'leasehold'.

If Beckham is 'fully tax resident' in Britain, as he claims, he would be taxed on the benefit-in-kind of the Miami apartment. The peculiarity of Beckham's denial of any special tax arrangements is the £2.7 million purchase by Beckham Brand of paintings for the flat. The artworks were declared as a tax-deductible purchase. But claiming that allowance was expressly forbidden by HMRC on 6 April 2017.[3] HMRC would have levied £553,000 tax on Beckham as a 'benefit in kind' (BIK). Note 7 of the consolidated accounts of Beckham Brand Holdings suggests that the extra BIK tax was not paid.[4]

The Miami apartment represented a standard arrangement, his adviser said. The apartment is owned by Beckham Brand, as is the art within it. 'A market rent is charged for personal use of the apartment.' No figure which corresponds to a reasonable annual market-rate rent for the apartment is immediately apparent in Beckham Brand accounts, an expert indicated in response.

Settling into Miami, Beckham took delivery of 'Seven', a 94-foot yacht built in Italy by Ferretti. With five stateroom bedrooms, a speed of 30 knots and a four-man crew, it was valued new at about £15 million. Conscious that opulence would deny him a knighthood, the media adopted Beckham's under-valuation of his latest toy at £5 million.

His luxurious lifestyle did not mirror success at his football club. Construction of the academy, the stadium and public amenities had not started.[5] To meet the time-limit for the first season starting in March 2020, Jorge Mas had signed a 50-year rent-free lease for the 18,000-seater Lockhart Stadium in Fort Lauderdale. To Mas's disappointment, Beckham's attempts to build a team were floundering.

After exciting the fans with promises of signing big stars, Paul McDonough, the sporting director, had failed to sign notable players. He seemed destined to start the season with an incomplete squad.[6] The first match against LA Galaxy ended in 1–0 defeat. The second match against DC United was lost 2–1. In a panic to score results, younger players were abandoned and the club brought in older players, including: the Mexican attacking midfielder Rodolfo Pizarro for $12 million; another midfielder Blaise Matuidi, a French international; and the Argentine international striker Gonzalo Higuain from Juventus. The revived hopes were dashed. In the first two away matches, Miami were again defeated. Not only did the three foreign players appear to be disappointments, but the club had secretly broken the MLS rules by under-reporting the transfer fees of Matuidi and four other players. That serious offence remained concealed.

Beckham showed no signs of despondency or concern on arriving at Brooklyn's 21st birthday party in his English country home in Great Tew. Despite the spread of Covid and an imminent lockdown, the party went ahead. Stormzy was the star performer.[7]

By then, Brooklyn had broken with Hana Cross during a tearful argument at a London party. He had also earned a reputation of having an 'astonishing success rate with girls', including Lottie Moss, the younger half-sister of model Kate Moss. To protect himself he was told by his parents to 'dish out' non-disclosure agreements 'indiscriminately'. As usual he refused, especially on behalf of his latest flame, an American billionaire's daughter called Nicola Peltz.

The 25-year-old actress, the youngest of Nelson Peltz's ten children was once the devoted owner of 11 dogs. At the Tew party, obviously attached to Brooklyn who was four years younger, they sang a duet that each other was 'the love of my life'. A bedroom selfie posted before the party, captioned Black Heart, showed Nicola in a bra and

Brooklyn shirtless. Peltz was tattooed on his chest. The Beckhams' spokeswoman declared that Brooklyn's parents 'have very much given this relationship their blessing. They think he's landed on his feet.'

Pointedly, the spokeswoman also said that Posh and Becks kissed on the dance floor. 'He also grabbed Posh's bum,' their spokeswoman added. Four months later, Brooklyn and Nicola announced their engagement with a £250,000 diamond and emerald ring. Next, they bought a £7.5 million home in Beverly Hills.[8]

The Beckhams assumed that they would be immediately accepted by Nicola's parents, Nelson and Claudia. They had consorted with Hollywood stars and believed the Peltzs would greet them like all celebrities, as royalty. That was an understandable mistake by the foreign visitors. Neither of the Beckhams recognised the cultural chasm separating them from the Peltzs. The difference between Florida's aristocrats and Californian celebrities was not just money, although that difference was stark. The Beckhams' estimated £250 million fortune hardly compared with Nelson Peltz's £1.8 billion. His 27-bedroom 130-acre property, High Winds in Bedford outside New York, had an ice-hockey rink, and his £76 million mansion in Palm Beach relegated the Beckhams' Cotswold property to the status of a very modest abode.

More fundamentally, the Beckhams were baffled by the Peltzs' values. Although both shared a self-made heritage, the difference was the levels reached by their respective success. The couple from Essex had nothing in common with a prominent Jewish family renowned as Republican fundraisers. The Peltzs expected their neighbour Donald Trump to accept an invitation to their daughter's Palm Beach engagement party. No British politician would be on the Beckhams' guest list. Neither Nicola nor Claudia was interested in Victoria's suggestion of an engagement party in London, a wedding in St Paul's cathedral or in Italy, a wedding dress made by her workshop, or Gordon Ramsay in charge of catering.

Indeed, Claudia Peltz had little interest in Victoria's involvement in arranging any of the celebrations. The Peltzs knew how to organise parties with a budget to dwarf the Beckhams' hospitality. While the Beckhams' parties cost at most £200,000, and were often part-funded by magazines, the Peltzs expected to spend millions of pounds on the wedding. By the time Victoria understood her position, she was faced with a more serious challenge.

At the beginning of the Covid lockdown in March 2020, Victoria had taken government money to furlough 30 of her staff.[9] Her request for taxpayers to fund 80 per cent of her staff's wages, about £250,000, was exposed within weeks. The optics of the Beckhams flaunting their new £14 million Miami flat and their £35 million Holland Park house, and also taking taxpayers' money, evoked splenetic fury.

'The fucking Beckhams,' raged Ricky Gervais. 'Sorry I'm done with them now. Shame on them.' Piers Morgan stoked the furore: 'Sorry, this furlough scheme was not for prima donna millionaires like you.' Eyewitnesses in their Cotswold home revealed that the criticism had plunged the 'dreadfully tense' Beckhams into 'crisis mode'. Victoria complained it was the 'worst week of her life'.[10] Clearly, she had forgotten Rebecca Loos. Her publicist Nicola Howson suggested that she hunker down, hoping the blizzard of criticism would pass. The tactic failed. Within days, Victoria reversed her decision. 'Posh is devastated by the backlash she's faced,' said her spokeswoman. She blamed her fellow directors for seeking the payments. Haemorrhaging money, she made another 20 staff redundant. For once she did not publicise Beckham's 45th birthday party on Instagram, except to say, 'He ate a bacon butty.'

And then, despite the lockdown, it was back to selling her products. Her promotion of a £140 cell-rejuvenating moisturiser attracted particular carping. Her YouTube image, said her critics, suggested a remarkable amount of work to her nails, face, hair and possibly also lip-filler and Botox. Had she, they wondered, broken lockdown rules?[11] If that were true, the police never showed any interest in the allegations.

Beckham was wheeled out to deflect the barbs. Posing in beekeeping gear with three of his children in his Cotswold garden, he held a scythe against a country landscape, He epitomised 'cottagecore', a new rural lifestyle. In order to interpret his latest stunt, academics were wheeled-out to define Beckham as a romanticised ideal of masculinity. Little more was heard about the scythe, Cotswold chic or the bees, except when they popped up in a brief sequel in his Netflix series, and when Victoria recommended using bee pollen as a cure for wrinkles.

To escape from their accumulated problems, Victoria and her children joined Beckham in Miami for Christmas.

Inter Miami was in a crisis. Admitting naivety and inexperience, Beckham had failed to build a winning team. The club lacked suitable accounting and marketing departments, had not signed a shirt sponsor and was still losing most matches. Beckham had also been unable to broker amicable relations between his two investors Marcelo Claure and the Mas brothers. The Bolivian appeared to resent the Cubans' greater wealth and influence in Miami, and ultimately over the club's destiny. Following a fierce argument, Claure mounted a bid to undermine Jorge Mas.[12]

A whistleblower told Claure that the team's managers had concealed from Dan Garber and the MLS the high transfer fee for Blaise Matuidi and had under-reported the foreign players' salaries. Claure was shocked by the secret breaking of the MLS's rules. After confronting Mas, McDonough and Beckham at a series of stormy board meetings he was convinced that all three were aware of the impropriety, including Beckham, the 'director of soccer operations'.

The crisis was aggravated by the imminent $26 billion merger of Sprint with T-Mobile. As a director of several billion-dollar corporations, Claure could not be a party to dishonesty. 'This is my team,' he told the Mas brothers and Beckham. 'It's you or me.' Clare's next step was draconian. On legal advice he told the MLS's Don Garber about the illegal payments. Once his fellow directors heard of this, all three owners knew that the MSL was certain to impose sanctions for the unprecedented breach of the rules.

Beckham's anger towards Claure was not concealed. Eyewitnesses who heard him at the meetings and thereafter had the firm impression that he felt 'betrayed' by Claure. While football for Claure and Mas was a hobby, for Beckham it was his life. He saw nothing wrong, it appeared, in pursuing his dream of owning and managing a club at any cost, even if the rules were broken. The saga would leave Claure unable to utter publicly a single good word about Beckham.

Garber had every reason to be shocked by Claure's revelations. Not only was the MSL undermined but Beckham's reputation was endangered. Garber's bigger problem was to resolve the war between Claure and Mas before the scandal became public. After intense secret negotiations it was agreed that Paul McDonough, the sporting director, would be fired. The reasons were withheld. The public would hopefully believe that his departure was triggered by the bad results.[13]

McDonough's resignation on 9 December 2020 predated by four months the public disclosure of the 'crime'. McDonough would take the blame for the secret payments. 'I had full knowledge of what was going on,' he said, 'and participated in conversations and setting things up.'[14] McDonough's humiliation raised questions about Beckham's culpability. McDonough agreed not to say whether Beckham, the 'director of soccer operations', was involved in those conversations or knew about the deception. Beckham remained silent and Garber repaired the damage.[15] His solution was Claure's departure. He lacked the money and connections among Miami's fixers to develop the club. Moreover, he was chairman of WeWork, a multi-billion-dollar company heading towards bankruptcy. Mas would stay in charge of Inter Miami, and as the club's managing owner take the blame.[16]

To remove Claure's veto over the club's development, in September 2020 Beckham bought back 5 per cent of the shares for £11.2 million ($15.4 million). Since he had just bought out Fuller, he borrowed more money for the purchase.

On the day of McDonough's resignation and the coach Diego Alonso's departure, Beckham had posted an iconic photograph of himself in the gym. His head was thrown back, his rippling chest muscles glistened, and his eyes were closed in ecstasy. Among the 1,735,183 who 'liked' the shot was Victoria. 'Wow, wow, wow,' she commented. 'My inspiration in the gym.'[17]

McDonough was replaced by Chris Henderson as 'chief soccer officer and sporting director'. Curiously, two years earlier Henderson had been rejected by Beckham in favour of McDonough, although Henderson, a former professional player with 79 caps for America, was Seattle's experienced manager.

Beckham's old friend Phil Neville, who had originally been in the Manchester United team with him, was appointed as the head coach. 'It's nothing to do with him being my friend,' said Beckham.[18] Neville's previous five coaching or managerial appointments had all proved unsuccessful, but despite his repeated failures he was blessed with an 'imitable capacity to keep falling into more lucrative jobs,' wrote the Guardian's Jonathan Liew. The many who asked, 'Just how does he keep doing it?' got no satisfactory answer.[19] Effusive with praise, Beckham told the Miami Herald, 'Phil has made a huge difference.'[20]

CHAPTER 31

LOSS-MAKING DEALS

Securing more money from new sponsors for the Beckham Brand was becoming a problem. Although his stable included Adidas, Haig, Tudor, Coty, AIA insurance and Sands hotels and casinos, was paying him annually about £30 million, Beckham pondered the dearth of major brands offering new contracts. Fearful that he might not have sufficient money to fund the Beckham lifestyle, he lowered his standards.

In June 2020 he had launched Guild Esports, a video gaming company, with Esports' executive chairman Carleton Curtis. In the midst of Covid, virtual sporting competitions and gaming in football, Formula 1 and other sports had become a $1.1 billion global business through streaming. The industry was expected to be worth $1.56 billion by 2023. Curtis predicted that with Beckham's sponsorship, Esports' video games, clothes and branding would become one of the biggest of their kind in the world. In September, their prospective floatation valued the company at £50 million.[1]

David Beckham Ventures (DBV) invested $319,000 for a 4.74 per cent stake in the company. In exchange for being the fourth largest investor he agreed to make personal appearances and allow his name and image to be used to promote the business. As payment, Curtis agreed with Dave Gardner that Beckham would receive 15 per cent of all the net proceeds of merchandising and sponsorship. In the first year he would receive a minimum of £2,250,000, escalating to £4 million in the fifth year. Thereafter he would be paid annually £13 million.

In November he also signed a three-year contract to become the brand ambassador of Gemforex, a small retail offshore currency trader. Founded in Japan in 2010, Gemforex operated under a licence issued in Mauritius, a lax regulatory regime. Targeting clients in the

Far East, especially the Japanese and Chinese, Beckham was promised over £1 million a year in the deal brokered by British businessman Stephen Pearson of Sports Media Gaming (SMG).[2]

Beckham also became a Brand Ambassador for the Californian video game company EA Sports. Reports that he was paid £40 million over three years to represent FIFA were described by EA Sports as 'completely sensationalised and are in no way accurate'. His relationship with Electronic Arts quickly soured.

Other investments Beckham made were also faltering. OTRO, the global football subscription website for football fans, and supposedly worth £50 million, would fold. Beckham lost his stake. Despite that setback he invested in Lunaz, an indebted company electrifying classic cars. Within the first months of his involvement, the company's debts nearly doubled to £11 million.

Undeterred, he agreed with actor Mark Wahlberg to promote F45, a fitness company. Under their agreement Beckham would be annually paid £1.3 million ($1.5 million) plus shares worth $20 million. Wahlberg predicted that once F45 was launched on the stock exchange, the company would be worth $634 million and Beckham's shares were predicted to triple in value. His relationship with Wahlberg had been sealed during a family holiday with Victoria in Canada. Within weeks Beckham complained that he had not received the first tranche of shares, theoretically worth $11.3 million, from Wahlberg. Months later the shares were worth just $1.9 million. Beckham would claim he was owed $5 million on the first anniversary.[3]

Amid those loss-making deals, Beckham's accounts once again threw up a mystery. In 2021, Beckham personally sold to David Beckham Ventures (DBV) a stash of unnamed shares for £250,000. His stake was then instantly revalued by DBV at £1,812,000. That transaction was not explained in the accounts. All a misreading of the accounts, his people said. Independent expertise stands firm on this: an investment of £250,000 was bought that year and revalued by a multiple of 6.25 times in the year.

At his business manager Dave Gardner's behest, Beckham had also invested in Cellular Goods, the manufacturer of skincare and athletic recovery products made from legal cannabis. The British founder, Alexis Abraham, told him that he was raising £8 million to value the company at £20 million. Beckham invested £250,000 (through DBV).

On flotation in February 2021 his shares were worth £5 million. Then they began to slide. One year later the shares had dropped from £19 to 65 pence, a fall of 96 per cent.[4]

To some, Gardner's judgement in the investment circus was questionable. Nevertheless, Beckham's reliance on him appeared to be unconditional. That year Gardner split from his second wife, actress Liv Tyler, after seven years of marriage.[5]

Beckham's only conventional sponsorship deal was a contract with Maserati. One of the immediate beneficiaries was Romeo. With his bleached-blond hair, the one-time Yves Saint Laurent model was seen driving through Mayfair in a new Maserati – his 18th birthday present. Shortly after this, Romeo landed a deal to promote Puma, posed for *L'Uomo Vogue* and, thanks to his father, was playing with Inter Miami reserves. His switch to a footballing career had been helped after Beckham had bulldozed the £30,000 tennis court in their Great Tew home and built a football pitch. Romeo's training regime was being tested.

At the same time, Brooklyn won a contract to front the Superdry fashion label, and with Nicola Peltz a contract to wear Pepe Jeans. Both basked in reports that each contract was worth £1 million.[6]

In contrast, the problems plaguing Victoria's business could no longer be concealed. In 2020 sales were static at £38.3 million and Victoria Beckham Holdings (VBH), combining fashion and beauty, lost a further £16.5 million. (Fashion lost £11.8 million and cosmetics lost £4.7 million.) VBH's accumulated debts rose to £66.3 million.[7] Although Victoria had borrowed £9.2 million from Beckham she praised her new director Marie LeBlanc for getting her business into its best-ever shape. 'This is not a vanity project and commercial is not a dirty word,' she said.

And yet once again she changed direction. 'Baggy' and 'comfort' clothes were abandoned and she returned to 'make the most of a great bum and a good waist, to celebrate being a woman'. Highlighting her new vision she also contradicted herself: 'I guess it was a sign of insecurity, wearing very tight clothes.'[8]

Beckham was left to pick up the pieces. The income from Qatar was his lifeline. The 2020 revenues of his holding company, BBH, soared from £11.4 million to £34.3 million and his net profits rose 65 per cent from £11.6 million to £19.1 million. The revenue from sponsorship through DBV, including the Qatari annual payment, was up from £11.4 million in 2020 to £34.3 million. Among the many unresolved questions was the statement that dividends of £12.1 million were paid in 2020 by Beckham Brand Holdings but the accounts only showed £7.1 million paid out. Inexplicably, £5 million had apparently disappeared![9] That left one problem – sorting out Fuller's legacy.

In the blowback of Fuller's management was the bankruptcy of Bruce Rockowitz's Global Brands. The administrators in Bermuda declared that the Group had lost no less than $1.5 billion. The same amount that Rockowitz had predicted Beckham's sales would reach in 2020.

In 2021, Seven Global Holding Company Limited (SGHCL), jointly owned by Beckham and Rockowitz's Global Brands, was declared bankrupt owing $53.8 million to Beckham's companies, Seven Global LLP and DB Ventures. Over the previous years, possibly for tax reasons, Beckham had not taken the profits from their joint company, Seven Global Holdings. Instead, Beckham had advanced the profits as a loan to Global Brands. The Hong Kong company's bankruptcy exposed that expensive error. To settle the debts, recover his money and regain total control over his brand, Beckham's advisers embarked on a complicated series of manoeuvres costing Beckham about $45 million in cash and distributions. The accounts did not explain how that debt was fully repaid. Or what happened to the outstanding $9.8 million. Employing accountants solely to resolve that particular mess cost Beckham about £400,000 that year. His accounts do not readily explain the ultimate fate of $53.8 million of Beckham's income.

That was not the only financial difficulty Beckham dealt with. Belatedly, Seven Global's highly paid accountants admitted that after 2019 they had failed to recover $11.3 million from the German government. The money had been withheld by the German authorities in a dispute about taxes. For Beckham, always apparently concerned to save money by legally minimising his taxes, that loss would have been painful if he knew about it. But that assumed he was actually told about the 'loss'. The evidence suggested that he was unaware of the 'loss' and it would be forgotten by his accountants until they were unexpectedly reminded of it in late 2023. At least the anguish paved the way for a potentially profitable future. He had found a new adviser and fixer prepared to pay cash for his brand and take the risk.

Beckham's saviour was James Salter's Authentic Brands Group (ABG). Salter, a 60-year-old Canadian, had used a multi-billion-dollar fund to buy entertainment and retail companies including Brooks Brothers, Juicy Couture, Izod, Ted Baker, JCPenney and Barneys in New York. Valuing itself at $12.7 billion and with ambitions to expand across the world, Salter wanted to use Beckham's image and 72.7 million Instagram followers (and 56 million followers on Facebook) to promote Authentic's 50 brands including his latest $2.5 billion acquisition, Reebok.[10] Salter's identification with sport was enhanced by his purchase in 2019 of *Sports Illustrated*, America's most popular sports magazine.

Beckham and Salter had first met nine years earlier. By 2020, Salter was Beckham's preferred partner rather than an American private equity group. Authentic brought the skills and infrastructure Beckham needed. His relationship with Salter was sealed during another lake-side summer holiday with Wahlberg in Muskoka, Canada.

Beckham agreed to sell 55 per cent of his brand (DBV) to Salter for $269 million. Beckham claimed that he received $200 million in cash and shares worth $69 million. His spokeswoman also claimed that the $200 million was paid to Beckham Brands Ltd and distrib-uted to shareholders, but BBL's accounts do not show the receipt of $200 million. She also claimed that the money was used to buy out Fuller, buy back his rights from Global Brand and buy more shares in Inter Miami. The British corporate accounts are either too opaque to trace those transactions, or the millions flowed through another corporation.

Since Beckham's football club, Miami Beckham United, was regis-tered in Delaware, a state that allowed shareholders not only to benefit from secrecy but also from not imposing corporate tax on interest and investment income, he had the potential to benefit from the state's tax laws on his windfall. Except that his highly-paid tax advisers claimed that he was 'fully tax resident' in Britain.

His advisers used the landmark sale to Authentic to reorganise his business completely. That was necessary after Global went bankrupt. To continue his business, he needed to buy out Global's shares in his brand. Organising the financial manoeuvres for the restructuring of his companies would cost Beckham over £3 million in legal and accountancy fees.

In every sense the next accounts in December 2021 concealed as much information as legally possible.[11] As the director of at least 19 companies in Britain and more abroad, Beckham and his financial advisers had created a succession of inter-company trades and inter-company loans. In 2021, BBH's inter-company debt increased to £19.9 million. Those internal transactions left threads that are difficult even for specialists to follow, not least because the various companies' financial years ended at different dates. Honest suspicion that complexity was an end in itself was fuelled by the inordinate number of companies he controlled for total annual earnings that rarely exceeded £40 million. By comparison, if Dior owned the same number of companies for its annual revenues of £60 billion it would comprise about 30,000 active companies.

To outsiders, the late return of statutory filings of Beckham's accounts at Companies House appeared to be endemic. Over the years his companies incurred several fines for late submission of the statutory returns. But his auditors' conduct appeared to cause Beckham little concern. His spokeswoman said it was standard practice born of the inherent complexity of the arrangements.

The principle culprit was Footwork Productions Ltd, a company at the top of his commercial pyramid, overseeing BBH and seven other companies. Repeatedly, BBH failed to file its statutory accounts on time. On 8 March 2022, Footwork was threatened by the regulator at Companies House with being struck off or closed down unless required paperwork was filed.

After the 2021 accounts were filed, Beckham's tax advisers completed a series of complicated manoeuvres to restructure his business, casting another smokescreen over his finances. Creating a classic pyramid structure, at the top of the tree was Footwork Productions Ltd (FPL), wholly owned by David Beckham. Beneath that was David Beckham Ltd, a dormant company, and Beckham Brand Holdings Ltd (BBHL). In turn, BBHL owned Beckham Brand Ltd (BBL).

In parallel, a new company, DRJB Holdings, was created. It is 45 per cent owned by Footwork Productions Ltd (FPL) and 55 per cent by Authentic Brands. DRJB Holdings owned DB Ventures Ltd (DBVL) and has a share in Seven Global Holdings. To further stymie those seeking the unvarnished truth about Beckham's operations, DB Ventures Ltd owned no less than three film companies – namely, a

75 per cent stake in Studio 99 Ltd, which in turn wholly owned two subsidiaries, the White Ball Film Company and Project 237 Ltd.

And to confuse matters further, his publicists claimed that DB Ventures (DBV) controlled his brand operations; and that his loans to Victoria had been injected into VCB Holdings (VCBH) but were ultimately owned by DRJB Holdings. In that part of the restructuring, £12.2 million of Victoria's debt to David was wiped out in an unusual dividend payment by BBH. Simultaneously, BBH was used to shelter a bewildering money-go-round. Although the group lost £13.3 million after the sale of 'assets', it paid £46.4 million as a dividend from profits that fell from £47.4 million to £12.4 million.

In what looks like a lawful tax-saving exercise, part of the dividends were paid to Global. Intriguingly, Beckham appears to have invested £25 million in the company. Indeed, he seems to have had access to huge amounts of cash. He also lent Footwork Productions Ltd (FPL) a further £3.5 million, allowing the company to pay off a £12.5 million loan. His total loan to FPL was £16.75 million.

Yet another company, David Beckham Holdings (DBH) owned part of his share of Inter Miami football club and his Miami property. By the end of 2022, DBH owed Beckham £6.5 million. How that debt arose is unclear from the publicly available accounts. With that, another layer of complexity was added.

On 8 September 2022, FPL passed an odd resolution. Two £1 shares were divided into 2 million shares nominally worth £0.000001 pence each. On the same day, after another restructuring, a further 814,726 shares were created and issued to Beckham. That manoeuvre had followed the restructuring of DRJB Holdings, one of Beckham's new companies. DRJB issued 25,281,200 ordinary shares of £0.0001 and 23,021 preference shares of £0.0001, which were bought for £31.6 million. Initially, those shares were unequally divided between three owners: Beckham, Footwork and Authentic Brands. The upshot was that Salter, through ABG-Beckham LLC, owned 54.96 per cent of Beckham's brand and the rest was owned by Beckham's company, DRJB Holdings. That streamlining had the effect, arguably, of hindering outsiders seeking information, partly because his accountants did not list DRJB Holdings as the owners at Companies House, but as David Beckham (16.32 per cent) and Footwork (28.72 per cent).[12]

To add to the mystery, Beckham Brand Holdings almost doubled the amount paid to its 21 employees from £2.9 million to £5.1 million.[13] The trigger was a huge profit splurge from his brand. In 2022, the income of DB Ventures Ltd (DBVL) soared from £34 million to £57.3 million. The company's profits rose from £17.2 million to £25.6 million. But the administrative expenses doubled from £16.8 million in 2021 to £31.6 million. That was only partly accounted for Beckham increasing his income from £2 million to £10 million. The additional £5 million of costs were not explained.

One shadow over his new arrangements was a growing dispute about the faltering business with Mark Wahlberg. After the family summer holiday in Muskoka, Beckham lost his patience. He and Salter would issue a writ on 19 October 2022 to recover the $20 million sponsorship payment Wahlberg allegedly owed. Beckham's ambition to be a businessman was being challenged.

CHAPTER 32

THE WEDDING

Nelson Peltz discovered he had little in common with the Beckhams, and as the celebrity couple settled in Miami their attraction to the billionaire scarcely increased. Peltz was not a football fan and he didn't admire losers. Inter Miami, he heard, was a turkey. By April, Phil Neville had failed to turn the team's fortunes around. With only two wins from 11 matches there was little to cheer, even after a desperate victory on the eve of his daughter's wedding. 'He launched a brand not a team,' a leading commentator said of Beckham.[1]

One headline was particularly embarrassing. The MLS announced a $2 million fine on the club for failing to report the excessive payments to five players and for concealing Blaise Matuidi's high salary. Jorge Mas was personally fined $250,000. He blamed McDonough outright. 'Paul had extreme authority,' said Mas, excusing himself as a non-expert. He was fined for failing to disclose immediately the over-payments. Claure had disclosed them to the MLS.

The MLS's sanction included a compulsory cut of the club's budget by 25 per cent for two years. That limited the purchase of any new player until 2023. Many talented players were forced to leave the club. Fans gave up and turn-out fell. Beckham was cleared of wrong-doing.

Privately, Mas realised Beckham's limitations. He appeared to be neither a businessman nor a club manager in control of the staff. Beckham's critics would say that he had proved himself to be an unreliable show-pony. His judgement was questioned.

Many American Jews were disquieted by Beckham's enthusiasm for Qatar. 'Qatar really is an incredible place,' Beckham had told his 77 million followers.[2] He ignored Qatar's financing of Hamas and other terrorist groups openly committed to the destruction of Israel. Many others were struck by the country's dubious human rights record, especially its criminalisation of homosexuality and its cruel misogyny in the suppression of women. A majority were unimpressed by Beckham's explanation on a visit to Doha's stadiums that he would use the 'power of football to inspire positive change' and 'believes in Qatar's commitment to progress'.[3] Beckham's contract to represent Qatar was criticised in the media as 'unforgivable', 'morally bankrupt' and 'sportswash'. Some Americans believed that Beckham was best marginalised.

Victoria had also found little in common with Claudia Peltz. The 67-year-old former star model, and the mother of eight of Peltz's ten children, had been surprised that a security detail had arrived to 'sweep the place'[4] before the Beckhams paid their first visit to her home. Claudia would be reluctant to understand Victoria's sense of self-importance, brand of humour or her exaggerated boast of commercial success. In Claudia Peltz's eyes, said her friends, Victoria's small fashion business was an indulgence.

Despite the Covid pandemic Victoria's sales in 2021 had grown from £36 million to £41 million. Her beauty product sales, up £5 million to £7.3 million, had been hailed by Toledano as a breakthrough.[5] In the same period, Dior's cosmetic sales had tripled to over £6 billion. That year Louis Vuitton's annual sales were 17 billion euros and Chanel's 11 billion euros. Victoria was not helped by media reports that the £490 black leggings sold in Dover Street could be bought on Amazon for £10. True or not, the report was damaging.

But at least the improved cost-controls had reduced the company's (VBH's) annual losses from £15.6 million in 2019 and £10.5 million in 2020 to £5.9 million losses in 2021. Despite that improvement, for the first time the auditors issued a statutory warning – a 'material uncertainty' – amounting to a question whether her company could continue operating. Their stark message had been prompted by HSBC's demand that she repay a £10 million loan. Beckham and the other shareholders had been forced to lend her a further £9.2 million. Her clothing company now owed £53.9 million to Beckham, although his company accounts showed debts of just £29 million. Her auditors did not explain that discrepancy in the public accounts.

Ralph Toledano had to believe that NEO's £30 million investment was not lost. Optimistically he predicted that by 2024 her sales would increase from £40 million to £100 million.[6] Toledano's forecast was pushed out to the media by her publicists. The bad news was that the numbers of followers pressing 'like' on her posts had fallen by half. Similarly, viewers of her lipstick promotions had fallen from 869,984 viewers to 127,953. Unable to afford a traditional live catwalk show for London's Fashion Week, she posted photographs of her latest range on her Instagram site. Just 72,826 of her 29 million followers watched. For over an entire year no magazine had featured her on their cover.[7] She persevered nonetheless.

Victoria was compelled to slash her prices again. Expensive accessories were sold off at huge discounts in TK Maxx. A £1,199 dress was priced at £199 but, even so, few buyers appeared. Months later she slashed prices again. Sunglasses were cut from £139 to £55 and the price of a Reebok bra from £75 to £37.50.[8] Her accumulated debt in 2021 rose to £66.3 million.[9]

Victoria's underlying problem never changed. Her clothes were judged to be well made but were starkly similar to cheaper brands. In a competitive market she defined her style as herself. Few rich, sophisticated women had been persuaded to identify with Victoria Beckham. Previously, few dared to tell her that truth but the businesses' latest finances compelled her to listen to criticism, not least from her director Marie LeBlanc. Once again she staged another relaunch, but without thanking LeBlanc for any success.[10]

'Miami,' Victoria admitted, 'opened my eyes to the fact that looking feminine and curvy is so important to many women.' Women, she had discovered after 14 years working in fashion, 'want shape – boobs and a bum'. She aimed for 'as good a bottom as I can get', working out every day at six in the morning.

Victoria did not invite Claudia Peltz to her 47th birthday lunch at singer Pharrell Williams' new hotel on South Beach. Kim Kardashian, her guest, guaranteed publicity. There was still much to learn about the business of being a celebrity family.[11] Thankfully, Beckham's partnership with James Salter could provide the necessary financial and social breakthrough.

Beckham's relationship with Salter had introduced him to the heart of the American billionaire world. In the transition over the past 20 years from Tony Stephens to Simon Fuller and now Salter, Beckham was no longer just a face for hire, a footballer or a celebrity, but a combination of all three – a player inside a corporate empire. To confirm his new status, he featured with Salter at a *Sports Illustrated* party in Miami. Serena Williams and the great quarterback Patrick Mahomes were the star guests.[12] The event attracted little publicity. The media focus had switched to Brooklyn Beckham's wedding.

With their 13.2 million Instagram followers, the durability of Brooklyn's relationship with Nicola excited curiosity, especially about her father's attitude towards a 23-year-old playboy. The billionaire remained discreet.

After abandoning photography, Brooklyn had decided to copy his parents' friend Gordon Ramsay. Cooking, he believed, was easy and lucrative. Introducing himself as a celebrity chef he first featured in an eight-minute video making a sandwich. To film *Cookin' with Brooklyn* had required a crew of 62 people. Five cameras focused on the star as he spread mayonnaise over a slice of bread. 'It does help to be creative,' he told the camera as he smeared a bagel with coleslaw and topped it with hash browns. Fortunately, a member of the crew supported by nine producers held a cribsheet to help him identify the utensils as he fried an egg and placed it on top of the bread. The recipe, he told viewers on the morning television show, had been guarded by his family for 'generations'.

In the next episode Brooklyn made spicy tomato spaghetti. His recipe was uncomplicated. The pasta was dropped into boiling water. Once it was cooked and drained he poured the sauce over the pasta from a jar. In one episode, viewers spotted a wine cork floating in ragu. It was, he explained, to tenderise the meat.

The next instalment was roast beef with Yorkshire pudding. The beef was clearly uncooked and the pudding had collapsed. In another show, a cheese sandwich was toasted with a blowtorch. 'I'm not a professional chef,' he explained. He cooked because 'it takes my mind off anything that's happening'. But the chef appeared to be untroubled. Millions of his followers tuned in and showered him with near-universal praise. In Brooklyn's world, celebrity did not require unique talent. What counted in winning followers were his image, lifestyle and attitude towards people. Millions admired those qualities in Brooklyn, including the moment he posed in pink trousers to promote Wendy's burger chain, which happened to be owned by Nelson Peltz.[13]

As the magazine deadline for the wedding closed, Brooklyn's publicists delivered a coup: the cover of Variety's 'Young Hollywood' issue. The headline, 'Brooklyn Peltz Beckham, Heir of Britain's Other Royal Family' buzzed among his growing followers, 14 million on Instagram. Variety's interviewer shamelessly praised the chef's fish and chips, even though Brooklyn's efforts had succeeded only on his third attempt. The magazine did not mention that Superdry had ended its contract with Brooklyn.[14] Nelson and Claudia Peltz would have disliked any criticism of their new son-in-law. To their delight, the couple's love of publicity was satisfied when Tatler featured Nicola on its front cover as 'The New Mrs Beckham'.

The weeks before the three-day celebration for 300 guests at the Peltz's ocean-front estate in Palm Beach were plagued by a blizzard of emails, anguished conversations and recrimination. Successive wedding planners had exhausted the patience of Nicola and Claudia. Nelson Peltz believed that one firm of planners had 'hoodwinked' his wife. He issued a 188-page lawsuit to recover £129,000 for their incompetence and drunken behaviour. They would counter-sue and accuse Peltz of being a 'billionaire bully' who called his own daughter's marriage a 'shit show'. Both women agreed to conceal the true cost from Nelson, especially after he wanted the wedding cancelled. If they did spend £3 million instead of the agreed £2 million, then he was unlikely to notice it for some time. There was even a cynical rumour that Nelson Peltz was insulted by the £3 million estimate. Nothing less than £15 million was satisfactory.[15] At least he recouped some money by selling the picture rights to Vogue. Guests were asked not to take any photographs.

Few outsiders were interested whether everyone enjoyed themselves on 9 April. In the post-Covid era of Russian atrocities in Ukraine and the criminal charges thrown at their neighbour Donald Trump, many were looking to be entertained by any missteps, real or fabricated, during the event. Some noticed that Tom Cruise and Katie were not at the wedding; and that the Beckhams were not seated at the top table; and that the rabbi twice called Brooklyn 'David'. Gossips mentioned that Brooklyn had signed a pre-nuptial agreement; that Nicola had spent $83,000 on her hair and make-up; and that Nicola complained about the flowers: 'They aren't white enough.'

British observers noticed that Ted Beckham arrived with his new blonde wife Hilary, while Sandra was alone, and that the 'star-studded guest list' highlighted Gordon Ramsay and Eva Longoria. Mischievous gossips wrote that singer Marc Anthony had dedicated his first song to start the dancing to Victoria and Brooklyn. Nicola, they smiled, had fled in tears. Whether that was true was irrelevant. By the end of the day Nicola had recovered. She was driven by Brooklyn around Palm Beach in a 1954 Jaguar XK140 electrified by Lunaz for £350,000, a present from Beckham. With considerable schadenfreude, outsiders were left at the end of the party with an impression of reeking debris strewn across the manicured Peltz lawns. The most notable legacy was Nicola's relationship with Victoria.

Nicola did not hide her dislike of Victoria. She no longer posted 'likes' of Victoria's posts. Only five out of Victoria's 131 posts after the wedding scored her approval. Nicola chose to ignore the birthdays of David and Harper. In retaliation Victoria liked only six of Nicola's 36 posts and ignored *Vogue*'s wedding and honeymoon photos. Her Instagram congratulations mentioned Brooklyn only.[16] Everyone noticed that Brooklyn refused his parents' offer to summer on their new boat. Instead he sailed across the Mediterranean on Nelson Peltz's glittering gin-palace. Nicola, said Brooklyn, was his 'number-one priority'. He renamed himself Peltz Beckham. Understandably, Victoria was hurt.

By September, Nicola's warfare with Victoria was undisguised. In an interview with *Grazia* she accused Posh of 'ghosting' her after reneging on her original offer to make a wedding dress. 'Days went by,' Nicola said, 'and I didn't hear anything.' To read in the media that she didn't want to wear Victoria's dress, whimpered Nicola, 'hurts my feelings'. Finally, Victoria admitted that her workshop could not have made it. Most suspected that the reason was money. Satisfying Nicola's demands, the money-conscious Victoria had feared, would require endless transatlantic trips. The cost would have been too high and there would be nothing but grief in return. Nicola got married in a Valentino dress instead.[17]

'We don't do that in this family,' Beckham told Brooklyn after reading Nicola's interview. Washing the family's dirty linen in public damaged the brand. Brooklyn, it appeared, no longer wanted to be associated with his own family. Among the 80 tattoos carved on his body, many were devoted to his wife. 'She always cries when I get another tattoo,' he said.[18]

Wisely, Victoria saw no advantage in continuing a public spat. To make peace she invited Nicola and Brooklyn to her first Paris show in three years in October 2022. 'Paris is the ultimate dream,' posted Victoria, hoping for success. The show was held in the unspectacular Church of the Val-de-Grace on the Left Bank. Most eyes were fixed on the families as Victoria's models paraded the lead design, tagged as 'a sexy dress that's easy to wear'. Sitting apart from his family, Brooklyn and Nicola looked uncomfortable, especially after Beckham entered with 11-year-old Harper wearing a £2,000 silk-and-lace dress. Harper hugged Brooklyn, but not Nicola.[19]

Sitting in the front row, Lady Mary Charteris looked particularly debonaire. Only those who recalled Glastonbury in 2017 would raise their eyebrows quizzically and wonder what precisely her presence meant.

At the end of the show Victoria burst into tears as Nicola and Brooklyn left without staying for the Beckham family steak and chips dinner at Girafe, near the Eiffel Tower.[20] The couple returned to the George V hotel where Claudia Peltz was waiting. Tellingly, Nicola did not post any messages about the show, but posted 'No family is perfect.' Four weeks later Nicola continued the spat. 'I was really excited to wear it,' she said about the disputed Beckham wedding dress, 'And I didn't end up wearing it.' Victoria replied that she never promised to make the dress.[21] Eventually the feud burned itself out, and Victoria was back in London. Despite tabloid gush and Anna Wintour's presence at the show, Victoria's collection was largely ignored outside Britain. Booth Moore of *Women's Wear Daily* commented: 'It did seem to cherry-pick some inspiration from others. Hopefully she can settle on and evolve a more palpable design language of her own.' Victoria's publicist forlornly promoted her 'presence' in Paris, at a small outlet on the second floor of the Printemps department store. Even Victoria eventually admitted disappointment. 'It almost reignited the brand,' she said.[22]

In the backwash of the wedding, the Beckham–Peltzs' fame soared. Brooklyn would feature on the cover of *New York Magazine* as 'The

Year of the Nepo Baby', and the couple would promote their new 'throuple' relationship with actress Selena Gomez. As usual, the backstory was bewildering. Gomez had not been invited to their wedding and she had dumped her friend Francia Raisa despite her being the donor of a kidney to Gomez in 2017.[23] But the threesome's friendship was passionate.

Seventeen-year-old Cruz was not as fortunate after the wedding. Desperate to establish himself, he had earlier that year been photographed bare-chested in his pants with his jeans around his ankles. 'Proud Dad,' Beckham posted about his son's appearance in *i-D* magazine. Sporting two tattoos, Cruz said his ambition to be a musician had started in 2008 when he appeared with his mother on stage during the Spice Girls tour.[24] At the wedding he and his parents persuaded Marc Anthony to help start his pop career. Introduced to KODA, a Ghanaian Gospel singer and songwriter, Cruz recorded 'If Everyday Was Christmas'. Later that year the song was released. It was not a hit.[25]

Disappointment was always concealed from outsiders. In the Beckhams' full-throttled dash to replicate the Kardashians' mammoth publicity machine, every appearance of their four children was accompanied by both David and Victoria posting messages of their pride and support. All the Beckhams' earlier reservations about using the children to promote the brand had disappeared. 'So proud,' wrote Beckham about Harper. 'So cool' posted Victoria about Cruz, who would be pictured at Paris Fashion Week wearing a £32,000 Rolex watch. 'So proud' posted Beckham again when 20-year-old Romeo signed to play for Brentford's B team.[26] Harper was roped into the publicity during a trip to Venice with her father. In return for exclusive photographs of the pair on a gondola, the newspaper mentioned that David was wearing DB Eyewear.[27]

Throughout those months as he settled in Miami, Beckham still hoped to secure a knighthood. In one last blast, his publicists persuaded the *Sun* that he finally qualified for the honour. Ingenious Media's tax avoidance schemes, reported the newspaper on its front page, had been cleared by a judge. HMRC, stated the *Sun*, had been beaten in the courts, so Beckham had been cleared; and HMRC had dropped the 'red' tag that prevented Beckham from receiving a knighthood. The honour was deserved, not least because he had also given £50 million to charity, supported the *Sun*'s Poppy campaign, visited the Chelsea pensioners (once), was a massive royalist, and three years earlier had paid £12.7 million in tax. 'He loves the Queen,' blasted the newspaper. 'That alone should qualify him for a knight-hood.'

Among the newspaper's erroneous claims was that HMRC had been defeated in the courts. On the contrary, three judges had upheld HMRC's case against Ingenious's investors with the exception of one minor issue. Like other investors, Beckham had to pay the outstand-ing taxes which HMRC had demanded. And in 2021 his corporate accounts were more opaque than ever. Brand Beckham's accounts reported losses, plus a £19.9 million inter-company debt, but also a reduction of the company's debts to Beckham himself from £11.2 million to £3 million. Similar adjustments among all his companies were unexplained in the accounts themselves.

One peculiar discrepancy was his accountant's presentation of his corporate history. HMRC expects companies to set out comparable figures over the past years so that the trends are clear. Unusually, Beckham's previous returns for his four main companies were materi-ally changed every year. To outsiders it could easily have appeared that his tax arrangements were not crystal clear. But nothing obvi-ously illegal jumped off the page either. Once again, despite the *Sun*'s support, his knighthood was not forthcoming.[28]

Nevertheless, the public mood favoured Beckham. His announce-ment of a £1 million donation to UNICEF, for Ukrainian children after the war broke out, added to the goodwill.[29] And then he pulled off a blinder. While other celebrities took advantage of a VIP speedy entrance to pay homage to the Queen lying-in-state in Westminster Hall, Beckham's publicist tipped off the media that he had quietly joined the 12-hour queue to say farewell. 'I grew up in a household of royalists,' he explained, once his presence was disclosed. His grand-father always thought of the monarch when they sang the National Anthem at international matches, and his 'Nan' was a staunch loyal-ist. As he bowed his head to the Queen's coffin, any doubts about the humble patriot's down-to-earth character were brushed aside. Not only in Britain but across the world.[30]

Two months later it all turned sour.

CHAPTER 33

QATAR

Beckham's financial future was now in Miami, a booming haven for money-makers. From his penthouse he gazed over the sunlit ocean and enjoyed the embrace of an uncritical social circle, which included the social gadfly Dave Grutman. Among the restaurants that the 49 year old owned was Papi Steak serving $1,000 steaks in a gold brief-case. Like so many ambitious socialites in Beckham's life, Grutman positioned himself next to the star in photographs to promote his own brand.

As for Beckham, he seemed oblivious to his wife, who was commut-ing between London and New York with Ken Paves, her hairdresser, and occasionally arriving in Miami without Harper to maintain the appearance of a marriage. There was sadness in the photos she posted of herself wearing a jumper with the slogan 'All I Want for Christmas is David Beckham' and David wearing wet underwear on his birthday with the caption, 'You're Welcome'. No one seemed bothered by a photograph taken during his recent visit to Macao accompanied by Angelababy, a Hong Kong actress. In the couple's new life, so much depended on Beckham's financial success.

His deal with Qatar promised to boost his fortune. Extraordinary secrecy imposed by Qatar prevented any outsider discovering his esti-mated £15 million annual fee. The mystery was compounded after Beckham's spokeswoman denied to the *Financial Times* that the money was paid into one of his acknowledged companies.

However, on the eve of the 2022 World Cup there was no secret about Beckham's commitment to Qatar. Throughout the capital Doha, Beckham's face beamed from billboards and screens. In an artfully shot video 'Visit Qatar' he promised that the competition would be a platform for 'progress, inclusivity and tolerance'. Paid to voice sincerity, he praised the fans for contributing to how 'the modern and traditional fuse to create something special'. For those in any doubt about his endorsement of the monarchy that punished same-sex activity with seven years' imprisonment, he addressed those at the government's youth festival in Doha. 'Today is your day to dream' and 'The pitch will be a platform for progress.'[1] In return for millions of pounds he preached that football would provoke conversations to improve sympathy and understanding for the gas-rich state.

Millions of people across the world believed Beckham's message. The critics mostly were in Europe, especially Britain. The *Sun* led the charge against the hypocrites – Beckham, Gary Lineker, Robbie Williams, Joe Lycett, Black Eyed Peas and other celebrities who had damned Qatar after 2012 but then flocked to profit from the contest. After Beckham posted a selfie on Instagram just before England's game against the USA, the *Mirror* seethed that 'It's called Greed. How much money do you actually need?' To hit back against the 'epic' hypocrites, Beckham's publicists briefed against model Vogue Williams for calling their own employer a 'shitebag'. Earlier that year, they revealed, Williams had posed on a free promo-tour in the Maldives where gays are also imprisoned.[2]

Beckham's critics assumed that his behaviour would irreversibly damage the brand.[3] But Beckham knew better. After all the controversies since 1998 – the World Cup red card that year, Rebecca Loos, the hacked emails, tax avoidance and so much more – he calculated that memories were short. Regardless of the headlines the criticisms would evaporate and his popularity would be restored. He always found ways – or a stunt – to re-legitimise himself.

Unexpectedly during the competition he flew 7,600 miles from Qatar to Boston to join the new Prince and Princess of Wales, William and Kate, and President Biden to celebrate the launch of the royals' environmental Earthshot prize.[4] Hours after publicly kissing Kate on her cheek, Beckham was flying back to Qatar, a 15-hour journey. Coincidentally, on the same day, Harry and Meghan were seeking to wow Americans during an event in New York. Inevitably the Sussexes were overshadowed by the constellation in Boston. Beckham had got his revenge for the Sydney snub.

As the dust settled he had good reason to believe that his Qatari millions were safe. But the commercial cost was noticeable. None of the bidders to buy Manchester United wanted to pay for his support, and his Qatari contract broke his relationship with AIA, the Asian insurance company, and Diageo. Some in the whisky headquarters who were proud that Diageo had funded Queer Britain, a London museum, were displeased by Beckham's anti-LGBTQ+ stance in Qatar.

Their antagonism was bolstered by Beckham's failure to sell Diageo's spirit. After nine years, his celebrity blue bottle had captured only 0.2 per cent of the market. Like his fragrances, Haig Club crashed. Few young people believed that Beckham genuinely enjoyed drinking whisky or wanted to be identified with a retired footballer's favourite tipple. He could rue that George Clooney's Casamigos Tequila, created in 2013, had been sold in 2017 to Diageo for $700 million plus $300 million depending on sales. To smother the negativity, Beckham claimed that he had ended the relationship in order to create his own brand. That has not yet materialised.

Any other celebrity would undoubtedly have suffered permanent damage from the criticisms, but Beckham's unique mastery deflected the barbs.

Inter Miami's third season was not a success. Out of 63 games, the team had won 19 matches and lost 35. They had scored 64 goals and let in 104 and were bottom of the table. The club and Beckham were floundering. Reflecting the declining interest in the club, Jorge Mas could only extract a paltry $4.5 million annual fee from the cryptocurrency XBTO to sponsor the players' pink shirts. In 2021, Beckham admitted that Mas was his saviour. Riding to the rescue, Mas launched his plan.

In September 2021, both Masayoshi Son's and Marcelo Claure's stakes were bought by the Mas brothers. The record price for the 52.5 per cent was about $630 million. To Claure's satisfaction it was the highest value of any MLS club. Claure's only public utterance was self-congratulatory: 'I fulfilled my dream to set up a football team in Miami and then I moved on to my next dream.'

The Mas' purchase was part financed by a $140 million loan from Ares Management, which was a $260 billion global fund. Described as a 'preferred equity investment', the loan apparently also allowed Beckham to buy back another 15 per cent of the shares, bringing his stake to 25 per cent. Mas held 75 per cent of the shares. How

Beckham financed his purchase of the extra shares remains a mystery. The transactions are not reported in any of his British-registered companies. That raises questions about his financial arrangements in America.

With Claure removed, Mas began negotiating with city officials the final details of the $1 billion development of Freedom Park complex for the stadium. The risks remained considerable. An unsuccessful team with poor revenues would not justify a $1 billion development. One year later the city granted Mas all the permits he needed to build the stadium complex.

One fortuitous coincidence of Beckham's presence in Qatar was the visit of Francis Suarez, Miami's mayor. On 14 December 2022, Suarez watched the match between France and Morocco with Beckham. Thrilled to be Suarez's host, Beckham posted a photo of the two together with the text, 'Miami Boys in town.' The visit closely followed Suarez's approval of the Freedom City stadium complex. Everyone knew that Jorge Mas had secured permission for the development with Suarez's help to get the necessary votes. The mayor's enemies quickly asked whether Beckham had given Suarez a free ticket. That would be illegal, because Beckham was registered as a Miami city lobbyist. He was caught in the middle of a *Miami Herald* investigation of the mayor's alleged sleaze. Principally, Suarez was accused of accepting free gifts and foreign travel to the Middle East for himself and his retinue from those who wanted his support for building projects in Miami.[5] Naturally, the mayor denied any wrongdoing. The newspaper's investigation continued as Inter Miami emerged from a grim period.

Over the previous three years Mas had been negotiating a contract with Lionel Messi and his brother.[6] The world's best player with 468 million Instagram followers, Messi was a marketing dream, as Mas knew. Sales of shirts, tickets and merchandise would finance his investment. Helpfully, Messi's wife Antonela Roccuzzo wanted to live in their ocean-front home near Miami, close to her father. As a paid influencer for Dior, Louis Vuitton, Guerlain and others, she had 36.3 million followers, about 6 million more than Victoria. Her life, she believed, would be better in America than in Saudi Arabia, which had offered Messi about $400 million to sign a short contract.

Among the many obstacles Mas encountered to seal the deal with Messi was the star's scepticism about American football. With Beckham's help, the 36 year old could be reassured that much had changed since Beckham joined LA Galaxy in 2007. Then, the MLS consisted of 13 teams. In 2022, it had 29 teams. Back then MLS sold the television rights to ESPN for $8 million a year. Now, Apple paid $250 million a year. The annual minimum wage had also increased to $67,360. With the players' average pay standing at $250,000, the quality of the game had markedly improved. In 2007 the MLS had agreed that Beckham could buy a franchise for $25 million, but in 2022 the MLS sold the franchise for the 30th team to be based in San Diego for $500 million. With the 2026 World Cup destined to be played in the USA, Canada and Mexico, American football's future was sure to be lucrative.

Refusing to take 'No' for an answer, Mas spoke about paying Messi around $200 million for four seasons, plus a share of the merchandising profits. As the months passed, the contract period reduced to two and a half years. During the negotiations over the last eighteen months, Mas agreed to pay Messi about $120 million, plus an income from Apple TV, sales of Adidas and proceeds from the ticket and shirt sales. Finally, if he stayed until the end of the contract, he would be entitled to buy shares in the club.

Mas knew that one player alone could not make a complete difference on the field. Even a genius like Messi. As an added incentive, Mas agreed to fire Phil Neville and recruit the Argentine coach Gerardo 'Tata' Martino and two Latino players from Barcelona.

On 7 June 2023, Messi finally signed for Miami. Beckham's world was electrified. Two weeks later the curtain rose for Messi's debut match. No Hollywood scriptwriter could have perfected the events played out in front of Kim Kardashian, Serena Williams and other stars in the hospitality suite.

In the 94th minute, Inter Miami were awarded a free kick against Cruz Azul, a club based in Mexico City. The score was 1–1. Messi was given the chance to take the last shot of the match. At the end of a spine-tingling display, the Argentinian mesmerisingly curved the ball over the wall of Cruz Azul players into the left-hand corner of the net. The perfection of the goal reduced Bend-It-Like-Beckham to tears.

And then Victoria appeared. The diva put her arms around Beckham's neck, searched for the camera, pouted and posed.

One month later, thanks to Messi's astonishing play in the following six matches, Inter Miami won the League Cup trophy in a dramatic penalty shoot-out. Thereafter it was downhill for the club. Messi was injured and the club finished the season at the bottom of the league. But the profits were already pouring in to finance the new stadium.

More important for Dan Garber, the combination of Messi and Beckham had made Inter Miami the MSL's global showcase. America's soccer community believed the trajectory was ever upwards. Nothing could go wrong.

CHAPTER 34

SMOKE AND MIRRORS

'Golden Balls' was humiliated. A rictus grin could not conceal his embarrassment. Jeering fans were drowning out his words, despite multiple amplification over the Tannoy speakers.

Packed into the Hong Kong Stadium on 4 February 2024, 38,000 fans were outraged. They had paid up to £400 a ticket and flocked to see the great Lionel Messi play for a guaranteed 45 minutes against a local team. Instead, the Argentinian had sat grumpily on the bench throughout the match. Ignoring loud chants of 'Messi', he sulked, chewed gum, yawned and refused even to wave at the booing crowd as he walked back into the dressing room after a drab game.

Beckham walked on to the pitch. 'I would like to say thank you very much for the incredible welcome' he said. Chants of 'Refund' drowned him out. The Beckham Machine had lost control. Money, vanity and greed had ripped off the mask of the Miami team's goodwill visit.[1]

The showcase match between Inter Miami and Hong Kong had been agreed between Beckham and Tatler Asia's chief executive Michael Lamunière in May 2023. During Beckham's promotional trip to open the Londoner hotel in Macao, he had agreed with Lamunière to bring Inter Miami to Hong Kong.[2] Lamunière planned to use the prestige match to establish Tatler XFEST as the annual host to 'celebrate the best of Hong Kong'. As part of the deal Beckham also agreed to feature on *Tatler*'s front cover. His self-portrayal for the magazine's interview was memorable: 'I just want to be remembered as a nice person. Humble, generous and hardworking – that's the gist of it.'

Lamunière had agreed with Inter Miami's business chief, Xavier Asensi, that Messi would be the star attraction. The Argentinian's appearance guaranteed a sell-out within one hour of tickets going on sale. For Asensi the match was part of Inter Miami's launch as a global brand. In the week before the match, pink shirts were on sale throughout pink-painted Hong Kong. Messi's face shone from hundreds of poster boards. 'Money grab' was among the less generous descriptions of Asensi's promotion of Messi.[3]

Expectations were high when the team landed in their chartered aircraft. 'Messi mania is sweeping Hong Kong,' reported CNN. The following night, Beckham had smilingly posed for selfies and signed autographs at *Tatler*'s star-studded Miami-themed party at the X-Club in Cardinal Point. 'Becks adds star power to the city,' gushed another television report.[4] By then Beckham knew that Messi would not be playing, but he kept it secret. The tour, he knew, was falling apart.

Two weeks earlier, the team had set off on a 25,000-mile, five-nation pre-season journey in America and Saudi Arabia to play seven matches. The team had not yet won a single match. At its previous stop in Saudi Arabia, Miami had been defeated 4–3 by Al-Hilal and was then crushed 6–0 by Al-Nassr. Although Cristiano Ronaldo, Al-Nassr's star player, was unfit to play, Messi's team were embarrassed by three goals scored in the first 12 minutes. At the end, a medical team declared that Messi was suffering from a hamstring injury.[5]

Beckham and Miami's managers decided not to reveal the bad news to *Tatler*'s Michael Lamunière, or anyone else in Hong Kong, after the team descended from their plane at the airport. None of the locals knew why Miami's players refused to pose long enough for photographers, and why Messi did not shake hands with the welcoming dignitaries.[6]

Two days later, during the final countdown to the match, the secret inside the exuberant stadium remained undiscovered. While mingling on the pitch with local celebrities, including the actor-singers Tony Leung and Carina Lau, Beckham knew that the star players – Messi and Luis Suarez – would sit on the bench as substitutes but would not be called upon. The team manager Gerardo 'Tata' Martino decided that the risk to their ageing legs, knees and hips was too great.

Until the last ten minutes of the lacklustre match Beckham's hosts still believed that Messi would play.[7] Unsurprisingly, even without Messi, Miami won the match 4–1. The fans were outraged. They had mainly bought tickets for a unique opportunity to see Messi play. At the end, booing fans gesticulated with thumbs down and shouted 'Refund'. Deaf to reality, Beckham warbled on the pitch that 'We look forward to coming back one day to entertain you even more.' No one saw the new tattoo on his leg: a Miami pink heron.

The media reaction about the 'calamitous' weekend and a 'messy public relations nightmare' damned Messi for snubbing Hong Kong's leader during the trophy award ceremony, and for 'ignoring *Tatler*'s pleas' that at least he walk around the pitch. By then, the team had flown on to Tokyo.

During the next match against Japan's Vissel Kobe, Messi and Suarez unexpectedly played after half-time. 'A slap in the face to Hong Kong,' screamed *Tatler*'s spokesman. Fans in Kobe's half-empty stadium witnessed a goalless draw ending in Kobe winning the penalty shoot-out. Messi did not kick one shot at goal. Jorge Mas's prediction that signing Messi would transform the MSL looked threadbare. 'WHY HONG KONG HATES MESSI' was the *South China Post*'s headline.[8] 'All petulant in pink, like some thuggish flamingo,' the newspaper quoted its own managing editor, Yonden Lhatoo. Beckham, scorned Lhatoo, was 'feckless', 'clueless' and a 'selfish jerk'.[9]

Beckham had not flown to Japan. Instead, to fulfil his sponsorship contract, he had dashed to Qatar to play padel in Doha. At the end of the week he surfaced at his Oxfordshire home. In a familiar damage-limitation exercise his Instagram post showed him wearing a heavy coat and a hat in a chicken coop. 'The excitement of finding eggs,' he or his publicist wrote, 'is pretty amazing.' Among the scathing comments from Asia was a question: 'Will the chickens come home to roost?' Beckham was not concerned. After a lifetime of turbulence, another bout of criticism barely bothered him.

Only months earlier, on 4 October 2023, Beckham's global reputation had soared. A four-part Netflix series describing his life had sparked huge praise and big audiences. Filmed over two years by the American actor Fisher Stevens, the series was full of star interviews and produced what the *Daily Telegraph* called, 'a superb, unexpected, complex portrayal – both of an era and an unexpectedly complex man'. The *Daily Mail* called it 'David Beckham's slick hagiography.'[10] Both sides agreed that the Beckhams had produced a superbly crafted glossy advert. For the majority of viewers the Beckhams emerged as a wonderful couple.

Most viewers had been struck by David Beckham's emotional description of overcoming the vitriol levelled at him after his red card against Argentina in 1998. Many were also impressed by recordings of Beckham repeatedly scoring spectacular goals. In the series he never missed. Not even once. Others were enthralled by the 'heart-warmingest theme' of 'a long-enduring marriage between two people who seem genuinely to enjoy and admire one another'. Beckham emerged from the series universally loved, while Victoria was generally praised despite the accusation in one quotation published by the *New Yorker* magazine of being a 'charmless empty gobshite'.[11]

Closer examination revealed that the series was flawed by distortions. 'Scandals are sanded down or unmentioned altogether,' reported the *Daily Mail*, 'conflict minimised, personal flaws and failings airbrushed away and history rewritten.' The director was accused of a deliberate blurring of reality. Football matches were wrongly described, Glenn Hoddle's reputation was trashed by the prejudicial edit of his post-match 1998 press conference, the Qatar deal was ignored, and a *Daily Mirror* front-page headline was cropped to remove the assertion by Rebecca Loos's brother that Beckham did indeed have an affair with Loos.

In the director's edit of the interviews, Beckham inaccurately pleaded that his transfer to Madrid was involuntary. 'I got sold overnight,' he blabbed. Again inaccurately he said that he had moved to Spain without consulting Victoria. With similar imprecision Victoria said that the move to Madrid was 'a shock'. She refused to move to Madrid because there were no schools for her very young children. She forgot to mention that she had stayed away in a bid for stardom with Damon Dash.[12] And both overlooked Tony Stephens' long negotiations with Real Madrid.

After hours of filming, Fisher Stevens had edited a sequence of moody interviews about Beckham's affair with Rebecca Loos. Remarkably, Loos was not mentioned by name. Both Beckhams agreed about the consequence of his relationship. For Victoria it was the 'hardest' time of her life because 'it felt like the world was against us.' Mournfully, David asserted that he felt 'physically sick every day. Victoria means everything to me,' he said. 'To see her hurt was incredibly difficult. But we're fighters. And at the time we needed to fight for each other.'

Most noteworthy was Beckham's soulful blame of the media for their troubles – how newspapers had invaded his privacy by exposing his affair with Loos. Viewers were unaware how every week the couple had begged the media for attention, and how journalists had been summoned to Courchevel in 2004 to photograph their bliss.

The series convinced the audience that the illusion of innocent hurt, diligently manufactured by the Beckhams, was real. Indeed, the series' success proved that the public wanted to believe that the myth was reality. The truth about his hypocrisy was ignored, except by Rebecca Loos. Beckham's fantasy annoyed Loos. Beckham, she complained from her home in Norway, 'portrays himself as the victim' and had cast her as 'a liar'. All a bit odd, she thought, considering that soon after the affair was exposed, they had met again at a Madrid hotel.[13]

Amid the accolades for the series, those multiple flaws tended to be ignored. The reputations of the Beckhams glowed, especially across America and Asia. This was the moment, Victoria believed, to secure positive headlines for her business.

In March 2023, Ralph Toledano had announced that Victoria's company had finally turned a corner. Over the following months her publicists mentioned a £200,000 profit, which was not quite so impressive on a turnover of £58 million but was billed as a huge step forward.[14] The truth was different.

Most of the Beckham companies were due to file their 2022/3 accounts on 31 December 2023. British companies file their accounts on HMRC's website electronically. They are published automatically and instantly accessible to everyone, including journalists. But the Beckhams' advisers delivered the accounts to HMRC either by post or by hand. They would only be electronically available on 16 January. Until then, the Beckhams' publicists were free to spin their good-news story.

Just as planned, the *Daily Mail*'s headline on 30 December reported that Victoria's business had earned a £200,000 profit. Unreported was how the £200,000 profit had been conjured by Victoria's accountants using a technical measure called EBITDA. First, the accountants had taken a premature 'write back' on the Dover Street shop.[15] Next, they raised the value of the stock by 135 per cent, although sales had only increased by 44 per cent.[16] In reality, Victoria's business in 2022 made a loss of £2.964 million, and to stay in business she had borrowed an additional £6.9 million. After cancelling some loans owed to Beckham, she still owed her shareholders a hefty £50 million. Trust in the accounts was further challenged by a series of errors.[17] Noticeably, her auditors and accountants increased their annual fees by 28 per cent and 42 per cent.[18]

David Beckham's accounts were similarly confusing, at least to those without weeks to spend understanding them. Beckham's publicists hailed as proof of his enduring legacy that he had earned a record £72.5 million in 2022 against his £34 million income the previous year. 'Record profits' was the media's banner headline. Most of the additional income was assumed to come from Qatar. Again, none of the newspaper reporters had been able to read the details of the accounts. Even if they had, no outsider could have understood the jigsaw puzzle presented in the accounts of DRJBHL, the new company jointly owned by Beckham and Authentic Brands, boasting the £72.5 million headline.

The year had been dominated by the recovery of Beckham's ownership of his brand from Global, the unfortunate deal Simon Fuller had negotiated with Bruce Rockowitz that ended after Global's bankruptcy. Beckham apparently paid Global's administrators £38.2 million ($45 million) to recover its 51 per cent ownership of Beckham's brand.[19] To register the payment and new ownership, DRJBHL undertook a confusing sequence of transactions – a 'cash' merry-go-round. In 2022, DRJBHL's 'cash' reserves were increased from £4.22 million to £32.2 million. And yet it was not real 'cash' but preference shares bought by Beckham and Authentic in 'cash' (£31.5 million). Yet after DRJBHL received the 'cash' for the shares, the same 'cash' was instantly repaid to Beckham and Authentic as $38.8 million.[20] The 'cash' merry-go-round was not explained by the directors or auditors, and it is possible that it also legally saved taxes.

According to an old accountancy saying, 'Turnover is vanity, profit is sanity, and cash is reality.' The absence of real 'cash' in DRJBHL exposed the unreality of the expensive corporate restructuring which, according to the accounts, cost much of Beckham's £72 million income.

The churn – also funded by Beckham's personal loans – raised further questions. A statement in DRJBHL's accounts declared that no directors had been paid in 2022.[21] That was not the complete picture. DRJBHL's subsidiary, David Beckham Ventures (DBVL), had paid substantial salaries to directors, including £10 million to Beckham.

And then there was another apparent contradiction. The accountants recorded a company asset of 'goodwill' valued at £38.2 million. That was the sum paid to recover the brand rights from Global. The £38.2 million goodwill, stated the report, would be written off over the following 20 years.[22] Yet in the same accounts, no less than £7 million (20 per cent) was instantly 'written off' or amortised. The inconsistency was not explained.

That question was amplified by unexplained riddles throughout the accounts of Beckham's other companies. Among them was the payment of a $7.8 million 'overhead fee' by Beckham's company DB Ventures (DBVL) to Authentic.

Among other inexplicable costs was DBVL's agreement to buy unspecified investments from David. They were instantly revalued downwards by £1.3 million, a 78 per cent loss. Rather than Beckham personally bearing the loss, it seems that the company was used to write off £1.3 million against tax.[23] Similarly, the company bore the loss of £1.5 million from speculating in cryptocurrencies.

A further transaction during 2022 legally to avoid tax was the sale by David and Victoria of David Beckham's image rights to DBVL for $10 million. The Beckhams benefited because the $10 million they received would be taxed at the lower capital gains tax of 28 per cent rather than as income tax at 45 per cent. The report failed to explain how the $10 million value was assessed. To further minimise tax, David also sold his personal share in Studio 99 to DBVL for $5 million. Since Studio 99 and its subsidiaries at the end of 2022 had lost about £1 million, the valuation was not explained.

All those manoeuvres, whether properly executed (which cannot be known from inspection of the accounts alone), were unlikely to help Beckham's bid for a knighthood. His quest for an honour, it appeared, had been finally quashed by self-interest. His fortune, he knew, was secure once JP Morgan Chase agreed to sponsor Inter Miami's stadium and the club's annual revenue was predicted to soar from $56 million in 2022 to $200 million in 2024.

The public has never demanded answers about Beckham's finances. For his fans, Beckham was the working-class boy from Chingford.

Few seriously resented him for his four stunning homes – in London, Oxfordshire, Miami and Dubai – his countless luxury cars, about 40 employees and, after loans, his estimated £250 million fortune. He and Victoria epitomised the best of self-made Britons who, despite their celebrity, savoured family values. Only a minority were suspicious about their breathless lust to rank among the global superstars.

With supreme self-confidence the attention seekers had perfected a formula for smiling and saying almost nothing beyond self-congratulation. While the couple offered little that was new or original, theirs was a triumph of publicity over curiosity. They were icons for those who demanded from their heroes little more than glamour and the compelling reassurance that two ordinary people had made good. That success was diligently plotted.

Forever fearful of reaching a tipping-point, they had both successfully swerved away from every disaster. Neither was prepared to be taken hostage by their mentors. Both had been silently ruthless towards anyone challenging their survival. Their victims and critics were silenced by non-disclosure agreements and by the power of the Beckhams.

Beyond his remarkable good looks, Beckham's image of stubborn determination had won him global approval. Made famous by football and the nostalgia for a tattooed lad enjoying his manly bravado, Beckham's smiling embrace of the public deflected the successive pitfalls that would have destroyed other celebrities. Repeatedly, his transgressions had been ignored by billions of football fans who hailed his devotion to their sport.

Thanks to Simon Fuller – wilfully ignored in the Netflix series – Beckham had capitalised on the explosion of football's value. His global brand, reinforced by the move to Los Angeles, had become an enduring strength as a role model. Despite the widespread disproval in Europe of his relationship with Qatar, his fans in Africa and Asia were largely unconcerned. The threat of serious repercussions evaporated. Nestlé's decision to choose Beckham to promote Nespresso confirmed his invulnerability.

Yet his status and survival would have been washed away without Victoria's determination to maintain the illusion of a happy family. Suffering his adultery and absences she steadfastly protected the brand. In return he continued to finance her vanity business. Her tiny fashion house is unlikely ever to be genuinely profitable, but her supporters fully approve her steely ambition regardless of the monotonous repetition in promotional interviews.

Images are their message, not least at Victoria's 50th birthday celebration at London's Oswald nightclub on 20 April 2024. The army of photographers on the Mayfair pavement were spoiled for choice as the Beckhams' 100 guests, including all the Spice Girls and Tom Cruise, walked through the club's small door. Among the few stars missing was Nicola Peltz. Apparently, Nicola had unexpectedly returned to America. But it did not dent the Beckhams' joy as Victoria emerged at 2.30 a.m., carried piggyback by her husband to a waiting car. No one compared this with his gesture to help Victoria suffering from a broken foot with the same antic for photographers in Courchevel exactly 20 years earlier. Goodwill towards the Beckhams suffocated any cynicism.

Although vulnerable to sudden blasts of reality, for many the Beckhams' extraordinary prosperity is a particularly modern story of aspiration and ambition fulfilled. The Beckhams' flaws are a magnifying mirror for some of their fans' own weaknesses, whilst the Beckhams' strengths and will power continue to be qualities many wish to emulate. For their critics, the Beckhams' illusion of substance conceals their indifference to much beyond themselves. In that sense, they personify the superficiality of contemporary celebrity. Yet, for millions of their followers, it is the unparalleled success of the creators of the House of Beckham that excites admiration and offers everlasting entertainment.

ENDNOTES

Abbreviations used:

DB/David Beckham; DM/*Daily Mail*; ES/*Evening Standard*; G/*Guardian*; Ind/*Independent*; Mos/*Mail on Sunday*; Mir/*Mirror*; NoW/*News of the World*; Obs/*Observer*; S/*Sun*; SM/*Sunday Mirror*; ST/*Sunday Times*; Tel/*Telegraph*; Times/*The Times*; VB/Victoria Beckham

CHAPTER 1. GLASTONBURY, JUNE 2017

1. S 18.10.17; MoS 22.10.17 (Hind); Mir 18.1017 (Boshoff) https://www.dailymail.co.uk/femail/article-4990708/Look-Posh-David-s-new-chum-racy-Lady.html
2. S 24.6.17
3. S 27.1.19 (Moodie)
4. S 27.6.17 (Wootton)
5. S 17.10.17
6. SM 2.3.03
7. SM 19.9.05 (Todd); SM 12.2.06; Mir 25.5.16; MoS 22.10.17 (Hind)
8. S 27.6.17 (Wootton)
9. Mir 1.10.09 (Hudson)
10. S 27.6.17 (Wootton)
11. https://www.dailymail.co.uk/femail/article-4990708/Look-Posh-David-s-new-chum-racy-Lady.html

CHAPTER 2. MADRID, JULY 2003

1. S 15.10.01
2. S 5.7.03
3. SM 11.4.04
4. S 21.6.03; SM 29.6.03 (Malone)
5. Carlin *White Angels* p.91
6. S 4.8.03; SM 3.8.03
7. SM 10.8.03
8. SM 10.8.03; S 6.2.98
9. SM 10.8.03
10. S 28.8.03
11. Carlin p.201

12. S 30.8.03

13. S 27.8.03

14. Mir 28.9.07

15. NoW 22.6.03

16. NoW 24.8.03

17. NoW 24.08.03

18. Footwork Productions Ltd, year-end 2003, accounts Note 6; turnover fell in 2000 to £558k and soared in 2001 to over £3 million, rising to £3.5m in 2002 and £18.7 million in 2003.

19. Mir 29.9.18 (Boshoff)

CHAPTER 3. LONDON, JULY 2023

1. Carlin pp.59ff; Andy Bernal *Riding Shotgun*

2. NoW 2.9.01

3. S 1.9.01

4. DB p.89; S 9.10.97

5. S 10.10.97 (Woolnough)

6. Footwork Productions Ltd income in 1999 was £828,000 and his income £365,000.

7. S 20.3.97

8. Confidential source

9. S 3.11.97

10. S 26.1.98

11. VB *Learning to Fly* p.375

12. S 13.1.00 (Mohan)

13. S 12.4.04

14. NoW 18.4.04

15. NoW 18.4.04

16. Sunday People 18.4.04

17. S 9.1.02

18. NoW 2.9.01

19. S 20.3.02

20. S 11.2.02

CHAPTER 4. FLASHPOINT

1. S 1.8.97

2. S 21.5.98 (Woolnough); S 29.5.98

3. S 1.3.00 (Ross)

4. S 2.7.98

5. S 9.6.97

6. S 3.3.98; S 1.10.98; S 17.11.98; S 7.1.00

7. S 21.5.98; DB p.74; S 23.4.98

8. S 24.6.98

9. S 3.2.98

10. S 22.6.98

11. S 27.6.98
12. S 29.1.17; DIDiscs
13. Obs 2.11.03
14. S 1.7.98
15. S 1.10.98; S 14.5.99 (Howard)
16. S 5.3.99
17. S 3.5.99; S 17.5.99; S 27.5.99; S 1.6.99
18. S 18.10.99
19. S 7.1.00
20. S 14.8.99
21. NoW 26.8.01
22. S 21.6.00; S 18.12.99
23. S 11.10.99; S 26.5.99

CHAPTER 5. SEPTEMBER 1999

1. S 24.9.99; S 25.9.99
2. S 14.6.99; S 2.12.99
3. S 19.6.03
4. Alex Ferguson *My Autobiography* p.239
5. DB p.159
6. S 1.1.99
7. DB p.201
8. S 14.7.99; S 1.3.00
9. https://hbr.org/2013/10/fergusons-formula
10. S 22.2.00
11. SM 27.2.02
12. Mir 28.9.07 (Boshoff)
13. S 9.2.00
14. S 26.2.00
15. S 7.1.00; S 20.4.00
16. S 12.6.00; S 19.6.00
17. S 21.6.00; S 22.6.00
18. VB p.495; DB p.214
19. S 3.3.01
20. Ind 16.10.03; NoW 9.11.03
21. SM 30.12.01 (Graham)
22. S 28.6.03
23. S 31.1.00 (Ross)
24. S 6.3.02; S 18.05.00
25. Michael Crick *The Boss*
26. Beckham, St John's Wood speech, 2.7.23
27. S 21.3.00 (Mohan)
28. S 13.5.00
29. Mir 26.4.07 (Hadley & Simpson)
30. SM 27.6.04; SM 14.5.00 (Malone); SM 6.5.01 (Malone)

CHAPTER 6. REVIVAL

1. S 15.3.01
2. S 23.1.01
3. S 19.5.01
4. GQ (June 2002)
5. S 19.6.01; S 30.6.01 (Mohan)
6. S 8.10.01
7. NoW 7.10.01; NoW 25.11.01 (Harrison)
8. SM 12.5.02
9. SM 29.12.02
10. Beckham, S 30.8.03
11. S 6.5.16
12. Parkinson interview (September 2001)
13. NoW 1.4.01
14. SM 22.4.01 (Malone); S 6.3.02 (Mohan); S 16.4.03; SM 10.3.02 (Hyland)
15. Mir 29.3.12; Mir 8.7.16 (Boshoff)
16. NoW 3.3.02
17. SM 22.2.04; SM 29.2.04 (Malone)
18. VB p.375; VB p.49; Mir 29.3.12; Mir 8.7.16 (Boshoff); NoW 3.3.02; SM 22.2.04; NoW 1.4.01
19. NoW 29.3.12; Mir 8.7.16 (Boshoff); NoW 3.3.02; SM 22.2.04; NoW 1.4.01
20. S 28.7.99 (Mohan); S 8.1.02; NoW 9.9.01; SM 6.8.00; S 20.11.01
21. Andrew Morton *The Beckhams* p.210
22. SM 6.8.00
23. Morton pp.144ff; SM 5.11.00 (Malone)
24. S 8.6.99
25. S 30.6.01 (Mohan); S 22.9.01 (Mohan); SM 15.8.05; W magazine 1.7.07
26. NoW 2.9.01; SM 20.2.00 (Hyland)
27. SM 2.9.01; SM 2.9.01, quoting autobiography
28. SM 16.9.01; S 10.12.02; S 12.12.02 (Mohan); SM 18.6.00 (Hyland)
29. DB *My World*
30. SM 15.10.00 (Hyland)
31. NoW 26.8.01; S 6.2.01
32. S 22.9.01; Parkinson interview 2010; S 13.3.03

CHAPTER 7. DISMAY

1. Ind 12.4.02
2. Morton p.208
3. S 7.2.02
4. S 9.2.02 (Mohan)
5. SM 10.3.02 (Hyland)
6. NoW 21.10.01
7. SM 18.4.01 (Hyland & Meyers)

8. SM 10.11.02
9. S 12.3.03
10. G 13.5.2002
11. G 13.5.2002
12. 'The Broken Metatarsal – A 2000s Football Podcast' https://audioboom
.com/posts/7736427-danny-mills-partying-with-beckham-and-steps-andscaringing
-wingers https://www.planetfootball.com/in-depth-mills-becks-pre-world-cup
-party-upsetting-englands-man-utd-players
13. SM 2.6.02
14. S 8.6.02; NoW 9.6.22
15. SM 23.6.02; S 29.6.02
16. SM 4.8.02

CHAPTER 8. DOUBLE-DEALING

1. S 11.12.03
2. Neville LinkedIn post 9.10.23
3. DB p.358
4. S 4.3.03
5. SM 15.6.03 (Weatherup)
6. S 26.3.03
7. NoW 29.6.03
8. Carlin p.49
9. S 25.4.03 (Custis)
10. SM 22.6.03
11. S 30.4.03
12. SM 16.1.00; NoW 21.11.04
13. S 15.4.03
14. S 31.5.03
15. S 30.5.03 (Newton)
16. S 31.5.03 (Mohan)
17. BBC 13.6.03
18. S 5.5.03; NoW 22.6.03
19. S 11.6.03 (Custis)
20. SM 8.6.03 (Smith)
21. GQ 3.3.19
22. S 12.6.03; S 14.6.03 (Mohan); SM 15.6.03
23. S 5.6.03 (Custis)
24. S 18.6.03; SM 22.6.03; Carlin p.88
25. NoW 9.11.03
26. NoW 22.6.03 (Harrison)
27. NoW 4.4.04; NoW 3.3.02 (Harrison)
28. S 10.4.04; S 23.9.08 (Newton); S 16.6.07
29. SM 11.4.04
30. NoW 2.11.03; SM 6.7.03; S 7.5.03 (Newton)
31. NoW 15.6.03

32. SM 27.7.03
33. VB p.145
34. G 12.2.05 (Poole)
35. Sean Smith *Victoria Beckham* p.145
36. G 12.2.05 (Poole)
37. VB p.257
38. VB p.243
39. VB p.448
40. S 30.8.03

CHAPTER 9. MARRIAGE CRISIS

1. Netflix, *Beckham* episode 3
2. SM 14.9.03 (Todd)
3. G 21.8.03
4. NoW 21.9.03
5. S 25.9.03
6. NoW 2.11.03
7. DM 1.11.03 & 29.11.03 (Wansell)
8. S 3.9.03
9. S 22.9.03 (Newton)
10. Times 2.12.08
11. Times 2.12.08, quoting VB autobiography
12. DM 26.5.07 (Boshoff)
13. DB p.423
14. DB p.111
15. NoW 4.4.04 (Thurlbeck); S 5.4.04
16. S 5.4.04; SM 11.4.04; NoW 18.4.04
17. NoW 18.4.04
18. MailOnline 21.5.20, article number 7701589
19. VB pp.301, 308, 316
20. NoW 4.4.04
21. NoW 28.9.03
22. SM 28.9.03 (Todd); NoW 28.9.03; NoW 28.9.03 (Atkinson)
23. NoW 28.9.03
24. NoW 28.9.03
25. SM 11.4.04 (Todd)
26. S 30.9.03 (Worden)
27. NoW 1.5.04 (Gibson – sent mistakenly to her phone)
28. SM 11.4.04 (Todd)
29. Neville Thurlbeck *Tabloid Secrets* p.245

CHAPTER 10. WRECKAGE

1. S 5.4.04
2. SM 26.10.03
3. SM 5.10.03
4. NoW 26.10.03

5. SM 26.10.03 (Todd)
6. ES 14.4.04
7. New Idea 31.12.13
8. S 3.11.03 (Worden)
9. Mail 8.11.03
10. S 15.11.03; DM 8.11.23
11. SM 9.11.03 (Hyland)
12. S 8.4.06; S 2.11.07
13. S 10.11.03 (Newton)
14. SM 9.11.03
15. S 17.11.03; SM 11.4.04
16. Campaign 28.11.03
17. SM 12.12.04 (Todd); NoW 24.10.04 (Loos)
18. NoW 4.4.04; S 20.12.03
19. NoW 4.4.04; S 20.12.03
20. Parkinson interview, broadcast 29.11.03
21. SM 2.11.03
22. S 18.12.03; NoW 14.12.03
23. S 20.12.03 & S 24.12.03
24. S 5.1.04
25. NoW 11.1.04
26. https://www.theguardian.com/football/2004/may/26/newsstory.sport3
27. S 30.8.03
28. Tel 24.10.03
29. DB p.445
30. S 15.10.03; SM 19.10.03
31. Ind 16.10.03 (Worden)
32. Unofficial partner podcast with Richard Gillis 2020
33. NoW 18.4.04
34. SM 1.10.00 (Hyland)

CHAPTER 11. DARKEST HOUR

1. G 29.12.03
2. SM 30.11.03; Carlin p.325
3. SM 15.2.04
4. NoW 22.2.04
5. S 24.2.04
6. SM 14.3.04; SM 28.3.04
7. NoW 1.5.04 (Gibson)
8. S 9.4.04
9. NoW 14.3.04
10. Morton p.192
11. Smith p.153
12. NoW 4.4.04
13. Thurlbeck p.260
14. James Hanning with Glenn Mulcaire *The News Machine* p.105

15. Mir 25.4.05
16. DB p.471
17. NoW 18.4.04 (Singh)
18. SM 18.4.04 (Todd)
19. DB pp.470, 472
20. SM 18.4.04 (Todd)
21. NoW 18.4.04
22. NoW 18.4.04
23. S 5.4.04
24. S 6.4.04
25. VB p.431
26. S 6.4.04
27. Mark Frith *The Celeb Diaries* p.158; VB p.304
28. VB p.9
29. NoW 18.4.04 (Singh)
30. SM 11.4.04 (Malone)
31. DB p.145; Morton p.16
32. S 9.4.04
33. SM 25.4.04
34. NoW 6.6.04, Spanish TV interview

CHAPTER 12. ALONE

1. S 12.4.04 (Newton)
2. S 13.4.04
3. ES 14.4.04
4. Mir 18.4.04 (Malone)
5. S 14.4.04 (Moore)
6. S 17.4.04 (Newton)
7. *Sunday People* 18.4.04
8. S 19.4.04
9. SM 2.5.05 (Todd)
10. NoW 23.5.04; S 24.5.04; *Marie Claire* (May 2004); W magazine
11. SM 25.4.04 (Todd)
12. Carlin p.329
13. Grant Wahl *The Beckham Experiment* p.38
14. S 21.10.05
15. VB p.222
16. https://companycheck.co.uk/company/OC308659/INGENIOUS-FILM
-PARTNERS-LLP/companies-house-data https://www.accountancydaily.co
/client-public-eye-accounting-fame https://companycheck.co.uk/company
/OC308659/INGENIOUS-FILM-PARTNERS-LLP/companies-house-data

CHAPTER 13. LAST CHANCE

1. S 13.5.04
2. S 27.5.04

3. SM 27.6.04 (Todd)
4. S 15.6.04; S 24.5.04; *Marie Claire* (May 2004)
5. SM 23.5.04
6. S 17.5.04; SM 4.7.04
7. SM 12.10.04
8. DB p.318
9. *Vanity Fair* (July 2004); NoW 23.5.04; SM 7.4.06
10. SM 10.5.05
11. S 20.11.04
12. SM 4.7.04 (Todd & Kerins)
13. SM 30.5.04
14. S 26.5.04 (Custis)
15. NoW 12.10.03
16. SM 27.6.04 (Todd)
17. S 14.6.04
18. SM 13.6.04
19. S 5.7.04
20. S 26.6.04
21. S 26.4.04; SM 27.6.04
22. SM 27.6.04
23. SM 4.7.04 (Todd & Kerins)
24. S 5.7.04; SM 27.6.04
25. NoW 4.7.04
26. SM 27.6.04 (Todd); NoW 7.11.04; S 3.7.04
27. NoW 1.8.04
28. NoW 16.5.07
29. S 2.7.04; S 14.9.04
30. S 6.7.04 (Newton)
31. S 6.7.04
32. SM 1.8.04 (Todd)
33. NoW 25.7.04

CHAPTER 14. SEX SCANDAL

1. DM 19.7.04
2. S 31.7.04
3. *Vanity Fair* (July 2004)
4. SM 12.10.04
5. NoW 12.9.04
6. S 22.4.06
7. Mir 29.9.18 (Boshoff)
8. SM 2.5.05 (Todd)
9. NoW 1.5.05, 8.5.05 court hearing
10. S 3.11.04 (Newton)
11. NoW 1.5.05, 8.5.05 court hearing
12. S 22.9.04

13. SM 26.9.04; S 1.10.04 (Newton); SM 10.10.04 (Todd)
14. S 5.10.04, quoting *Gala* magazine; S 7.10.04 (Newton)
15. SM 3.10.04 (Todd)
16. SM 10.10.04
17. S 12.10.04
18. NoW 17.10.04
19. SM 12.12.04 (Todd); NoW 24.10.04 (Loos)
20. SM 13.8.00
21. S 13.10.04 (Howard)
22. S 13.10.04 (Howard); S 16.10.04 (Kelly)
23. S 22.10.04
24. S 18.11.04 (Howard)
25. S 22.11.04 (Beauchamp)
26. S 22.11.04
27. NoW 17.10.04
28. NoW 5.12.04
29. SM 14.11.04
30. S 2 & 3.11.04
31. S 12.11.04
32. NoW 12.4.05
33. SM 14.11.04 (Todd)
34. NoW 28.11.04
35. SM 12.12.04 (Todd)
36. SM 9.3.05 (Todd)
37. SM 9.3.05 (Todd)
38. NoW 5.12.04
39. SM 20.6.05
40. NoW 1.5.05, 8.5.05 court hearing
41. G 12.2.2005
42. S 24.12.04; NoW 26.12.04; SM 26.12.04

CHAPTER 15. SHAME

1. *PR Week* 11.3.05
2. S 10.7.09
3. SM 10.3.05 (Kerins)
4. S 8.5.05; SM 6.6.05; S 19.6.05
5. NoW 5.6.05
6. SM 10.3.05; S 30.4.05 (Beauchamp)
7. SM 5.5.05 (Todd)
8. NoW 12.4.05 (Singh)
9. SM 25.4.05; NoW 25.4.05; S 27.4.05 (Newton)
10. SM 2.5.05
11. S 27.4.05 (Newton)
12. S 27.4.05
13. S 2.5.05

14. Mir 6.2.17
15. SM 2.5.05 (Todd)
16. Ind 17.6.09
17. S 30.4.05
18. Mir 2.6.06
19. S 2.5.05
20. S 2.5.05
21. S 19.4 04; S 3.7.04
22. NoW 18.4.04
23. S 27.9.14
24. S 12.5.05
25. S 19.9.05
26. SM 21.8.05 reporting *Chic* magazine
27. SM 15.8.05
28. S 7.6.05 (Newton)
29. S 28.6.05; SM 3.7.05
30. NoW 31.8.06
31. S 19.8.05
32. S 14.9.05
33. S 13.10.05
34. S 17.1.06
35. S 3.2.06
36. S 21.10.05
37. S 23.1.06; S 29.1.06
38. SM 4.6.06
39. S 22.4.06
40. S 9.4.06
41. S 27.10.05; S3.11.05 (Newton); NoW 22.12.05
42. NoW 20.4.06; S 9.5.06; S 11.5.06
43. S 21.10.05; NoW 8.2.06; S 15.2.06 (Newton); S 27.2.06 (Newton)
44. S 23.12.05

CHAPTER 16. DOWNFALL

1. SM 17.12.06
2. S 23.5.06
3. SM 17.7.05 (Todd); NoW 24.5.06
4. S 23.5.06
5. S 31.5.06
6. SM 11.6.06
7. S 4.5.08
8. SM 10.12.06
9. S 22.6.06
10. SM 2.7.06 (Malone)
11. SM 2.7.06
12. S 27.6.06

13. NoW 6.7.06
14. NoW 6.7.06
15. S 4.7.06
16. DM 3.7.06
17. S 3.3.07 (Sean Custis)
18. Parkinson interview (December 2007)
19. S 4.7.06
20. S 13.8.07
21. S 13.8.06 (Newton)
22. SM 12.1.03
23. S 17.8.06
24. S 13.8.06; S 17.8.06
25. NoW 26.10.06; S 28.9.06
26. NoW 22.11.06 (Kastrinakis)
27. S 21.9.06, quoting GMTV interview
28. S 8.10.06 (Beauchamp); SM 22.10.06
29. S 1.11.06
30. SM 2.7.06; SM 13.4.06, quoting Australian *Harper's Bazaar*
31. SM 13.4.06, quoting Australian *Harper's Bazaar*; S 25.11.06, quoting GMTV interview
32. SM 12.11.06
33. Morton p.155
34. S 2.11.06
35. S 23.8.06
36. Apple 'Business of Fashion' podcast 2022
37. S 26.8.06
38. S 14.9.06
39. S 1.9.06
40. S 2.11.06
41. *Women's Wear Daily* 10.6.18
42. S 2.1.07

CHAPTER 17. SALVAGE

1. NoW 6.6.07; NoW 22.11.06; S 9.9.06; S 12.12.06
2. NoW 15 & 22.11.06
3. NoW 27.9.06
4. Mir 11.1.07
5. Wahl p.34, quoting *Forbes* magazine
6. Mir 11.1.07
7. Mir 12.1.07
8. Mir 12.1.07 (Holt)
9. S 16.1.07
10. S 16.1.07 (Beauchamp); S 21.1.07
11. S 17.1.07 (Beauchamp); Mir 12.1.07 (Holt)
12. S 19.1.07 (Beauchamp); S 20.1.07 (Beauchamp)
13. SM 1.4.07

14. S 16.6.07
15. S 16.1.07; SM 14.1.07 (Kerins)
16. S 25.1.07
17. S 22.7.07 (Newton)
18. S 7.2.09 (Kelly)
19. S 28.2.07; Mir 28.2.07 (Hedley); S 2.3.07
20. S 13.2.07 (Beauchamp)
21. S 12.10.06
22. S 3.3.07
23. Mir 26.5.07; SM 27.5.07
24. NoW 30.5.07
25. Mir 30.5.07 (Holt)
26. SM 3.6.07
27. SM 3.6.07
28. SM 15.10.06 (Todd); Mir 19.1.07 (Hedley)
29. Mir 28.2.07 (Hedley)
30. SM 11.3.07; S 16.5.07
31. Mir 1.3.07 (Hedley)
32. Mir 1.3.07 (Hedley)
33. S 16.5.07; Mir 9.6.07
34. Mir 21.5.07
35. SM 13.8.00
36. https://www.straight.com/article-88444/silver-jeans-heat-up-with-label
-1921-and-a-spice-girl
37. S 9.6.07 (Custis)
38. S 13.6.07; S 27.4.07 (Beauchamp)
39. S 16.6.07
40. DM 26.5.07 (Boshoff)
41. NoW 6.6.07 (Harrison)
42. Mir 23.6.07
43. SM 1.7.07; NoW 18.7.07
44. Mir 4.5.07 (Hadley & Simpson)
45. Mir 23.7.07; Mir 28.6.07
46. S 22.7.07; Mir 30.6.07; S 30.6.07
47. S 17.11.06
48. S 17.7.07
49. DM 8.2.16
50. https://www.greg.gg/webCompSearchDetails.aspx?id=s0jrWx8s2SE=&r
=0&crn=&cn=Frantzen%20Partners&rad=ContainsPhrase&ck=False
51. Confidential source
52. Confidential source

CHAPTER 18. PHONY

1. VB p.487
2. S 17.7.07
3. Mir 30.5.07

4. S 22.6.07
5. S 7.6.07 (Newton); Mir 9.6.07
6. DM 26.5.07 (Boshoff)
7. NoW 16.4.08
8. NoW 23.1.11 (Malone)
9. Mir 1.6.07 (Hedley)
10. SM 15.7.07; S 2.8.07
11. Mir 24.7.07; Mir 16.7.07 (Hedley)
12. DM 28.9.07 (Boshoff)
13. S 21.7.07
14. SM 22.7.07
15. https://www.theguardian.com/culture/tvandradioblog/2007/jul/18/victoriabeckhamcomingtoame
16. SM 6.12.10; SM 29.7.07; Mir 17.8.07
17. S 22.7.07 (Newton); S 1.8.07
18. Mir 13.7.07; S 15.6.07; Mir 15.9.09
19. S 22.7.07 (Newton)
20. Wahl p.3; S 17.7.07 (Smith)
21. (Sold in 2018 for $33 million) Mir 8.6.07
22. Mir 14.7.07 (Hadley)
23. DM 28.9.07 (Boshoff)
24. S 18.10.07

CHAPTER 19. AGONY

1. Mir 16.7.07; SM 15.7.07
2. S 18.7.07
3. Mir 19.6.07
4. SM 15.7.07
5. S 22.7.07
6. Wahl p.74
7. Mir 19.7.07; S 20.7.07
8. S 24.7.07
9. S 18.8.07; Mir 20.8.07
10. Mir 31.8.07; DM 28.9.07 (Boshoff)
11. S 24.10.07
12. Mir 19.11.07
13. Wahl p.81 & p.97
14. Wahl p.176
15. Wahl p.140
16. DM 25.10.08 (Boshoff)
17. G 19.5.08
18. Mir 12.9.07
19. NoW 29.8.07 (Atkinson)
20. S 21.12.08; SM 19.10.08
21. Mir 29.9.07

22. Mir 9.10.07; S 27.10.07
23. NoW 21.11.07
24. SM 11.11.07
25. SM 18.11.07
26. Mir 26.11.07; S 29.11.07
27. S 30.11.07, quoting NoW
28. Mir 21.11.07; S 21.11.07
29. S 23.11.07; NoW 28.11.07
30. Mir 28.11.07
31. Mir 24.11.07; SM 23.12.07
32. S 15.11.07; Mir 27.11.07
33. S 3.11.12
34. S 30.11.07; NoW 28.11.07 (Singh)
35. SM 02.12.07; Mir 19.10.07
36. DM 28.9.07 (Boshoff)
37. SM 25.11.07
38. Mir 3.12.07 (Hedley & Simpson); SM 7.4.06
39. S 20.1.207; Mir 17.1.08; Mir 21.12.07; S 14.5.08 (Smart)

CHAPTER 20. CHEAPSKATE

1. Wahl p.151
2. Wahl p.221
3. *The Grocer* 17.10.09
4. *The Grocer* 17.10.09
5. file://C:/Users/tombo/AppData/Local/Microsoft/Windows/INetCache/Content.Outlook/QQR557G8/The_%20Grocer%2017102009.pdf https://www.easier.com /29272-david-beckham-academy-findus-launch-megao3.html https://www.thegrocer.co.uk/sainsburys/its-goldenballs-just-don't-mention-those-fish-fingers-/223408.article
6. Mir 1.2.08 (McGovern)
7. Mir 1.2.08 (Holt)
8. S 2.2.08
9. Mir 9.1.08
10. S 5.2.08 (Howard)
11. S 28.3.08; Mir 10.3.08
12. Mir 10.3.08
13. S 1.4.08
14. S 6.4.08
15. S 17.10.09; NoW 6.2.08; SM 10.2.08
16. S 2.3.08
17. S 14.3.02
18. *Vogue* (April 2008); S 23.9.08 (Newton)
19. *Harper's Bazaar* (October 2009)
20. Mir 24.1.08 (Turner)
21. Mir 3.8.09 (Moodie)

22. Mir 7.5.08; Mir 14.5.08 (Moodie)
23. Confidential source
24. *Times* 2.12.08
25. Samantha Conti https://wwd.com/wwd-masthead/samantha-conti/ https://wwd.com/runway/fall-2023/paris/victoria-beckham/review/
26. VB p.375
27. Mir 11.9.08 (Ward); S 10.9.08 (Kelly)
28. S 26.5.10 (Connolly); Times 29.6.10 (Armstrong)
29. *Times* 2.12.08 (Armstrong)
30. S 30.8.08 (Smart); NoW 28.9.08
31. Mir 14.5.08 (Moodie)
32. Mir 27.7.08
33. S 23.4.08 (Smart); S 30.5.08
34. Mir 27.7.08
35. S 24.9.08
36. S 14.6.08
37. Mir 20.9.09 reporting Whoopi Goldberg interview
38. https://www.allure.com/story/victoria-beckham-cover-story
39. S 29.9.08
40. S 17.10.09; NoW 30.11.08
41. S 16.6.10 (Smart)
42. S 5.7.08
43. 2008 BBL accounts
44. S 23.1.10

CHAPTER 21. MORE CAPS
1. S 24.6.08 (Howard)
2. S 11.7.08
3. Wahl p.272
4. Wahl pp.254, 263
5. Wahl p.280
6. S 22.9.08
7. Wahl p. 264
8. Mir 29.6.08 (Moodie)
9. Mir 5.2.09; NoW 15.2.09
10. SM 6.7.08
11. NoW 15.2.09
12. S 27.1.09
13. S 7.3.09
14. SM 29.3.09 (Bobby Charlton won 106 caps for England)
15. S 11.6.09
16. *Times* 29.11.23
17. S 4.5.09 (Smart)
18. Mir 31.10.09
19. S 11.8.09; Mir 18.3.08

20. NoW 5.7.09
21. S 17.6.09 (White)
22. Mir 30.12.09
23. Mir 1.10.09

CHAPTER 22. FOOLED

1. S 17.10.09 (Smart)
2. NoW 10.1.10
3. NoW 8.11.09
4. S 14.11.09
5. S 4.12.09
6. S 16.1.10 (White)
7. Mir 16.2.10; Mir 11.3.10; SM 24.1.10; S 26.1.10; S 11.3.10
8. S 22.01.10
9. Mir 14.1.10 (Moodie); Mir 18.1.10; Mir 6.8.09; NoW 16.8.09
10. S 24.3.10; Mir 25.3.10
11. S 16.1.10 (White); S 2.4.10 (White); S 8.4.10 (White); S 2.6.10 (White)
12. NoW 11.7.10
13. Mir 10.9.10 (Hudson)
14. S 7.10.10; S 9.10.10, quoting *Marie Claire*
15. Mir 17.5.10
16. S 13.8.10 (White & Custis); SM 15.8.10
17. S 21.12.10; S 23.12.10
18. S 25.9.10 (White)
19. S 16.2.11; S 11.4.11; SM 21.2.11
20. Mir 7.12.15
21. Mir 2.6.14
22. Mir 2.6.14
23. SM 12.12.10; DM 17.9.10 (Venice massage parlour)
24. S 2.7.12
25. S 23.9.08; NoW 6.6.10

CHAPTER 23. MIXED MESSAGES

1. DM 13.8.10; NoW 23.5.10
2. https://podcasts.apple.com/us/podcast/ruthies-table-4-david-beckham
-part-1/id1585413971?i=1000549627692
3. S 13.8.10
4. S 16.8.11
5. C:\Users\tombo\AppData\Local\Microsoft\Windows\INetCache\Content
.Outlook\QQR557G8\C7F55BIC-95BA-4104-B1F7-39A9A34B58E6(002).png
6. S 16.8.11; Tel 21.1.12; Harper's Bazaar (May 2012)
7. SM 19.9.10
8. *Times* 16.1.10
9. S 29.11.11
10. S 29.3.12; Mir 20.1.13 (Moodie); Mir 29.4.13

11. Mir 29.4.13

12. S 13.8.13; SM 3.2.13; Mir 28.1.13; *Elle* magazine (May 2012); *Harper's Bazaar* (May 2012)

13. SM 7.7.11; S 8.8.11

14. SM 12.2.12; S 20.12.10; SM 5.2.11; S 26.12.18 (Wootton)

15. DM 1.6.13 (Boshoff)

16. Mir 26.2.12

17. S 13.9.14; Mir 25.10.14

18. S 12.7.11 (Samson & White)

19. https://www.motor1.com/news/173852/evoque-designer-slams-victori -beckham/

20. SM 19.2.12

21. *Der Spiegel* (August 2013); S 6.2.17

22. S 23.11.11

23. NoW 4.1.11

24. MoS 11.11.18

25. SM 15.4.12; Mir 8.1.13

26. S 3.12.12

27. Mir 2.12.12

28. S 6.12.12

29. https://www.fourfourtwo.com/features/who-owns-psg-everything-you -need-to-know-about-paris-saint-germains-qatari-chiefs

30. Mir 1.2.13

31. https://wwd.com/feature/bruce-rockowitz-global-brands-group -10343769/#!

32. GQ 3.3.19

33. Mir 7.2.13

34. Mir 2.3.13; Mir 5.3.13; S 2.3.13

35. Mir 9.11.13; Mir 29.1.14

36. https://www.bloomberg.com/news/articles/2022-02-12/super-bowl-ad -lawsuit-hits-delivery-agent-david-beckham-underwear Mir 16.3.13

37. Mir 21.3.13; Mir 21.6.13

38. S 24.1.13 (White)

39. SM 31.3.13

40. Mir 4.4.13

41. Mir 17.5.13

42. S 18.5.13 (White)

43. Mir 4.4.13

44. Mir 7.5.13; SM 9.5.13; S 20.5.13

45. Mir 31.10.13

CHAPTER 24. KNIGHTHOOD

1. *Der Spiegel* (August 2013)

2. S 10.11.13

3. Mir 10.12.13; S 30.11.13; Paris *Vogue* (November 2013)

4. SM 20.11.13
5. S 9.7.14; Football Leaks: Black Sea EIC2016 (3.2.17)
6. S 6.10.13 (White); DM 16.8.16
7. S 9.8.12 (Smart); Morton p.155
8. MoS 5.2.17 (Hind)
9. Mir 30.12.13
10. S 4.2.17; Mir 30.12.13; S 26.12.18 (Wootton)
11. Mir 9.4.14
12. S 4.2.17
13. S 4.2.17
14. S 16.3.15
15. S 13.4.14 (White); S 29.4.14
16. S 4.2.17
17. Mir 11.6.14; Mir 26.10.15
18. *Der Spiegel* 2015; Football Leaks: Black Sea EIC2016 (3.2.17)
19. S 7.2.17
20. DM 17.6.15
21. Football Leaks: Black Sea EIC2116 (3.2.17)

CHAPTER 25. FASHION FOLLIES

1. Mir 19.2.14; *Allure* magazine (March 2014)
2. S 12.3.16 (White)
3. Mir 9.10.15; S 26.9.14; G 24.9.14; S 18.2.15
4. S 24.12.14 (Wootton)
5. S 28.10.14
6. S 17.3.19, quoting FT 16.3.19
7. S 13.6.15; Mir 17.3.15
8. Mir 19.2.14; *Allure* magazine (March 2014); Mir 10.7.14; *Vogue* (July 2014)
9. ST 16.4.23
10. S 11.2.13
11. Mir 17.4.14 (Moodie)
12. G 28.1.14
13. https://www.google.com/gasearch?q=victoria%20beckham/keep%20fit%20routine&tbm=&source=sh/x/gs/m2/5
14. S 1.9.15; S 17.10.22
15. S 17.9.15 (Wootton); S 29.9.15 (Wootton); S 4.8.15
16. S 9.12.15
17. S 17.2.13
18. G 9.2.14 (Cartner-Morley)
19. S 4.11.14; S 10.9.15 (Fahey); S 10.1.15; S 12.9.15
20. *Harper's Bazaar* (May 2012); Mir 11.11.14; S 25.11.14
21. S 4.1.03; S 29.1.15 (Wootton); Mir 27.2.15; Mir 7.12.15
22. Mir 7.12.15; S 2.5.15 (White); Mir 4.5.15 https://www.chinadaily.com.cn/celebrity/2015-05/04/content_20614224_2.htm

23. SM 16.8.15; S 25.11.14; Mir 12.1.19; S 8.8.15 (Wootton); S 10.9.16; S 15.9.15; S 22.12.15 (White)

24. S 9.12.15

25. S 4.2.17

26. S 15.9.15

27. S 23.9.15

28. S 22.9.15 (Wootton); S 27.9.15 (Brankin); S 15.11.15; Mir 13.11.15; DM 26.9.15

29. S 19.11.15

30. G 18.4.19; Mir 7.10.15; *Grazia* magazine (October 2015)

31. S 10.11.15 (Wootton)

32. *Glamour* 29.10.15; Cl 6.6.23

33. Victoria Moss, 13.11.15; S 25.5.98

34. *Glamour* 9.11.15

35. S 1.1.16; S 15.11.15

CHAPTER 26. COUNTDOWN

1. S 10.2.16; SM 14.2.16

2. S 23.3.16; S 20.3.16; S 11.2.16; S 1.5.16; S 3.5.16

3. S 12.4.16; SM 14.2.16 (Boyle)

4. S 12.4.16 (Wootton)

5. S 26.2.16 (Wootton); SM 6.3.16; S 20.5.16; S 15.6.16; S 6.7.16; S 13.9.16; S 10.2.16; Mir 19.8.16 (McPhee, Watts); S 13.12.16; S 2.9.16 (Wootton); MoS 21.7.19; DM 12.7.16 (Boshoff)

6. S 14.9.16; S 7.12.16; S 8.12.16; MoS 4.8.19

7. Mir 15.4.16 (Retter)

8. Mir 2.9.16, quoting *Vogue*; Netflix 2023

9. Mir 3.10.16, quoting *InStyle*; VB p.516

10. Times 15.2.16

11. Times 12.9.16

12. G 12.9.16

13. *Times* 12.9.16

14. S 17.3.19, quoting FT 16.3.19; S 12.3.16 (White)

15. E.g. in BBH's 2016 accounts, the accruals increased by £541,000. And see Note 30 of the accounts, which lists four material changes. One change in the 2017 accounts is tacked on as a sub-note to 'Tangible Fixed Assets'.

16. https://www.leaguescup.com/news/inter-miami-cf-and-david-beckham-s-role-from-foundation-to-glory-in-five-years; Beckham, St John's Wood speech, 2.7.23

17. https://edition.cnn.com/2013/10/30/sport/football/football-david-beckham-club-owner/index.html#

18. *SportsPro* 29.1.20

19. S 15.12.13; Mir 3.6.14; S 5.12.15; htps://www.intermiami.news/club/stadium/ https://www.sportsbusinessjournal.com/Articles/2023/08/04/ares-management-inter-miami-investment.as https://intermiami.news/club/ https://

www.intermiami.news/club/club-history/ https://www.espn.com/soccer/story
/_/id/37544133/mls-announces-david-beckham-expansion-team-miami https://
www.ft.com/content/5d55d1fa-727d-11e9-bbfb-5c68069fbd15 https://www
.intermiami.news/club/trphy-history/

20. https://youtu.be/0E2G7YLIWDo?si=4eBbcg_35JHuzXBq https://www
.bloomberg.com/news/videos/2015-03-27/global-brands-focused-on-affordable
-luxury-brands-ceo http://mobile.ytsports.cn/news-520.html https://youtu.be
/2KoROgp2Rq4?si=gYCn1i_lx7Xx4VRP https://www.scmp.com/magazines
/post-magazine/fashion/article/2027452/why-david-and-victoria-beckham-have
-thing-hong-kong

21. BBH's profits increased from £10 million to £31 million and Footwork's
profits were £11.4 million.

22. https://www.bloomberg.com/news/videos/2015-08-12/rockowitz-china-s
-move-positive-for-global-brands-ltd-

23. https://wwd.com/feature/bruce-rockowitz-global-brands-group-1034
3769/#!

24. https://youtu.be/0E2G7YLIWDo?si=4eBbcg 35JHuzXBq https://youtu
.be/0E2G7YLIWDo?si=4eBbcg 35JHuzXBq https://www.bloomberg.com/news
/videos/2015-08-12/rockowitz-china-s-move-positive-for-global-brands-ltd-
http://mobile.ytsports.cn/news-520.html https://www.youtube.com/@
CNBCInternationalTV

25. S 20.3.16; S 31.3.16; S 22.12.16; S 8.1.17
26. GQ 17.3.16
27. S 26.9.97
28. S 29.1.17

CHAPTER 27. THE STORM

1. SM 5.2.17; MoS 22.10.17 (Hind)
2. Mir 10.2.17
3. S 6.2.17
4. P.58 Global Brands 2019 annual report
5. SM 10.12.17; S 12.2.17; S 22.7.17 (Wootton)
6. S 14.3.17; S 29.12.16; S 20.4.17
7. S 10.5.17; S 14.5.17; S 21.5.17; S 27.5.17; S 17 & 18.10.17
8. S 15.5.17; S 16.5.17
9. Mir 12.7.17; Mir 19.7.22
10. Mir 26.4.07 (Hadley & Simpson); S 2.9.17
11. See interview, S 17.10.17
12. Notes 17 & 32 BBH 2017 accounts show benefit of Entrepreneurs
Allowance Relief, and CGT at 20 per cent rather than 45 per cent income tax
13. G 19.1.17 (Cartner-Morley)
14. Times 11.9.17
15. Mir 31.12.17
16. https://www.bloomberg.com/news/videos/2015-03-27/global-brands
-focused-on-affordable-luxury-brands-ceo

17. G 8.1.18
18. S 13.10.19; S 27.4.20
19. G 2.9.17
20. G 2.9.17; https://wwd.com/beauty-industry-news/fragrance/coty
-architects-bernd-beetz-and-stephen-mormoris-start-a-new-fragrance-business
-1203131132/
21. S 8.9.17; S 5.9.17
22. https://www.chinadaily.com.cn/celebrity/2015-05/04/content_20614224
_2.htm http://www.china.org.cn/arts/2015-05/04/content_35481625_3.htm
https://www.scmp.com/magazines/post-magazine/article/1512660/six-degrees
https://www.hollywoodreporter.com/news/music-news/ricky-martin-david
-beckham-coco-699490/ https://www.thestandard.com.hk/section-news/section
/11/256329/Husband's-'affair'-triggered-Coco's-downward-spiral
23. https://www.harveynichols.com/news/feature/house-99-by-david
-beckham/ https://www.harveynichols.com/news/feature/house-99-by-david
-beckham/
24. Mir 28.11.17; S 8.3.18
25. *Women's Wear Daily* 19.6.18 (Conti)
26. MoS 1.4.18
27. MoS 30.12.18
28. Mir 18.1.18
29. G 12.2.18
30. S 4.2.18; S 5.2.18 (Wootton)
31. S 6.2.19
32. MoS 14.10.18 (Hind)
33. S 2.2.18 (Wootton); Mir 9.2.18; S 12.2.18 (Wootton); S 7.3.18
(Wootton)
34. *Times* 12.2.18 (Murphy)
35. *Times* 18.2.19 (Murphy)
36. C:\Users\tombo\AppData\Local\Microsoft\Windows\INetCache\Content.
Outlook\QQR557G8\HotelShangri-La Santa Monica Relaunches its Famous
Rooftop Bar ONYX (002).png
37. G 18.4.18; G 4.3.18
38. S 8.3.18
39. https://edition.cnn.com/2013/10/30/sport/football/football-david
-beckham-club-owner/index.html https://www.cnn.com/2013/05/18/sport
/football/football-psg-beckham-farewell-game/
40. SportsPro 14.12.17
41. S 27.2.20
42. https://sportslulu.com/inter-miami-owners-percentaghttps://www
.miamiherald.com/sports/article254311828.html
43. SportsPro 29.1.20
44. G 30.1.18
45. G 11.5.18
46. S 1.5.18; S 5.5.18 (Wootton)

CHAPTER 28. WARFARE

1. M 5.1.19; DM 12.1.19 (Boshoff)
2. DM 9.6.18
3. DM 5.9.18 (Boshoff)
4. Mir 11.6.18
5. S 18.7.20
6. S 21.6.18; S 5.8.18; S 21.10.18 (Moodie)
7. SM 10.6.18
8. S 24.6.18; S 2.9.18
9. MoS 12.8.18
10. S 10.9.18 (Boyle); S 4.9.18 (Wootton)
11. MoS 9.9.18 (Hind)
12. https://www.dailymail.co.uk/tvshowbiz/article-6129603/Victoria-David-Beckham-star-second-VOGUE-cover-dismissing-split.html
13. https://www.nzherald.co.nz/entertainment/why-david-beckham-refused-to-pose-for-vogue-cover-family-shot/2FW7O6LNZ2CKZWRC26ZBTWZZE/ July 2018
14. S 29.6.18; S 6.7.18
15. DM 2.9.18
16. S 10.12.99; S 18.12.99; Morton pp.128ff
17. GQ 3.3.19
18. S 4.10.18; S 7.9.18; S 29.9.18
19. Mir 28.9.18
20. Mir 19.10.18; S 19.10.18
21. S 21.10.18 (Moodie)
22. G 19.1.19 (Cartner-Morley)
23. S 21.10.18 (Moodie)
24. Mir 22.10.18
25. Tom Bower *Revenge* p.237
26. S 17.9.18; BBC Radio 2 interview
27. G 15.9.18; G 17.9.18; S 12.12.18; G 15.9.18
28. *Closer* magazine 30.4.19
29. http://lottejeffs.com/wp-content/uploads/2017/04/Victoria_Interview.pdf

CHAPTER 29. A NEW YEAR

1. DM 27.4.19
2. S 30.12.18 (Moodie); S 27.1.19 (Moodie)
3. https://www.ft.com/content/006d1bb6-0d40-11ea-b2d6-9bf4d1957a67
4. MoS 17.6.18 (Hind)
5. Acted according to Chapter 10 of part 17 of Companies Act 2006
6. S 11.5.19
7. GQ 3.3.19
8. MoS 4.11.18 (Hind)
9. https://find-and-update.company-information.service.gov.uk/company/11043864/persons-with-significant-control

10. Beckham, St John's Wood speech, 2.7.23
11. GQ 3.3.19
12. GQ 3.3.19
13. S 1.2.19. Inter Miami appoint Kin to get sponsorship sales. Kin is Oliveira and Matthew Kay.
14. DB Instagram, ING7333
15. GQ 3.3.19
16. https://www.youtube.com/watch?v=bF014EUJrSI
17. G 19.1.19 (Cartner-Morley)
18. G 19.1.19 (Cartner-Morley)
19. S 26.1.19; S 3.2.19
20. S 16.1.19; G 18.1.19
21. S 8.2.20; Vogue 20.8.20 (Devaney); S 17.1.19
22. S 29.12.19 (Moodie); S 29.3.20 (Moodie); MoS 6.10.19 (Hind)
23. http://lottejeffs.com/wp-content/uploads/2017/04/Victoria_Interview.pdf
24. G 18.2.19; S 20.2.19
25. S 6.1.19; S 12.3.19; S 14.7.18; S 12.1.20
26. S 17.3.19, quoting FT: S 3.7.19; S 21.7.19 (Moodie)
27. G 30.11.19
28. S 10.5.19
29. S 8.3.19 (Wootton)
30. S 14.10.18 (Moodie); DM 23.5.19
31. SM 11.11.18; S 3.11.18 (Wootton)
32. S 2.6.20; S 7.4.21; S 14.6.19; S 8.10.19; S 31.3.19; S 5.5.19; S 17.5.19 (Moodie); S 20.5.19 (Wootton); Mir 19.6.19; DM 23 & 26.3.19 (Boshoff)
33. S 10.7.19 (Boyle); S 3.11.19 Moodie; Mir 23.7.19 (Hudson)
34. S 26.5.19 (Moodie); S 3.11.19 (Moodie); MoS 16.6.19 (Hind)
35. https://www.allure.com/story/victoria-beckham-cover-story
36. Mir 5.9.19; S 10.8.19; S 27.8.19; SM 1.9.19
37. MoS 19.4.20
38. S 29.11.19
39. Mir 29.8.20; S 24.8.20 (Boyle)
40. Imogen Edwards-Jones *Fashion Babylon* (re Tom Ford wanting to stop VB wearing their clothes) https://wwd.com/business-news/business-features/victoria-beckham-profit-beauty-fashion1235561589/#utm_medium=social&utm_source=email&utm_campaign=social_bar&utm_term=wwd.1678184036971.c09855c9-202f-4175-b436-fba1ff4db349&utm_content=bottom&utm_id=1235561589
41. https://hiec.com/heads-up-with-marie-leblanc-ceo-victoria-beckham/
42. S 26.01.20 (Moodie)
43. Mir 20.4.20 (Kindon)

CHAPTER 30. MIAMI

1. Thor Bjorgolfsson *Billions to Bust – and Back* p.84
2. https://www.glistatigenerali.com/capitali_imprenditori/superciuk-lultimo-eroe-vichingo/

3. EIM21895, 6.4.17, Example 4

4. The employer's NIC for social security costs was £596,000. That matches the employee's wages but it is not sufficient to cover the additional employer's NIC charge if Beckham paid the additional NIC on £250,000 income tax for the BIK.

5. Mir 27.8.21

6. https://sbisoccer.com/2020/12/on-mis-mcdonoughs-poor-execution-of -inter-miami-vision-likely-led-to-early-exit https://www.intermiami.news/club /owners/ https://www.intermiami.news/news/

7. S 9.3.20

8. S 17.9.19; S 3.11.19 (Moodie); S 14.11.19; S 9.3.20; S 9.4.20; S 12.7.20 (Moodie); Mir 11.7.20

9. MoS 19.4.20

10. MoS 26.4.20 (Hind)

11. S 1.5.20; Mir 1.5.20; S 22.4.20; S 30.7.20 (Moodie); G 30.7.20; S 21.6.20 (Moodie)

12. *The Athletic*, 9.6.21 & 17.8.21 (Tenario); *Miami Herald*, 26.11.23 & 27.11.23 https://www.sportspromedia.com/news/inter-miami-jorge-jose-mas -david-beckham-shareholders-ares-investment-mls/= https://www.intermiamicf .com/news/inter-miami-cf-announces-mas-brothers-beckham-increase- ownership-stake-in-the-cl https://www.miamiherald.com/sports/mls/article 197169104.html

13. https://www.mlssoccer.com/news/paul-mcdonough-stepping-down-inter -miami-cf-sporting-director

14. Felipe Cardenas 13.11.23; https://theathletic.com/5058191/2023/11/13 /paul-mcdonough-mis-usl/ https://sbisoccer.com/2020/12/on-mis-mcdonoughs -poor-execution-of-inter-miami-vision-likely-led-to-early-exit

15. SM 28.6.20; G 4.7.20; S 20.7.20

16. S 8.2.21

17. David Beckham post at 11.18 a.m. on 9.12.20

18. S 23.1.21

19. G 8.1.21 (Liew)

20. *Miami Herald* 27.2.21

CHAPTER 31. LOSS-MAKING DEALS

1. G 10.9.20; G 27.6.20; https://www.esportznetwork.com/david-beckham -launches-new-company-guild-esports/

2. G 30.11.21

3. https://www.yahoo.com/entertainment/david-beckham-sues-fitness -company-230903752.hyml https://www.businesswire.com/news/home /20220321005376/en/F45-Investor-DavidBeckham-Supports-the-continued -Growth-of-the-Brand-as-Partner-of-the-Latest-UK-Studio-in-High-Street -Kensington https://metro.co.uk/2022/10/20/david-beckham-and-greg-norman -sue-fitness-chain-f45-training-for-20m-17605177/

4. S 5.2.21

5. S 3.11.21 (Moodie)

6. S 28.12.21; S 7.11.21
7. S 18.2.21. In 2021, Victoria Beckham Ltd's accumulated losses were £50.3 million.
8. G 14.1.21
9. Note 13, BBH accounts 2019/20
10. https://chainstoreage.com/authentic-brands-group-acquires-majority-stake-david-beckham-brand https://www.ft.com/content/a0829b2a-e5fb-4e6b-a9c0-142529c0a56d
11. https://finance.yahoo.com/news/abg-jamie-salter-buying-building-050101527.html
12. See Note 4, 2022 returns Footwork Productions Ltd, and filing at Companies House
13. Note 7, 2021 BBH accounts

CHAPTER 32. THE WEDDING

1. *The Athletic* 7.8.21
2. S 4.9.22
3. Mir 27 & 28.10.21
4. DM 10.9.22
5. Tel 31.12.22
6. SM 14.8.22
7. MoS 3.10.21 (Hind)
8. SM 14.11.21; S 13.1.23
9. Mir 10.1.23
10. https://www.laineygossip.com/victoria-beckhams-public-facing-rigidity-revealed-to-be-greatest-skill-in-allure-cover-profile/77345 https://www.allure.com/story/victoria-beckham-cover-story
11. https://www.newidea.com.au/victoria-beckham-new-hell https://www.theguardian.com/fashion/2020/sep/21/victoria-beckham-cancels-catwalk-show-as-not-appropriate https://www.theguardian.com/fashion/2022/jan/14/victoria-beckham-fashion-brand-vb-body https://www.businesswire.com/news/home/20220321005376/en/F45-Investor-David-Beckham-Supports-the-Continued-Growth-of-the-Brand-as-Partner-f-the-Latest-UK-Studio-in-High-Street-Kensington https://metro.co.uk/2022/10/20/david-beckham-and-greg-norman-sue-fitness-chain-f45-training-for-20m-17605177/ https://www.theguardian.com/lifeandstyle/2020/jun13/victoria-beckham-i-guess-it-was-a-sign-of-insecurity-wearing-very-tight-clothes? https://i.guim.co.uk/img/media/e4d95bd8394a17fbd7a4c8e1129b31a4d0a555b6/00-17312941/master/1731.jpg?width=120&quality=85&dpr=1&s=none
12. *Hello!* magazine 7.5.22
13. Mir 11.2.22; DM 26.5.23
14. G 18.8.22; S 18.7.22
15. S 12.4.22 (Moodie)
16. Mir 7.9.22; DM 22.7.2020
17. S 23.9.22; *Grazia* (October 2022)

18. DM 30.9.22 (Boshoff)
19. DM 1.10.22 (Boshoff)
20. S 1.10.22; MoS 2.10.22
21. S 31.10.22; ST 30.10.22
22. Tel 22.3.23 (Armstrong)
23. S 19.1.23; Mir 3.1.23
24. DM 23.2.02 (Boshoff)
25. S 25.8.22; Mir 6.10.22
26. S 19.1.23; Mir 21.1.23
27. MoS 12.6.22
28. S 30.12.21 (Moodie)
29. Mir 9.3.22
30. S 17.9.22

CHAPTER 33. QATAR
1. G 15.11.22; G 18.11.22
2. MoS 18.12.22 (Hind)
3. SM 27.11.22; Mir 19.11.22; SM 27.11.22; Mir 19.11.22; SM 27.11.22; Mir 19.11.22
4. S 3.12.22
5. https://www.miamiherald.com/article282921823.html
6. https://www.mlssoccer.com/news/how-lionel-messi-could-transform-mls-and-clubs-most-likely-sign-him-andrew-wiebe

CHAPTER 34. SMOKE AND MIRRORS
1. https://uk.sports.yahoo.com/news/lionel-messi-no-show-ignites-153904463.html https://www.campaignasia.com/article/tatlers-messi-mess-hong-kong-event-plunges-into-chaos-without-star-player/494175 https://www.dailymail.co.uk/sport/football/article-13043635/David-Beckham-BOOED-40-000-angry-fans-chant-refund-Lionel-Messi-left-bench-Inter-Miamis-pre-season-win-Hong-Kong-XI.html https://www.scmp.com/sport/football/article/3250908/lionel-messis-hong-kong-trip-becomes-greatest-let-down-all-time-goats-day-bench-leaves-inter-miami https://theathletic.com/5249529/2024/02/04/inter-miami-hong-kong-messi/?source=user_shared_article https://www.scmp.com/sport/football/article/3251170/lionel-messi-fiasco-hong-kong-moves-next-stage-grief-social-media https://www.miamiherald.com/sports/mls/inter-miami/article285077787.html?deviceId=D7F6DC20-FB35-42B6-8A9D-B9ADAB179ACC&tempKey=value https://www.ft.com/content/02c035dc-4f8a-4e78-a86e-7811835a9dab
2. https://www.tatlerasia.com/lifestyle/entertainment/david-beckham-october-cover https://www.tatlerasia.com/lifestyle/sports/david-beckham-tatler-xfest-football-match-inter-miami-hong-kong https://www.tatlerasia.com/lifestyle/sports/look-ahead-inter-miami-rise-xfest-match
3. 'Morning Footy' CBS sports podcast, Feb 2 (USA); Podcast: Miami Total Football Radio

4. https://www.youtube.com/watch?v=oOXgTGQJgUE
5. https://theathletic.com/5245193/2024/02/03/inter-miami-tour-messi/?source=user_shared_article
6. https://www.youtube.com/watch?v=SzXsed7RJDY
7. https://uk.sports.yahoo.com/video/hong-kong-sports-minister-assured-082747784.html
8. 15.2.24
9. https://www.scmp.com/video/yonden-lhatoo
10. DM 5.10.23 (Callahan)
11. New Yorker 19.10.23
12. Mir 23.10.23
13. MoS 22.10.23
14. Times 22.3.23
15. VBHL accounts 2022, Note 21, p.34
16. £3.14 million in 2021 to £7.35 million in 2022
17. VBHL accounts 2022, Note 5 shows depreciation of tangible fixed assets as £673,000 but Note 12 states the figure as £766,500. Note 5 states the amortisation of tangible fixed assets was £715,000 but Note 11 states it was £621,500.
18. VBHL accounts 2022, Note 6, p.24, auditors' remuneration
19. Namely, Seven Global LLP
20. DRJBHL 2022 accounts, Note 14, p.33
21. DRJBHL 2022 accounts, Note 9, p.30
22. DRJBHL 2022 accounts, Note 2.11, p.25
23. DBVL 2022 accounts, Note 13, p.24

ACKNOWLEDGEMENTS

Writing unauthorised biographies has become a speciality of mine. The research followed a predictable pattern. Inevitably, many people associated with the Beckhams were told not to speak to me. I did not trouble to ask the Beckhams for an interview. Over the past 30 years, both have given hundreds of interviews. In their hyper-guarded operation they try to control both the message and their media profile. They were certain to deny access to an independent writer.

Discovering the truth while denied access to the subject of the book depends on the trust of reliable witnesses and the determination to unearth what, for different reasons, has been concealed. Fortunately, many agreed to help on condition of anonymity.

In writing this book, no one was more important than Claudia Wordsworth, an outstanding, determined researcher and an invaluable guide to previously untold aspects of this extraordinary story. As always, Claudia exceeded all expectations. I owe her a great debt.

At the outset of the research I consulted a remarkable group of journalists – all experts on all aspects of the Beckhams' lives. Over the years, very often to the Beckhams' fury, they have written exposés for the tabloids. Generously, they filled in what was missing from the published record, confirmed their published stories and pointed me in the right directions. Naturally, many of their names appear in the book, but I won't thank them individually.

Many others gave me information and asked not to be named. Indeed, this book was noteworthy for the number of people who asked to remain anonymous. Clearly, I am indebted to all of them.

I was fortunate that Alan Samson, an outstanding publisher, agreed to edit the manuscript. Alan surpassed expectations, not least thanks to his remarkable expertise in football.

As always, I am especially grateful to my loyal agent Jonathan Lloyd of Curtis Brown, an outstanding friend and ally.

My publishers have been hugely supportive, especially indefatigable lawyer Simon Dowson-Collins, publisher Adam Humphries, outstanding picture researcher Fiona Greenway, project editor Georgina Atsiaris and proofreader Dawn Booth.

The most important thanks are due to Veronica, my wife, best friend, wise consigliere and irreplaceable supporter. Without her, as always, this book would not have been written.

London, June 2024

PICTURE CREDITS

INDEX